Religion in the Egyptian Novel

Edinburgh Studies in Modern Arabic Literature
Series Editor: Rasheed El-Enany

Writing Beirut
Samira Aghacy

Autobiographical Identities in Contemporary Arab Literature
Valerie Anishchenkova

The Iraqi Novel
Fabio Caiani and Catherine Cobham

Sufism in the Contemporary Arabic Novel
Ziad Elmarsafy

Gender, Nation, and the Arabic Novel
Hoda Elsadda

The Unmaking of the Arab Intellectual
Zeina G. Halabi

Post-War Anglophone Lebanese Fiction
Syrine Hout

Prophetic Translation
Maya I. Kesrouany

Nasser in the Egyptian Imaginary
Omar Khalifah

Conspiracy in Modern Egyptian Literature
Benjamin Koerber

War and Occupation in Iraqi Fiction
Ikram Masmoudi

Literary Autobiography and Arab National Struggles
Tahia Abdel Nasser

The Arab Nahḍah
Abdulrazzak Patel

Blogging from Egypt
Teresa Pepe

Religion in the Egyptian Novel
Christina Phillips

Occidentalism
Zahia Smail Salhi

Sonallah Ibrahim
Paul Starkey

Minorities in the Contemporary Egyptian Novel
Mary Youssef

edinburghuniversitypress.com/series/smal

Religion in the Egyptian Novel

Themes and Approaches

Christina Phillips

EDINBURGH
University Press

Edinburgh University Press is one of the leading university presses in the UK. We publish academic books and journals in our selected subject areas across the humanities and social sciences, combining cutting-edge scholarship with high editorial and production values to produce academic works of lasting importance. For more information visit our website: edinburghuniversitypress.com

© Christina Phillips, 2019, 2021

Edinburgh University Press Ltd
The Tun – Holyrood Road
12 (2f) Jackson's Entry
Edinburgh EH8 8PJ

First published in hardback by Edinburgh University Press 2019

Typeset in 11/15 Adobe Garamond by
Servis Filmsetting Ltd, Stockport, Cheshire

A CIP record for this book is available from the British Library

ISBN 978 1 4744 1706 8 (hardback)
ISBN 978 1 4744 8388 9 (paperback)
ISBN 978 1 4744 1707 5 (webready PDF)
ISBN 978 1 4744 1708 2 (epub)

The right of Christina Phillips to be identified as author of this work has been asserted in accordance with the Copyright, Designs and Patents Act 1988 and the Copyright and Related Rights Regulations 2003 (SI No. 2498).

Contents

Series Editor's Foreword — vi
Acknowledgements — x

Part 1
1 Introduction: Religion and the Novel — 3
2 The Religious Other — 34
3 The Secular Scripture — 77

Part 2
4 Introduction: Religion, the Egyptian Novel and the New Literary Sensibility — 113
5 Intertextual Dialogues — 122
6 The Coptic Theme — 153
7 Mystical Dimensions — 189
8 Feminist Perspectives — 219

Conclusion — 254

Works Cited — 260
Index — 279

Series Editor's Foreword

Edinburgh Studies in Modern Arabic Literature is a new and unique series that will, it is hoped, fill in a glaring gap in scholarship in the field of modern Arabic literature. Its dedication to Arabic literature in the modern period, that is, from the nineteenth century onwards, is what makes it unique among series undertaken by academic publishers in the English-speaking world. Individual books on modern Arabic literature in general or aspects of it have been and continue to be published sporadically. Series on Islamic studies and Arab/Islamic thought and civilisation are not in short supply either in the academic world, but these are far removed from the study of Arabic literature qua literature, that is, imaginative, creative literature as we understand the term when, for instance, we speak of English literature or French literature. Even series labelled 'Arabic/Middle Eastern Literature' make no period distinction, extending their purview from the sixth century to the present, and often including non-Arabic literatures of the region. This series aims to redress the situation by focusing on the Arabic literature and criticism of today, stretching its interest to the earliest beginnings of Arab modernity in the nineteenth century.

The need for such a dedicated series, and generally for the redoubling of scholarly endeavour in researching and introducing modern Arabic literature to the Western reader, has never been stronger. Among activities and events heightening public, let alone academic, interest in all things Arab, and not least Arabic literature, are the significant growth in the last decades of the translation of contemporary Arab authors from all genres, especially fiction, into English; the higher profile of Arabic literature internationally since the award of the Nobel Prize in Literature to Naguib Mahfouz in

1988; the growing number of Arab authors living in the Western diaspora and writing both in English and Arabic; the adoption of such authors and others by mainstream, high-circulation publishers, as opposed to the academic publishers of the past; the establishment of prestigious prizes, such as the International Prize for Arabic Fiction (IPAF) (the Arabic Booker), run by the Man Booker Foundation, which brings huge publicity to the shortlist and winner every year, as well as translation contracts into English and other languages; and, very recently, the events of the Arab Spring. It is therefore part of the ambition of this series that it will increasingly address a wider reading public beyond its natural territory of students and researchers in Arabic and world literature. Nor indeed is the academic readership of the series expected to be confined to specialists in literature in the light of the growing trend for interdisciplinarity, which increasingly sees scholars crossing field boundaries in their research tools and coming up with findings that equally cross discipline borders in their appeal.

Unlike in the West where religion has been on the retreat since the Renaissance and is almost invisible in society, religion still plays an important role in the life of individual and society in Egypt, and for that matter the rest of the Arab world. Religion has a presence in the daily life of people: in their thinking, in their speech, in their actions, in what they eat and what they drink, in what clothing they wear, in who they can marry, in who can inherit the deceased and how much, etc. etc. People base their morality on religious edicts, and judge themselves and others according to how truly pious or hypocritical they are. And when it comes to gender, if at all possible, you'd better be a man, because religion does not believe in the equality of the sexes. All that and we're only speaking about standard mainstream religion, but if you are a disgruntled, alienated and socially disadvantaged citizen, then you might end up rejecting the society that rejected you together with its 'domesticated' religion, and become radicalised, puritanical, a 'religious' fundamentalist, and a violent 'reformer' of society according to your own brand of religion: in other words, what we like to call a 'terrorist'. All that is within the supposedly 'homogeneous' Muslim community, but when society is actually composed of two religious communities, one a dominant Muslim and the other a substantial Christian minority, as is the case in Egypt, then the scene has the potential of even higher drama, in the absence of democracy, civil society institutions and an enlightened education system. The bloody confrontation often making news these days between a militarised Egyptian state and the Muslim Brotherhood and other 'religiously' inspired radical groups is a powerful reminder of 'religion' in society.

If religion has such a mighty presence in the life of individuals and society, you would expect novelists to reflect that in their writing. And that they have done, since the genre established itself in Egypt in the early years of the twentieth century, and continue to do unabatedly today. There is no better place to learn about the intellectual engagement with the role of religion in the life of modern Egyptians than in the novel. Attitudes to religion and its portrayal will differ substantially depending on where the novelist stands ideologically, e.g. how secularised, and whether a man or woman. In the fiction of Naguib Mahfouz (one of the novelists studied in the current monograph), for instance, which chronicles the life of Egypt in the twentieth century, you can read the story of the rise of political Islam from the 1930s to the 1990s from an antipathetic standpoint. But on the other hand, the last three decades or so have witnessed the rise of what came to be known as 'Islamic literature', mostly second-rate narratives by untalented writers devoted to the propagation of traditional Islamic values. A different perspective yet again can be found in the fiction of Salwa Bakr (again treated in the present monograph). As a woman writer and a Marxist, she has little patience for the religiously sanctioned injustices inflicted on women by society and makes no secret of that in her ideologically laden but beautifully accomplished writing. She succeeds artistically where Egypt's great Feminist and older and better-known writer, Nawal Saadawi has failed: turning vehemently felt convictions into good art.

The prevalence of religion as a theme in Egyptian fiction from its inception to the present day is phenomenal, in true measure to its dominance in people's life, and no amount of scholarly investigation can do it justice. To the existing body of writing, this monograph contributes a systematic examination of the phenomenon in Egyptian fiction in light of modern literary theory that includes a fresh reading of some seminal texts coupled with an approach to less studied and some very new texts – such as *Azazeel* (2008) by Yusuf Zeidan – offering a balanced selection of writers, classical and new, male and female, Muslim and Christian.

Professor Rasheed El-Enany, Series Editor,
Emeritus Professor of Modern Arabic Literature,
University of Exeter

Acknowledgements

I begin by thanking Philip Stewart who, in his office in the Department of Plant Sciences at the University of Oxford, inspired in me a fascination with Arabic literature and gave me the bright idea to do a PhD, and who has remained a support and correspondent ever since. I owe an enormous debt of gratitude to Professor Sabry Hafez, my PhD supervisor, who has opened many doors to me and has been a wonderful support and mentor for many years now. Likewise to Professor Rasheed El-Enany who guided this project through publication and has been a fine friend and source of encouragement. A brilliant series editor! I thank the British Academy for funding the initial stages of this research under their postdoctoral fellowship scheme and the University of Exeter for granting me study leave to finally finish it. I would also like to thank the editorial and production team at Edinburgh University Press for their hard work and patience, and my colleagues at the Institute of Arab and Islamic Studies, University of Exeter, for their support, friendship and motivation. Most of all I would like to thank my marvellous husband Adam Zoubir who has made it all fun, my children Zain, Penny and Luke, and my parents and sisters.

For Adam, Zain, Penny and Luke

PART I

1

Introduction: Religion and the Novel

Religion and literature have comingled in the Middle Eastern context for centuries. The sacred texts of monotheism, the Torah, Bible and Qur'an, not only constitute literary artefacts in themselves but have spawned whole genres and shaped literary creativity in manifold ways. The Qur'an, for example, is understood as consummate in style as well as message. Its meaning is not simply a matter of revelation but dependent upon the myriad literary structures and devices – syntax, rhythm, rhetoric, narrative, repetition, voice, image, symbol, allegory, intertextuality, etc. – it employs. Even the most literal believers would concede this, since as the perfect Word there is no dismantling of Qur'anic form and content. Arabic poetry, which was already well established by the advent of Islam, incorporated religious themes early on, especially in the Umayyad and Abbasid panegyric, and developed an ascetic genre which derived specific inspiration from Qur'anic ideas, images and phrases. Sufi poetry in both Arabic and Persian has reached impressive artistic heights, drawing on Qur'anic imagery and concepts and transforming the pre-Islamic poet's arduous journey through the desert into a mystical path to the Divine. In another perspective, Syrian cultural theorist and modernist poet Adunis (ʿAli Ahmad Saʿid) proposes Arabic poetry to be a form of liturgical repetition (*takrār taqsī*) by virtue of the linguistic inimitability it shares with the Qur'an, which has lent *jāhilī* verse a belated religious colouring.[1] Hadith studies, such as the *Sahih*s of Bukhari and Muslim, and exegeses (*tafāsīr*) of Tabari, constitute some of the landmarks of classical Arabic literature, while even profane works, such as the *maqāma*s of al-Hamadhani and al-Hariri and compendiums of al-Jahiz, are interwoven with Qur'anic allusion and quotation and manifest Islamic themes.[2] Virtually all classical Arabic texts begin with pious preambles and dedications and include scriptural quotation in their pages. Into the modern era, Arabic fiction and poetry has plundered scripture and sacred myth for themes and symbols and creatively engaged with religion to communicate contemporary messages.

Beyond historical specificities there are more fundamental ways in which literature and religion intersect. (Here I should note that I am referring to religion and literature in their broadest senses, as cover terms for a variety of texts, practices and phenomena, which in the case of religion includes revelation, doctrine, ritual and theology, and in the case of literature indicates highly valued verbal expression, that is, texts, either written or oral, which society values and preserves.) For a start, religion and literature overlap in terms of subject matter. While science, history and philosophy deal with facts and verifiable reality, religion and literature are geared towards the intangible, ethereal and abstract. They deal with human experience, existential truths, esoteric meanings, and spiritual and emotional well-being. Scientific thought and empirical discourse proceed through logic and reason and produce knowledge about the external world; religion and literature depend more on imagination and intuition to nourish understanding of the human condition. While literature and religion pose a threat to scientific discourse in one sense, contradicting and undermining its painstaking discoveries and methodology, in another sense they complement it, picking up where science and empiricism leave off. Jabir ʿAsfur makes this point for story when he draws attention to its ability to explain that which is unaccounted for by scientific logic,[3] and it is one of the reasons why the famous Egyptian novelist Najib Mahfuz eventually chose literature over philosophy. In his words the writer transforms philosophy into something the human soul can experience.[4]

In dealing with non-empirical reality, literature and religion employ similar methods and draw on similar resources. For example, imagination occupies a central place in both. Without falling into a romantic concept of man's radical creativity we can say that imagination enables man to think the 'unconditioned', to borrow from Kant. The material world is locked in space and time and understood through empirical methods and knowledge. God, the self, feeling, hope and aspiration lie outside these limits and are figured by the imagination. In the words of Paul Ricoeur, whose theory of narrative opens up new ways of thinking about scriptural and textual revelation, imagination 'has a prospective and explorative function in regard to the inherent possibilities of man'.⁵ In other words imagination augments experience. It permits us to think what is beyond verifiable experience, and it is to our imagination that religion and literature appeal when they speak of worlds which we have not or cannot experience ourselves. Belief in God and the afterlife, just like belief in Shahrazad's story-cycle in *Alf Layla wa Layla* and ᶜAshur al-Naji's heroic and spiritual quest in *Malhamat al-Harafish*, requires a suspension of disbelief and openness to other worlds and modes of being. Of course there is a qualitative difference here, for the suspension in the case of literature is temporary. As James Wood writes, 'Belief in fiction is always belief "as if". Our belief is itself metaphorical – it only *resembles* actual belief, and is therefore never wholly belief'.⁶ Whereas religious belief implies something more profound and enduring, namely faith. Yet faith in God, embracing prayer and doctrine, readiness to follow Alice through the keyhole and weep with Hypa in ᶜ*Azazil*, all of these things call on a cognitive faculty beyond reason.

If imagination permits us to think beyond verifiable reality, poetic language permits us to speak it. Descriptive language, which facilitates ordinary communication and serves empirical discourse so well through close correspondence between sign and reference, is of limited use to a discourse centred on an entity that stands outside language (i.e. God) and for literary expression, which turns on the gap between signifier and signified. Literature distorts language and reality in order to express more profound truths. Scripture, theology and other kinds of religious discourse, though they may utilise empirical registers for certain purposes, move away from denotative language and descriptive methods when communicating esoteric and transcendental meanings. Religion and literature, we can say, tend towards *metaphor*. I am not talking here about Aristotelian displacement and substitution but the kind of dynamic interaction of object and terms envisaged by Max Black.⁷ Metaphors are not about perceiving similarities so much as creating them. The juxtaposition of disparate terms, and the tension arising thereof, stretches understanding beyond the literal. Thus metaphors are cognitive instruments for communicating meaning beyond literal language and experience. And it is this ability to stretch language that makes metaphor and metaphorical language an indispensable tool for religious and literary discourse. Metaphor is the most suitable means of speaking about that which lies beyond logic and human experience, hence its critical role in revelation. From a literature perspective, metaphor functions both to produce meaning in a micro sense, that is, on the level of word, sentence and discourse in a given text, and on a macro level to resolve the problem of reference that has troubled literary expression since the emergence of structuralism and its insistence on the autonomy of the text and strictly relational character of language. Literary texts refer to the world metaphorically. They create possible worlds which speak of experiential reality but are not a mirror image of it. They are imaginative reconfigurations of the world, which the reader integrates with his/her own lived experience, thereby activating the metaphor. As such the reader facilitates aesthetic reference, contributing the essential link between the text and the world, which naturally varies from person to person. In fact, insofar as literary texts create new possibilities, so theorists like Ricoeur see a revelatory function. Literary texts open the reader to new modes of being in the world, and 'this referential function of poetic discourse conceals a dimension of revelation in a nonreligious, nontheistic, nonbiblical sense of the word'.[8]

Ricoeur's revelatory concept of literature is highly abstract and beyond the scope of this study. What matters here rather is the function of metaphor and dependence on metaphorical reference characteristic of literature and religion alike. For just as literature inhabits the poetic, so the divine messages of the sacred texts of Islam and Christianity are figured metaphorically. In his seminal study, *The Great Code*, Northrop Frye shows how a literal reading of the Bible is misreading. The Bible narratives do not refer to historical events but to spiritual truths. Regardless of the historical veracity or otherwise of its material, the Bible's contents were selected and shaped in order to communicate particular messages and therefore call for a metaphorical reading. Thomas Aquinas recognised this feature of Christian scripture when he defined its *sensus literalis* as its intended meaning: 'When Scripture speaks of the arm of God, the literal sense is not that he has a physical limb, but that he has what it signifies, namely the power of doing and making.'[9] A similar argument is made for divine anthropomorphism by the Muʿtazilites and in Ibn Rushd's (Averroes') theory of *taʾwīl*, and is of course the basis of all symbolic readings of scripture. Comparison of the same myth as appropriated by different religious traditions demonstrates the validity of the argument that sacred stories are related for their signified not literal meaning. One need look no further than the story of Joseph as it appears in the Bible, Qur'an and Sufi texts.

Metaphor and metaphorical reference are not only characteristic of revelation but suffuse the realm of doctrine and constitute the basic a priori of discourse about God. The fact that the Divine stands outside language, that there is nothing, no word in our linguistic repository capable of capturing the essence of God, means that discourse about Him is necessarily indirect, via tropes and figures.[10] The Persian poet Rumi was well aware of this when he composed the lines 'Neither words, nor any natural fact / Can express this [esoteric reality]'.[11] Even for theology, which manifests less verbal limits insofar as its themes and explanations may run ad infinitum and be endlessly refined, metaphor is a liberating force and at times a necessity. '[I]t is because no language is completely transparent upon reality, providing unambiguous "names" for clear-cut "things", that the indirect mode of reference employed in literature constitutes some of the most effective theology', observes T. R. Wright.[12] In the realm of doctrine too metaphor is indispensable. Christianity and Islam are faiths beyond reason since many of their basic doctrines cannot be grammatically expressed except in the form of metaphor. Christ *is* God, the concept of the Trinity, the oneness and many-ness implied in *tawḥīd*, and the simultaneous transcendence and omnipresence of Allah, all of these rest on metaphorical thinking.

If metaphor is a fundamental strategy of religious and literary discourse, so too is *mythos* or story. For it is from story that faith and literature derive their vitality. The sacred texts of monotheism make extensive use of story, drawing on both its emotive power and the essential role it plays in human being and identity. The Qur'an includes legends and narratives of pre-Islamic prophets, adapted to its message, and relates disaster stories as a mechanism of dissuasion. Beyond the Qur'an, stories from *al-sīrat al-nabawiyya* (prophetic biography) and *qiṣaṣ al-anbiyāʾ* (tales of the prophets) have long sustained believers. It goes without saying that stories affect us more immediately and profoundly than other modes of expression, through their aesthetic quality and appeal to the senses and because they address the underlying laws of experience. It is precisely awareness of poetry's power to persuade that led Plato to banish poets from his Republic and why fiction is closely censored by authoritarian regimes and paranoid dictators. Stories also play a dynamic role in human being and identity. We make sense of our lives by fitting them into a wider narrative. '[V]irtually all our basic convictions about the nature and meaning of our lives find their ground and intelligibility in some form of overarching, paradigmatic story', writes Michael Goldberg.[13] If our lives are not to seem trivial they must be situated in a narrative, a sacred story or some other narrative carried by a community, like nationalism. Sacred stories, or we could say master stories, are dwelling places. We inhabit them and through them make sense of our lives. The function of myths, writes Frye, is to 'tell a society what is important for it to know, whether about its gods, its history, its laws, or its class structure',[14] and literature is its successor. Literature takes over from myth the function of relating man to his surroundings. Man's need for story is thus an existential fact of human being. Moreover, it is at those points where myths and individual lives intersect that stories become redemptive. Conversion occurs at the moment when a person discovers the interconnection between their own story and the master story of revelation,[15] when the subject awakens to a story broader than one's own. Finally, and not unrelated, is the spiritual function common to literature and religion. Without entering into pragmatic theories of literature or following Matthew Arnold in suggesting that poetry can perform all the functions of faith, religion and literature have in common the capacity to nourish the believer and/or reader spiritually and emotionally. They provide comfort, pleasure, validation, escape, and as such fulfil a basic human need.

Given the many areas of overlap of religious and literary discourse historically, methodologically and epistemologically, the purported incompatibility of religion and literature in modern times, and of religion and the novel in particular, is striking. Faith and the modern form of the novel are uncomfortable bedfellows. Wood sees modern fiction as the 'enemy of superstition, the slayer of religions'.[16] Siddiq writes that 'radical scepticism toward religious dogma may be intrinsic to the novel as a literary genre'.[17] In the case of Arabic literature, having coexisted happily with Islam for centuries, a chasm has opened up in the last hundred or so years such that works which combine the two in a pious sense, literature that springs from or exhibits Muslim sentiment, are less than canonical and relegated to a sub-category, *al-adab al-islāmī*, within, or rather alongside, the canon of modern Arabic literature, even as sales of this faith-inspired literature often outweigh those of the secular mainstream.[18] The same phenomenon exhibits in English literature, where only a handful of religiously motivated writers have broken into the canon, C. S. Lewis and G. K. Chesterton foremost among them. It is no doubt in recognition of this problematic that theorists on the side of faith habitually expand the field of religious poetics beyond the committed corpus. Najib al-Kilani, a well-known author and critic in the field of *al-adab al-islāmī*, does not limit Islamic literature to religiously oriented works and Muhammad Qutb, brother of famous Muslim Brotherhood leader Sayyid Qutb, includes non-Muslim works in his discussions of Islamic art.[19] On the Christian side, T. S. Eliot's call to read ethically is a programme for all literature, as are the literary approaches of T. R. Wright, Michael Edwards and Luke Ferreter.[20] Attempts to rehabilitate religio-literary discourse have had virtually no impact on the literary mainstream, which remains steadfastly tethered to a secular aesthetic in both the Arab and European context.

One way of understanding this rift in the Arab case is in terms of shifting literary values and canon revision. The *nahḍa*, or cultural revival that began in Egypt in the nineteenth century, transformed literary tastes and values away from traditional forms like the *maqāma* and *risāla*. As Michael Allen explains in his study of sites of reading in colonial Egypt, *adab*, which once upon a time denoted cultivated knowledge and refined taste and conduct, was redefined under the auspices of the *nahḍa* to mean literature in a different sense, which included the hitherto foreign forms of the novel and short story. Nineteenth-century Egypt witnessed transformations in print culture, education, concepts of authorship and ideals of textual practice which brought new literary forms to the fore along with a new kind of intellectual, the modern cosmopolitan, whilst simultaneously devaluing pre-existing culture and texts which in the past exemplified literariness. 'In order for nineteenth-century Egypt to be seen as moving forward, it reinvents those traditions from which it claims to develop', writes Allen.[21] In practice this meant assigning negative value to traditional texts and representatives, many of which could be classed as religious. For what is valued in the discourse of nineteenth- and twentieth-century Arab modernity and its cultural products is reason, intellectual freedom, scepticism and secularism, and what is found distasteful is fundamentalist rhetoric and religious conviction. The novel and short story, which spearheaded the new literature, are troubled by master narratives, or at least metaphysical master narratives (these genres in their early Arabic formulation have little problem with the grand narratives of nationalism and modernity, which are only later called into question). Something about transcendent deferral and faith jars with modern literary aesthetics, which leads us to the question of secularism and the novel.

The novel is a secular form. This widely held assumption is rooted in classical theories of the genre which locate its beginnings in the emergence of modern society. Ortega y Gasset and Georg Lukacs' method of contrasting the epic and novel leads to a concept of the latter as a decentred form, a genre emptied of God. The novel is the literary embodiment of metaphysical angst, a genre structured on the principle of search, lacking as it does a transcendent orientation. The world of the novel is a created reality and as such destined to be reformulated in every novelistic work. Its heroes are alienated individuals in search of meaning, which can never be resolved except on a microscopic level. The novel has no totality, no overarching myth; if an overarching myth is implied, as for example in *al-adab al-islāmī*, its aesthetic is compromised. It celebrates individualism, interiority and human agency, the temporal and mundane over the transcendent and cosmic. As Watt writes in regard to the conditions constitutive of the novel's emergence, 'individual experience replaces collective tradition as the ultimate arbiter of reality'.[22] Likewise Jabir ʿAsfur, who emphasises the novel's pluralism and anti-authoritarian character and echoes Lukacs when he refers to it as *malḥamat al-ʿarab al-muḥdathīn* (the epic of the modern Arabs), describes the novel as the art form that 'strives to understand the age and its complex transmutations from the *perspective of the individual*' (my italics).[23] The novel as a form is man-centred, rational, contingent, sceptical, intellectually free – details which put it in the camp of secularism and modernity, a correlation implicit in ʿAsfur's proposition of *zaman al-riwāya* (time of the novel) as the condition of contemporary Arab culture; 'a time of enlightenment, which means the primacy of reason in attaining knowledge, acceptance of the logic of science in explaining the world, and liberating the [kind of] thought that interrogates everything …'.[24] The correlation is also ostensibly supported by the pattern of the novel's emergence in different locations and languages, that is very often in tandem with the nation-state, that entity which typically involves the substitution of sacred ties and theocentric culture with civic bonds, linguistic unity and geographical borders. Studies of the latter not only identify the critical role that the novel plays in constructing (and at a later stage deconstructing) national imaginaries, but also the ideological reciprocity of novel and nation, for example in relation to concepts of time, knowledge, ethics and history, which has contributed to their synchronous development.

Yet the equation of the novel and secularism is far from straightforward. It is a thesis which, like Frederic Jameson's concept of third world literature and national allegory, has a good deal going for it, in the sense that it sounds about right or reflects our general reading experience, but is nevertheless thoroughly troublesome. Part of the problem lies in the inherent instability of the novel and secularism as ongoing projects. The novel did not appear one day fully formed but emerged over a long period, and the same applies to secularism. In the Arabic context the presumption of the novel's secularism is frustrated by the ideological flux that characterises the form in its early period. The nascent Arabic novel, even when it has a clear secular motivation, as in the case of Muhammad Husayn Haykal's *Zaynab* (1914), which has been read as an expression of Egyptian liberal nationalism in the early decades of the twentieth century, is far too contradictory. Nationalist ideals mix with Islamic affiliation, human agency coalesces with divine intervention, producing a fascinating record of cultural and intellectual instability but not a secular text as such. Moreover, even once the Arabic novel has matured, in the sense that it has assumed a form which aligns with global definitions of the genre, and a range of phenomena manifest to merit referring to it as secular, this is hardly the end of the journey or a fixed situation. The novel and secularism are discourses which continue to develop and define themselves against competing narratives and according to changing realities and pressures. There is also the issue of precursors and prototypes. Secularism and the novel may well extend further into history than is generally assumed, especially on flexible definitions. Frye's archetypal criticism perceives an ancient tradition of secular literature, Bakhtin's analysis of the novel allows for premodern examples, and for those who view secularism as an outgrowth of rationalism there are numerous classical strands in both the Arab and European traditions.

The European association of the novel and secularism creates a further complication. Neither can be considered indigenous forms in the sense of hitherto unknown organic outgrowths of a native tradition, if such a thing is even possible. They are, rather, assimilated discourses adapted to new milieux. This is not to deny the Arabic novel its Arabo-Islamic literary ancestors or to ignore secular themes in Arabo-Islamic tradition, such as religious tolerance and pluralism, the Muʿtazilite school, and the philosophy of Ibn Rushd. Nor is it to imply that the Arabic novel and Arab secularism are identical to their European counterparts. Literary forms and political and philosophical thought systems are dynamic discourses with their own histories and circumstances, but at the same time they are part of a wider ideological and discursive context which makes for constant evolution and redefinition. Here is not the place to discuss origins or enter the minefield of literary genealogy,[25] but what we can say is that the Arabic novel as a form, especially in the early period, which for our intents and purposes takes in the first half of the twentieth century, carried with it the spectre of the West, whether or not the West was explicitly mentioned or thematised in a given work, and that this put the Arabic novel on the defensive from the start, as though it had to ever assert and vindicate its existence, which places it in a particular position with regard to tradition and, by extension, Islam, as a component part of the latter but of course by no means confined by it.

The same is true to an extent of Arab secularism, which likewise emerged as a discourse under the auspices of the *nahḍa* and is closely bound up with the process of modernisation and statehood. Rooted in Christian heritage and the European Enlightenment, secularism in an Arab and Egyptian context should be viewed against a background of western hegemony and occupation, independence and Islam; not an organic phenomenon so much as a means to achieve certain goals, at least in the first instance. The Levantine Christians – men like Butrus al-Bustani (1819–83), Farah Antun (1874–1922), Ahmad Faris al-Shidyaq (1805–87) and Shibli Shumayyil (1850–1917) – began to argue for the delimitation of Church authority in the nineteenth century. They discerned early on a connection between western civilisational progress and the separation of religion and politics, and were particularly motivated by this ideal as a minority group and in light of local sectarian strife, specifically the Mount Lebanon Civil War of 1860. An uncoupling of religion and state offered this group a route into mainstream society and they did not hold back in their attacks on Church authority.[26] At the same time Islamic reformers Jamal al-Din al-Afghani and Muhammad Abduh sought to adapt modern political concepts, like democracy, freedom and pluralism, to the Islamic model, opening the way for social change, and 'secular' intellectuals, like Qasim Amin (1863–1908) and Lutfi al-Sayyid (1872–1963), as well as writers of early Arabic modern fiction like Muhammad Husayn Haykal (1888–1956) and Taha Husayn (1889–1973), both also public intellectuals, promoted secular ideals under the purview of liberal nationalism. It was the latter that in the end provided the most critical impetus. The ideology of liberal nationalism, which replaces religious ties with citizenship, more than anything served to embed secular ideals in Arab life and politics. The rise of the Wafd, Egypt's first secular party, and 1919 revolution, with its slogan 'Egypt for Egyptians' (*miṣr li'l-miṣriyyīn*), marked a turning point in the story of Egyptian nationalism, while the 1923 constitution enshrined secular ideals of citizenship in law. ᶜAli ᶜAbd al-Raziq's (1888–1966) famous treatise, *Al-Islam wa Usul al-Hukm* (1925), which refuted Islam as a political system, raised a storm but its basic premise was already taking shape in the administrative fabric and state institutions of Egypt. Further impetus was provided by Gamal Abdel Nasser's pan-Arabism and socialism, where a distinction arises between Arab and Egyptian secularism but the dismantling of religious authority at state level remains the same.

I have been talking about secularism so far in the basic sense of the separation of religion and politics, or more specifically the emptying of public institutions and social space of religion. Such understandings only go so far where the novel is concerned, however. For example, a novel like Tawfiq al-Hakim's *ᶜAwdat al-Ruh* (1933) or Najib Mahfuz's *Bayn al-Qasrayn* (1956) may represent this reality as an effect of verisimilitude or as a projection of an ideal, but this does not in itself make the novel secular. Setting and character may engender secular ideals but they do not necessarily constitute genre ideology. Nor does the separation of religion and state and assignment of faith to the private realm cover secularity. The latter is not only extremely difficult to achieve – can we really demarcate public and private? can behaviours and practices be truly limited to one or another social space?[27] – but it is only one dimension of the secular, which we might understand, following Talal Asad, not as a doctrine or political structure but as an epistemology, and further as a range of possibilities which may or may not manifest all at once in a literary text. Science, reason, humanism, intellectual freedom, religious pluralism, mechanical time, the sovereign self – all of these are manifestations of the secular, but they are not essential components, nor are they necessarily exclusive to secular space. Egyptian scholar Abdelwahab Elmessiri, who has written much on secularism, refers to it as a world outlook 'that forms the unconscious basis and implicit frame of reference for our conduct in public *and* in private' (my italics).[28] Charles Taylor, another key theorist in the area, sees secularity in terms of the conditions of belief. A secular society is one that has moved away from a situation of unproblematic belief to a situation in which belief is regarded as one option among many: 'Secularity in this sense is a matter of the whole context of understanding in which our moral, spiritual or religious experience and search takes place'.[29] A secular society is one where any and every position is possible – religious fanaticism of any creed, militant atheism and everything in between, and where everyone is charged with selecting, even creating, their own meaning and belief system. Secularity implies disenchantment, a shift from a transcendent frame to an immanent frame, which may be closed or open. Belief in transcendence is possible but not necessary, likewise unbelief. Thus Taylor overcomes problematic assumptions such as the secularisation thesis and socio-historical specificity of secularism and secularity. There is no compulsory waning of belief in a secular society. This may occur, as in the case in parts of Europe, but it is not a prerequisite. Moreover, while secularism as a socio-political doctrine has its roots in Latin Christendom, the conditions of belief model can be applied to other contexts and forms.[30]

It is in terms of Taylor's conditions of belief that it is possible to describe the novel as a secular genre. The novel's secularity, we can say, lies in its conditions of belief and immanent frame. Genres are Weltanschauungen, ways of seeing, and for the novel this means seeing sceptically, humanly and, for the most part, rationally. Genres embody a particular conception of man in the world, which in the novel translates to alienation and the buffered self.[31] The novel is an a priori expression of disenchantment and sovereign man. The world is impersonal, its meaning is supplied, not pregiven or transcendent. Moreover, meaning is plural. The novel is heteroglossic; it allows to speak the full spectrum of voices even when it exhibits bias towards one viewpoint. Religion is not disallowed from its pages but it is filtered through novelistic consciousness, which is sceptical and maintains a critical distance. Faith is possible but as one of several options. The Arabic novel is bursting with religious themes and signifiers. Pious characters, holy spaces, divine reference, sacred imagery, scriptural intertextuality, mystical themes – these are all permitted but they are filtered through a secular lens. The same is broadly true of the Arabic short story, which is a distinct genre but springs from the same socio-historical matrix. It appeared around the same time as the novel in Egypt, though it was quicker to artistic maturity, and the factors conducive to its emergence were precisely those factors which facilitated the birth of the Arabic novel, namely a rise in literacy, spread of secular education, development of national consciousness, expansion of the press and, crucially, a change in worldview. Theorists of the short story link it to modernity and although Frank O'Connor argues in a seminal study that the difference between the short story and the novel is more ideological than formal, the divergence to which he is referring relates to its typical hero (an outsider) and his/her relation to wider society, not the sceptical, rational attitude characteristic of both forms.[32] The short story is the genre of individuation and eccentricity. It necessarily deals with fragments rather than the whole, and with individual rather than collective identity. Moreover, as Hafez writes, 'the quest for "identity" that the short story articulates is not for the "identity" that one inherits but for an "identity" that one chooses'.[33] In other words, it is profoundly man-centred and meaning is once again supplied, not inherited or pre-existing. The short story, we might say, is a variation of modern narrative discourse which is secular as an effect of its conditions of belief. We might also note, in the Arab and Egyptian context, the fluidity of narrative genres among the literary pioneers, since short story writers and novelists were often one and the same, which makes for a certain thematic and ideological continuity between the early Arabic novel and short story.

Literary secularism is not static and stable, however. It must constantly figure itself against its other: religion. Religion and secularity, whilst not reverse mirrors to one another, are locked in a relationship of mutual definition and dependence. Talal Asad writes that 'Any discipline that seeks to understand "religion" must also try to understand its other'.[34] His account of secularity, like Charles Taylor's *A Secular Age* (2007), involves a good deal of discussion of religion and belief, just as arguments by nineteenth- and early twentieth-century Arab secularists could not but engage with religious themes and debates. One way of understanding this interlocking relation in the context of the Arabic novel is in terms of intersubjectivity and alterity. Religion in the secular space of the novel is the *other*, not in the sense of an exotic unknowable figure like the third world subject in colonial discourse, but as an entity against which the secular is articulated and takes shape. Just as the Occident is constructed by the Orient, and vice versa, so secularism and secularity in the Arabic novel are formulated in dialogue with, and often contradistinction to, religion and religiosity. Such a trajectory onto the Arabic novel's secularism not only provides the terms for its elaboration, for as Part 1 of this study will show, the ambivalence and anxiety implied by alterity, and cultural alterity in particular, aptly describes the dynamic between the secular and religious in the Arabic novel, but also illuminates a dimension of postcolonial identity which has sometimes been obscured by the coloniser/colonised dialectic. In other words, whilst replicating several characteristics of colonial otherness, the religious other calls into question a fundamental structure of postcolonial scholarship in an Egyptian and Arabic context, namely its valorisation of the East/West binary.

The other, as we know, is constitutive of the self. Continental philosophy and psychoanalysis, two disciplines which take selfhood as an object of study, arrive at this conclusion. Following through Kant's concept of unified consciousness but rejecting his transcendental self and insisting instead that self-construction is a process performed by the human subject, Hegel ascertained that self-knowledge requires the presence of an other.[35] The journey into the reality of Hegel's self is contingent upon recognition, a task which can only be performed by an other. Consciousness is thus a necessarily reflexive function that implies a process of mutual acknowledgement between the subject and object. From the publication of the *Phenomenology of the Spirit* (1807) onwards, intersubjectivity has been both a fundamental principle and problem for philosophers in the European tradition, from which postcolonial theory springs. Heidegger's principle of *Mitsein*, intended to abolish the tendency to solipsism in western philosophy, makes the relationship with others the very essence of what it means to be a self. The philosophy of Levinas is essentially an ethics of the other, a phenomenological description of the encounter between the self and the Absolute Other which pre-exists self-consciousness.[36] For Sartre the self has a masochistic desire to be limited by the other whose presence is a prerequisite for self-consciousness.[37] More recently, Ricoeur has used grammatical and narrative analyses to characterise the self and other as interdependent and work through an ethics of this relationship.[38] Within the field of psychoanalysis Jacque Lacan's mirror stage is constructed on the concept of the other; the birth of the Ego is the realisation of others, and of the self as an other, and a relationship of rivalry or conflict emerges therefrom.

Theories and approaches differ but there is little doubt about the intrinsic role of the other in self-formation. And when the formation of the secular is at issue then it is hardly surprising that religion occupies this space. As the sceptical, humanist, secular discourse of the novel takes shape, so religion is othered. What this means in practice, and in the early Arabic novel in particular, when Arabic novelistic consciousness is in its infancy and on the defensive, is that religion is self-consciously displaced and critiqued. The novel as a secular form, as a new conception of man in the world and expression of disenchantment and immanence, engenders and articulates an epistemological break whereby the entity that constituted the framework (that is, religion and a religious worldview) becomes an object within another larger framework (that is, the discourse of the novel and a secular worldview), a transition from subject to object in other words. Religion is ousted from subject position and objectified, or re-formed as an object. Textual examples of this include characters reflecting on belief, which figures faith as optional, or discussing God and religion from the outside, revealing the kind of critical distance that is absent in axiomatic belief. Articulating secularity in the Arabic novel also habitually entails religious criticism. Although religious criticism is by no means inherent in secularism, nor indeed exclusive to it, the literary evidence reveals it to be a common accompaniment – from Shidyaq to Mahfuz to Yusuf Zaydan, religion and its institutions repeatedly come under attack. One explanation here may well be that, although religious criticism is not an essential component of the secular, an antagonistic relation with the other is part and parcel of intersubjectivity and alterity.

The birth of the self in Lacanian thought is dependent upon the emergence of the other as bitter rival. Sartre's self/other relation, structured around emotional alienation and enslavement, is fundamentally conflictual.

Postcolonial studies, which has long been involved in the question of otherness, has made similar findings. This scholarly field's valorisation of the East/West opposition and preoccupation with the colonial other has frequently obscured the role that religion has played, and continues to play, in postcolonial identity, including in the Arab context, and there are, moreover, compelling arguments to dispense with the other as a discursive category, on the logic that it simply reinforces and perpetuates divisions we should be seeking to eliminate.[39] Yet Edward Said and Homi Bhabha's diagnosis of a hostile relation is instructive with regard to the religious other in the Arabic novel, especially insofar as this hostility is shot through with contradictions. Colonial discourse, in their analysis, is simultaneously thrilled and repelled by the Orient. Colonial discourse figures the Orient as regressive and base whilst at the same time it is titillated by its exotic difference. 'The Orient at large ... vacillates between the West's contempt for what is familiar and its shiver of delight in – or fear of – novelty', writes Said.[40] The religious other may not excite the secular subject or represent novelty, but there is certainly a good deal of tension attendant in the rejection and displacement of religion in the (early) Arabic novel, for example in ongoing divine invocation by 'secular' characters, references to fate and destiny by 'objective' narrators, and nostalgia for religious forms. There is also the problem of dependency. Bhabha elaborates on this aspect of colonial discourse in his analysis of the stereotype, which is its major discursive strategy but rests on a spurious concept of fixity. The very employment of the stereotype, and its endless repetition, exposes the coloniser's inability to exist without the other and thus betrays a certain restlessness in the colonising psyche. The stereotype, he writes, 'is a form of knowledge and identification that vacillates between what is always "in place", already known, and something that must be anxiously repeated'.[41] Thus Bhabha reads the dependency of self/other as indicative of a certain lack in the subject and as a signifier of anxiety. Turning back to the Arab context and religious other, this dependency, of the secular self upon the negation of the religious other, and the restlessness it presupposes, is evidenced in repetitive religious criticism on the pages of the Arabic novel and, more acutely, in the apparent recanting of some of its key practitioners – writers like Muhammad Husayn Haykal, Taha Husayn, ʿAbbas Mahmud al-ʿAqqad and ʿAbd al-Rahman al-Sharqawi, who, having pushed a secular agenda in critical and literary works, including novels, for a good part of their careers, began at certain junctures to publish Islamic texts (*islāmiyyāt*), works which deal with Islamic themes and appeal to religious sensibilities.

There are points of departure between the colonial other as described in postcolonial theory and the religious other as it manifests in the Arabic novel, however, which should be noted before I turn to its practitioners and an explanation of the chapters and rationale of the study. For a start there is the issue of temporality. The other in colonial discourse is located, for the most part, in the past or at least outside of modernity. Colonial discourse conceives of modernity on a temporal arc and as teleology such that the other is figured as primitive and 'backward' or regressive, on a course towards the modern space occupied by the coloniser, even though imperial power will always work to exclude it. As such colonial discourse artificially conflates geographical and temporal space. The same teleology is assumed in the early Arabic novel, where the religious other is likewise cast as regressive and located in the past. But there is a difference here, for this past *exists* and what we are dealing with is not a discursive invention so much as a reconstruction, a revaluation of cultural space and traditional forms and recasting of the latter as regressive. The distinction here is belonging and knowledge, which is present between the secular self and religious other but not so much its colonial counterpart. This leads to a second critical observation. Central to the colonial other is its unfamiliarity, whereas the religious in the Arabic novel is all too familiar. It is more like an aspect of the self that is purposely dissociated, or at least subdued as a new identity and future is envisaged. The religious other is thus produced *through* knowledge, not in the absence of it.[42] It is an insider forced out, and any out-of-placeness associated with it is assigned or invented. Thus, while novelty and unfamiliarity make the colonial other an object of desire, ambivalence in relation to the secular subject and religious other in the Arabic novel derives from familiarity and proximity. Contradictions in the secular discourse of Muhammad Husayn Haykal, Tawfiq al-Hakim and others are often residue, an effect of the hitherto intrinsic role of religion in culture, language and psyche such that it lingers on even as it is replaced as axial orientation.

Earlier I noted that the question of the Arabic novel's origins is not at issue here. Literary genealogies are complicated and frequently revised in light of new priorities, and in the case of the Arabic novel the debate has been amply covered. Instead, by way of introduction to the push and pull between religious and secular discourse in the early Arabic novel, which constitutes the scholarly thrust of Part 1 of this study, I will instead pause briefly to consider the philosophy, self-image and aspiration of the first Egyptian novel writers, since these have a direct bearing on the shape and content of the genre in its early period. The first thing to note in this regard is the progressive character of the first novelists, or rather intellectuals, since in many instances we are dealing not with vocational artists so much as intellectuals and men of letters who turned to literature as one of various channels through which to fulfil their perceived social function and communicate reformist messages. Men like Haykal and Taha Husayn were part of a new intellectual elite, which came to the fore in the early years of the twentieth century and actively sought change along European lines. This group was secular educated, or at least partially so, and most had spent time in Europe and read Auguste Comte, John Stuart Mill, Hippolyte Taine, Ernest Renan and other European philosophers and historians in vogue at the time. Though their backgrounds differed and they adopted a variety of methods and opinions, they were united in their ambition to see Egypt modernised and by a self-image that saw themselves, the intellectuals, as social leaders charged with educating the people and effecting change. As such they represented the vanguard of society, but not an uncontested one. For the first decades of the twentieth century were characterised by ideological ferment, with conservative elements opposing rapid change and religious voices openly hostile to the secularising discourse of these men, which made for heated debate in the newspapers of the time. The first Egyptian novels did not reflect and express the common experience and collective aspiration of Egyptians so much as the themes and concerns of a particular intellectual group, who were locked in a discursive struggle with conservative and religious strands of society – the traditional intellectual elite, who commanded the sympathy and respect of the majority and had more symbolic capital. This naturally placed religious and orthodox critique high on the agenda in the early Arabic novel, as a critical obstacle in the way of modernity. In other words, not only is religion an other in the Arabic novel on the basis that the form is by nature secular, but also because secular values, or values perceived to entail secularism such as science and nation, were among the priorities of its practitioners.

Nationalism was a key theme and concern of this group. Modern Egyptian nationalism traces to the nineteenth century and ᶜUrabi revolt of 1882 and gained momentum through the British occupation and World War I. Yet independence was hardly a unified and unifying goal for Egyptians. Up to the 1919 revolution many still saw the future of Egypt within a wider Islamic caliphate, and even after independence, which was granted by the British in 1922 with conditions, there remained plenty of questions and disagreements over the identity and direction of the Egyptian nation, with Arab, Islamic, Egyptian and minority identities all vying for space and recognition. Up to the early 1930s the intellectual elite favoured a specifically Egyptian identity. They developed a liberal territorial nationalism based around environmental determinism and Pharoanic heritage, drawing on the idea that there existed a unique Egyptian spirit and personality which was shaped by the land and had its roots in ancient Egypt, before Roman and Arab invaders. The prominence of nature and the *fellāḥ* theme in works like *Zaynab*, *ᶜAwdat al-Ruh* and even *Al-Ard* are an expression of this. From the 1930s the Pharaonic theme dwindled as Arabo-Islamic heritage reasserted itself. However, shifting nuances and identity politics are less important here than the extent to which the novel became a conduit for a nationalist imaginary whose principle feature was replacement of the religious ties with civic bonds. Salama Musa, a leading expositor of secular nationhood, saw the rise of nationalism as part of an historical evolution which had taken place in Europe and was underway in the Middle East.[43] Religion was no longer a basis for community. It was now a matter for the individual; 'private faith is the religion of the future'.[44] The patriotic bond (*al-rābiṭa al-waṭaniyya*) had replaced the religious bond (*al-rābiṭa al-dīniyya*).[45] Similarly, in his famous work *Mustaqbal al-Thaqafa fi Misr* (1938), Taha Husayn writes that religious unity is not the foundation for political community and nation (nor indeed is language), and is keen to promote religious plurality. The Coptic Church is a pillar of the Egyptian nation and the Copts, as Egyptians, have the same rights and responsibilities as all their countrymen.[46] These ideas were widespread in the intellectual elite of the time. The first writers of novels in Egypt were nationalists who used the novel to foster a national consciousness which was secular at its core, which again pushes religion up the agenda as a discourse in need of redefinition and reimagining in a new social order.

Also worthy of mention is the self-conscious project of fashioning a national literature (*al-adab al-qawmī*) which the early novelists were involved in. Independence meant not only political sovereignty but cultural autonomy. Egypt needed its own national literature, which for a group that was broadly speaking reacting against tradition meant new genres and directions. Ahmad Dayf first introduced the idea of a national literature in a lecture at the Egyptian university in 1918 and Haykal sketched the theoretical outline in an essay published in *Al-Siyasa* on 18 March 1925, drawing on the themes of territorial nationalism, and rehearsed the theory in several writings thereafter.[47] Literature and the environment are interdependent in his analysis. National literature is the product of place, time and character and has a role to play, along with education, in nurturing the nation, as the American example demonstrates. Egypt has been remiss in this respect, too attached to classical Arabic literature in its wide sense, which lacks the specificity of a national canon, or even foreign literature, while Egypt's writers and poets do not draw inspiration from Egyptian sources. Thus Haykal calls for a concerted effort to uncover the national personality (*dhātiyyat al-umma*) and for an Egyptian national literature that combines the nation's past and present and draws on, and reflects, its milieu: to produce a genuine national literature 'we must describe our lives and the lives of our ancestors and the environment which cultivated us and the legacy hidden within us'.[48] Authenticity and the Egyptian nation are thus everything in the new literature, and its mutual guarantors. Moreover, *al-adab al-qawmī* is charged not only with reflecting life but with vital functions, including fostering national sentiment among Egyptians. The relevance of the national literary project for our purposes is that it figures the novel, as a critical genre within the new literature, as a formal vehicle for a nationalist, and by extension secularising, project. The very writing of novels in the early period is a nationalistic performance and self-conscious substitution of traditional literature and its values.

* * *

As an effect of the above nation features prominently in the coming discussion, especially in Part 1, which explores the emergence of the Egyptian novel as a secular genre and the role of religion within it. Drawing on theoretical concepts laid out in this introduction, specifically the secular conditions of belief of the novel and intersubjectivity as a critical tool for understanding the religious/secular dialectic, as well as nation formation as a vital frame informing and influencing story, theme and approaches to the sacred, I explore manifestations of the secular, both on the level of content and form, in the early Egyptian novel and corresponding representation of religion in various forms. Chapter 2 (The Religious Other) identifies religion as a key problematic in early examples of modern Arabic narrative discourse in Egypt before embarking on an in-depth discussion of the religious/secular opposition in seminal works by Haykal, Taha Husayn and Tawfiq al-Hakim. I explore how texts like *Zaynab* (1914), *Al-Ayyam* (vols 1 and 2; 1929, 1933), ʿ*Awdat al-Ruh* (1933) and ʿ*Usfur min al-Sharq* (1938) promote national and secular values on the level of story and character, but undermine these values through self-contradiction and slippage, and how religious patterns remain deeply embedded in characters' thought and behaviour even as formal religion is subjected to harsh critique and theocentrism is displaced as ideology. Chapter 3 (The Secular Scripture) continues in a similar vein, focusing now on mature works by Najib Mahfuz and ʿAbd al-Rahman al-Sharqawi, which offer further perspectives on the interdependence and co-imbrication of the religious and secular. I explore the trilogy (1956–7), *Al-Ard* (1954) and *Muhammad Rasul al-Hurriyya* (1962) as different culminations of the secularisation process implied by nation formation, and the conflict and tension inherent therein, examining methods of religious displacement and othering, strategies of demystification, lines of religious critique, symbolic trajectories, as well as spiritual yearning, apologetics and theological conundrums as they appear in these works. The evidence is that into maturity, as the secular aesthetic in the Egyptian novel stabilises, religion remains a contested site.

Having discussed the religious/secular dialectic at length in Part 1, Part 2 focuses on religious themes and approaches in the modern Egyptian novel. I begin this section with an introduction to literary developments from the late 1960s (Chapter 4), specifically the *turāthī* trend and ascendance of experimental narrative strategies, in the context of wider cultural shifts around this time, including the religious resurgence, and how all of this affected the representation of religion on the pages of the Egyptian novel. I then move to selected themes and close readings of novels from the early 1970s. In Chapter 5 (Intertextual Dialogues) I explore how Jamal al-Ghitani reworks elements of Ibn Iyas' Egyptian chronicle to bring out themes relating to the collusion of religion and power in *Al-Zayni Barakat* (1971) and how messianic thought and prophetic myth are deconstructed in Mahfuz's *Malhamat al-Harafish* (1977). I analyse the reimagining of Christ's crucifixion in ʿAbd al-Hakim Qasim's short novel *Al-Mahdi* (1984) as a comment on modern-day religious violence and the practice of scapegoating, and discuss religious conflict in the text as an example of René Girard's mimetic rivalry leading to communal self-purification through sacrifice. I also explore the dialogue with Islamic eschatology and dream narrative in *Turaf min Khabar al-Akhira* (1984) by the same author, examining how the scene of the interrogating angels and pattern of judgement in the afterlife are transformed to communicate social and religious themes. In Chapter 6 (The Coptic Theme) I explore Bahaʾ Tahir's *Khalati Safiyya wa'l-Dayr* (1991) as a complex allegory of religious tolerance and read Idwar al-Kharrat's *Turabuha Zaʿfaran* (1986) as an example of Deleuze and Guattari's concept of minor discourse whilst paying attention to Christian scriptural reference and themes of religious tolerance and Coptic identity. I then turn to two historical novels centring on Coptic protagonists, *Al-Bashmuri* by Salwa Bakr (1998) and *ʿAzazil* by Yusuf Zaydan (2008), to examine how they rewrite history from a Coptic perspective in order to redress the historical marginalisation of Egypt's Christians and destabilise certain myths of history and nation. Religious tolerance, religious violence and religious criticism as represented in these works are also examined. In Chapter 7 (Mystical Dimensions) I revisit Mahfuz's trilogy, rereading Kamal's infatuation with ʿAyda in terms of the Sufi's love affair with God. I explain the turn to Sufism post-1967 in terms of its symbolism and identity as marginalised discourse and of certain overlaps in Sufi vision and the new literary sensibility before exploring in detail the mystical content of two further works by Mahfuz. I read *Hikayat Haratina* (1975) as an inversion of the Sufi path and exploration of mysticism as a solution to social ills and metaphysical angst, and *Asdaʾ al-Sirat al-Dhatiyya* (1995) as a reimagining of spiritual autobiography and embodiment of the limits and possibilities of Islamic mysticism. The structure, language and intertextual dialogue with Sufi writing in these two works are considered as ways of challenging unitary discourse and communicating postmodern themes. In Chapter 8 (Feminist Perspectives) I explore *Suqut al-Imam* (1987) and *Jannat wa Iblis* (1992) by Nawal Saʿdawi as feminist dystopias which employ unconventional narrative techniques to augment the dystopic effect and take issue with the founding texts of monotheism as historic vehicles for female oppression. I refer briefly to Salwa Bakr's rehabilitation of Zulaykha in *Wasf al-Bulbul* (1993) before exploring *Al-ʿAraba al-Dhahabiyya la Tasʿad ila al-Samaʾ* (1991) by the same author as a critique of religion via the trope of madness, paying attention to how religion, as belief, custom, institution and law, is implicated in the plight of women in the text. The discussion also takes in the Alifa Rifʿat's stories as a rare example of Islamic literature admitted to the canon. Each of these four chapters begins with a contextual introduction.

As the chapter breakdown reveals, the study is ambitious but by no means exhaustive. The possibilities for studying religion in the Egyptian novel are many, and the scope of material immense. Therefore I have chosen to focus on some key themes and on a selection of novels which exemplify these. Readers may reasonably question the choice of texts and note omissions and perhaps some repetition. The texts in Part 1 have been analysed many times over. Yet while many scholars have noted religious criticism and nationalist themes in these works, and while religion and secularism are acknowledged as critical debates in the decades during the period in which they were produced, what is lacking in modern Arabic literary scholarship is a focused study of the religious/secular dialectic as it is played out in the early Egyptian novel, taking into account the wider question of the form's secular aesthetic, and, moreover, recognising, and analysing, the cross-contamination of the religious and secular in this context. Similarly, although Mahfuz and Saʿdawi are favourites in modern Arabic literary studies, I concluded that their contribution to certain themes (Sufi, feminist) is too significant to ignore for the sake of avoiding favoured writers, though in the case of Mahfuz, and excepting the trilogy, it was possible to opt for lesser known works for close reading of mystical content without overlooking critical features and discussion points. On the other hand, a novel like Jamal al-Ghitani's *Kitab al-Tajalliyyat* is relevant to the discussion of Sufi themes in Chapter 7 and may seem strangely absent, but because it has been closely analysed by Ziad Elmarsafy under the Sufi rubric in a recent book in this series I have chosen to omit it here and would recommend that the reader visits his *Sufism in the Arabic Novel* for further elaboration on mystical dimensions in Arabic literature in general and in the work of al-Ghitani in particular. The same applies to Mahfuz's *Al-ᶜAʾish fi'l-Haqiqa* (1985). Ibrahim ᶜAbd al-Majid's *La Ahad Yanam fi Iskandariyya* (1996) would likewise fit well in the Coptic chapter as a late twentieth-century exploration of Christian–Muslim relations in Egypt, but in the end I opted for *Khalati Safiyya wa'l-Dayr* (1991) as the text through which to exemplify post-1967 approaches to inter-community cooperation. Word limit and duplication account for the many other works that have not made it into this study.

If religion is an enormous topic in modern Arabic literature, this partially explains why I have limited the study to Egypt. Modern Arabic literature takes in the verbal art of several countries and there is no denying the rich and productive dialogue that takes place across this corpus and its co-affinities. Yet at the same time, insofar as I have endeavoured to study literature in context and inasmuch as I understand art to be deeply involved in its environment, then some cultural and geographical limits were necessary. The national trajectory is essential for understanding approaches to religion in the early Arabic novel as the coming chapters will illustrate, but Arabic literature takes in multiple nationalisms, each developing at its own pace, according to idiosyncratic conditions and local histories. I therefore limited the study to Egypt in order to take advantage of the national and cultural context in its specifics. For instance, 1967 was a cataclysmic event across the Arab world, but its repercussions were felt differently in Egypt and elsewhere. Likewise, the Christian theme in modern Arabic literature has a specificity in Egypt, by virtue of its Coptic history, that is not shared by other regions of the Arabic-speaking world. I might cautiously also note the pioneering and central role Egypt has played in the development of modern Arabic literature through its various phases. Muhammad Siddiq writes that 'The Arabic novel in Egypt encapsulates and epitomises the characteristic formal traits, thematic interests, and cultural and structural constraints of the Arabic novel in general ...',[49] though this should not of course be taken to imply homogeneity.

Readers might also question my focus on the novel rather than poetry or the short story, or perhaps the three forms together, which would surely yield fascinating results for the artistic representation of religion. A combined approach is, however, beyond the scope of this project, and left with the three as distinct forms the novel is the obvious choice, not only because of its ascendency in the last century – Jabir ᶜAsfur, as noted, refers to the modern period in Arabic culture as *zaman al-riwāya* – but because the novel's aesthetic puts it into a particular relation with religion, which makes the role and representation of religion in its pages all the more interesting. The novel more than any other modern art form eschews dogma. Though the short story and modern poetry partake in the secular aesthetic of the novel, by virtue of their brevity and fragmentary character they tolerate faith more easily. A key question in this study is how religion makes its way back into the pages of a narrative form that has effectively renounced it, which is not so easily posed in the case of the short story and poem. I should at this point qualify this as *canonical* narrative form and reiterate that this is a study of the Egyptian novelistic canon. *Al-Riwāya al-islāmiyya* (the Islamic novel), which belongs to the aforementioned sub-canonical field of *al-adab al-islāmī*, does not form part of the discussion due to its popular character and aesthetic weakness. While this genre is significant, not least because of its wide readership, it calls for a different set of analytical techniques and, to my mind, a cultural studies, rather than a literary text, approach. There is also the problem of beginnings. While I begin my exploration of religion in the Egyptian novel with *Zaynab*, I do not, as mentioned, insist on *Zaynab* as the first Arabic novel nor deny premodern examples of the form, and while I make much of the secular aesthetic of the novel and the shifting Weltanschauung which accompanied its emergence, I do not insist on secularity as an exclusively modern condition nor deny secular themes in premodern literature; these are the theoretical premises upon which the study is based but they are not final statements and should be understood as part of an ongoing debate about the nature, form and manifestation of the religious and secular in different milieux.

Religion is huge in its connotation and as a cover term seems clumsy in an academic context, where precision is preferred. Yet it is also a convenient way of referring to the myriad set of texts and practices, including revelation, doctrine, scripture, ritual, myth and theology, with which the Arabic novel engages. I have endeavoured to specify the aspect of religion under discussion where appropriate but religion, the religious and the sacred are nevertheless inescapable as general terms and I hope do not cause confusion or appear lacking in definition in the coming pages. Likewise, are secularism, secularity and the secular. The first is a political ideology and social structure, the second a state or condition and the third an adjective applied to either. I try to maintain these distinctions but some overlap is unavoidable here as in all discussions of the secular. For example, while I argue that the novel's secularity is essentially a matter of form and textual ideology, I nevertheless pay attention to secular themes and expressions on the level of plot and in the discourse of characters in the early part of the study in order to complete the picture and show as many dimensions of the religious/secular dialectic as possible. I might also, again cautiously, add that, away from matters of political dogma and away from sociology, secularity and secularism are to an extent interchangeable terms in a literary context. Amardeep Singh's literary secularism covers a range of phenomena in his study of that name, aligning in the end with Edward Said's concept of secular criticism.[50] Finally, I would like to acknowledge a structural question I struggled with, namely the place of women's writing in this study. Like many Arab women writers I tend to reject women's writing as a category – why should literature by women be approached as a subject of special interest and why should this body of work be defined by the gender of its author, when other texts are classed by theme, technique, genre, time period, and so on? By devoting a chapter to women writers am I not perpetuating a methodological approach that I do not necessarily support? But at the same time when it comes to matters of religion it is clear that Arab and Egyptian women have a particular voice and contribution and that a section dedicated to feminist perspectives is appropriate, and that while the latter does not in theory imply women-authored texts, in practice it is predominantly women who have championed the cause therefore Chapter 8 has, in effect, become a chapter on women's writing. I should also say a quick word about translation. Most of the texts studied here have been translated into English and these have been used alongside the Arabic. Some translations take more liberties than others however, and in a literary study the priority when quoting material is to stay as close to the original as possible. Therefore when quoting I have largely used my own translations, not because they are superior but because, having started on this track in Part 1, where the English translation of the Arabic texts is freer, it seemed appropriate to continue, so as not to fall into an exercise of linguistic comparison and translation studies. This also means that any flaws in translation, as in the rest of the study, are entirely my own.

Notes

1. Adunis, 'Khawatir hawl Mazahir al-Takhalluf al-Fikri fi'l-Mujtamaʿ al-ʿArabi', *Al-Adab* (Beirut), May 1974, pp. 28, 29.
2. On the Qur'an's influence on classical Arabic literature, see A. M. Zubaidi, 'The Impact of the Qur'an and Hadith on Medieval Arabic Literature', in A. F. L. Beeston, T. M. Johnstone, R. B. Serjeant and G. R. Smith (eds), *Arabic Literature to the End of the Umayyad Period* (Cambridge: Cambridge University Press, 1983), pp. 322–43. On the Qur'an as literature, see Issa Boullata (ed.), *Literary Structures of Religious Meaning in the Qur'an* (Abingdon: Routledge, 2000); Thomas Hoffmann, *The Poetic Qur'an: Studies on Qur'anic Poeticity* (Wiesbaden: Harrassowitz, 2007); Mustansir Mir, 'The Qur'an as Literature', *Religion and Literature*, vol. 20, no. 1 (1988), pp. 49–64; Shawkat Toorawa, 'Hapless Hapaxes and Luckless Rhymes: The Qur'an as Literature', *Religion and Literature*, vol. 41, no. 2 (Summer 2009), pp. 221–7. On the Qur'an and modern Arabic literature, see Stefan Wild, 'The Koran as Subtext in Modern Arabic Poetry', in Gert Borg and Ed de Moor (eds), *Representations of the Divine in Arabic Poetry* (Amsterdam and Atlanta: Rodopi, 2001), pp. 139–60; Toorawa, 'Modern Arabic Literature and the Qur'an: Creativity, Inimitability … Incompatibilities?', in Glenda Abramson and Hilary Kilpatrick (eds), *Religious Perspectives in Modern Muslim and Jewish Literatures* (London: RoutledgeCurzon, 2005), pp. 239–57.
3. Jabir ʿAsfur, *Zaman al-Riwaya* (Damascus: al-Mada, 1999), p. 76. ʿAsfur is drawing on Jonathan Culler here.
4. See opening quotation of ch. 3, Ghali Shukri, *Al-Muntama: Dirasat fi Adab Najib Mahfuz* (Cairo: Dar al-Maʿarif, 1969), p. 207. See also Menahem Milson, *Najib Mahfuz: The Novelist-Philosopher of Cairo* (Jerusalem and New York: St Martin's Press and Magness Press, 1998), pp. 32ff, and *On Literature and Philosophy: The Non-Fiction Writing of Naguib Mahfouz*, trans. Arab Byrne with intro. by Rasheed El-Enany (London: Gingko Library, 2016). An illuminating essay in this collection, 'Art and Culture', originally published in *Al-Majalla al-Jadida* in August 1936, explores the remit of art, and the permissibility of intellectual matter alongside its traditional aesthetic and emotional functions, concluding that art can encompass all of these things, whereas knowledge (rational, philosophical) has its limits (pp. 135–9).

5. Paul Ricoeur, *History and Truth*, trans. Charles A. Kelbley (Evanston: Northwestern University Press, 1965), p. 127.
6. James Wood, *The Broken Estate: Essays in Literature and Belief* (London: Pimlico, 1999), p. xiv.
7. Max Black, *Models and Metaphors* (Ithaca, NY: Cornell University Press, 1962).
8. Paul Ricoeur, *Figuring the Sacred: Religion, Narrative, and Imagination*, trans. David Pellauer (Minneapolis: Fortress Press, 1995), p. 222.
9. Thomas Aquinas, *Summa Theologica*, 1a. 1, 10. Cited from Janet Soskice, *Metaphor and Religious Language* (Oxford: Clarendon Press, 1985), p. 86.
10. Soskice, *Metaphor and Religious Language*, p. 63. Soskice goes on to interrogate this assumption.
11. Jalal al-Din al-Rumi, *The Essential Rumi*, trans. Coleman Barks and John Moyne (London: Penguin, 1995), p. 10.
12. T. R. Wright, *Theology and Literature* (Oxford: Basil Blackwell, 1988), p. 10.
13. Michael Goldberg, 'Exodus 1:13-14', *Interpretation: A Journal of the Bible and Theology*, vol. 37, no. 4 (1983). Cited from Wright, *Theology and Literature*, p. 83.
14. Northrop Frye, *The Great Code: The Bible and Literature* (New York: Harcourt, 1982), p. 33.
15. See Wright, *Theology and Literature*, pp. 84–5.
16. Wood, *The Broken Estate*, p. xiv.
17. Muhammad Siddiq, *Arab Culture and the Novel: Genre, Identity and Agency in Egyptian Fiction* (London: Routledge, 2007), p. 102.
18. Reuven Snir, *Religion, Mysticism and Modern Arabic Literature* (Weisbaden: Harrassowitz Verlag, 2006), p. 21. See ch. 1: 'Synchrony: Islamist Literature', pp. 21–36. See also Fedwa Malti-Douglas, *Medicines of the Soul: Female Bodies and Sacred Geographies in a Translational Islam* (Berkley, LA, and London: University of California Press, 2001), pp. 5–9. Malti-Douglas notes a permeability between the two literary corpora but suggests the religious side to be the more porous (pp. 5–6).
19. Malti-Douglas, *Medicines*, pp. 6–7; Najib al-Kilani, *Al-Islamiyya wa'l-Madhahib al-Adabiyya* (Beirut: Muʾassasat al-Risala, 1983), pp. 117ff; Muhammad Qutb, *Manhaj al-Fann al-Islami* (Beirut and Cairo: Dar al-Shuruq, 1983), pp. 212ff. Other studies of *al-adab al-islāmī* include: Muhammad Hasan Burayghash, *Fi'l-Adab al-Islami al-Muʿasir: Dirasa wa Tatbiq* (Beirut: Muʾassasat al-Risala, 1998), and his *Nahw Adab Islami: al-Qissat al-Islamiyya al-Muʿasira*

(Amman: Dar al-Bashir, 1992); Sabir ʿAbd al-Dayim, *Al-Adab al-Islami Bayn al-Nazariyya wa'l-Tatbiq* (Zaqaziq: Dar al-Arqam, 1990); Najib al-Kilani, *Afaq al-Adab al-Islami* (Beirut: Muʾassasat al-Risala, 1985); Ahmad Bassam Saʿi, *Al-Waqaʾiyya al-Islamiyya fi'l-Adab wa'l-Naqd* (Jedda: Dar al-Manara li'l-Nashr, 1985); Christian Szyska, '"Illa al-Ladhina Amanu wa Amilu al-Salihat wa Dhakaru Allah Kathiran": Hawla Mafhum "al-Adab al-Multazim" ʿinda Udaba al-Harakat al-Islamiyya', *Al-Karmil: Abhath fi'l-Lugha wa'l-Adab*, vol. 20 (1999), pp. 33–62.

20. Michael Edwards, *Towards a Christian Poetics* (London: Macmillan, 1984); Luke Ferreter, *Towards a Christian Literary Theory* (London and New York: Palgrave Macmillan, 2003); Wright, *Theology and Literature*.
21. Michael Allen, *In the Shadow of World Literature: Sites of Reading in Colonial Egypt* (Princeton and Oxford: Princeton University Press, 2016), p. 7.
22. Ian Watt, *Rise of the Novel: Studies in Defoe, Richardson and Fielding* (London: Chatto and Windus: 1957), p. 14.
23. ʿAsfur, *Zaman al-Riwaya*, p. 42.
24. Ibid. p. 15. ʿAsfur formulates his *zaman al-riwāya* with reference to poetry, which was the ascendant art form until the *nahḍa*, and refers to the novel as *dīwān al-ʿarab al-muḥdathīn* (p. 10).
25. Wen-Chin Ouyang gives an overview of the debate about origins in *Poetics of Love in the Arabic Novel: Nation-State, Modernity and Tradition* (Edinburgh: Edinburgh University Press, 2012), pp. 10ff.
26. See Nazik Saba Yared, *Secularism and the Arab World (1850–1939)* (London: Saqi Books, 2002), p. 196. See also chs 2 and 3 and Azzam Tamimi, 'The Origins of Arab Secularism', in Azzam Tamimi and John L. Esposito (eds), *Islam and Secularism in the Middle East* (London: Hurst and Company, 2002), pp. 13–28.
27. See Talal Asad, *Formations of the Secular: Christianity, Islam, Modernity* (Stanford: Stanford University Press, 2003), pp. 8–12, where he discusses the possibilities for reading a sacred text like the Bible purely as art and the complex motives of religious violence: 'Is motivated behaviour that accounts for itself by religious discourse ipso facto religious or only when it does so *sincerely*?', asks Asad. Abdelwahab Elmessiri makes a similar point. The state, along with multinational corporations and pleasure industries, have penetrated deeply into our private lives, such that even dreaming is no longer a spontaneous activity. Elmessiri, 'Secularism, Immanence and Deconstruction', in Tamimi and Esposito, *Islam and Secularism*, pp. 52–3.

28. Elmessiri, 'Secularism, Immanence and Deconstruction', p. 2. See also *Al-ʿAlmaniyyat al-Juzʾiyya waʾl-ʿAlamaniyyat al-Shamila*, 2 vols (Cairo: Dar al-Shuruq, 2002).
29. Charles Taylor, *A Secular Age* (Cambridge, MA, and London: Belknap Press of Harvard University, 2007), p. 3.
30. See Charles Taylor, 'Modes of Secularism', in Rajeev Bhargava (ed.), *Secularism and Its Critics* (Oxford and Delhi: Oxford University Press, 1998), pp. 31–53.
31. Taylor, *A Secular Age*, pp. 37ff.
32. See introduction to Frank O'Connor, *The Lonely Voice: A Study of the Short Story* (Cork: Cork City Council, 2003 [1962]), pp. 1–24. O'Connor argues that the hero of the short story tends to be an individual from a 'submerged population group', an isolated type, whereas in the novel there is invariably a process of identification between character and reader and, by extension, society, even if this relation is a hostile one.
33. Sabry Hafez, *The Quest for Identities: The Development of the Modern Arabic Short Story* (London, San Francisco and Beirut: Saqi Books, 2007), p. 37.
34. Asad, *Formations of the Secular*, p. 22.
35. G. W. F. Hegel, *Phenomenology of the Spirit*, trans. A. V. Miller (Oxford: Clarendon Press, 1977), para. 179, p. 111: 'Self-consciousness exists in and for itself when, and by the fact that, it so exists for another; that is, it exists only in being acknowledged'.
36. See Emmanuel Levinas, *Totality and Infinity: An Essay on Exteriority*, trans. Alphonso Lingis (Pittsburgh: Duquesne University Press, 1969) and *Otherwise than Being: or Beyond Essence*, trans. Alphonso Lingis (Pittsburgh: Duquesne University Press, 1998).
37. Jean-Paul Sartre, *Being and Nothingness*, trans. Hazel E. Barnes (London: Routledge, 1996), p. 237: 'In order to make myself recognised by the Other, I must risk my own life. To risk one's life, in fact, is to reveal oneself as not-bound to the objective form or to any determined existence – as not-bound to life'.
38. See Paul Ricoeur, *Oneself as Another*, trans. Kathleen Blamey (Chicago and London: University of Chicago Press, 1990).
39. Robert J. C. Young, 'Postcolonial Remains', *New Literary History*, vol. 43, no. 1 (Winter 2012), pp. 36–9.
40. Edward Said, *Orientalism* (New York: Vintage, 1979), p. 59.
41. Homi Bhabha, 'The Other Question: Stereotype, Discrimination and the Discourse of Colonialism', in *The Location of Culture* (London and New York: Routledge, 2004), pp. 94–5.

42. Sara Ahmed makes a similar argument for the stranger, who she argues is recognised and tasked to embody that which the community wishes to expunge from its purified space. '[T]he stranger is produced as a figure that is distinct from the (philosophical) body, only through a process of expulsion: the stranger "comes to be" as an entity precisely by prior inhabiting of that philosophical body, or the body of the community "that knows".' *Strange Encounters: Embodied Others in Post-Coloniality* (London and New York: Routledge, 2000), p. 56.
43. Israel Gershoni and James P. Jankowski, *Egypt, Islam, and the Arabs: The Search for Egyptian Nationhood, 1900–1930* (New York and Oxford: Oxford University Press, 1986), p. 140.
44. *Al-Yawm wa'l-Ghad* [1928] in Salama Musa, *al-Muʾalifat al-Kamila* (Beirut: Maktabat al-Maʿarif, 1998), p. 662. Also p. 379: 'People exaggerate the religious bond (*al-rābiṭa al-dīniyya*), which in fact has no value outside of language and nation'. Salama Musa cites the fact that there are Muslims in China and Christians in South American and Australia who are of no interest to Muslims and Copts in Egypt as evidence of the weakness of the religious bond as a basis for community.
45. Salama Musa, 'Al-Wataniyya wa'l-ʿAlamiyya', *Al-Majalla al-Jadida* (March 1930). Cited from Gershoni and Janowski, *Egypt, Islam, and the Arabs*, p. 140 and n. 68.
46. Taha Husayn, *Mustaqbal al-Thaqafa fi Misr* (Cairo: Matbaʿat al-Maʿarif, 1938), pp. 16, 481, 484.
47. Haykal, 'Al-Adab al-Qawmi', *Al-Siyasa*, 18 March 1925; *Fi Awqat al-Faragh* (Cairo: Maktabat al-Nahda al-Misriyya, 1968 [1925]), pp. 350–6. See also essays in Haykal, *Thawrat al-Adab* (Cairo: Dar al-Maʿarif, 1978 [1933]), e.g. 'Al-Adab al-Qawmi' (which differs from the 1925 piece of the same title), 'Al-Taʾrikh wa'l-Adab al-Qawmi', 'Muhawilat fi'l-Adab al-Qawmi'), and Gershoni and Janowski, *Egypt, Islam, and the Arabs*, pp. 191–227. A manifesto for a new national literature, signed by Muhammad Zaki ʿAbd al-Qadir, Muhammad Amin Hassuna, Muhammad al-Asmar, Zakariyya ʿAbduh, Mahmud ʿIzzat Musa and Muʿawiya Muhammad Nir, was published in *Al-Siyasa* on 28 June 1930.
48. Haykal, *Thawrat al-Adab*, p. 122.
49. Siddiq, *Arab Culture and the Novel*, p. 4.
50. Amardeep Singh, *Literary Secularism: Religion and Modernity in Twentieth-Century Fiction* (Newcastle: Cambridge Scholars Press, 2006); Edward Said, 'Secular Criticism', in *The World, the Text, and the Critic* (Cambridge, MA: Harvard University Press, 1983), pp. 1–30.

2

The Religious Other

Haykal's *Zaynab*, published in 1914, is generally named as the first novel in Arabic.¹ The designation is related to *Zaynab*'s break with *maqāma*, realism and novelistic strategy and is by no means uncontested. *Adhra᾽ Dinshaway* (1906), *Hadith ᶜIsa ibn Hisham* (1907), as well as earlier works by Salim al-Bustani, Francis Marrash and Farah Anton, have been proposed for the accolade, and Bouthaina Shaaban and Hoda Elsadda point to contributions by women like Zaynab Fawwaz and Labiba Hashim which have been wrongfully overlooked.² But I am not concerned here with first works so much as the emergence of the Arabic novel as a secular form and what this means for the representation of religion in its pages, and in this regard *Zaynab*, with its hybrid secularism and unconscious theism, invites attention. *Zaynab* consciously promotes Egyptian identity over religious affiliation for the first time in Arabic fiction, co-opting the novel into the wider nationalist secularising project of the author. Yet *Zaynab* was preceded by a series of narrative texts – modern *maqāma*s and eclectic prose works – which establish religion as a critical problematic in modern Arabic fiction before the novel took hold. For example, *Al-Saq ᶜala Saq fi-ma huwa al-Fariyaq* (1855) by Faris al-Shidyaq is explicitly negative about Syrian Christianity. Early in the first volume the narrator notes that although not a book of religious criticism *Al-Saq* will nevertheless illustrate the impoverished learning of the Church and the impasse this creates.³ In fact the Church's faults turn out to be many in al-Shidyaq's literary portrait. The Maronite Patriarch and his clergy are represented as a hypocritical and ignorant group, monasteries a sanctuary for the lazy and unproductive. I referred in the previous chapter to the author's support for the segregation of religious and political authority. Here al-Shidyaq shows, through anecdotes and scathing commentary, why he so despises the clerical establishment, that 'confederacy of cretins' (*maʿāshir al-sufahāʾ*),[4] who imprisoned and tortured his brother, possibly to death, for converting to Protestantism.[5] The latter event, addressed in an extended and vitriolic tirade at the end of the first volume, not only shows a dark and sinister side to the Church but highlights the conflict between faith and individual freedom. Back in Egypt, renowned editor, poet, writer and nationalist, ʿAbdullah al-Nadim (1843–96), was concerned with the corrupting effects of modernity and European influence on traditional life. His moralising short narratives in *Al-Tankit wa'l-Tabkit* and *Al-Ustadh*,[6] insofar as they address themes like the proper performance of religious obligations, ill effects of alcohol, ignorance about religion, and false piety, represent Islam as a system of ethics under threat.[7] Another prominent journalist who turned his hand to fiction, Muhammad al-Muwaylihi (1858–1930), satirises Islamic institutions and representatives – ignorant clerics, pious charlatans, defective Sharia courts, etc. – in *Hadith ʿIsa ibn Hisham* (1907), which fuses the classical *maqāma* with contemporary content.[8] ʿIsa and the Pasha's encounter with the Azhar shaykhs in particular suggests a severe disconnect between the religious establishment and modern life, while their tour of the law courts reveals a hybrid legal system struggling to cope with the pressures of change. ʿIsa is left insisting that, no, the Sharia has not been abrogated, it just needs to adapt to modern times. His defence here and elsewhere aligns with themes and ideas promoted by Jamal al-Din al-Afghani and Muhammad Abduh such that *Hadith* becomes in places a vehicle for Islamic reformist messages. The narrative engenders, among other things, anxiety over the future of Islam in a fast-changing world.

Hadith opens with a dedication (*ihdāʿ al-kitāb*) which signposts its Muslim sensibility. The book is dedicated to al-Afghani and Abduh, among others, and a letter from the former is extracted in which al-Muwaylihi's success as a writer is attributed to God. The form of the quotation, uncritically inserted as the conclusion to the dedication, implies an acceptance of the views expressed therein, including the God-given nature of the author's talent. This is followed by a preface invoking the blessings of God on Muhammad and his family, thus situating the text in a trajectory of Islamic heritage, which is borne out by reference and quotation in what follows, as well as the Islamic reformist theme. *Al-Saq*, too, for all its caustic criticism of the Church, opens with divine invocation and makes frequent reference to God as ordaining or decreeing this or that. Though the Maronite clergy are under attack and the author would see the Syrian Church stripped of its political power, the Islamic State, in the form of the Ottoman Sultanate, of which the author's home of the Levant formed a part, is not questioned and the work is unquestionably theocentric. These works are conceived in a God-centred world in which belief is taken for granted and a religious community is assumed. This changes with *Zaynab*, which opens not with religious invocation but an epigraph of a country scene and proceeds to promote a national imaginary based on territorial kinship. At the same time its strategy of realism and novelistic presentation moves Arabic fiction in the direction of the secular, though this is by no means a simple course.

Zaynab's author, Haykal, who published one other novel (*Hakadha Khuliqat*, 1955), in addition to numerous critical articles and biographies of great men, was a liberal nationalist and vocal secularist in the early decades of the last century and played a prominent part in public life as a politician, journal editor and intellectual through to the 1950s.[9] Born in Kafr Ghannam in the Mansoura district to a family of ʿ*umda*s (village mayors), he was sent to Cairo aged seven to attend a government primary school and continued his education all the way to the Sorbonne, where he studied law (1909–12).[10] The tensions emerging from this trajectory, between traditional village life and a modern secular future, are the subject of *Zaynab*, in particular with respect to love and the possibilities of the cosmopolitan intellectual finding it in a satisfying mutual form when the Egyptian woman remains uneducated and locked away. Haykal came under the influence of Lutfi al-Sayyid (whose nephew he became through marriage) and Qasim Amin in his youth, during which time he began to write articles for *Al-Jarida* and self-consciously assume the role of a public intellectual, and the ideas he developed at this time, for example on Egyptian nationhood and female emancipation, filter through onto the pages of *Zaynab* through the drama and its not very subtle narrating voice. Haykal's relationship with religion, like certain others of the Egyptian intellectual elite in the first quarter of the last century, was not a straightforward one. In his early writing he tends to view Islam as an obstacle to progress whilst positing Pharoanic heritage as the root of Egyptian authenticity and Europe as the model of science and intellectual progress. He reflects on religion's social and moral function in his diaries and insists on the separation of religion and state.[11] Yet in the 1930s, having pursued a rather negative discourse on Islamic institutions and religion hitherto, he wrote a biography of the Prophet and an account of his own pilgrimage to Mecca, suggesting a change of heart. These would be followed by studies of the Orthodox caliphs Abu Bakr, ʿUmar and ʿUthman in the 1940s.[12] The switch was not unique to Haykal and scholars have questioned the religiosity behind these works, identifying rather a political motivation and cynical attempt to reach more devout elements of the population, but even so they indicate instability and conflict in the author's position. In *Zaynab*, on the other hand, written during a period of intellectual self-confidence and in the spirit of liberal nationalism, there is no attempt to cater for religious sensibilities and pious readers. Yet there is fluctuation and incongruence in the secularism which the text is presumed to engender, both as national allegory and as a novel, which attests that a transition to modernity is not a swift and easy mutation but a process rife with contradiction and variation and that the novel as a form is not as secular as it is conventionally assumed.

Zaynab tells the story of Hamid, a secular-educated urban youth, who bears a clear resemblance to the author, and his search for love during the summers he spends in his family village. His efforts are centred on Zaynab, a peasant girl and, as such, an unsuitable match who is herself embroiled in a tragic love story, and his cousin ʿAziza, who has the correct credentials in terms of class and upbringing but with whom he cannot forge a meaningful relationship due to rules of segregation and who is also, like Zaynab, married off against her will. The story takes a highly romantic shape and ends without resolution. ʿAziza vanishes into a mysterious marriage, Hamid disappears to complete his search alone and Zaynab dies of an illness linked to heartbreak.

Insofar as secularism, as a pluralist discourse, implies heteroglossia and polyphony in fiction then *Zaynab* does well. The narrative is multi-voiced and although the narrator adopts an authoritative, often didactic tone, he does not subsume every attitude and position into his purview. The ideological spread may be limited by chronotope, for we have only the inhabitants of a single Egyptian Muslim village at the turn of the last century, but within this group we have rebels and conformists, traditional and modern, orthodox and popular, and some variations thereof, coexisting in a multi-discursive space.

The nation, for example, actuates feelings of hope in Hamid, who envisages future glory and views Ibrahim's conscription into the army, which will not involve the farmer in anything as significant as revolt against the occupiers or combat with the enemy, in a broad trajectory of national progress; never mind the apparent insignificance of the tasks, '[Ibrahim] would at least be representing his nation and her army'.[13] But for Ibrahim the Egyptian nation is largely irrelevant and his conscription is simply the latest mechanism for the exploitation of the *fellāḥ* (Egyptian peasant). It has nothing to do with national service for him. He regards his military calling as 'just a job' and an effect of an unjust system which demands submission of the poor to the needs of the rich and powerful.[14] Scholars have written about *Zaynab* in the context of political imaginary, as one of those texts which perform the critical task on the path to nationhood of constructing and disseminating a national consciousness. Jeff Shalan explores *Zaynab* as an expression of territorial nationalism rooted in the *fellāḥīn*, whereby the critical lens applied to the lives of the peasants and conventions of love and marriage is an extension of the liberal nationalist thought of its author and his party.[15] But the nation is hardly a unitary discourse or common ideal for the characters themselves. Most are indifferent to it, while for Ibrahim it is simply another power structure profiting from his labour, the next phase in ongoing oppression of the impoverished masses. *Zaynab* may construct a national imaginary through the thought process of Hamid and vision of the narrator, who valorises the Egyptian countryside and *fellāḥ* to this end, but it does this in a multi-discursive context where voices against or indifferent to the nation speak too.

If secularism implies scepticism, then *Zaynab* also takes steps in the right direction. Its protagonist, Hamid, is an intellectual reflective type, who receives his secondary schooling in a secular institution in Cairo and returns to the village with a modern worldly outlook. As such we have in our central character a secular symbol. However, although Hamid's interior monologue includes much musing and speculation, this does not ultimately extend to faith, which casts doubt over his secular mindset, since secularity starts from a position of doubt. If Hamid's education and conflict with traditional life and the conventions of marriage make him a modern secular representative in the text, there is conversely little evidence that he regards theism in a secular manner, that is, as something which man opts into as opposed to a pre-given fact or natural phenomenon. Towards the end of the story Hamid joins a Sufi brotherhood and is quickly disillusioned. The narrator has indeed pre-empted this with intrusive commentary mocking its leader, Shaykh Masʿud, and condemning the Sufi solution before it has been acted upon. We are even told that Hamid himself has never approved of the group and his short-lived membership is portrayed as an act of desperation, a reaction to his hopeless predicament in love.[16] The episode as a whole, notwithstanding its suspect position in the plot, as an example of religious avowal/disavowal, suggests the optional character of religion and shows Hamid adopting a critical attitude towards it. But religious ritual and theism are not synonymous, and while Hamid views rural mysticism from a critical distance and is able to opt in and out of it, the same does not apply to belief in God. In fact the less educated, less worldly traditional representative, Zaynab, is the only character in the text to reflect on the supernatural as something which may or may not exist: 'maybe it is true that there is in people's souls a divine compartment that perceives what the senses do not and guides our hopes and draws our life's path for us', she says to herself as she ponders her feelings for Hamid.[17] Her meditation here, albeit isolated in her wider stream of thought, which consists in the main of musing on her lovers and her personal plight, places the supernatural in object position, a matter of reflection as opposed to an a priori fact.

We see no such reflection in Hamid, whose worldview, notwithstanding a sceptical attitude towards certain elements of religious practice, is theistic. Hamid's habit of praying in the mosque is not especially significant in this regard and can be viewed in the context of religion as culture and community, part of the fabric of village life. Nor is his disgust when he discovers his uncle and other villagers flouting the Ramadan fast of great import with respect to his Weltanschauung since the behaviour is condemned as disregard for custom and tradition as much as anything; his uncle offers him a cob to eat 'as though to demonstrate the extent of his indifference to the obligation (*farḍ*) that his entire family had performed for generations'.[18] It is the character's thought process and language that are of interest here and that problematise him as a secular representative. Hamid's interior monologue includes divine reference and statements about the mysteries of the universe which leave little doubt that the character is thoroughly theistic in outlook. He sees the world and the people in it as subject to higher forces, which although not understood are pre-given, in the order of things in a way that is not true of religious practice, which as we have seen he is able to view more critically. These higher forces include evil as much as good, and an illuminating example of Hamid's transcendent ascription is the way in which he frames the interlude with the farm girl whom he falls upon without invitation or prelude, even if she happens to respond with enthusiasm. Rather than taking personal responsibility, which would be a humanist response, he attributes his actions to Satan and a power beyond himself. 'Woe to existence that the world is arranged in this ill-fated way', he repines on his way to the canal, where he jumps into the water to cleanse himself and asks God's forgiveness.[19] The episode not only exemplifies the character's belief in the supernatural, but shows too that he subscribes to a scriptural concept of women and evil and that he further models his behaviour on religious paradigms. The sacred texts of Abrahamic religion link women and evil in multifarious ways, beginning with the founding myth of Adam and Eve. Women are accomplices of Satan, and examples of them thwarting men and spreading evil in scripture are many. Hamid, who elsewhere in the text expresses regret at the injustices suffered by women,[20] reverts to this vision of women when he reacts to the peasant girl with statements like 'Woman is a cursed devil (*shaytān*), a snare laid for poor men to blindly fall into!'.[21] This is not just a misogynist viewpoint but a religio-misogynist one, since the linking of woman and *shaytān* has roots in Islamic discourse, and the association of woman and snares has a Qur'anic precedent in verse 29 of *Surat Yusuf*. Hamid's word *ḥibāla* (snare) is but a synonym for *kayd*, a term which Zulaykha's husband applies to the whole of womankind in the Islamic story of Joseph.

The theme continues as Hamid 'cleanses' himself in the canal, which casts the encounter with a female body as sinful and something to be excised. The canal scene transcribes the scriptural pattern of sin–purification–forgiveness onto the narrative. Hamid is structuring his actions around religious concepts. Also noteworthy in this regard is that Hamid alludes to his predicament in terms of a fall. 'Woe to women who hurl us down from high rank and majesty', he complains to himself.[22] While the reference is ostensibly to social standing, the imagery, the sense of disgraceful descent, in conjunction with the notion of woman as evil, sex as sin, and guilt cleansed with water, makes this another example of the character's deep imbrication with scriptural structures of thought and experience. He returns to the concept again when he asks, 'have I come this far to sink to the very lowest level on account of a working girl, however beautiful she may be?'[23] If Hamid is the spokesman of modernity in the text, then modernity for him does not exclude religious belief. This need not be surprising, for most understandings of modernity today reach the same conclusion. But it does run counter to Haykal's early reflections on religion as an historical stage and of science taking its place in the modern era.[24] In the context of an embryonic form and first foray into novel-writing, one suspects that Hamid the character has come out more religious than Haykal intended, and that perhaps the author was better at articulating a modern secular position in his journalism and polemic than in fiction, with its ambivalence and unintended effects. Moreover, if Hamid is a representative of secularism in the text, then it is a rather messy version thereof, for he has the ability to perceive only certain kinds of religion from a critical distance whilst exhibiting naïve theism and reproducing religious structures and paradigms in his own thoughts and behaviour.

Hybrid or piecemeal secularism also applies to the narrator of *Zaynab*. While the text works as an expression of liberal nationalism on one level, and significantly does away with the religious framing of *Hadith ʿIsa ibn Hisham* as described, the narrating voice frequently works against the secular attitude implied in the nationalist dimension. Although not a character himself, the narrator of *Zaynab* is highly conspicuous. He frequently intervenes in the text to interpret events and set characters' actions and emotions in context. In these moments he represents an extension of the author, and it is here that he is at his most secular, in a sceptical, critical sense. For example, during Shaykh Masʿud's visit to the village the narrator adopts a critical approach to mystical practice and describes the worshippers in a manner that recalls Haykal's early view of religion as a source of comfort for the less educated. Masʿud's followers are depicted as a deranged rabble, duped by their charlatan shaykh:

> The moon above looked down on them calmly, as though smiling mockingly and ridiculing their madness, and the silent night returned the moans that rose from them as they all called to God until their voices grew hoarse. Neither the heavens nor the earth responded and their exertion was futile.[25]

Their faith is an act of ignorance, their prayers useless. The narrator also adopts a critical stance on religion in scenes around Zaynab's illness, where he speaks reproachfully of Umm Jaziyya's method of treatment, a form of exorcism, and the supernatural explanations of country folk: 'Most people think that the sick person has been touched by the evil eye or simply has a cold' [as opposed to something serious like tuberculosis],[26] he explains to the reader, lamenting the habit of not calling a medical doctor until it is too late or not at all. In Zaynab's case, Umm Jaziyya and the family burn alum and imagine that they see a familiar figure in the shapes of the flames. The irony here is that, while the narrator is disparaging of this practice and interpretation, he himself attributes Zaynab's illness to melancholy and tragedy in love, which hardly replaces superstition with science.[27] He correctly names her illness as consumption and evidently supports modern medicine as the appropriate course of treatment, but betrays the spirit of science represented in this position with his romantic interpretation of the causes. The doctor, incidentally, does not live up to his scientific values either. He urges Zaynab to tell her story as a means to a cure and includes fresh air at sunset in her treatment plan, which again tends towards the romantic. As a representative of science and modernity he is less than inspiring. Indeed he does not even prioritise his patient upon arriving in the village but rather chats with the magistrate at length about politics before enquiring after the reason for his urgent summons.

A secular-nationalist theme develops in the narrator's portraits of the *fellāḥīn* as at once symbols of timeless Egypt and as caught in a class struggle, though again we find contradictions. Ibrahim represents the archetypal *fellāḥ* in the text (while most of the others appear as a group). The narrator describes him as a pawn in an exploitative power structure which will endure in the absence of class action, imposing a socialist materialist interpretation on the experience of the peasant, which is secularising insofar as it breaks away from fatalist understandings of experience.[28] This angle is short-lived, however, for within a couple of paragraphs the same narrator tells us, still in reference to Ibrahim's plight, that there is no escape from fate and recommends that 'we be satisfied with our lot and forget our ordeals'.[29] Similarly, the nationalist theme in the narrator's discourse, which manifests in particular in statements about the *fellāḥīn*, whose 'steadfastness (*jalad*) traces back to ancient times and has passed from Pharoanic *fellāḥ* through to the *fellāḥ* of Ismail's time to the *fellāḥ* of today',[30] is secularising in the sense that it posits a national community over a Muslim one, but conflicts with suggestions by the narrator of higher powers controlling life on earth, which ultimately undermine the notion of a self-governing people forging their own future. For example, the following statement by the narrator hardly allows man charge of his destiny:

> Our days on earth, with their happiness and pain, sadness and joy, are out of our control. They are in the hands of another [power] – and in the moments when we sense this power we shudder as we sense our inability to embark on anything we want to by ourselves.[31]

The phrase 'our days on earth' (*ayyāmunā ʿalā al-arḍ*) naturally also carries with it a vision of this life as a prelude to another.

When he is not intervening with explanations and digressions, the narrator's language suggests a theistic worldview, or at the very least a psyche in which religious structures and motifs are deeply embedded. He refers to creation (*al-khalq*), which inscribes a particular understanding of the world on the text, and employs cosmic imagery and religious analogies. He describes Zaynab's future as a torment of hell and compares worshippers at a distance to 'phantoms swirling amidst the jinn or angels drawing together'.[32] Elsewhere daybreak is described as 'the god of fire and light'[33] and the sun as a great disc 'moving between the heavens and earth as though shaken from its bed by angels'.[34] In other literary contexts, such as Najib Mahfuz's trilogy, employing religious imagery to describe profane objects and experience functions to secularise the sacred (see Chapter 3), but here it simply intones the mental structures of the narrator and the extent to which they are infused with religion and myth. As he theorises the appropriateness of marrying one's own kind, the narrator brings in imagery from the creation myth of Adam and Eve: 'the longing in our chest for the partner that was eternally separated from us on the day when Eve was created from Adam's rib makes us look to our own class and people as brothers'.[35] The imagery here not only confirms the ingrained nature of religious stories in the thought of the narrator, but introduces the concept of marriage as sacred return. Whether consciously or not, the narrator recasts marriage, which is a central ambition and tenet in the narrative, as a reconstitution of the originary pair. While there are secular themes in the discourse of the narrator, in the form of materialist interpretations, nationalism and religious criticism, his vision and psyche are imbued with religious paradigms and tend towards theism. In common with Hamid, although he views religious practice and certain religious beliefs from a critical distance, transcendence is assumed and constitutes part of his optic lens.

But what does transcendence mean in *Zaynab*? For the most part we are not talking about theism in an Islamic mould. The narrative develops an ethics of love and individual fulfilment which has little to do with religious prescription and morality, and though it may include scenes of worshippers at the mosque and references to God in the speech of the characters, these are strategies of verisimilitude and characterisation and do not necessarily form part of the ideology of the text. Transcendence in *Zaynab* refers rather to the mysterious workings of the universe, hidden forces and nature in particular. Nature is an agent and mystical power in the novel. Hamid and Zaynab are seen in communion with it at certain points, and it is to nature that Hamid turns for comfort and meaning in times of despair and to escape modern life, such that nature, rather than religion, becomes the alternative to modernity and materialism. The sanctification of the countryside in *Zaynab* recalls the pantheism of the English romantic poets, but this is no theology of nature. What we have is a displacement of divinity onto nature, which in turn becomes a symbol of Egyptian authenticity and vehicle for nationalism. In other words, religious spiritualism based on divinity is replaced with nationalist spiritualism focused on an Egyptian pastoral. It is noteworthy in this regard that Zaynab the *fellāḥa*, another symbol of nation in the narrative, merges with nature at times and in these moments is attributed mystical power too. In the opening pages we are told that 'Nature excelled in Zaynab', and that walking in the countryside at night one might find oneself magnetically drawn to the sound of her singing and virtually put into a trance state by the beautiful tones.[36] That which heralds or assists the nation – the countryside with its crop heritage going back to the Pharaohs and/or the *fellāḥ* with similar ancestry and symbolic too of the nation's fertile maternal element – is thus elevated to mystical heights in the text. What we have here is a confluence of nature, nationalism and divinity in the service of Egyptian nationhood and the first hints in an Arabic literary context of nationalism as religion, a concept which is further developed in Tawfiq al-Hakim's ʿAwdat al-Ruh (1933).

Transcendence in *Zaynab* might also refer to the author–God complex. Though themes can assist, the novel's secularity ultimately depends on its internal contingency, on it functioning as a self-contained reality in which the drama is organic and the plot is driven by character and governed by rational laws, and which crucially masks the controlling hand of the author. These are the essential ingredients of a nascent novel genre, as attested by the way in which early attempts at novel-writing in Arabic, as in other languages and contexts, are evaluated, with non-self-conscious authorial intrusion regarded as a weakness, as distinct from the deliberate and ironic signposting of the author found in postmodern fiction. The corollary of this is that heteroglossia and polyphony, which are constitutive of secularism in fiction, are highly valued in the early modern novel. The author of *Zaynab* is, however, highly visible, no doubt as an effect of Haykal's limited experience of the form. He is visible in the discourse of the narrator, where the latter's explanations and digressions are a channel through which Haykal communicates his views and ideas, for example on marriage and nation. This is true, to an extent, of Hamid's discourse too.[37] The author is also visible in the shape of the story, that is, in the palpable crafting of the narrative to facilitate certain meanings and messages. The abrupt visit of Shaykh Masʿud to the village, for example, looks suspiciously like a device to enable criticism of Sufism in the countryside and of hypocritical holy men. Hamid's short-lived membership of the brotherhood does not fit with the character as we know him (we are even informed of his long-time disapproval of the group) and the episode is barely believable in context. Likewise the retelling of Hamid's story, first in his confession to Shaykh Masʿud and then in his letter to his parents, constitutes excess in the text and reveals the labouring hand of the author. Other less than credible details, such as the conscious rational way in which Zaynab apparently selects Ibrahim as the object of her affection juxtaposed with the all-consuming romantic love that ensues, and Hamid's all too easily alternating love and ability to forget Zaynab and ʿAziza at appropriate points, also point to an architect beyond the text, manufacturing events and details to fit messages and themes. Zaynab's decision-making is included to give Haykal the opportunity to comment on the suitability of pairing with one's own kind while Hamid's love story as a whole is manifestly engineered as a conduit for commentary on love and marriage. Such visible manipulation of the narrative exposes the controlling hand and creative power of the author, an entity external to the world of the text, which compromises the work's secularity. Of course every novel has an author and the notion of an organic self-propelling novelistic reality is a fallacy, but the hypervisibility of the author in *Zaynab* makes this fallacy harder to maintain.

The theistic language and attitude of the narrator and other characters in *Zaynab* not only complicate the text's secularism but, perhaps unwittingly, raise some theological problems. *Zaynab* is well known for its representation of ideological conflict between tradition and modernity, village and city, but insofar as the narrative is infused with theistic attitudes and reference to destiny it also underscores a tension between divine will and religious law on the one side and (human) nature on the other, with marriage as the key site of conflict. For a start, although the characters ignore this point themselves, marriage is an institution whose conditions, including the submissive role of women within it, the limited possibilities of escape for the wife as compared to the husband, are enshrined in Sharia. Thus when marriage becomes a source of misery and imprisonment, as is the case for Zaynab, what we are dealing with is a clash of nature and religion, human volition and divine law. The same applies to the veil, which ʿAziza regrets and sees as a curb on her freedom, and female confinement, which negatively affects her health.[38] These customs, which society imposes and which trace back to the Qur'an and hadith (even as some of them predate Islam), ostensibly produce suffering and reveal a disjunction between religious law and human nature and ambition in the text. Zaynab's marriage, furthermore, raises the question of predestination and divine benevolence. It is regarded by many characters, and indeed the narrator at times, as God's will that Zaynab should marry Hassan. Is it then also God's will that Zaynab should suffer torment and anxiety such that she falls sick and dies? For this is where the marriage ultimately leads in the text. 'Oh Lord, if you wanted to give Hassan to [Zaynab] why did you not incline her heart to love him?', the narrator laments,[39] underscoring the fundamental cruelty of the situation and hinting at a problem in the Islamic tenet of *qadar* (divine fore-ordainment) and the question of God's benign intent. For what kind of God is it who would will such a catastrophic union?

In fact, it is only Zaynab in the text who sees a human hand in her plight and blames her parents, though even this is mixed with reference to God as the controlling power in her destiny. No one else departs from the narrative of divine decree, which ultimately absolves them of guilt. The reader, on the other hand, is reminded of the false consciousness and relinquishment of responsibility of a society that defers everything to God.

The first volume of *Al-Ayyam* by Taha Husayn, another landmark in modern Arabic literature, published fifteen years later in 1929, is in a different league to *Zaynab* aesthetically. It possesses an artistic consistency and stylistic authority that is lacking in the earlier work and, while there is ideological tension, it is less crude than the contradiction and incongruity in Hamid and the narrator's discourse. Authorial intrusion is here excused by the autobiographical format, which inserts the author's voice in the text in a manner which is acceptable to the reader, and didacticism is permitted by the fact that the story is addressed to a child, the author Taha Husayn's daughter. As such *Al-Ayyam* feels more like the kind of novel we are used to reading than does *Zaynab*, which is ironic given that it was not intended as such but was written, and is generally labelled, as an autobiography. But *Al-Ayyam*'s provenance need not deter us here, for this masterpiece of modern Arabic literature sits as comfortably as a novel as it does as an autobiography, not least because it employs novelistic strategies which point towards a *pacte romanesque* as much as anything else.[40] For instance, the narrative refers to the protagonist in the third person, concealing the identity between subject and author and enabling the reader to identify with the protagonist in a way he/she might not the voice of a famous Egyptian intellectual. Certain devices, such as the metaphor of blindness, which operates on many levels as Fedwa Malti-Douglas has shown, and meaningful juxtapositions, which encourage us to interpret events and images for their meaning more than their historical content, also facilitate a novelistic reading.[41] It is also significant that the subject remains nameless in the first two volumes (1929, 1939), so that the biographical detail is extra-diegetic, communicated by material external to the text, and that the text has been included in many studies of the Arabic novel as testimony to its contribution to the form.

I deal with the first two parts of *Al-Ayyam* only here, since the third and final volume was not written until much later and therefore belongs to a different period.⁴² These volumes tell the story of a blind boy's journey from ignorance to enlightenment, especially with respect to religious practice and knowledge. Education provides the narrative thread, which in turn thrusts institutions like the Qur'an school (*kuttāb*) and the Azhar into the forefront and opens the way for a thorough critique of them.⁴³ The story begins in a village in Upper Egypt, where popular religion and superstitious belief reign supreme and religious instruction, the only kind of learning available, is in the hands of a corrupt parochial shaykh, known as Our Master (*sayyidunā*). The protagonist as a young boy starts out in harmony with this environment but his critical acumen and sharp insight, enhanced no doubt by his position as observer, often sitting quietly on the periphery of action and gatherings as a neglected blind boy, increasingly set him apart from the majority. He longs to break out of the village strictures and at thirteen is sent to the Azhar, whose orthodox learning confirms to him the misconstrual that is popular belief and practice. But he is soon disillusioned with this institution too thanks to its petty shaykhs, fossilised knowledge and narrow method. He turns to self-guided reading and seeks out liberal mentors, eventually finding intellectual freedom and spiritual satisfaction in literature and the newly established (secular) Egyptian university. *Al-Ayyam* (vols 1 and 2) is then a story of disenchantment. The world is gradually stripped of its myth and magic and the boy exchanges a traditional and superstitious mindset for a rational modern outlook. In the opening pages the narrator recalls the boy's fear of demons (ʿ*ifrīt*, pl. ʿ*afārīt*) who come out at night and can only be escaped by covering one's face, but as the narrative proceeds he discovers the falsity of popular belief and magic, after he experiments with spells from the book of Diyarbi, and sees how the amulets and incantations of his mother and Sayyiduna serve no purpose in the event of his sister's and brother's illness. When news of a shooting star (*najm dhū dhanab*) arrives from Cairo the countryside prepares for calamity and when the appointed time passes uneventfully, the Azharites gloat because they denied the story from the start, the bearers of the Qur'an (*ḥamlat al-qurʾān*) insist it was a near miss thanks to God's mercy and people's supplications, and the Sufis argue it would have occurred were it not for the mediation of saint Qutb al-Mutawalli.⁴⁴ In other words each group interprets and reinterprets the event to fit their particular version of truth, which in turn casts (religious) truth as narrative. At the Azhar, we meet shaykhs with poor grasp of the books they teach and who are petty and intolerant of modern subjects. The narrator sums up the futility of its pedagogy when he remarks of a line in *Talkhis al-Miftah*, 'How much has been said on this one sentence in abridgements, elaborations and expansions, and in commentaries, annotations and reports, when [its meaning] is patently clear and free of ambiguity and obscurity'.[45] These details demythologise the institution. The Azhar loses its holy aura and comes to represent instead a relic of the past.

Disenchantment is linked to secularism in the discourse of modernity and *Al-Ayyam* is also a story of secularisation. For the boy's transcendence of the environments he is born into and adopts by virtue of his disability is a signifier of secularism.[46] First he oversteps popular religion so that it becomes a belief system within the wider frame of reference of orthodox Islam, which he in turn exceeds so that it too becomes a belief system within a broader rational scientific Weltanschauung, in which critical principles are applied to everything, including religious texts, and which epitomises the secular. The critical faculties of which we see glimpses in the early part of the narrative come to subsume everything by the end of the text; a sceptical rational approach takes over so that everything is viewed through a scientific lens, a secular lens. A corollary of this is that religion is compartmentalised, in effect assigned to different spaces which the protagonist transcends ideologically. Popular belief is contained in the village, orthodox Islam in the Azhar, and our rational critical protagonist moves freely in and out of these spaces. Thus religion is symbolically delimited. It becomes an entity in a wider frame.

Human agency and individualism are further signifiers of secularism in the text. While in *Zaynab*, fate and destiny govern much of the drama and the characters seem at times like pawns in a cosmic plan, in *Al-Ayyam* characters, and increasingly the protagonist himself, drive the story, in which is embedded a growing individualism and which in turn engenders man as master of his destiny, a secular index. The protagonist's father is the guiding hand to start with, sending him to various religious instructors in the village, then his brother, who determines which classes he attends in Cairo and his physical whereabouts in the city at any given time, then the subject himself. Meanwhile the protagonist gradually distinguishes himself as an exceptional individual. The first sign of this is in the opening pages, when as an experiment he breaks with custom and takes his food with two hands. He is batted down on this occasion but as the narrative proceeds the protagonist relishes distinction. In the magic experiment referred to above, he chooses not to share his discovery with his friend, lending him superiority over him, albeit covert, and he later takes pride in becoming a voice of dissent in the village, decrying texts like *Al-Dalaʾil* and magic practice to anyone who will listen. He continues to mark himself off from the crowd at the Azhar, challenging his teachers and getting himself expelled from various classes. Even when he is de-registered and in effective crisis, he marks himself off from the other members of his radical student trio by reacting differently and not seeking immediate amendment. The selection by the author of episodes which demonstrate his difference from, and (intellectual) superiority over, his peers is motivated no doubt by the kind of self-portrait Taha Husayn was trying to achieve in writing *Al-Ayyam*, of a pioneering intellectual overcoming particular hurdles, but in narrative and ideological terms it also functions to signpost human agency and individualism in a theocentric setting and as such tends towards the secular.

Secularism, as I have argued, is not a monolith or unitary discourse, and in a literary context in particular, where it manifests as an attitude or epistemology as opposed to a political doctrine or administrative imperative, its form and nuance varies. In this regard, the literary theme in *Al-Ayyam* is significant. The protagonist finds intellectual freedom and spiritual fulfilment in literature, which he immediately understands calls for an approach different to that employed on the religious and legal texts of the Azhar curriculum. In so doing he touches upon a critical distinction between literature and religion; the centrifugal/centripetal dichotomy. Literary truth tends towards plurality, religious truth towards singularity, leaving aside postmodern approaches to the latter. While religion and literature have much in common in the realm of myth-making, narrative strategy and spiritual nourishment, their approach to meaning is, broadly speaking, diametrically opposed, hence the general incompatibility of religious belief and modern fiction described in Chapter 1. What is interesting here is that the intellectual freedom that the protagonist finds in literature, and which dovetails with the secular value system he acquires in the second volume, obtains from a premodern context. It is the works of Sibawayh, Zamakhshari, Mubarrad and the stories of *Alf*

Layla wa Layla and *sīra*s of ᶜAntara and Sayf ibn Dhi Yazan which break the shackles of Azhar-style knowledge and open up new vistas to him. The literary and the secular are paired in *Al-Ayyam* and have a crucially premodern reference, at least in the first instance (the protagonist goes on to read modern fiction and European translations and access new worlds through these works too). Thus the text departs from the standard equations of secularism and modernity, secularity and modern art, and offers something more akin to Northrop Frye's secular scripture, that tradition of literature which existed alongside sacred stories from the very beginning but was profane in character. Taha Husayn identifies a freedom and irreverence in the literary imagination which projects the secular into premodernity, and premodern literature in particular.

There is another story here, or another way of thinking about the secular/religious dialectic in the text, and this is in terms of a transition from subject to object, or better a reconceptualisation of religion as the other. Religion in *Al-Ayyam* becomes an other, not, as mentioned, in the sense of a mysterious thrilling figure but as an entity against which the secular rational discourse of the protagonist takes form. Identity and nationhood in Arab and Egyptian literature have often been understood in the context of imperialism and western influence. Many are the works of Egyptian fiction in which European characters and symbols function to demarcate difference and reflect on national and individual identity, and many are the studies which analyse the dynamics of this relationship. There is of course no denying the prominence of the western other and its hold on the Arab and Egyptian literary imagination, but at the same time, as discussed in Chapter 1, the valorisation of the figure of the West has obscured the role of religion in Arab and Egyptian self-definition in the literary corpus.[47] *Al-Ayyam* 1 and 2 is a case in point. With its specific reference to historical figures and representation of contemporary debates and tensions, and with a protagonist whose journey from ignorance to enlightenment, tradition to modernity, has a clear, albeit simplistic, symbolic value, *Al-Ayyam* is one of those modern texts that narrate the nation, and this narration involves othering religion through processes of displacement, objectification and critique. I referred above to the shifting ideological framework of the text, from religious to secular, and to the spatial delimitation of religion. These are strategies of displacing and objectifying Islam, of representing it as an object of discourse within a wider (secular) frame. Another key strategy is religious criticism which, although by no means essential or exclusive to secular discourse, frequently accompanies it and here has the effect of desanctifying and discrediting religious representatives and institutions.

For example, the education trajectory, as noted, handily leads to negative reflection on the *kuttāb* and Azhar. Sayyiduna is ignorant and hypocritical and represents the worst of rural religion. His portrait is so grotesque, filtered as it is through the naïve consciousness of a young boy, that he can only be abhorred by the reader. The shaykhs of the Azhar, though better versed in the Qur'an and classical sources, are no less ineffective as teachers, as noted. With the exception of the Imam's (i.e. Muhammad Abduh's) followers, their explanations are superficial and often nonsensical. They are characteristically petty and resistant to empirical methods and modern ideas, as evidenced by the poor treatment of its progressive teachers, including Muhammad Abduh and El-Marsafy. A good deal of the second volume is taken up with Azharite portraits and denigration of its world of knowledge. Autobiography is an exercise in self-construction. The author selects details from his past and experience to construct a particular image of himself. This is how we must understand the presence of so many negative religious types in the text, that is, as part of an effort to demonstrate what the author is not, what he has grown away from and rejected. These religious representatives are the author's others, figures against whom he defines himself but who also vie with him, or with what he stands for, in the cultural space of the text and beyond. Likewise, religious knowledge in its popular superstitious and conservative forms, which also receives significant attention in the text, as it is displaced comes to represent the other of the sceptical secular thought system which the protagonist acquires in the second volume and which forms the retrospective lens of the narrative as a whole.

But othering is never clean and simple, and the other is never a pure form. The rejection of a discourse or entity, especially when that discourse or entity has previously constituted part of the subject's Weltanschauung or experience, is a messy process coloured by slippage. In *Al-Ayyam* we see this in the persistence of religious expression and the ambivalent character of the Azhar. With regard to the former, references to God and destiny and

Islamic formulae are not a problem when they are contained in the speech of a character, since in these instances they simply represent and reflect the worldview of a given individual and thus belong to literary verisimilitude. Even when the boy-narrator invokes God or attributes agency to the Divine it does not compromise the secular theme since it is specific to the character at a particular moment in his life; indeed a decrease in divine reference over the course of the text in the discourse of the protagonist is a measure of his disenchantment and gradual embrace of modern secular forms. But the voice of the narrator and protagonist merge in the second volume, once the latter has mentally divorced himself from the thought and value system of the Azhar and adopted modern critical methods, and divine references in this section of the text are more troubling. They are admittedly sparse – in the final pages the protagonist-narrator remarks at the end of the academic year that 'God alone knew how happy and delighted he was when the first signs of summer appeared …'[48] and the others in the last chapters consist of invocations for the deceased – but they nevertheless betray the secular spirit championed in the latter part of the second volume. Literary secularism demands rational narrative and does not easily tolerate theological reference. Even when unconscious, divorced from spiritual import and/or formulaic, divine reference on a narrative level represents a dilution or contradiction in the secular. Fedwa Malti-Douglas detects a hint of Qur'anic style in the language of *Al-Ayyam*.[49] Phrases like '*wa shuyūkh al-ṭarīq, wa mā shuyūkh al-ṭarīq* ('And the Sufi shaykhs, what are the Sufi shaykhs?') and '*wa lākin al-Alfiyya! wa mā adrāka mā al-Alfiyya*' ('The *Alfiyya*! What will inform you what the *Alfiyya* is?') possess a scriptural echo and denote the subject's deep involvement with Islamic structures, which again attests that their displacement is no easy process.[50] Similarly the Azhar, which is of course plentifully criticised in the text, is an ambivalent figure. The protagonist finds peace and security in its precincts,[51] and even after he has switched allegiance to the Egyptian university he feels nostalgia for it.[52] Malti-Douglas remarks on the symbolism of the Azhar pillars. They project a sense of rigidity but also of protection.[53] It is also in the Azhar that the protagonist first encounters progressive thinkers, like Muhammad Abduh and El-Marsafy, and discovers radicalism. This institution, which the protagonist ultimately rejects and whose learning and values become the other of his secular scepticism and modern intellectual outlook, is then not without positive attributes and essentially provides the means by which the protagonist exceeds its otherwise constricting space. As such the rejection of the Azhar is shot through with contradiction. The same applies to the village as the premier site of religious malpractice and superstition. The protagonist abandons it for the city and rejects its mentality wholeheartedly, yet in the second volume it becomes an arena for intellectual freedom and unfettered reading away from the Azhar and its stifling curriculum.⁵⁴

In his work on the stereotype in colonial discourse Bhabha detects dependency. The presence of the stereotype and its unceasing repetition points to unease and instability in the coloniser. This very same dependency, of the self upon the negation of the other, is apparent in the author's critical engagement with the religious establishment in *Al-Ayyam*, as well as when Taha Husayn's intellectual output is considered in its entirety. The same applies to Haykal. For both men were social reformers, supporters of a basically secular concept of Egyptian identity and nationhood, and both men couched their discourse of reform in negative religious rhetoric. Haykal, as mentioned, promoted a vision of the Egyptian nation rooted in its Pharoanic past in the 1910s and 20s. He criticised the ᶜ*ulamāʾ*, supported ᶜAbd al-Raziq's controversial treatise *Al-Islam wa Usul al-Hukm* (1925), which denied Islam a political function, and echoes themes from the secularisation thesis when he speaks of religion in terms of stages of civilisation.⁵⁵ Taha Husayn, similarly, preceded the first volume of *Al-Ayyam* with his controversial study, *Fi'l-Shiᶜr al-Jahili* (1926, On Pre-Islamic Poetry), in which he applied scientific methods to the study of pre-Islamic poetry and questioned the validity of the Qur'an as an historical source, and sought to explain the emergence of Islam in positivist terms, and around the same time published a series of essays entitled *Bayn al-ᶜIlm wa'l-Din* (Between Science and Religion), which argue, among other things, that religion has no place in twentieth-century political life.⁵⁶

The persistent presence of Islam in Haykal and Husayn's secular-oriented writings points to a lack in the new discourse – namely its dependency upon the negation of traditional Islamic authority – and betrays a certain anxiety in its advocates. This anxiety would be revealed in drastic fashion in the 1930s, when fear of the religious other prompted a change in the literary outputs of both Haykal and Husayn. In 1933 Taha Husayn published the first of three volumes of *'Ala Hamish al-Sira* (On the Margins of the Prophet's Biography),[57] a book of imaginative tales based around the life of Muhammad, and in 1935 Haykal published *Hayat Muhammad* (The Life of Muhammad), another biography of the Prophet, which he followed with *Fi Manzil al-Wahy* (1937, On the Site of Revelation) and a series of studies of the Rashidun caliphs in the 1940s.[58] This switch to Islamic subjects is not necessarily indicative of newfound religious commitment, as Louis Awad, Muhsin al-Musawi, Charles D. Smith and others have argued. Rather, the turn in both instances was motivated by a desire to reach new areas of the population and to counter accusations of atheism levelled at the authors.[59] Husayn prefaced *'Ala Hamish al-Sira* with an introduction that makes clear that what is to follow is an exercise in spiritual, not intellectual, nourishment. He criticises advocates of reason who ignore man's emotional needs but does not question their distrust of the stories themselves. Instead he argues that there is a difference between those who direct stories about early Islam to the mind, on the basis that they are historical fact, and those who direct them to the heart, on the basis that they provide emotional sustenance.[60] The collection should also be viewed in the context of the controversy sparked by *Fi'l-Shi'r al-Jahili*, as part of an effort to restore the author's damaged reputation.[61] Likewise, it is unclear how much religious sentiment is behind Haykal's studies. They were written, at least in part, to counter charges of atheism that were being levelled at his party, the Liberal Constitutionalists, at the time and in an environment in which politics was increasingly intertwined with religion.[62] For in the aftermath of the 1919 revolution and 1923 constitution, when the euphoria of independence died down, the liberal nationalism that carried these events through began to waver and religious voices and ideals, which the nationalist furore had suppressed for a time, came to the fore once more. The climate of the 1930s was one of disillusionment with parliamentary government and the liberal secular values that stood behind it. The years after independence were characterised by an ongoing struggle between the Palace, Wafd, Liberal Constitutionalists and Azhar and their internal power politics. Meanwhile the Muslim Brothers and Misr al-Fatat (Young Egypt Party) gained popularity and religious tensions flared up between Christians and Muslims. The champions of liberal secular values found themselves increasingly out of step with popular sentiment, as well as in the firing line of the religious establishment. In this climate Haykal's own party, the Liberal Constitutionalists, whose newspaper *Al-Siyasa* he edited, changed its policy and began to present itself as the chief defender of Islam in Egyptian politics, whilst accusing its opponent, the Wafd, of a Coptic conspiracy. Haykal's biography of the Prophet, and the studies that followed, can be viewed in the context of this policy shift and in response to some of the accusations levelled against him and his party.[63] *Hayat Muhammad* is not a traditional *sīra*. It opens with a polemical account of Christian–Muslim relations and makes clear that what will follow is a strictly scientific study, 'developed on the western modern method, and written for the sake of truth alone'.[64] It argues that the West is lacking in spirituality, but even as it posits Islam's superiority in this area it remains steadfast in its elevation of science as the highest value in modern times. There is a problem in the author's stated approach, for Haykal relies on the Qur'an uncritically, which essentially undermines his scientific method. But it is nevertheless written with a scientific attitude, dealing with the Prophet as a human and leaving out the miracles attributed to Muhammad, and promotes science and reason as method. In a chapter added to the second edition, Haykal quotes Muhammad Abduh that 'man is not a convinced Muslim unless he has reasoned out his religion, known it in person, and become personally convinced of its truth and validity'.[65] In other words, Islamic faith is personal and preceded by reason. *Fi Manzil al-Wahy* and Haykal's studies of the Rashidun caliphs are similarly concerned to limit religion and promote reason. The former, in Charles D. Smith's analysis, develops a concept of spirituality based on Bergson's theory of intuition such that the Prophet's mission becomes an expression of a universal human faculty,[66] and the caliphal studies analyse Islam's initial strength and subsequent decline, and deny Muhammad and his successors temporal authority.[67] These works should not be understood so much as a reversal or retraction of secular values as an encroachment onto religious space by secular intellectuals, and further as an expression of the potency of the religious other. Haykal, Husayn, as well as Ahmad Amin, Mansur Fahmi, Mahmud Taymur and ʿAbbas Mahmud al-ʿAqqad,[68] in their prolific writing careers and in an environment of politico-ideological struggle could not but address themselves to Islam.

A similar expression of the potency of the religious other is found in

Haqqi's famous short novel *Qindil Umm Hashim* (1944), where a character makes the difficult journey away from religion only to recant later.[69] Ismail travels to Europe where he falls under the spell of western civilisation and abandons the Islamic belief he grew up with – 'religion became for him a fable invented to control the masses'[70] – only for his faith to re-emerge once back in Egypt. Moreover, as he resumes his faith so he backtracks on scientific method by incorporating the oil of the saint's lamp into a clinical setting and relying 'on God [first] then on his knowledge and hands',[71] thus subordinating science to religion, an effective reversal of his position in England, where reason served to undermine religious truth. Notwithstanding the artificiality of the synthesis proposed – as Muhammad Siddiq notes, the happy ending is more an act of 'authorial will' than artistic necessity – *Qindil* reads not only as a deconstruction of the secularisation thesis and rejection of the sequential concept of tradition and modernity, but as an expression of the power of the religious other, such that a character is able to completely suppress the massive exercise in demystification he has undergone. In the period before his re-conversion Ismail experiences acute cultural and psychological alienation which makes the secular scientific route untenable for him. He cannot in the end break with faith.

If *Al-Ayyam* and *Qindil* represent the push and pull between religious and secular discourses on a plot level, Tawfiq al-Hakim's *'Awdat al-Ruh* (1933) enacts a different kind of religious displacement, which entails not so much ideological conflict or transition but a co-option of religious forms into the national imaginary, such that nationalism becomes itself a kind of religion.[72] *'Awdat* follows the coming of age of young Muhsin through unrequited love and political awakening in the lead up to the 1919 revolution, whilst allowing other characters to assume centre stage at different times. As such *'Awdat* is a communal novel where *Al-Ayyam* was an individual story. Ideological transition is here represented not so much in an individual character's intellectual journey as in the varying levels of tradition, religiosity, modernity and European influence of a wide cast of characters, as well as, less consciously, in slips in the secular language of Muhsin and the narrator. For in common with *Zaynab*, the otherwise secular protagonist, who is the closest voice to the author's own in the text, and the otherwise invisible objective narrator are found attributing events to God in certain places, which goes against the rational premises of secularism and indicates, especially in the case of the narrator whose voice engenders the ideology of the text, a worldview wavering between human agency and transcendent causality.

The first part of ʿAwdat is given over in large part to the love story. Muhsin and his uncles are rivals for Saniyya's affection and are all left heartbroken when she becomes engaged to another admirer. Yet romantic love is but a precursor for a greater, more productive love in the form of nationalism and patriotism. In their forlorn state Muhsin and his uncles rally around one another and the brotherhood, which was significantly and symbolically disrupted by the French-mannered girl, is restored. They begin to work together on revolutionary pamphlets, united in a new purpose and love of country. Thus ʿAwdat is a story of conversion: from romantic lover to national activist. Muhsin and his uncles relinquish a pathetic love and false god for an active, unifying love of the nation. And this nation is no less a deity. While nationalism often displaces religion in the sense of pushing it to the periphery or delimiting it to the private realm, here the displacement takes shape in substitution. Nationalism all but becomes a religion in in the novel.[73] Egypt in ʿAwdat is divine, a mythical entity comprised of a sacred territory and sacred community. As a sacred territory it combines the timeless Nile Valley with its annual floods and luscious vegetation and the miraculous Pyramids, while its sacred community is focused primarily on the *fellāḥ*, the Egyptian peasant or farmer, who is idealised and celebrated as a superior figure. The Egyptian peasantry possesses a 'tremendous spiritual power' and a special innate knowledge located in the heart and passed down from the Pharoanic peoples who ploughed the same blessed earth 8,000 years ago. This in contradistinction to the European, whose knowledge is acquired and therefore superficial. 'Get one of these peasants and remove his heart and you'll find the residue of ten thousand years of experience and knowledge',[74] the French archaeologist explains to his sceptical English friend, whereas do the same to a European and you will find it empty.[75] The modern *fellāḥ* is a direct descendent of the ancient Egyptian, through a pure lineage (thanks to inhabiting the same villages for thousands of years), and like his ancestor has enormous capabilities: 'Do not be surprised if these people, who stand together, share the same nature and are agreeable and prepared to sacrifice themselves to produce another miracle like the Pyramids', the archaeologist prophesises.[76] They are simply in need of a messiah, one of their own men who will 'embody all their feelings and hopes and be their ultimate symbol'.[77] What we have here is not far from a chosen people, a unique group with special attributes and a special destiny. Dmitry Merejkovsky, whose *Les Mystères des Orients* (1925) was one of the novel's influences, writes that all religions express the same truth of a god who dies and rises from the dead.[78] This is the shape of the Egyptian nation in the text; a dormant force lying fallow until Saʿd Zaghloul comes to inspire it to rise up, to rebirth, at the end of the narrative. The patriotic hero of nationalism mirrors the saviour or prophet of traditional religion.

Further parallels exist on the level of ritual, prayer and sacrifice. The preparation and drinking of tea by the peasants is depicted as a holy ceremony, the teapot an idol on an altar.[79] The songs of the peasants are communal hymns and their harvest labour an act of worship and sacrifice.[80] And just as Abraham was willing to sacrifice his son upon divine request in the Bible, so the nation, as deity, makes absolute claims on its people, including fighting or dying for it. *ʿAwdat* screens the violent aspect of nationalism, which again links it to religion, especially insofar as the scapegoat mechanism lies at the heart of both.[81] Just as male–female relations and love in the novel come in a romantic sanitised form, so the text sticks to the emotive and positive aspect of nationalism. But sacrifice is touched upon nevertheless. The ancient Egyptians gave their lives in the construction of the Pyramids, and Muhsin and his cohort (Salim, ʿAbduh, Hanafi, Mabruk) are faced with the gallows. Al-Hakim deflects the crude horror here through humour. From their prison cell they spy the morbid apparatus, one large one small, and turn the situation into a joke about the mini gallows specially designed for Muhsin.[82] The scene demonstrates the group's willingness to die for the nation, to sacrifice themselves for a transcendent concept, whilst masking the monstrosity with comedy.

As nationalism becomes a virtual religion in *ʿAwdat*, the question arises as to what becomes of traditional religion, which in this case means Islam. In its popular form, it is mocked through the character and superstitious methods of Zanuba and Shaykh Simhan, and excessive faith is broadly associated with lack of education and lack of worldliness in the text. But more than religious critique in the style of *Zaynab* and *Al-Ayyam*, *ʿAwdat* sketches a new category of religion that has themes in common with Pharaonic belief and Sufism and reimagines Islam in the context of nationalist ideology. In the scene on the train, Islam is reinterpreted as 'an emotion of mercy, goodness of the soul, and unity of hearts', with nothing to do with religious or sectarian differences.[83] As such Islam becomes a quality in which all faiths and groups can share, a national ethics more than a religion in a conventional sense. The narrative is framed by the Osiris myth, with the insinuation that Egypt too is a deity on the brink of rebirth, and opens with verses from an ancient funeral lament referencing unity and eternity. The oneness of being emerges as an essential truth in ʿAwdat, whilst the Divine in a traditional monotheistic sense is notably absent from its message. When Muhsin comes across a calf and baby suckling together he is struck by the oneness of creation and realises that 'awareness of the unity of the universe is awareness of God',[84] an epiphany that notably comes to him via the heart, not the intellect. The ancient Egyptians had it right with their animal deities and closeness to nature. 'Isn't every creature made by God? ... Doesn't everything reveal its maker and every craft reflect its craftsman?'[85] We are reminded of Ibn ʿArabi's *waḥdat al-wujūd*, that oneness which fuses God and creation and lies behind mystical union (the text uses an approximate phrase: *waḥdat al-kawn*).[86] ʿAwdat replaces monotheism with mysticism and co-opts Islam to its nationalist agenda by jettisoning all but an integral inclusive ethic.

This co-option and substitution effects a not dissimilar displacement as was seen in *Al-Ayyam*. ʿAwdat does not include high doses of religious critique, nor a conscious journey away from traditional Islam and theological knowledge as such, but the centre is nevertheless wrested from traditional religion as nationalism takes over and mysticism replaces monotheism as a way of understanding God and creation. On the other hand, secularity implies intellectual freedom, and the religious character of nationalism and its elevation as ideology in the text complicates the secular aesthetic. Literary secularism allows for all possibilities and in this regard ʿAwdat's nationalism is not very accommodating. Indeed the spiritual theme and proselytising character of ʿAwdat makes it an almost religious novel. Given the critical acclaim with which ʿAwdat was met and its continuing canonical status one can only conclude that the novel genre is more hospitable to authoritarian discourse and religious-like themes than its equation with secularity suggests.

A less dogmatic, more philosophical stance is adopted in *ʿUsfur min al-Sharq*, published by the same author a few years later (1938), which sees Muhsin travel to Europe as a student.[87] A secular theme emerges on a narrative level in the privatisation of belief and in the conversations between Muhsin and Ivan, who El-Enany notes is based on a real acquaintance of the author,[88] which approach religion as an object and suggest a vantage point outside of it. Although we do not see any evidence of prayer or the kind of godly reference associated with pious characters in Arabic fiction here, Muhsin by his own account is thoroughly believing. Indeed 'If [he] had felt for a moment that he was completely alone, that heaven did not exist … he would not have been able to bear living for a single day!'[89] But Muhsin's faith is idiosyncratic, as it revolves not around Allah in an orthodox sense but Sayyida Zaynab, the granddaughter of the Prophet, whose famous mosque and square are located in the centre of Cairo and who is the textual opposite to earthly European Suzy in the text.[90] When he forgets his faith it is Sayyida Zaynab whom he has forgotten, and when he suffers or succeeds Sayyida Zaynab is the cause. She is his guardian angel and the focal point of his religion, and as such takes the traditional place of God.[91] But the interesting point here is not so much the displacement of Allah per se, nor even the feminisation of the deity, so much as it is the extent to which Muhsin has devised his own version of divinity and the sacred. His faith is individual and private. It does not conflict with mainstream Islam (Zaynab is of course a popular saint in Egypt and sought out by many) but Muhsin nevertheless picks and chooses from the wellspring of Islam that which suits him, and his self-styled belief reads as an expression of secularity by firmly locating faith in the private realm. There is also, notably, almost no connection between Muhsin's private faith and the Islam that he discusses with Ivan elsewhere in the text. Religion is at once diverse and compartmentalised; there are many versions of it and individual faith is a private matter. Another trajectory onto this is the protagonist's categorical separation of the sacred and worldly realms and clear assignment of divine and human agency to heaven and earth respectively. Though a philosopher and dreamer himself, he is in no doubt that society is man-made and that the solution to human suffering is not the promise of paradise but social justice. In an extract excluded from the two Arabic editions (1938, 1964) but included in the French and English translations, which al-Hakim helped prepare, Muhsin, in conversation with Ivan, draws up a model of secularism based on Islamic authority. He quotes Rashidun caliph ʿUmar's advice to a man who left his mule in the hands of God. '[F]irst tie your donkey with a stout rope and then commit him to the care of God', a statement which carries the meaning that man must create his own solutions. He also quotes Muhammad's response to a question as to whether his defence plan against the Quraysh is inspired by God: 'God will not intervene in this affair', responds the Prophet. In other words, worldly matters are man's problem.[92] The quotations, aside from endorsing secularism, demonstrate the profound involvement of the religious and secular realms. For not only does Muhsin adopt an Islamic methodology – proving a point through prophetic example is a mainstay of theological argument in Islamic scholarship – but unwittingly makes the case for secularism via religion, so that the former springs from the latter. The irony is deepened when in the same passage he states the virtual reverse; the prophets 'all thought of a certain social justice which would inspire those who followed and push them toward more extended horizons'.[93] The impression here is that the worldly preceded the sacred, that it was the prophets' social messages that facilitated prophethood and crowned them as messengers. Whichever way you look at it, the social and sacred, secular and religious, are deeply intertwined.

Ivan and Muhsin's conversations are largely taken up with religion. Religion is the paradigm through which Ivan theorises the superiority of the East, which he equates with spirituality as compared to the morally vacuous, materialist West. Muhsin is not necessarily in agreement with this conclusion but together they explore and evaluate Christianity and Islam as belief systems from a critical distance, which immediately places them in object position. Of course religious critique is possible within a theistic worldview, but the empirical stance adopted by Ivan and Muhsin, basing their conclusions on knowledge and data as opposed to feeling and personal attachment, and their material focus, in the sense that the truth claims of Christianity and Islam are not at issue only their method and approach to worldly affairs, in addition to the virtual absence of any connection between Islam as described by the two men and Muhsin's own Islamic faith, which is contained in his own private space – all of these things constitute a secular approach. The divergent conclusions drawn by Ivan and Muhsin, for example the latter's deconstruction of the former's valorisation of the spiritual East in the final pages, are based on observation and learning. Ivan does not commend Islam (and Christianity) because he accepts its message but because it is a system which provides hope and meaning. And Muhsin's comments on Islam are not related to his faith but to factual observation and knowledge, for example when he describes the role of social reform and the behaviour and attitudes of contemporary Muslims.[94] In other words, even the believer here approaches the religious question through a rational lens. Religion is discussed and critiqued in a secular frame using secular methods. Religion's truth claim is irrelevant, for the real concern, and only measurable aspect, is its contribution to society and the welfare of man in this life. In this regard, Ivan's attempts to believe and the lax Catholicism of André, the son of Muhsin's landlady and a pragmatic foil to him, are also relevant. The former casts religion as a discourse to opt into, from the starting point of a wider critical or secular frame, while the latter provides an example of socialised or secular religion. As Ivan laments the collapse of religion Muhsin suggests that he build his faith on the essence of sacred books without intermediary. The Russian rejects the idea. He has tried to believe but his conscience will not let him. Although he does not find his way to religion, the act of trying and the presence of conversion as a possibility paints religion as discourse. This is not to suggest conversion only occurs in secular space, but that the critical distance occasioned by its literary representation makes visible religion's discursive character. On the other hand, André treats the funeral of his friend's son-in-law as a social obligation more than a religious rite and tells his friend that 'We enter [a church] like we enter a cafe'.[95] His flattening of church and cafe is a general comment on religion in Europe, on the West's assumed irreverence and desacralisation of religious insignia, and Muhsin's experience entering Christian space is quite different. But the contrast in itself confirms the individual character of religion, that it means different things to different people. Belief is a multifarious phenomenon and personal affair.

Meanwhile institutional religion is under attack. In another passage suppressed in the original publication but reintroduced later, Muhsin recalls an Azharite friend in Paris who leers at women and whose mind is closed to culture, and whose religious knowledge is in any case superficial.[96] The other common trait of the Arabic literary shaykh, greed and materialism, is represented here by the guardian of the Sayyida Zaynab mosque, whose eyes are ever fixed on the offerings box and other material objects in the holy space. 'Why do people insist God needs Persian rugs to furnish his houses?' Muhsin asks himself, as he reflects on the falsity of such adornment and on inflexible rules and traditions which detract from the essence of religion.[97] His friend Ivan, on the other hand, remarks on the treacherous wealth of the Christian Church and characterises it as a capitalist system (*niẓām rasmālī*).[98] These criticisms, by now not unfamiliar, undermine institutional religion, rendering it folly and vanity and are, incidentally, widespread in the early Egyptian short story too. Hafez identifies the corruption of traditional religious shaykhs as a major theme in the work of the Taymur brothers, Muhammad and Mahmud, and Mahmud Taha Lashin.[99] Filtered through the consciousness of Muhsin and Ivan, these criticisms indicate both critical distance and a clear distinction between formal religion and the subject's private faith, which does not come under scrutiny. The effect is secularising insofar as impugning religion pushes it to the margins, for even if secularism does not demand religious denigration, it does require its demotion, and criticism assists in this respect. This is buttressed by *ʿUsfur*'s style and form, which consist in mundane prose and narrative realism. Much of the text is channelled through the thoughts and memories of Muhsin, whose language is functional, if romantic in places. There is no imploring the Divine here, nor the religious formulae which creep so easily into characters' dialogue as a feature of everyday Arabic. Moreover, the plot is realistic and reasoned, if somewhat theatrical in places. The occasional shifts of consciousness away from Muhsin to secondary characters and tendency to intellectualise and over-explain are examples of artistic weakness, but gone are the inelegant coincidences of *Hadith ʿIsa ibn Hisham* and *Zaynab* that betray the controlling hand of the author and compromise the secular spirit by announcing the presence of an external power or creator. Instead we have largely coherent characters, some with additional symbolic value which al-Hakim manages well enough not to render them flat or artificial. And gone are the suggestions of divine intervention, fate and destiny. In view of the above, there is little opposition to classifying *ʿUsfur* as secular literature and the text broadly lends credence to the association of the novel and secularity common to theories of the genre. As a measure of its maturity, the tension attendant in the literary secularism is here not in incongruence and contradiction, but rather emerges in conscious features of the narrative, such as a theme of nostalgia for transcendence, an engagement with religion as myth and image (a cosmological code), and a profound linkage of art and the sacred.

Through the discourse of Ivan, the text postulates the critical role of religion in the maintenance of hope, meaning and morality in the world. Heaven is a great leveller, a wonderful gift from the eastern prophets, for 'whoever is deprived a share of paradise on earth, his claim is safeguarded in the paradise of heaven'.[100] Science, industry and political ideologies like Marxism and fascism have destroyed heaven and bequeathed a moral and metaphysical vacuum. Ivan is an idealist and in fact the narrative cannot conclude without Muhsin deconstructing his friend's utopian hyperbole. The East is not perfection nor spirituality personified. Its holy men are materialistic and modernity in a Euro-mould is almost a religion in itself: 'It might be possible these days to eradicate the grandeur of heaven from the mind of the Eastern man ... but it is absolutely impossible to eradicate the grandeur of "modern European science"'.[101] There are no pure sources and no more 'East' as such.[102] Ivan's concept of the Orient is an artificial construct based on stereotypes, just as André and his wife Germaine's allusions to *Alf Layla wa Layla* and Suzy's reference to an uncouth Oriental (*sharqī mutawaḥḥish*) point to preconceived images based on orientalist representation more than observation and reality.[103] But the point here is the intrinsic value of, and nostalgia for, religion and the order and meaning it offers in the modern world. Ivan yearns for spirituality and transcendence, over which he believes the modern West has run roughshod. Ivan's physical decline is a reflection of psychological breakdown in the absence of a myth to live by. Even as Ivan scorns the priest who visits him in his final hours, so he cannot survive without transcendent hope and meaning. Even as the text diffuses secularity and promotes science, embedded in its pages is a feeling of nostalgia and sense of the powerful draw of the sacred. Any shift in Weltanschauung away from religion is going to be painful and disorienting.

If sacred yearning is encoded in the narrative, so too is a mythical register, which similarly points to a deep-seated attachment to religion, this time in the form of sacred stories and cosmology. Heaven (*samāʾ*) is mentioned often and more than God figures transcendence in the text. The prophets' message is a discourse on heaven in Ivan's analysis: 'The real miracle is that [the Near Eastern prophets] offered people another world filled with angels with beautiful white wings …' where 'mankind can live a richer and fuller life than in the real world'.[104] The shift from an omnipotent Being to a superlunary utopia is indicative of the motivation behind the characters' interest in religion, that is in the context of society. There is no sense of a journey to God here, or of serving the Almighty, which is the essence of faith and religion in many understandings; instead we have heaven as an ideal and deferred reward, a reality to aspire to or consolation for worldly suffering. The motivation is decidedly social. The heaven motif also feeds into a cosmological code, which associates positive values in the text, such as beauty, art and joy, with celestial space, as contrasted with the earthly character of things like work and relationship troubles, and which uses a metaphor of ascent/descent, or the Fall, to elaborate Muhsin's experience. The gate to the ticket office where Suzy sits every day is the Gate of Paradise (*bāb firdaws*)[105] and she looks down 'from her lofty height' (ʿ*alyāʾihā*).[106] When Muhsin first strikes up conversation with Suzy he is worried about her leaving 'without him having said anything that would fix this fleeting relation to earth'.[107] And his two-week affair with Suzy is described alternately as a sojourn in paradise and journey to earth, according to the protagonist's shifting mood and values, for Muhsin does not remain static in the text but is on a learning journey such that his outlook is different in the pre- and post-Suzy phases. Having elevated Suzy to the position of a demi-god, their affair is a mixture of heaven and hell; like Adam on earth, Muhsin experiences pleasure but pain too, when the philosopher-dreamer becomes jealous and anxious lover.[108] He now 'lives in "reality"', which is further confirmed by the fact that he abandons his books as he plunges into a relationship with the French girl. Yet when Suzy spurns Muhsin in favour of her boss Henri, he is 'like Adam expelled from paradise (*al-janna*)',[109] cast out of heaven for committing an indeterminate sin for which there is no pardon.[110] She has offered him ambrosia to taste and the water of Kawthar to drink, and then pushed him out of heaven.[111] In a letter to Suzy he calls her his Eden (*janna*) and describes himself as excommunicated.[112] He now understands how Adam felt when he was cast out of paradise.[113] The language of the Fall is used to suggest how Suzy brought Muhsin into reality, down from his esoteric meandering into the world of pleasure and pain, but the moment the affair ends, the quotidian aspect is forgotten and the affair is equated with an experience of pure heaven. Muhsin's initial analysis turns out to be the more enduring, however, for as he returns to his cerebral pursuits post-Suzy and recalls his boyhood and Sayyida Zaynab, he (re)discovers serenity. He felt 'as though he had become light and was rising, departing from the earth and returning to heaven, to the heaven from which he had descended'.[114] Thus on a macro level, and despite the character's feelings at the time, the Suzy interlude represents descent, a less authentic period in the philosopher-dreamer's life when he 'lowered his gaze' (to borrow from Kamal ʿAbd al-Jawwad) and suffered the consequence. His newfound tranquillity is appropriately associated with renunciation, which also has a religious connotation. Muhsin withdraws from the world and lives on a diet of rice, thus the Adam metaphor becomes an ascetic analogy: Muhsin the seeker. Both imply Muhsin to be living by myths that originate in religion, that sacred stories and religious forms constitute a symbolic world which the protagonist, however secular his speech and behaviour, still inhabits.[115] They also reveal the usefulness of religion as a familiar source of symbol and image for the author to draw on to enhance meaning.

The cosmological code also intersects with the artistic theme. Besides its well-known reflection on the East/West conundrum, *ʿUsfur* is also the portrait of an artist, and moreover an artist-prophet. The author is not so forthcoming as to adopt this persona for himself, though there is no shying away from propagating an elitist vision of art and literature as the prerogative of a gifted few.[116] Rather Beethoven is brought in to channel the Sublime in the text and link art with transcendence. Beethoven's music is heavenly and angelic. Muhsin attends a performance of his Fifth Symphony and is deeply moved by the sacred atmosphere, which he compares to that of places of worship. The work is surely divinely inspired, he concludes.[117] Later he attends another concert, this time Beethoven's Ninth, which induces something like a mystical experience in him.[118] The German composer is likened to a prophet[119] and his art opens onto the Divine: 'it was as though the veil of heaven had opened up to bring to our ears the songs of Houris and the angels, together in eternal paradise, and the hymn of joy, that divine spark, the joy of souls residing in God'.[120] In a world in which mosques and churches are decked in superficial garb, religion is buried beneath rigid traditions, and holy men are distracted by concerns of the world, art emerges as a pure alternative and route to the sacred, another kind of mysticism. Moreover, if art is a trajectory onto transcendence, so it is dependent upon it.

> Heaven ... Paradise ... Hell! Strip our earthly world of these three words which derive from the East and our most splendid works of art would immediately fall apart! ... Every beautiful thing we have been able to create has been done so under the light of rays from the kingdom of heaven.[121]

Ivan suggests not only the divine provenance of art but its religious content. Without the myth, what is left of art? His words point to a symbiotic relation that cannot be undone without severe collateral damage. Though Ivan's point of reference is western art, the text envisages a world heritage of letters and creativity through Muhsin, who alludes to and quotes artists, poets and writers from Europe and the Middle East alike through the text.[122] Verses from Hafiz and Khayyam provide him with comfort and are pertinent to his experience of love, analyses of the Good Friday Spell from Wagner's *Parsifal* and words from Beethoven's diaries strike a chord with him as his search enters a new phase post-Suzy. The pattern of quotation and cross-cultural reference functions as a counter-discourse to the East/West dichotomy entertained by André, Suzy, Ivan and to an extent Muhsin too. Art and culture become a global currency that transcends national boundaries and continental divides, a common heritage of man, which might supersede religion as a spiritual solution.

Notes

1. I refer to the third edition, *Zaynab: Manazir wa Akhlaq Rifiyya* (Cairo: Dar al-Maʿarif, 1983). Translations my own with corresponding page numbers from John Mohammad Grinstead's liberal translation, *Zainab: The First Egyptian Novel* (London: Darf Publishers, 1989).
2. Hoda Elsadda, *Gender, Nation, and the Arabic Novel: Egypt 1892–2008* (Edinburgh: Edinburgh University Press, 2012), pp. xix; Bouthaina Shaaban, *Voices Revealed: Arab Women Novelists, 1898–2000* (Boulder, CO: Lynne Rienner Publishers, 2009), chs 1 and 2.
3. Faris al-Shidyaq, *Kitab al-Saq ʿala al-Saq fi ma huwa al-Fariyaq*, ed. and trans. Humphrey Davies (Arabic and English combined edition), *Leg over Leg of The*

Turtle in the Tree Concerning The Fariyaq, What Manner of Creature Might He Be (New York and London: New York University Press, 2006), vol. 1, p. 37.
4. Al-Shidyaq, *Kitab al-Saq ʿala al-Saq*, vol. 1, pp. 298–9.
5. Asʿad al-Shidyaq, brother of Faris al-Shidyaq, was imprisoned in the monastery at Qannubin after he converted to Protestantism and died there in the 1830s. Ibid. p. 346, n. 314.
6. *Al-Tankit wa'l-Tabkit* (6 June–23 October 1881); *Al-Ustadh* (23 August 1892–13 June 1893).
7. On Nadim's sketches, see Sabry Hafez, *The Genesis of Arabic Narrative Discourse: A Study in the Sociology of Modern Arabic Literature* (London: Saqi Books, 1993), pp. 113–29; Matti Moosa, *The Origins of Modern Arabic Fiction*, 2nd edn (Boulder, CO: Lynne Rienner Publishers, 1997), pp. 67–89.
8. First published in *Misbah al-Sharq*, the newspaper edited by al-Muwaylihi and his father, 1898–1902. A full study of the text is provided with the English translation by Roger Allen, *A Period of Time: A Study of Muhammad al-Muwaylihi's Hadith ʿIsa Ibn Hisham* (Reading: Ithaca, 1992). See also Ahmad Ibrahim al-Hawari, *Naqd al-Mujtamaʿ fi Hadith ʿIsa ibn Hisham* (Cairo: Dar al-Maʿarif, 1986); Roger Allen's updated translation and introduction in *What ʿIsa Ibn Hisham Told Us*, 2 vols (New York and London: New York University Press, 2015).
9. Studies of Haykal and his work include Yusuf Khulayf, *Al-Adab wa'l-Hayat al-Misriyya: Muhammad Husayn Haykal* (Cairo: Dar al-Hilal, 1993); Nabil Faraj (ed.), *Muhammad Husayn Haykal fi ʿUyun Muʿasirihi*, including introduction by Jabir ʿAsfur (Cairo: Matbaʿat Dar al-Kutub al-Misriyya, 1996); Charles D. Smith, *Islam and the Search for Social Order in Modern Egypt: A Biography of Muhammad Husayn Haykal* (Albany: State University of New York Press, 1983); David Semah, *Four Egyptian Critics* (Leiden: Brill, 1974).
10. See Smith, *Islam and the Search for Social Order*, ch. 2: 'The Formative Years: Haykal between Egypt and Europe, 1888–1922'.
11. See e.g. diary entries 1 and 25 September 1909 (in Haykal, *Mudhakkirat al-Shabab*, Cairo: al-Majlis al-Aʿla li'l-Thaqafa, 1996), and his essay 'Al-Din wa'l-ʿIlm', in Haykal, *Al-Iman wa'l-Maʿrifa*, ed. Ahmad Haykal (Cairo: Dar al-Maʿarif, 1964), pp. 11–40. Also Smith, *Islam and the Search for Social Order*, ch. 2.
12. *Al-Siddiq Abu Bakr* (Cairo, 1942), *Al-Faruq ʿUmar* (Cairo, 1944–5) 2 vols, *ʿUthman Ibn ʿAffan: Bayn al-Khilafa wa'l-Mulk*, pub. posthumous (Cairo, 1964), ed. Ahmad Haykal.

13. *Zaynab*, p. 221 (trans., p. 153).
14. Ibid.
15. Jeff Shalan, 'Writing the Nation: The Emergence of Egypt in the Modern Arabic Novel', *Journal of Arabic Literature*, vol. 33, no. 3 (2002), pp. 211–47.
16. *Zaynab*, pp. 243–4 (trans., p. 167).
17. Ibid. p. 42 (trans., p. 23).
18. Ibid. p. 44 (trans., p. 25).
19. Ibid. p. 172 (trans., p. 121).
20. e.g. ibid. p. 193 (trans., p. 135).
21. Ibid. p. 172 (trans., p. 120).
22. Ibid. p. 172 (trans., p. 121).
23. Ibid. p. 185 (trans., p. 123).
24. Haykal, *Mudhakkirat al-Shabab*, diary entry 1 September 1909; Haykal, 'Rijal al-ᶜIlm wa Rijal al-Din'; Smith, *Islam and the Search for Social Order*, p. 41.
25. *Zaynab*, p. 243 (trans., p. 167).
26. Ibid. p. 291 (trans., p. 200).
27. Ibid. pp. 291–2 (trans., p. 200).
28. Ibid. p. 223 (trans., p. 155).
29. Ibid. p. 224 (trans., p. 156).
30. Ibid. p. 29 (trans., p. 15).
31. Ibid. p. 40 (trans., p. 22).
32. Ibid. p. 76 (trans., p. 49).
33. Ibid. p. 151 (trans., p. 108).
34. Ibid. p. 168 (trans., p. 118).
35. Ibid. pp. 50–1 (trans., p. 29). Adam is brought in again as Hamid deplores the incident with the farm girl, where he refers to mankind as 'the tribe of Adam, between the angels and beasts' (p. 175, trans., p. 122).
36. Ibid. pp. 18–19 (trans., p. 6). The language in this passage is highly romantic.
37. See Hamid in a debate with friends about marriage, ibid. pp. 128ff.
38. *Zaynab*, p. 28 (trans., p. 14). ᶜAziza, we are told, has been weak from childhood and her confined life compounds this.
39. Ibid. p. 270 (trans., p. 183).
40. ᶜAbd al-Muhsin Badr discusses the difficulty of categorising *Al-Ayyam* (*Tatawwur al-Riwayat al-ᶜArabiyya al-Hadith fi Misr*, Cairo: Maktabat al-Dirasat al-ᶜArabiyya, 1963, pp. 297–300), with the opposite finding, that it is difficult to class as either novel or autobiography.

41. See Fedwa Malti-Douglas, *Blindness and Autobiography: Al-Ayyam of Taha Husayn* (Princeton: Princeton University Press, 1988).
42. I refer here to the 1996 edition (Cairo: Dar al-Maʿarif). Translations my own, with corresponding page numbers from the combined English translation: *The Days: Taha Hussein, His Autobiography in Three Parts*, trans. E. H. Paxton, Hilary Wayment and Kenneth Cragg (Cairo: American University in Cairo Press, 1997).
43. The education trajectory is a common paradigm in Arabic autobiography. See Tetz Rooke, *In My Childhood: A Study of Arabic Autobiography* (Stockholm: Stockholm University, 1997), pp. 97–102.
44. *Al-Ayyam*, vol. 1, pp. 107–9 (trans., pp. 63–5).
45. Ibid. vol. 2, p. 76 (trans., pp. 155–6). *Takhlis al-Miftah* is a fourteenth-century book on rhetoric by al-Qazwini.
46. Qur'an reader and religious instructor were common paths for the blind at the time, and this was the initial expectation for Taha Husayn too.
47. Beyond the literary corpus, Ibrahim M. Abu Rabi identifies Islam as an 'historical other' in modern Arabic thought, with the exception of its Islamic stream (which naturally takes the Muslim self as its starting point), whilst emphasising the critical role of Christianity, imperialism and the West in articulations of the self and nation in all streams of modern Arabic thought (Islamic, liberal, nationalist, leftist). See Ibrahim M. Abu Rabi, 'The Concept of the "Other" in Modern Arab Thought: From Muhammad Abduh to Abdullah Laroui', *Islam and Christian–Muslim Relations*, vol. 8, no. 1 (2007), pp. 85–97.
48. *Al-Ayyam*, vol. 2, p. 174 (trans., p. 226).
49. Malti-Douglas makes this observation as a correction to Edward Said's comments on *Al-Ayyam*'s style. See Malti-Douglas, *Blindness and Autobiography*, pp. 154–5 and ff.
50. Cf. Q. 101:1–2. *Mā adrāka* is a Qur'anic phrase. See Malti-Douglas, *Blindness and Autobiography*, pp. 154–5 and ff.
51. *Al-Ayyam*, vol. 2, pp. 14, 16 (trans., pp. 113–14).
52. Ibid. p. 181 (trans., p. 231).
53. Malti-Douglas, *Blindness and Autobiography*, p. 78.
54. *Al-Ayyam*, vol. 2, pp. 174–5 (trans., p. 226).
55. See notes 11 and 24.
56. Published in *Al-Hadith* (February–May 1927). Reprinted in *Min Baʿid* (Beirut, 1967). See Charles D. Smith, 'The "Crisis of Orientation": The Shift of Egyptian Intellectuals to Islamic Subjects in the 1930's', *International*

Journal of Middle East Studies, vol. 4, no. 4 (October 1973), pp. 396–7. Pierre Cachia gives an account of the *Fi'l-Shiʿr al-Jahili* episode in *Taha Husayn: His Place in the Egyptian Literary Renaissance* (London: Luzac and Company Ltd, 1956), pp. 145–9. *Fi'l-Shiʿr al-Jahili* was reprinted in 1927, with the offending segments expurgated, as *Fi'l-Adab al-Jahili*.

57. Vol. 2 (Cairo, 1933), vol. 2 (Cairo, 1937), vol. 3 (Cairo, 1938). I refer here to a later edition, published in 1962.
58. *Hayat Muhammad* started to appear in the form of articles in February 1932. *Hayat Muhammad* (Cairo: Maktabat Misr, 1935), trans. from 8th edn Ismail Ragi A. al-Faruqi, *The Life of Muhammad* (London: Shorouk International, 1983); *Fi Manzil al-Wahy* (Cairo, 1937). See note 12.
59. See Smith, 'The Crisis of Orientation'. Smith formulates his argument partly as a critique of the analysis of the same situation of Nadav Safran (*Egypt in Search of Political Community*, Cambridge, MA: Harvard University Press, 1961). Louis Awad analyses the turn to Islamic subjects as an attempt to placate the conservatives and gain acceptance, and as an effort to forestall rising fundamentalism (*The Literature of Ideas in Egypt*, Atlanta, GA: Scholars Press, 1986, pp. 187–8). With respect to Taha Husayn, Pierre Cachia rejects the idea that Husayn ever retracted the arguments of *Fi'l-Shiʿr al-Jahili*, since he continued to express them and the book was reissued under a different title with only a few alterations (*Taha Husayn*, p. 147). See also Albert Hourani, *Arabic Thought in the Liberal Age, 1798–1939* (Cambridge: Cambridge University Press, 1983), pp. 333–4; Muhsin al-Musawi, *Islam in the Street: Religion in Modern Arabic Literature* (Lanham, Boulder, New York, Toronto and Plymouth: Rowman and Littlefield Publishers Inc., 2009), pp. 23ff.
60. Taha Husayn, *ʿAla Hamish al-Sira* (Cairo: Dar al-Maʿarif, 1962), p. 11.
61. *Fi'l-Shiʿr al-Jahili* was attacked in several articles, lectures and books and Taha Husayn offered to resign his post from the university, though his offer was refused by the then rector, Lutfi al-Sayyid. Cachia, *Taha Husayn*, p. 60.
62. Smith, *Islam and the Search for Social Order*, pp. 109–13.
63. See ibid., ch. 4: 'The Road to Islam: Intellectual Developments, 1924–1933'.
64. Haykal, *The Life of Muhammad*, p. li. For discussion and analysis of the text, see Smith, *Islam and the Search for Social Order*, pp. 109–30; Antonie Wessels, *A Modern Arabic Biography of Muhammad: A Critical Study of Muhammad Husayn Haykal's Hayat Muhammad* (Leiden: Brill, 1972).
65. Haykal, *The Life of Muhammad*, p. 522.
66. See Smith, *Islam and the Search for Social Order*, pp. 132–5. Smith observes

how 'Despite his title, Haykal's emphasis was on Muhammad's actions and sayings as reflecting intuition, *ilhām*, rather than divine revelation, *waḥy*. The choice permitted Haykal to present Muhammad's deeds as justifying the use of one's own intuition, unfettered by religious interpretations, in the modern day' (p. 133).

67. Ibid. p. 135. On these Rashidun studies, see ibid. pp. 135–8.
68. ʿAbbas Mahmud al-ʿAqqad, *ʿAbqariyyat Muhammad* (1942).
69. For some analyses of *Qindil*, see M. M. Badawi, 'The Lamp of Umm Hashim, the Egyptian Intellectual Between East and West', *Journal of Arabic Literature*, vol. 1, pp. 145–61; Rasheed El-Enany, *Arab Representations of the Occident: East–West Encounters in Arabic Fiction* (London and New York: Routledge, 2011), pp. 67–73; al-Musawi, *Islam in the Street*, pp. 46–58; Muhammad Siddiq, 'Deconstructing "The Saint's Lamp"', *Journal of Arabic Literature*, vol. 17 (1986), pp. 126–45; ʿAli al-Raʿi, *Dirasat fi'l-Riwayat al-Misriyya* (Cairo: al-Dar al-Misriyya li'l-Taliʿa, 1965), pp. 157–78. Aside from *Qindil*, which was published in a volume with short stories under that title, Haqqi published three other short story collections (*Dimaʾ wa Tin* 1955, *Umm al-ʿAwajiz* 1956, *ʿAntar wa-Juliet* 1961).
70. Yahya Haqqi, *Qindil Umm Hashim* (Cairo: Dar al-Maʿarif, 1984), p. 30.
71. Ibid. p. 57.
72. I refer to the 1988 edition here: Tawfiq al-Hakim, *ʿAwdat al-Ruh*, 2 vols (Cairo: Maktabat Misr). Translations my own with corresponding page numbers from William M. Hutchins (tr.), *Return of the Spirit: Tawfiq al-Hakim's Classic Novel of the 1919 Revolution* (Washington, DC: Three Continents Press, 1990). Studies of al-Hakim and his work include: Paul Starkey, *From the Ivory Tower: A Critical Study of Tawfiq al-Hakim* (London: Ithaca, 1987); Ghali Shukri, *Thawrat al-Muʿtazil: Dirasat fi Adab Tawfiq al-Hakim* (Beirut: Dar Ibn Khaldun, 1973), and his *Tawfiq al-Hakim: Al-Jil wa'l-Tabaqa wa'l-Ruʾya* (Beirut: Dar al-Farabi, 1993).
73. For nationalism as religion, see Carlton J. H. Hayes, 'Nationalism as a Religion', in *Essays on Nationalism* (New York: The Macmillan Company, 1926), pp. 93–125. Also Rogers Brubaker, 'Religion and Nationalism: Four Approaches', *Nations and Nationalism*, vol. 18, no. 1 (January 2012), pp. 2–20; Ninian Smart, 'Religion, Myth, and Nationalism', in Peter H. Merkl and Ninian Smart (eds), *Religion and Politics in the Modern World* (New York: New York University Press, 1983), pp. 15–28; Anthony D. Smith, *Chosen Peoples: Sacred Sources of National Identity* (Oxford: Oxford University Press, 2003);

David Stevens, 'Nationalism as Religion', *Studies: An Irish Quarterly Review*, vol. 86, no. 343 (Autumn 1997), pp. 248–58.
74. *ʿAwdat*, vol. 2, p. 52 (trans., 179).
75. Ibid. p. 53 (trans., p. 180).
76. Ibid. p. 59 (trans., pp. 183–4).
77. Ibid. p. 59 (trans., p. 183).
78. See Benjamin Geer, 'The Priesthood of Nationalism in Egypt: Duty, Authority, Autonomy' (unpublished PhD thesis, SOAS, 2011), p. 249. Dmitry Merejkovsky's book was originally published in Russian in 1925. It was translated into French and appeared in Paris shortly after, where al-Hakim came across it. Geer explores the relation between religion and nationalism in the Egyptian context, drawing on Pierre Bourdieu to cast Egyptian intellectuals and leaders (specifically Nasser) as a priesthood of nationalism.
79. *ʿAwdat*, vol. 2, p. 40 (trans., p. 173).
80. Ibid. p. 39 (trans., p. 172).
81. Stevens explores the relation between religion and nationalism via the scapegoat in his article 'Nationalism as Religion' (see note 72).
82. *ʿAwdat*, vol. 2, pp. 205–6 (trans., p. 278).
83. Ibid. p. 13 (trans., p. 156).
84. Ibid. p. 35 (trans., p. 169).
85. Ibid. p. 36 (trans., p. 170).
86. Ibid. p. 35 (trans., p. 170).
87. I refer here to the 1988 edition (*ʿUsfur min al-Sharq*, Cairo: Maktabat Misr, 1988), which includes a few passages which were omitted from the original, perhaps because they were deemed too revealing of the author or too sensitive for the public at the time. See R. Bayly Winder's comparison of the two Arabic editions and its translations in the introduction to his translation of the text, *Bird of the East* (Beirut: Khayyats, 1966), pp. xi–xiv. Translations here are my own, with references to Winder's *Bird of the East*.
88. El-Enany, *Arab Representations of the Occident*, pp. 42–3. The same applies to Suzy (p. 44). See El-Enany's extended analysis of the novel, which refers also to *ʿAwdat* and other works by al-Hakim, pp. 41–51.
89. *ʿUsfur*, p. 106 (trans., p. 88).
90. Al-Musawi notes this oppositional relation (*Islam in the Street*, p. 191) as part of a wider exploration of the role of Sayyida Zaynab in the text (pp. 186ff).
91. There is a concomitant feminisation of divinity here inasmuch as the male

deity is replaced by a female saint, but this is not developed and probably unconscious.
92. *Bird of the East*, p. 72. See note 87. Bayly Winder proposes that this section (trans., pp. 72–3) was added for the benefit of French readers (it first appeared in the 1960 French translation) as the clarifications therein are superfluous for Arabic readers.
93. Ibid. p. 73.
94. Muhsin posits Islam as a social reform movement in the extract mentioned above (trans., pp. 72–3). The behaviour of contemporary Muslims is dealt with in his monologue pp. 190–1 (trans., pp. 166–8).
95. *ᶜUsfur*, p. 22 (trans., p. 12).
96. Ibid. pp. 78–9. The episode was reintroduced in the second edition (1964) and print runs since then. See note 87.
97. Ibid. p. 183 (trans., p. 136).
98. Ibid. p. 170 (trans., p. 147).
99. Hafez, *The Genesis of Arabic Narrative Discourse*, pp. 168, 202, 223–4. Hafez names various stories which touch on the theme, including: Muhammad Taymur, 'Dars fi Kuttab' (1922); Mahmud Taymur, 'Al-Shaykh Jumᶜa' (1925), 'ᶜAmm Mitwalli' (1926) and 'Al-Shaykh Sayyid al-ᶜAbit' (1926); Mahmud Taha Lashin, 'Mephistopheles' (1927), 'Al-Shaykh Muhammad al-Yamani' (1929) and of course the famous 'Hadith al-Qarya' (1929).
100. *ᶜUsfur*, p. 87 (trans., p. 69).
101. Ibid. p. 190 (trans., p. 167).
102. Ibid. p. 191 (trans., p. 167).
103. Ibid. p. 93.
104. Ibid. p. 102 (trans., p. 85).
105. *Bāb firdaw* [sic]. Ibid. p. 57 (trans., p. 41).
106. Ibid. p. 123 (trans., p. 103). Muhsin's friend André suggests he has ensconced her in a palace from *Alf Layla wa Layla* and imagines her looking down from the lofty height of her window.
107. Ibid. p. 75 (trans., p. 59).
108. See ch. 13.
109. *ᶜUsfur*, p. 135 (trans., p. 113).
110. Ibid. p. 138 (trans., p. 118).
111. Ibid. pp. 138–9 (trans., p. 118).
112. Ibid. pp. 146 (trans., p. 125).
113. Ibid. p. 147 (trans., p. 126).

114. Ibid. p. 156 (trans., p. 135).
115. On sacred stories as dwelling places, see Stephen Crites, 'The Narrative Quality of Experience', *Journal of the American Academy of Religion*, vol. 39, no. 3 (September 1971), pp. 291–311.
116. See e.g. *ᶜUsfur*, p. 84 (trans., p. 66).
117. Ibid. pp. 66–7 (trans., pp. 51–2).
118. Ibid. p. 167 (trans., pp. 143–4).
119. Ibid. pp. 166, 189 (trans., pp. 143, 165).
120. Ibid. p. 167 (trans., pp. 143–4).
121. Ibid. p. 102 (trans., p. 86).
122. Aldous Huxley, Jean Cocteau, Beethoven, Anacreon, M. Ernst on Beethoven, Saint-Saëns, Ishaq Mawsili, Jahiz, Hafiz, Khayyam among others.

3

The Secular Scripture

As the novel emerges in Egypt in the first half of the twentieth century, fashioned for the most part by an intellectual elite who were invested heavily in the ideology of modernity, it aligns increasingly with values and ideals associated with secularism and secularity, like reason, humanism, intellectual freedom, disenchantment and plurality. The same is seemingly true of the Egyptian short story, where religion retains a similarly strong presence but is approached in maturity, for the most part, as discourse. The plights of ʿAbd al-Karim in 'Arkhas Layali' (The Cheapest Nights) and ʿAbdu in 'Shughlana' (Hard Up) are manifestly socially determined, whatever the characters might think.[1] Their ascription of good and bad fortune to God becomes in the social realism of Yusuf Idris an expression of false consciousness, as indeed do manifestations of faith in many of his other short stories. 'Hadith al-Qarya' (Village Talk), heralded as the first artistically sophisticated example of the short form in Arabic, demonstrates the symbolic capital of religion and religious voices whilst subsuming them into a wider secular critique of traditional society and its leaders, the religious shaykhs, a pattern we see many times over in the years to come.[2] This is not to make comprehensive claims for secularity in wider Egyptian society during this period or later. The 1923 constitution established citizenship as the foundation of an independent Egypt, allowed for religious and political pluralism, and granted personal liberty and free speech to all Egyptians, and the Wafd party, which dominated government through the 20s, 30s and 40s, was founded on secular values and pursued secular policies in law, administration and education. But state ideology is not necessarily identical with popular ideology and the rise of religious sentiment and increasing intermingling of religion and politics in the 30s and 40s reveals a high degree of ideological instability. Moreover, the Islamic resurgence that gained momentum following the fall of Nasser raises questions about how far secular ideology was actually entrenched in the 50s and 60s, when Arab socialism was in ascendency and public space was virtually emptied of religion. A far more detailed assessment of secularism and secularity in Egypt, taking in not only governance, law and political ethics but rural spaces and social attitudes, is required to make such a claim. Nor is it to insist on a hard and fast rule about the novel and secularism, for there will always be exceptions. At the very least the canonical status of ʿAwdat al-Ruh and certain didactic works shows that the Arabic novel does not disallow authoritarian discourse in every instance. It is simply to observe that the perfection of an artistic technique by a group of writers ideologically committed to modernity and the nation-state produced a literary genre that embodies themes and strategies associated with the secular. This does not, as mentioned, translate into the defeat or erasure of religion or the religious other in the mature Arabic novel in Egypt. Rather religion maintains a significant presence, but this presence becomes more meticulous and rational. That is to say that religion does not seep in so much via unconscious slips and concessions to divinity and transcendent causality (though some residue is inescapable) but is self-consciously invited in as theme, image, symbol, metanarrative, spirituality and target of criticism. Writing the nation, a project in which many Egyptian writers have participated, involves engaging with religion, often in a negative sense, since nationalism implies a relegation of religious voices and authority, while verisimilitude requires the presence of religious representatives and forms. It is also in maturity that the Arabic novel becomes more attuned to religion as a productive repository of symbols and images and a means of catalysing and enriching meaning.

Najib Mahfuz's fiction, spanning six decades and consisting of over thirty novels and hundreds of short stories, includes examples of all the self-conscious methods of engaging religion in a literary context mentioned above. His trilogy, regarded by many as marking the coming of age of the Arabic novel, merits discussion here as a landmark expression of literary secularism and epic tale of disenchantment. Composed of *Bayn al-Qasrayn* (1956), *Qasr al-Shawq* (1957) and *Al-Sukkariyya* (1957), the trilogy tells the story of Egypt during a particularly turbulent period in its modern history, from shortly before the 1919 revolution until the middle of the Second

World War.³ It is, as others have noted, a national allegory *par excellence*, in which the story of the nation is narrated and represented through the discourse and drama of a family. Narrated, in the sense that the characters themselves provide a running commentary on national events and politics. Represented, in the sense that the main political and intellectual currents of the period are embodied and dramatised by the family and their close circle. Politics affects everyone and the crises of the nation – occupation, resistance, air raids, economic decline, clash of ideology, etc. – are the crises of the family. And if the trilogy is an allegory of the nation as it transitions from a traditional to a modern society, Mahfuz equates the former with theism and dramatises the religious dimension of transition so that, like *Al-Ayyam*, the narrative becomes the story of Egypt's journey from religiosity to secularity, with all the contradictions this entails. In other words, the novel maps the epistemological shift that accompanies and facilitates the birth of the modern secular nation, whereby religious belief and identity are subordinated to nationalist ideology and citizenship.

The most obvious expression of this is in the much discussed (and therefore only summarised here) disintegration of parental authority and increasing marginalisation of the mother and father. Amina, with her fortune-telling, superstition and legends, represents popular religion while ʿAbd al-Jawwad, a professed Hanbali, is conservative Islam. Within the nuclear family at the start of the text we have represented two main strands of Sunni Islam, to which we can add Fahmi's Islamic modernism. Religion in the trilogy is not unitary, as the alternate emphases of family members demonstrate, but the world of *Bayn al-Qasrayn* is unquestionably God-centred and crucially bound together by the sovereign command of ʿAbd al-Jawwad, the patriarchal exemplar of modern Arabic literature and a convenient symbol of God.⁴ The latter symbolism is intimated variously in the text, through this character's larger than life persona, authority and seeming infallibility in the first volume, as well as in the discourse of the narrator and characters. Amina, bound by the laws of patriarchal subservience, is plagued by conscience after visiting the shrine, in a manner reminiscent of a believer, and when she is eventually forgiven, Kamal, who was part of the plot and steered her off course into the path of danger, 'laughed like a sinner (*mudhnib*) granted redemption'.⁵ Amina's expulsion can further be read, following El-Enany, as a reference to the Fall and expulsion from heaven.⁶ Much of the text's religious displacement is enacted around Kamal, who grows apart from his parents in line with his religious dissociation. Contradictions emerge between Amina's inherited knowledge and Kamal's school lessons, and the legend of the tomb turns out to be false, thus popular belief unravels for the boy, and with it his mother's wisdom. She becomes a remnant of the past with whom he struggles for conversation. It is noteworthy, in light of what we have seen in *Zaynab* and *Al-Ayyam*, that popular religion is sympathetically portrayed in the trilogy. Gone is the scathing criticism born out of its injurious and even fatal connection to traditional medicine, and instead we have gentle mocking of its ignorance and nostalgia for the link it engenders with the past.

As a symbol of the divine ᶜAbd al-Jawwad's loss of authority over his family, which in turn signifies the nation, is a heavily loaded metaphor. The patriarch's grip loosens as his sons rebel and embrace new ideas. Fahmi refuses to renounce his political activism in a significant scene in which his father asks him to swear upon the Qur'an. Yasin comes into conflict with ᶜAbd al-Jawwad when he takes his first wife, Zaynab, to see the comic character Kishkish on stage,⁷ and his libido is apparently a force which neither father nor son can control. Kamal clashes with ᶜAbd al-Jawwad over his decision to become a teacher, and his whole path in life is a path away from the father and that which he represents, a tale of oedipal disentanglement as Siddiq has shown.⁸ As a celibate bachelor Kamal is the polar opposite of the indulgent ᶜAbd al-Jawwad, and the sceptical scientific thought system he embraces is an affront to the traditional Islamic outlook of his father, as is dramatised so effectively in the famous Darwin scene in which ᶜAbd al-Jawwad grills Kamal on his article for *Al-Fikr* magazine on *The Origin of Species*. As his progeny become masters of their own destinies, heading their respective households and making decisions without reference to him, ᶜAbd al-Jawwad's virility and physical strength are simultaneously in decline. He walks with a stick and is significantly spurned by the dancer Zanuba in favour of Yasin in the second volume, and by the third is old and weak and increasingly confined to the house, observing events more than driving them. The image of Kamal carrying him home in his arms after an air raid neatly epitomises the role reversal and filial ascendency. Centre stage is now occupied by the younger generations, Kamal and his nephews Ridwan, Ahmad and ᶜAbd al-Munᶜim, while

ʿAbd al-Jawwad is left pondering the effects of time. Moreover, with power no longer concentrated in one man, new voices come to the fore, including atheism, and these are notably no more or less valid than the religious stream in the family and society, where faith continues to be marked by variation and plurality (orthodox, popular, militant, moderate). By the third volume Islam is no longer a default position. ʿAbd al-Jawwad's grandchildren embrace or reject religion within the context of the nation, which more than Islam has become the unquestioned Weltanschauung. Even the Islamists in *Al-Sukkariyya* are nationalists. ʿAbd al-Munʿim, as an active member of the Muslim Brotherhood, represents militant Islam in the third volume and he is notably as concerned as his communist brother Ahmad with the overthrow of the British. At Ikhwan meetings Egyptian independence is a discussion topic and clear goal. This is the era before global jihad and transnational Islamic revival, when fundamentalist groups concerned themselves more with local issues and power than the abstract enemy and salvation.

Demystification is a component part of religion's displacement in modernity and is reflected here, in part, in the sons' discovery of their father's genial but irreligious side. Having only known him as a pious tyrant at home, Yasin and Kamal learn that their father is an indulging reveller outside the family residence. The irony is that exposure reveals something more rather than less pleasant; the oppressor becomes human, perfection is imperfection. Yasin is immediately relieved, since his god is now a mirror of himself rather than an unattainable ideal. But for Kamal the revelation produces confusion. Even if he can stomach ʿAbd al-Jawwad's unholy behaviour, the duplicity of it all is deeply distressing and constitutes no less than the denudation of an ideal and fall of an idol: 'your power is just a legend now', he laments.[9] Siddiq, drawing on psychoanalysis, notes the transference of object choice to ʿAyda as the father's image recedes. But ʿAyda too turns out to be a false god, another figure demystified in a further blow to religion and religious belief. Kamal assigns ʿAyda divine attributes and the imagery around her in the text leaves little doubt that she is another symbol of the divine, in particular a Sufi version thereof, as I will explore further in Chapter 7.[10] But ʿAyda turns out to be as brutal as ʿAbd al-Jawwad, at least psychologically. Lending no favours to female representation in Arabic literature, she is not far off a one-dimensional temptress who torments and exploits her pathetic lover. She mocks Kamal's physical appearance and uses him as a pawn to catalyse her engagement to Hasan Salim. On the occasion of ᶜAyda's wedding Kamal is deeply pained, not so much because she has escaped him but 'because she has descended from heaven, because she is wallowing in the mud after living grandly over the clouds'.[11] She is another 'cruel mocking god', or rather not a god at all, as Ismail points out more than once to his lovesick friend. But Kamal is an idealist and habitual seeker and the demise of ᶜAyda is simply the latest in a series of fallen icons punctuating his intellectual journey away from God. From a devout believer enamoured of al-Husayn and sacred legend in volume 1, he gradually extricates himself from myth and theism as the narrative progresses. It is of course no coincidence that his loss of faith is announced shortly after the ᶜAyda revelations, but it is actually science that deals the final blow. In the end it is not demystification that ousts religion but a thought system which supersedes the Logos, a thought system founded on scepticism and empiricism and which leaves matters of religion up to the individual, as myths and rituals to live by beyond the scope of science. As a signifier of this, as well as an effect of the psychological trauma occasioned by the loss of core beliefs and ideals, in his post-religious phase Kamal begins to doubt everything to the point of extreme malaise, which in turn casts a shadow over science and knowledge as paths to fulfilment. As one character comments, 'Religion has taken vengeance on you [Kamal]. You renounced it for higher truths but have returned empty-handed'.[12] But there is one entity that does not come under scrutiny as Kamal questions God, love, ᶜAyda, immortality, even science, and that is the nation. The figure of the nation is present in Kamal's conversations and consciousness throughout the text, but it does not become a target of his scepticism. As religion is relegated and science takes over as the path to truth, the nation remains as an uncritical frame of reference. And the nation for Kamal, in common with the wider narrative, is secular, a realm wherein religion is welcome but subsidiary, as is elaborated in dialogues with Riyad Qaldas, the one Coptic character in the text who, as a member of a minority, is naturally concerned with the equality of all Egyptians regardless of creed and ethnicity. Here again the nation emerges as a core value. By the end of the trilogy, the family, as societal microcosm, no longer rotates around a symbolic father and is no longer bound by belief, and its central thinker Kamal has self-consciously exchanged religion for science and secularism.

The binary pattern, that is the clear contrast of old and new, religion and science, Islamic community and nation-state in the narrative, in the context of selfhood and identity formation on the level of individual (Kamal) and nation (Egypt), brings us back to intersubjectivity and figuring the other. Secular scientific discourse and national consciousness emerge out of, and in contradistinction to, religion in the trilogy. Citizenship and democracy specifically displace the imperial order, that is, British occupation, and Islamic caliphate. Riyad Qaldas reminds us of the mechanics of the latter when he refers to the poll tax (*jiyza*) levied on non-Muslims in past centuries and the historic persecution of the Copts in a system which prioritised religious identity. At the same time, Kamal's newfound Weltanschauung is closely bound up with, and defined against, the religious worldview that preceded it and which accordingly becomes its other. For the other, as discussed, as both a philosophical and psychoanalytical category, is a figure against which the subject becomes aware of and defines itself. Like Hegel's master/slave, the self and other are locked in a relation of recognition and consciousness, though it may be uneven, asymmetrical and even one-sided. The emergence of the nation in the trilogy and Kamal's embrace of science and secular knowledge take place with reference to religion, which is repositioned on the margins as object and differential.

Othering implies exclusion and denigration; the other is peripheral and inferior. This quality is achieved in the trilogy, as in *Al-Ayyam* previously, by a strand of criticism which stigmatises institutional religion and underscores the incongruence of Islam and modern life. The kind of teaching offered at the *kuttāb* is once more regressive. Kamal's religious lessons consist of lectures on the jinn and rote learning the Qur'an, delivered by a shaykh who also abuses school boys. The ignorance and evil filters through the institutional apparatus to the city mosques and Azhar. Yasin refers to the debauchery and penchant for young boys of a preacher at al-Husayn mosque.[13] Shaykh Mutawalli ᶜAbd al-Samad, a persistent presence through the three volumes, displays the ignorance so often associated with popular religion in modern Arabic literature when he decries modern medicine. He bestows blessings in exchange for gifts and is gluttonous and hypocritical, reprimanding others for alcohol consumption whilst indulging in soft drugs himself. As such he draws attention to the idiosyncrasy of Islamic law, which ostensibly permits one form of recreational high whilst prohibiting another, and the ease with which sacred rulings can be applied in letter but not in spirit. He is also, like other Sufi figures in Mahfuz's fiction, practically useless and increasingly irrelevant, counselling prayer in times of crisis but providing no tangible support. His mad utterances as he drifts into senility reflect on the sound and status of the Sufi voice in modern life.

Islamic law becomes a key problematic and channel for criticism beyond the shaykh. Only those characters who bend the rules and reimagine God in their own image are able to live comfortably as Muslims. ʿAbd al-Jawwad worships Allah with all his energy and no one would doubt his sincerity, yet he drinks and fornicates in contravention of Sharia, on the logic that legalising his sexual adventures through marriage would negatively impact his children's inheritance. He cannot conceive of a wrathful God who would begrudge him harmless fun. ʿAbd al-Jawwad's idea that these are victimless crimes reveals a regressive understanding of gender dynamics and sexual power, but he evidently enjoys the sympathy of the author, given his positive portrayal and the amount of words given to explaining his actions and the depth of his faith, which is not only sincere but measured and thoughtful: 'it was an inherited faith in which there was no individual judgement (*ijtihād*). Yet his sensitivity, kindness, emotional life and sincerity had added a refined eminent feeling to it which kept it from being blind tradition or ritual induced by desire or fear'.[14] Statements like this read like a defence of religious conservatism backed by genuine belief, as distinct from the hollow piety of the orthodox establishment here and in *Al-Ayyam*. The faith and practice of ʿAbd al-Jawwad, Yasin and other bon vivants in the text become a correction to strict and puritanical Islam, which places a heavy burden on those who adhere to it.[15] Kamal is a case in point. The most pious of all the characters, except perhaps ʿAbd al-Munʿim in the third volume, he derives little benefit from his faith and his adherence to Sharia puts him out of step with his friends and society, as highlighted by the awkward scenes at the Pyramids and ʿAyda's wedding. For Kamal religion is an all or nothing affair – 'Either the Qur'an is true in its entirety, or it is not the Qur'an'[16] – which means he is not able to experience pleasure until he has forsworn Islam, especially when he rejects marriage lest it distract him from his quest for truth.

Religious criticism in the trilogy effectuates and rationalises the relegation of religion and its transposition as the other. Or rather institutional Islam, for this is not an unconditional denunciation of religion in its vast and diverse entirety so much as a strategy to reinforce institutional displacement in a national context. The goal is to facilitate and justify the emergence of a new epistemology and political community. Institutional Islam is othered as the nation comes to the fore and Kamal embraces science and secular values. But secularity is not atheism and modernity does not exclude religious belief. Popular religion remains strong as the narrative draws to a close in the person of Khadija, who takes over from Amina as matriarch albeit with a smaller remit, and the majority of characters remain believers. The secularisation thesis finds no support here. Moreover, an alternative to secular nationalism and modernity is pitched in the person of ʿAbd al-Munʿim, who as a member of the Muslim Brotherhood advocates a return to Islamic core values as the foundation for the nation-state. While the ideological progression of the family, marginalisation of the symbolic father and Kamal's own intellectual trajectory tend to equate tradition and religiosity, there is no corresponding pairing of modernity and godlessness – even in our champion of science and secularism, Kamal ʿAbd al-Jawwad, who never really abandons his search and whose discourse in his post-religious phase retains echoes of the sacred.[17] Kamal no longer believes in God in the third volume, but his language and reference in his post-religious phase tell a different story on occasion. For example, we are told that Kamal would sit with ʿAʾisha, who is a shadow of her former self following the devastating loss of her husband and children, and 'He would contemplate her silently for a long time, sadly [re]imagining the beautiful form now diminished which God created her in, and examining what it had become'.[18] The creationist terminology here conflicts with the Darwinism which the character professes elsewhere in the text and sits uncomfortably with his apparent atheism. When Jalila suggests that he pass on her regards to his father, Kamal exclaims, 'What a suggestion! It's enough to bring the Hour of Resurrection (*al-sāʿa*)'.[19] Upon hearing an update about ʿAyda from his friend Ismail, 'he wished at that moment that a miracle would fall from the sky so he could meet her, even just for a few moments'.[20] Just as divine invocation and references to God as a prime mover by character and narrator in *Zaynab* and *ʿAwdat* problematise the secular theme, so the same feature in Kamal's discourse warrants reflection.

But what we are dealing with here is not a reversal of credo so much as cross-contamination of self and other, which is not unexpected in instances of fission such as this, when self and other were not born separate. Given the character's categorical statements of religious disillusionment and the reformulation of his quest away from the sacred, Kamal's invocation and religious language in the third volume point rather to the embeddedness of sacred forms and structures in his consciousness, and the difficulty of cleanly extracting oneself from a framework that is deeply entrenched in thought and culture. They also signal language as a site of extreme blurring between the religious and secular. What is the status of divine reference in the discourse of an atheist? Kamal's utterances are not expressions of faith but insofar as they carry the spectre of faith and theism nor are they purely temporal. We might also add to the ambivalent status of religious expression by the character in the third volume, his anguish and disquiet at abandoning religious belief, even after he has transcended it intellectually, and his suffering as he intellectually grows away from his parents. He refers to his moments of enlightenment and demystification as a succession of tragedies, starting with the revelation about al-Husayn's tomb,[21] and outlines his heartache in a soliloquy to his parents: 'How unhappy I am today as I am liberated from your influence [mother], just as I will be unhappy tomorrow when I am liberated from my father'.[22] In fact, Kamal's search for truth is religious in everything but name. I will explore in Chapter 7 how his journey in volumes 2 and 3 of the trilogy can be read as a mystical adventure, following through the Sufi symbolism. But even without this, the quest motif, as mythologists have shown, is a thoroughly religious pattern, even if the goal ceases to be sublime along the way. Spurning marriage, lest it 'cause him to lower his gaze',[23] and dedicating his life to a search for truth, Kamal is a secular seeker, a profane pilgrim. His friend Ismail is not far off the mark when he comments: 'you still – even in apostasy – believe in truth, goodness and beauty and want to consecrate your life to them. Is this not what religion requests? How can you deny the root (*aṣl*) but have faith in the branches (*farʿ*)?'[24] While the movement of text and character is towards the secular, the structures remain religious.

There is a sense of this on the plane of ethics too. Alongside the secular spirit and humanist values of the trilogy, a certain Islamic ethic runs through the text, for example in the theme of repentance, which goes unchallenged.

When Jalila reveals her intention to perform the hajj to purify herself before Judgement Day her proposal is accepted as a natural next step by a usually sceptical Kamal. ʿAbd al-Rahim Pasha has the same idea and even plans to marry afterwards. The Pasha is Ridwan's mentor and, although his news is met with hilarity by his young companions, the need for repentance is not seriously interrogated. It is in textual terms appropriate that the homosexual politician should seek forgiveness. The scene, moreover, ends with the Pasha drawing an analogy between Ridwan's eschewal of women and an incurable disease (*maraḍ lā yuʿraf lahu dawāʾ*), implying aberration.[25] No doubt verisimilitude is a factor here and hajj is commonplace at Jalila's and the Pasha's stage in life. But it is noteworthy that it is these two characters, the prostitute and the homosexual, who are singled out for the adventure. The characterisation of Ridwan is also significant in this regard. He is defined in the narrative by his good looks, homosexuality and *wasṭa* (connections). He is introduced by his boyfriend Hilmi into the Pasha's entourage of young men and receives promotions and favours through this channel. Next to the serious characters of Kamal, Ahmad and ʿAbd al-Munʿim, Ridwan comes off as rather frivolous, which hardly challenges sexual stereotypes and religio-cultural homophobia. Also of note is how Zanuba is rehabilitated through marriage. She is accepted into the family and emerges as a model character in the third volume only after she has abandoned her promiscuous lifestyle and dedicated herself to Yasin and motherhood. Though these are minor details relating to minor characters, and the puritanical morality of Sharia does not escape criticism as described above, it is nevertheless possible to detect in the treatment of Jalila, the Pasha, Ridwan and Zanuba a moral stance informed by an Islamic ethic, or at the very least an opportunity missed to reverse or rethink Islamic ethics in a secular humanist mould, the starting point of which would be equality, mutual respect and individual choice. Why should 'transforming her life', in Jalila's case, involve making pilgrimage to Mecca?[26] Why link positive womanhood with monogamy and motherhood? Why should the homosexual be the least positive, least principled of the three nephews? Of course not every narrative choice and character trait speaks to the moral hierarchy, and deciphering the ethics of an epic work like the trilogy, in which realism and naturalism are key strategies, is a large task to which I cannot do justice here. But notwithstanding this, these details represent the cracks where Islamic ethics and religio-cultural bias peculate through the secular frame. Moreover they suggest morality and ethics to be another area in which the secular and religious are difficult to disentwine and where slippage and contamination can be expected.

The secular theme on the level of story is matched in the trilogy by secular form, which is what ultimately aligns the work with genre theory as described in the Introduction, even if a secularising plot line helps. Secular themes, as discussed, are not necessary to produce a secular text even if the coincidence of the emergence of the novel and the nation-state makes them commonplace in the Egyptian and Arabic novel's early period. In the trilogy we find the contingent world which Lukacs identifies as constitutive of novelistic production. The world of the text is self-contained and self-propelling. The third person narrator is now invisible for all intents and purposes. Gone are references to God and destiny in narrative sections, which cast characters in a drama controlled from above, and gone are the coincidences of early modern Arabic narrative discourse which betray the work of the author. The drama is ostensibly driven by the characters, whose actions are widely psychologised and organic. Thus Kamal and Yasin's encounter in the brothel, a dramatic moment and apparent coincidence, which conveniently leads into revelations about ʿAbd al-Jawwad, makes absolute sense in context; Yasin is out on the prowl as usual and Kamal self-consciously enters this space as he renounces Islam and embraces the next step on his spiritual journey. Likewise Budur's sudden reappearance, which draws Kamal back into the world and focuses attention on the issue of marriage once more, is acceptable in narrative terms, coming on the back of the Shaddad family's change in fortune and new lodgings. In other words, even the surprises in the trilogy are rationalised and accounted for within the parameters of the story. The exception is ʿAʾisha's excessive misfortune, for she loses her husband and all of her children to epidemic and childbirth. But since the deaths do not open up a particular trajectory in the text – for example, by leading to a discovery or facilitating a plot line – they do not undermine narrative logic or the text's contingency. These deaths are not plot devices so much as examples of life's misfortunes, which are not beyond the remit of realism.[27] There is of course no such thing as truly objective narrative in a novel, as in history and biography. The invisibility of the author is in the end a creative strategy to simulate independent and organic drama and masks the hand of the writer. The plot and characters of the trilogy are drawn and manipulated to produce certain meanings and effects, just as the real-life events of autobiography and history are crafted to tell a particular story. Narrative is constructed, and it is constructed according to a discursive position or ideology, which in the trilogy happens to be secular. Here too is the moment to register the concurrence of realism and secularity in literature. Simulated objectivity, logical progression, contingency and human agency in the trilogy are strategies of realism and part of what makes the trilogy secular. Realism, insofar as it values empirical observation, abjures the supernatural, valorises man and works through logic and mechanical time, is secular. Indeed a novel's success in realism might be a measure of its secularity. This would seemingly apply to *Zaynab* and *ʿAwdat*, where lapses in realistic strategy, moments when action and drama are attributed to supernatural forces, are precisely the details which compromise these works' secularity. The question going forward is what happens to the Arabic novel's secular aesthetic in its post-realistic phase. What is the dynamic between realism, modernism and literary secularism?

If contingency, objectivity and agency produce a secular feel, this spills over into the treatment of religious myth and imagery, which are present here but in a secular register. The narrative freely draws on sacred forms and images to communicate profane meanings and effects. As such they are stripped of their spiritual import and secularised, or at least their spiritual dimension is significantly diminished, for one must acknowledge that so long as the signifier remains so too do traces of its past lives, in this sense precluding any easy separation. The waiter's voice sounds 'like the call of a muezzin' in the street below the house in *Bayn al-Qasrayn*[28] and the reverence of ʿAbd al-Jawwad's sons at the breakfast table is compared to a scene in a mosque: 'The brothers sat down politely and humbly, heads bowed as though at Friday prayer', a description which of course bolsters the father's symbolism.[29] Jalila describes how she has had a hundred lovers, and her tambourine player adds: 'Plus five – like the five fingers of the Prophet's granddaughter Fatima held up to ward off the evil of infidels',[30] and, along with Zubayda, is more than once compared to a camel litter on pilgrimage to Mecca (*maḥmil*).[31] The nationalist movement and Fahmi's death are couched in religious language and Fahmi turns his appreciation of Maryam into something akin to the *dhikr* ritual: 'When he was alone, he would repeat her name as though it were one of the venerable Muslim Saints engraved in his imagination along with the ornamentation provided by legends'.[32] Not unrelated is the employment of divine invocation for impious purposes. ʿAbd al-Jawwad, for instance, uses worship as a euphemism. 'Can I hope we might pray together?', he says to Zubayda in a scene full of invocation and innuendo.[33] He quotes a hadith – 'If you have no shame, do what you wish' – encouraging his friend Ibrahim al-Far to follow ex-lover Zubayda into the bedroom.[34] Examples of this are plentiful and on the one hand are symptomatic of a cultural context in which religion is deeply ingrained as myth, image and language, feeding into the point about deeply entrenched structures and residue. On the other hand, the employment of religious imagery, analogies and phrases in temporal contexts with profane purport is secularising. The sacred is reoriented to the temporal.

Finally, before I move on to the push and pull between secular and religious discourse in the work of another significant writer of the time, ʿAbd al-Rahman al-Sharqawi, I should return to the discussion of the other briefly and note that the other is not singular. In the case of Kamal, every friend who takes a different path to him – Ismail the Muslim pragmatist, Fuʾad the opportunist, Riyad the Coptic artist – are potential others. But the concept really comes into play when the subject is locked in a difficult relationship or power struggle with another entity or foil, as is the case for Kamal with both religion and the West, the latter represented by the British occupier and ʿAyda Shaddad, whose Parisian influence and European education has left her better acquainted with Christianity than Islam. The British troops are of minimal import here, except to note the presence of the attraction/rejection dynamic associated with cultural alterity; Kamal cannot help admiring the enemy and oppressor. But ʿAyda is of interest for in her we have a composite symbol of mystical divinity and the West together. When Kamal transfers his object choice to ʿAyda, he turns his gaze away from Arabo-Islamic tradition and onto the West. His gravitation to the Shaddad mansion and obsession with ʿAyda figures the allure of the western other, and it is no surprise that his relationship with ʿAyda and her brother Husayn is marked by an uneven power dynamic which renders him forever outside and inferior. He is left behind in Cairo when the Shaddad and their circle summer on the coast and he is the last to learn of ʿAyda's engagement, as well as becoming the butt of jokes for the family. The West in ʿAyda is impressive and enthralling but immoral and cruel. But this is not the whole story, for embedded in this female western other is a mystical ideal (see Chapter 7), which complicates Kamal's rejection of Arabo-Islamic tradition and dismantles the equation of the West with pure materialism, which is sometimes the impression in modern Arabic fiction (cf. Ivan's discourse in ʿUsfur). Kamal's reorientation towards western science and values is not as clear cut as it might seem, and nor is the West necessarily godless and modernity devoid of spirituality.

The displacement of religion in the trilogy is achieved on a narrative level by a multidimensional secularising plot line and national allegory, which pushes religious identity into second place behind national identity. A radically different displacement is effected in ʿAbd al-Rahman al-Sharqawi's *Muhammad Rasul al-Hurriyya* (1962), which represents a meeting point for the religious biographies and studies by secular-oriented writers and the novel, a text in which these two strands of modern Arabic literary prose intersect.[35] Displacement here starts from within; al-Sharqawi takes a central text of Islam, the prophetic *sīra*, and grafts new meaning onto it, reorienting it to tell a new story, reimagining it in a poetic and secular register. Although artistically the work does not come near the trilogy, nor its author's other fiction, it merits discussion here as the culmination of the secularisation of scripture begun by the likes of Haykal, al-ʿAqqad and Taha Husayn in the 1930s, however they viewed or described their undertaking, and as a counterpoint to the literary secularism of the trilogy, secularisation through another trajectory so to speak. But before I examine this peculiar text in detail, it is worth pausing for a moment on another of al-Sharqawi's novels, which mirrors the religious displacement enacted in the trilogy but from a village perspective, namely his famous novel *Al-Ard* (1954).[36]

Al-Ard is widely regarded as the first genuine village novel in Arabic, in the sense that it is written from the *fellāh* viewpoint, as opposed to the urban intellectual perspective of *Zaynab* and *Yawmiyyat Nāʾib fi'l-Aryaf* (1937).[37] It was written shortly after the 1952 Free Officers revolution and is expressive of its nationalist socialist orientation, though the narrative itself is set in the early 30s, a time when cotton prices were suffering as an effect of the Depression and parliamentary government was in crisis following the suspension of the

1923 constitution and dissolution of parliament under Ismail Sidqi (Prime Minister of Egypt 1930–3). This is the explicit historical context of the story, referred to frequently in dialogue by characters, underscoring its nationalist dimension. *Al-Ard* tells the story of an unnamed Egyptian village and its attempts to face off government interference and oppression. In so doing it paints a vivid picture of the disenfranchisement of the *fellāḥīn* under Sidqi and of a community rooted in pastoral tradition and bound by shared interest and a common enemy. If the trilogy plots a national imaginary in a modern urban trajectory, then *Al-Ard* is its rural mirror. But this is not a simple city/village, modernity/tradition dichotomy so much as a struggle between corrupt government – the national ideal gone wrong – and a neglected community. Technology and signifiers of modernity are not bad in themselves but become so because of the way in which they are deployed to the exclusive benefit of officials and townsfolk and to the detriment of villagers, with the proposed highway as a case in point. Likewise modernity's conceptual opposite, tradition, in particular insofar as it designates religion, is not uniformly positive, even as the text's sympathies lie with the villagers and their way of life. Next to the urban drift of *Al-Ayyam* and *ʿAwdat*, with their implied conjunction of the city and progress, *Al-Ard* shifts attention back to the rural setting and locates the nation in the *fellāḥīn*, resuming the project of *Zaynab* but with the theme of revolution at the forefront and a dominant strategy of social realism.[38] The *fellāḥīn* represent authentic Egypt and the nation's core, struggling to preserve their identity and assert their voice under a self-serving establishment that has betrayed the values of the Wafd.

In this context religion once again becomes a problem. There is no crisis of belief here, nor much imagining of multiracial religiously plural nationhood. *Al-Ard*'s nationalism is more ethnic than civic; the nation resides unambiguously in the *fellāḥīn*. Fraternity is represented in solidarity in action, tolerance in the inclusion of the Bedouin outsider ʿAlwani and Nubian Sergeant ʿAbdullah, who comes from Aswan but is quickly absorbed into village life (albeit for a short period only for he is transferred once he becomes a friend to the villagers), but these are secondary to emphasis on the land and *fellāḥ*, and ʿAlwani is, besides, and reiterating a theme suggested in *ʿAwdat*, morally inferior to the farmers.[39] What we do see, however, as the community devises practical solutions to urgent problems, such as the reduction of their water source, arrest of their men and seizure of their land, is the almost complete futility of their spiritual leader, Shaykh Shinawi. Recalling some of his literary counterparts, the shaykh is petty, acquisitive, hypocritical and collusive. He is convinced to support the villagers' petition seeking a reversal of the punitive irrigation ruling only once ᶜAbd al-Hadi has promised to slaughter a goat in his honour[40] and he has blessings for Zanuba but not her sister Khadra, even though their paths are essentially similar but for a dichotomy of wealth.[41] When the Bey drafts a new petition inviting a road through the village, the shaykh is instrumental in gathering signatures and ensuring that no villager reads its contents before signing. Thus he dupes his congregation in the interests of power, since the proposed road entails loss of soil and livelihood for villagers. When government soldiers ambush the village the shaykh hides, and when a burial site is required for Khadra, the shaykh balks at the possibility of her sharing his plot.[42]

Yet more than these crimes and flaws, it is the shaykh's redundancy that condemns him in the narrative and renders him peripheral, in this aligning with some of Mahfuz's Sufis as well as the shaykh in Yusuf Idris' story, 'Al-Mishwar' (The Errand), who has nothing to offer al-Shabrawi when he turns up desperate at the Sayyida Zaynab mosque.[43] When disasters strike, Shaykh Shinawi offers cosmological interpretations and counsels prayer. The former are broadly dismissed by the village, even as they open up theological conundrums and underscore the co-optation, or attempted co-optation, of religion to control the masses and perpetuate an oppressive status quo. The water crisis, for example, is because God sends a curse on villages if they disobey Him and don't pray, according to the shaykh. He even draws an analogy with ᶜAd and Thamud, ancient tribes who in the Qur'an invite God's wrath by rejecting His messengers but have nothing in common with the villagers other than suffering.[44] The shaykh's explication is mocked by a community who are in no doubt as to the root of their suffering. Are they the only evil village? What about the landowners who don't pray or pay zakat (alms), who drink alcohol during Ramadan and violate young girls, whose land flows with water and whose storerooms are filled with grain? Is God not angry with them?[45] Such questions not only reveal the villagers' rejection of religious platitudes but point to an issue many theologians have grappled with and which surfaced already in *Zaynab*, namely causality and divine justice. If

God is the prime mover, why single out this particular village for punishment? Why do the poor suffer more in this world? And even in the absence of punishment, why is there suffering at all? The shaykh's calls to prayer are frequently ignored. Water before prayer is ʿAbd al-Hadi's response to the shaykh's repeat invitations to the mosque.⁴⁶ The latter jumps in the well to rescue the buffalo as Shinawi stands on the sidelines counselling prayer.⁴⁷

Like Shaykh al-Mutawalli in the trilogy, Shinawi's sacred discourse and archaic reference is irrelevant to the pressing problems of the day, and the instances of him being ignored or silenced inscribe religious displacement onto the narrative. ʿAbd al-Hadi, a man of action and embodiment of the *fellāḥ* ideal, a foil and virtual nemesis to Shaykh Shinawi, holds more influence among the villagers and takes precedence over the shaykh in the moral order. A more radical expression of religious displacement comes in the narrator and Wasifa's illicit encounters in the *muṣallā* (prayer place), which, given the multiple locations they might have chosen, can only be read as intentional and symbolic. More than once the pair retire to the *muṣallā* and come close to defiling its sacred space, though the shaykh interrupts on the first occasion and the narrator's fear of consequences puts a halt to the second.⁴⁸ These scenes are scandalous in an Islamic register and reflect not only the younger generation's disregard for religious tradition but an intentional overwriting of holy signifiers in the text. Siddiq writes that 'the diminution in the status of formal symbols of sanctity, spatial as well as thematic, paves the way for an alternative organisation of national space around the idea of the homeland: *waṭan*'.⁴⁹ Religion is displaced in favour of the national.

At other times religion is seen in a power struggle with secular authority and national discourse. When ʿAbd al-Hadi, a self-appointed leader whose focus is the here and now ('He dreamed of Paradise ... Paradise in this world!'),⁵⁰ leads a meeting to discuss the irrigation issue, the shaykh resolutely leads a portion of the farm workers off to the mosque, delaying proceedings until they return. Later, at the ʿUmda's wake, the voice of the Qurʾan reciter intoning verses of the holy text competes with a lawyer's critique of the regime and maltreatment of the farmers. As the lawyer preaches about parliamentary government, the farmers are lured by the sonorous tones of renowned reciter Shaykh Ibrahim.⁵¹ This scene of traditional religious and modern secular voices vying for authority over a physically present audience composed of common Egyptians is, incidentally, recurrent in the Egyptian short story, where it similarly serves as a succinct symbolic expression of the bigger ideological struggle and the paradoxical role of the masses within it, as the silent subject stuck in the middle, the group over which each side seeks authority and influence but which itself has no voice or agency. Yusuf Idris has a medical doctor expounding on human dissection while a preacher begins a sermon in his close vicinity, attracting his listeners away from him, in 'Abu'l-Hawl',[52] while Lashin's 'Hadith al-Qarya' depicts a failed attempt by a city dweller to address a group of villagers followed by their rapturous response to their own shaykh, with whom the symbolic capital resides regardless of his ignorance and self-interest. Religion's subversive potential is introduced here too, for Mahmud Bey's entrance coincides with seven readings of the verse 'Behold your donkey' (Q. 2:259), with the effect of ridiculing the magistrate in front of his subjects. Even when instructed to choose another verse the shaykh keeps going and the audience can no longer stifle their laughter. The magistrate is able to restore order within a few moments but the scene nevertheless suggests fragile authority. The power structure has weak points just as religion has a seditious quality. In this regard we might also note that Shaykh Shinawi himself has a rebellious past and joined the revolution in 1919.[53] The subversive aspect of religion is increasingly exploited by novelists from the 1970s, especially via the Sufi voice, and al-Sharqawi envisages a revolutionary role for religion in some of his short stories in *Ard al-Maʿraka* (1953).[54] Notwithstanding the aforementioned scene however, for the most part in *Al-Ard* the power struggle is between religious and secular discourse, between the shaykh's sacred rhetoric and the village's secular discourse of revolution and popular national ideal. What is interesting here is that, in contrast to the trilogy, the alternative to religion is less secular modernity than secular tradition. Tradition is celebrated, not denigrated as it is in *Al-Sukkariyya*, when Kamal implies that he would just as well see the Pyramids destroyed if their stones could be made useful today.[55] Whereas the problem in modern Arab intellectual discourse is often the uncoupling of religion and tradition, when tradition has a negative value and the challenge is to extricate revelation and spiritual practice from it and reimagine it in a modern world, which is roughly speaking what Haqqi unsuccessfully tries to achieve in *Qindil*, the opposite is the case here. The text seeks to preserve tradition (farming practice and village life) whilst abrading its Islamic element. The village setting sits on an axis with heritage and *fellāḥ* ancestry while the urban setting, for example of the trilogy, looks out to science and the West. The future in the village novel involves harnessing tradition; in the urban setting of the trilogy it involves assimilating the West, or its useful parts. Thus we have here two different vistas on the future and modernity. What they have in common is a power struggle with institutional religion (and God Himself in Kamal's case). Islam is criticised and displaced but ever present. Secular discourse, be it Kamal's scientific system and western proclivity or the traditionalism of al-Sharqawi's village, emerges and ever articulates itself with reference to religion.

When trying to regain control of the room amidst the Qur'anic verse fiasco at the ʿUmda's funeral the magistrate says, 'We will herd the Wafd into Hell on the Day of Resurrection'.[56] He is here misquoting *Surat Maryam* (19: 86: 'And we shall drive the sinners to Hell') and reorienting scripture to produce non-sacred meaning. This is the essence of the project in *Muhammad Rasul al-Hurriyya: Innama Ana Bashar Mithlukum* (1962). Al-Sharqawi takes the biography of the Prophet and uses it to communicate contemporary meaning, not so much by misquoting as selecting from *sīra* that which serves his message, as well as emphasising and embellishing as required. This work, even more than the trilogy, engenders the simultaneous rejection of, and dependence on, religion at the core of religious alterity and secular discourse. For the construction of a modern contemporary message here involves simultaneous deconstruction of a traditional religious one. If the trilogy represents one culmination of religious displacement on account of its epic proportions, secular aesthetic and national allegory, then *Muhammad*, by taking a central text of Islam and grafting new meaning onto it, represents another. The end product is far less artistically satisfying, no doubt because the author has hamstrung his literary project from the start with a constricting plot line and, as we will see, a contradictory set of goals, which are in the end more polemic than literary.

Al-Sharqawi retells the story of Muhammad in a novelistic context. Haykal stripped the *sīra* of its fantastical elements and presented a scientific account of events, notwithstanding his uncritical use of the Qur'an. He rewrote the story of the Prophet according to modern scientific values and historical methods as he understood them. Al-Sharqawi moves in the other direction, exploiting the poetic side of scripture which Frye and others identify as its essential characteristic, whilst at the same time preserving the rational spirit instilled in prophetic biography during the Haykalian detour. The shift from history to novel brings the relationship between these two discourses into focus. *Muhammad*, based on real events, exceeds definitions of history and fiction based on truth versus imagination. The events of al-Sharqawi's story are factual, or presumed factual, even if the dialogue is supplementary.[57] What matters far more than historical veracity is how the events are treated. Historiography seeks answers. It is an enquiry into what happened and interpretation takes place, for the most part, prior to its textual arrangement. The emergence of history as narrative marks the closure of a range of possible readings of events, hence the language of history is normally descriptive. Ambiguity in an historiographical context is a threat and reduced to a minimum, while language's characteristic polysemy, the habit of words to mean more than one thing, is delimited as much as possible. In Ricoeur's threefold analysis of mimesis, history stops at mimesis$_2$ (*configuration*), at the point when events are shaped into a narrative whole, and its truth claim is bound up with mimesis$_1$ (*prefiguration*). Fiction, on the other hand, is geared towards Ricoeur's third stage in the mimetic process (mimesis$_3$, *refiguration*), when the imaginative configuration produced in mimesis$_2$ is integrated into the lived experience of the reader and its full meaning is realised. Regardless of whether the events narrated are imaginary or factual, as part of a fictional text they are there to produce an effect and convey a particular message, or messages. The gap between signifier and signified may thus be great in fiction, and the signified in this context always comes second. The transposition of the *sīra* from history to fiction in *Muhammad* severs the link between the narrated events and their presumed occurrence in the past, between mimesis$_1$ and mimesis$_2$, and opens up the possibility to exploit the gap between signifier and signified. Al-Sharqawi seizes this opportunity to reimagine the *sīra* in the context of man's general struggle for freedom and fight against ignominy, and in particular to infuse the biography of the Prophet with nationalist and socialist messages, as Wessels and Badawi have observed.[58]

The title dismantles the divine link in the Prophet's customary designation, 'Muhammad Rasul Allah', inserting freedom (*ḥurriyya*) where God stood previously, and the emphasis in the text is on Muhammad the man. In the introduction al-Sharqawi explains his project as an attempt to fill a lacuna and write about the person, 'to portray the story of an individual whose heart was open to the suffering, hardship and dreams of mankind',[59] and to do so in the form of a story (*al-shakl al-qaṣaṣī*),[60] signalling to the reader that a novelistic reading is what is intended, a reading that focuses on effects more than facts, albeit unlikely to achieve a purely aesthetic reception given the highly familiar subject matter. In what follows, the author remains true to his word by presenting a full and humanising portrait of Muhammad, his character, thought processes, crises, personal charm and sense of humour, but goes a step further to emphasise that Muhammad was *merely* human.

> He was just a man ... a man like them who possessed no [special] advantage nor disadvantage and was not able to protect himself or others from sickness or death. He cried and laughed like them, and his body tired and displayed energy [just as theirs did]. He slept and got up in the morning, and he could be angry or content just like them. He experienced hunger and thirst, ate food and walked through markets. He did not know the Unseen nor was he able to perform miracles, for humans cannot be miracle-workers.[61]

This point is repeated at different junctures, including the subtitle: 'I am just a man like you', which comes from Q. 18:110 but, as Badawi notes, significantly omits the rest of the verse, which goes on to indicate divine inspiration.[62] Al-Sharqawi's Muhammad is not distinguished by special powers but by his message of freedom, justice and equality. The miracles that he is traditionally believed to have performed and the supernatural events surrounding his life are omitted, following Haykal's example, while much effort is expended in developing a picture of Muhammad as an impressive political leader, military strategist, democrat and diplomat.

All of this is crucial for Muhammad's emergence as a socialist hero. As Wessels notes, written during the ascendency of Gamal Abdel Nasser, the book is an attempt to rewrite the *sīra* according to the political ideals of the day.[63] Muhammad is less spiritual leader than ordinary individual who steps up from among the masses to lead his people in a popular revolution against capitalist-style exploitation and social inequality. In this context, the Quraysh, who rule Mecca by virtue of their wealth and abuse their positions for material gain, and later the Jews of Medina, who monopolise the markets there and pursue wealth in the absence of a moral code, hence their association with alcohol and gambling, emerge as obstacles to a just and free system. Mecca emerges in the early chapters as a capitalist centre whose spiritual, religious and cultural fabric is based on buying, selling and profit, and where the big merchants are sovereign and erect rules and traditions to safeguard their business interests.[64] Medina is portrayed as more progressive, at least insofar as moneylenders do not wield so much power over their debtors, and slaves and labourers have more control over their destiny, but the distribution of resources remains unequal and the Jews' accumulation of wealth and lack of morality in business represents a problem.

With Muhammad's chief enemies cast in a capitalist mould, the confrontation between them, as Badawi has argued, becomes a kind of projection onto Islamic history of familiar class war: 'So the struggle began, the rich defending their existence and the poor their right to dignified life and dreams of a better world'.[65] Muhammad's mission is a social one. When expositions of Islamic teachings are offered there is an emphasis on those values which cohere with socialism; freedom, justice, action, equality, fraternity, mutual cooperation and a duty to the poor seemingly take priority over fasting, prayer, *dhikr*, hajj and other traditional Islamic duties and practices that do not have such an obvious social benefit.[66] Jihad is 'striving in the way of God' but this means striving to liberate man[67] and is applied to communal labour, another recurrent motif and signifier of socialism, in the lead up to the Battle of the Trench.[68] It is also significant, as others have remarked, that the new order that Muhammad seeks to implement is as much the result of long meditations and consultation as it is the product of divine insight.[69] From an early age the character's dissatisfaction with life in Mecca is clear. He reflects on the situation and envisages a better world, in which there is no usury or exploitation of the poor but which will require a revolution. When the revelation eventually comes to him at Hira, it is in the form of a vision that essentially completes a process that began some time earlier. In al-Sharqawi's hands, the event of revelation amounts to an extraordinary dream.[70] Whereas Ibn Ishaq shows Muhammad experiencing revelation both in sleep and in waking, al-Sharqawi significantly limits it to sleep.[71] The allusion to Muhammad's time with the Banu Saʿd as an opportunity to learn a more refined Arabic is also noteworthy, for it enables the eloquence of the Qur'an to be attributable to Muhammad's learning, more than constituting a miracle in itself, as it is traditionally understood.

Muhammad is thus re-presented as the leader of a popular revolution and champion of socialist values.[72] Islam is treated selectively, reimagined as a programme for reform along socialist lines, with particular aspects of its teachings emphasised and details of the traditional *sīra* that do not support the theme, such as the *ghazwas* (battles) and miracles, played down or omitted. The victory of the Muslims over the Quraysh and Jews becomes the victory of socialist values over exploitative capitalism. The religious significance of Muhammad's biography is displaced in favour of politics and humanism. The latter further manifests in a materialist interpretation of familiar events. The hostility that Muhammad meets in Mecca is motivated by economic rather than spiritual considerations. Muhammad's message is opposed not because of attachment to the idols in the Kaaba but because it threatens the wealth generated by the Kaaba in the form of offerings and trade opportunities. Nowhere in the Meccan section do we find anyone standing up for the idols on emotional or spiritual grounds. Contrast this with the traditional account, where Muhammad's disparagement of the gods in the Kaaba is cause for major offence amongst the Meccans.[73] Likewise, in Medina, Muhammad's chief opponents are the Jews, not because of a clash of sacred values but because, as the richest group and as usurers, they stand to lose the most in the new order.[74] Here too the struggle between the two parties develops in the absence of any real spiritual or philosophical confrontation. Conversion also tends towards the material. The first group of Muhammad's followers, which consists mostly of the oppressed,[75] embrace the new religion because of its promise of freedom and equality, more than undue piety: 'the new teachings spread amongst women, slaves and workers', the narrative tells us after listing some of its material benefits specific to these groups, such as emancipation from slavery, entitlement to the wealth of the rich and women's rights.[76] Though the timing and sequence of the conversions is historically correct, the way in which they are represented, that is, in the absence of a spiritual narrative, leaves only material explanations. Furthermore, conversion is usually announced as a *fait accompli*, without much indication that it was preceded by much soul-searching on the part of the convert. The exception is ʿUmar ibn al-Khattab, but even here the change of heart is as much to do with the actions and example of others, namely the lengths to which an old woman emigrant to Abyssinia and his sister Fatima are willing to go in the name of Islam, as it is his realisation of the excellence and distinction of the Qur'anic extract that he reads for the first time at his sister's house.[77] The same account is related in many of the canonical texts but it is significant that al-Sharqawi selects this version of ʿUmar's story over others, for instance ʿAbdullah b. Abu Najih's, which has him converting after listening to Muhammad in prayer.[78] The Muslims' behaviour after submission to Islam also suggests the importance of economics in their list of priorities in al-Sharqawi's analysis. Time and again the author draws attention to discontent following the distribution of war spoils, while the payment of zakat is singled out as a cause for unrest once the new community is firmly established. Again, it is not that al-Sharqawi invents these details but that he selects them over others in his representation of the young Muslim community.

Just as al-Sharqawi reorients the sacred to novelistic meaning in *Muhammad*, so he rationalises *sīra* and re-presents man as the highest value in the sacred story. The Prophet's achievements in Mecca and Medina are the product of his particular (human) talents, more than the work of God. The Muslims' success at Badr and in the Battle of the Trench is down to clever planning, solidarity and courage. Al-Sharqawi displaces traditional understandings and sacred themes in favour of a new hero and ideal. Muhammad is referred to by the narrator by his first name or *kunya*, Abu'l-Qasim, rather than a religious title, and the religious formulae that usually accompany mention of the Prophet and his Companions are omitted. References to *rasūl Allāh* and *al-nabī* appear in dialogue but reflect back on the characters who utter them and do not necessarily form part of the ideology of the text. Qur'an quotation is kept to a minimum and when verses are cited they are modestly presented; ordinary speech marks are used but none of the customary typographic embellishment. As Badawi observes, 'there is generally nothing in the author's mode of narrative to suggest that he is quoting a revealed text'.[79] Moreover, while precise dates are rare, when months and years are specified the Gregorian calendar is preferred over the *hijrī* one. Time is mechanical and secular. Yet even as al-Sharqawi rationalises *sīra* and overwrites the sacred, so he confirms the interdependence of the religious and secular. The very fact that temporal nationalist messages are inscribed *onto* prophetic biography renders supersedure ambivalent. For the new meaning is visibly dependent on the old by virtue of the juxtaposition, and the sacred form remains, even if only as scaffolding. Though the sacred connotation has been largely excised, its shape and image persist. As such *Muhammad* is a textual embodiment of the co-imbrication and interdependence of the religious and secular.

Further contradiction and blurring is found in the book's apologetic theme. Aside from the literary motivation, al-Sharqawi tells us in the introduction that the work is intended for non-Muslims and undertaken as a national duty. In so doing he draws a link between Islam and the Egyptian nation, which in *Al-Ard* he conceived of as a territorial fraternity hindered by religious types and institutions, for the national duty to which he is referring is the duty to defend Islam and the Prophet against negative images circulating in western media and literature, a motivation he shares with al-ʿAqqad and al-Hakim before him.[80] The apologetics comes across in the text's representation of Muhammad's military campaigns, dealings with the Jews and involvement with polygamy. The *ghazwa*s are portrayed as a necessary evil. Even when the Muslim army fires the first arrows, the attack is explained as pre-emptive. In connection with the Battle of Badr we are told that 'Muhammad had decided to attack first … for attack was the best means of defence',[81] as compared to Ibn Ishaq's account, which reports that 'when the apostle heard about Abu Sufyan coming from Syria, he summoned the Muslims and said, "This is the Quraysh caravan containing their property. Go out and attack it, perhaps God will give it as a prey"'.[82] Al-Sharqawi is also careful to draw attention to the fact that the enemy is always invited to submit to Islam in advance of any confrontation, while Muslim acts of aggression off the battlefield are distanced from Muhammad and portrayed as unfortunate episodes in which he had no part. The attack on a Quraysh caravan by ʿAbdullah b. Jahsh and his men during the sacred months angers Muhammad and is seen as a categorical aberration.[83] There is of course no suggestion in the traditional account that Muhammad was behind this attack but it is significant that al-Sharqawi omits the events that followed, namely the absolution granted, with the help of the Qur'an, and Muhammad's acceptance of the spoils.[84] The same defensiveness characterises representation of Muhammad's dealings with the Jews of Medina. He is portrayed as patient and generous towards them but forced to employ harsh measures after every effort has failed and they have proved inexorable in their antagonism. The Jews of Medina are portrayed as continually involved in plots and schemes to thwart the Muslims and al-Sharqawi follows Ibn Hisham in blaming them for Muhammad's death.[85] Wessels, who also refers to the apologetic tone in the book, writes that 'Ash-Sharqawi has established his defence of Muhammad by painting the Jews completely black'.[86] At the same time, Muhammad's marriages are justified as acts of compassion or as strategic, and he is initially reluctant to replace his first wife, Khadija, after she died.[87] Thus the narrative intervenes in debates about polygamy and the status of women in Islamic society. Even before revelation Muhammad's vision of a new society includes equality of the sexes, and particular respect for women is stated explicitly:

> It was necessary to ... protect the dignity of women, as mother, wife, life partner and blood relative. She should not be given to a man for him to enjoy for a time and then discard and she should not be bestowed on several men at once! ... It was necessary to respect her pride thus she should not be married to anyone unless she has consented and she must be made his partner as a dignified human individual, who will support him and not just be a concubine for his pleasure ...[88]

With regard to the veil, al-Sharqawi aligns with the reformist school and supports an interpretation which limits its use to the women of Muhammad's household.[89] We might also note that several episodes demonstrate the ill effects of alcohol, leading up to and justifying its eventual ban in the sixteenth chapter.[90]

The apologetic theme and interest in Sharia, in the sense of reinterpretation and reform, show that, for all its demystification and reorientation of the *sira*, the book is nevertheless involved with theological matters and keenly interested in Islamic identity and tradition. While in *Al-Ard*, al-Sharqawi conceives of an Egyptian nation in which Islam was a negative element, *Muhammad* acknowledges, and in its narrative framework even foregrounds, a symbiosis between Egyptian and Islamic identity and tradition. National duty includes defending Islam against foreign deprecation, albeit a displaced Islam that we are dealing with now – Islam as identity and heritage more than spiritual reality. In this sense Islam is co-opted to the colonial struggle as a cultural marker and history to protect. Either way, the tension attendant in the text's intermingling of nationalist stimuli and religious apologetics, in combination with its employment of a sacred form to communicate temporal meaning, produces tension and embodies the complexity of the religious/secular dialectic.+++There is little to be gained from evaluating a secular aesthetic in *Muhammad*. The predictable plot and polemic diminish the artistic and intellectual freedom associated with literary secularism. There is little scepticism or polyphony here. The work's secularity lies in its theme and intention, in the secularisation of *sīra* on the level of story more than in its artistry. And even here there are slips and contradictions. Al-Sharqawi makes supplications in the final passages of the introduction, having quoted a hadith a few pages earlier,[91] and a *hijrī* date is included with the Gregorian one when signing the introduction, marrying sacred history and secular time.[92] There are occasions too when a sense of Muhammad as chosen or destined to play the role that he eventually assumes creeps in. Addressing Muhammad in the second person prior to revelation, the narrator encourages him to 'speak your words' and 'arise and preach',[93] and soon afterwards, back in the third person, states that:

> Life had prepared a place for [Muhammad] and was waiting for him … He must assume his anticipated place, armed with consummate understanding of the nature of his role, with a consummate idea of life and death, and with consummate comprehension of the needs of suffering men.[94]

The same impression is created by the sense of anticipation prevalent amongst the dissenting voices already present in Mecca – men like Waraqa b. Nawfal and others who 'believed deep down that someone would come deliver the final word that would light up the darkness and change the face of the earth …'.[95] The evidence again reveals the difficulty of demarcating religious and secular language and space.

Notes

1. Both stories published in *Arkhas Layali* (Cairo: Nahdat Misr, 2009 [1954]).
2. Mahmud Taha Lashin, 'Hadith al-Qarya', in Sabry Hafez and Caherine Cobham (eds), *A Reader of Modern Arabic Short Stories* (London: Saqi Books, 1988 [orig. pub in *Yukha Anna*, Cairo, 1929]), pp. 136–44.

3. I refer to *Bayn al-Qasrayn* (Cairo: Dar al-Shuruq, 2009), *Qasr al-Shawq* (Cairo: Dar al-Shuruq, 2006), *Al-Sukkariyya* (Cairo: Maktabat Misr, 1961). Translations my own unless stated, with corresponding page numbers from the published English translations: *Palace Walk*, trans. W. M. Hutchins and O. E. Kenny (New York and London: Doubleday, 1990); *Palace of Desire*, trans. W. M. Hutchins, L. M. Kenny and O. E. Kenny (New York and London: Doubleday, 1991); *Sugar Street*, trans., W. M. Maynard and A. B. Samaan (London and New York: Doubleday, 1992). Studies of Mahfuz's work are abundant. For religion in his fiction, see Bacima Ajjan-Boutrad, *Le Sentiment religieux dans l'oeuvre de Naguib Mahfouz* (Paris: Sindbad, 2008); El-Enany, 'Religion in the Novels of Naguib Mahfouz', *Bulletin of the British Society for Middle Eastern Studies*, vol. 15, nos 1–2 (1988), pp. 21–7; Muhammad Hasan ᶜAbdullah, *Al-Islamiyya wa'l-Ruhiyya fi Adab Najib Mahfuz* (Cairo: Dar Qibaᶜ li'l-Tibaᶜa wa'l-Nashr wa'l-Tawziᶜ, 2001).
4. The connection has been noted by many, including Mahfuz himself. See Sabry Hafez (ed.), *Najib Mahfuz: Atahaddath Ilaykum* (Beirut: Dar al-ᶜAwdat, 1977), p. 157. Mahfuz refers to ᶜAbd al-Jawwad's ability to harmonise two diametrically opposing personalities in one person, something of which only God is capable, and ᶜAbd al-Jawwad 'is himself a god'. Also, Siddiq, *Arab Culture and the Novel*, pp. 125ff; El-Enany, *Naguib Mahfouz: The Pursuit of Meaning* (London and New York: Routledge, 1993), pp. 81–3.
5. *Bayn al-Qasrayn*, p. 224 (trans., 191).
6. El-Enany, *Pursuit of Meaning*, p. 81.
7. Kishkish Bey was a character played by the Egyptian comic Najib al-Rihani (1889–1949).
8. Siddiq, *Arab Culture and the Novel*, pp. 120–39.
9. *Qasr al-Shawq*, p. 480 (trans., p. 373).
10. Siddiq too interprets ᶜAyda as symbolic of the divine, though he does not identify or develop a Sufi reading in this connection (Siddiq, *Arab Culture and the Novel*, p. 135).
11. *Qasr al-Shawq*, p. 409 (trans., p. 317).
12. *Al-Sukkariyya*, p. 101 (trans., p. 95).
13. *Bayn al-Qasrayn*, p. 476 (trans., p. 414).
14. Ibid. p. 50 (trans., p. 42).
15. See also Siddiq, *Arab Culture and the Novel*, pp. 122–5, in connection with Ahmad ᶜAbd al-Jawwad.
16. *Qasr al-Shawq*, p. 431 (trans., p. 335).

17. Another champion of science and secularism in the third volume is Kamal's communist nephew Ahmad.
18. *Al-Sukkariyya*, p. 189 (trans., p. 180).
19. Ibid. p. 203 (trans., p. 194).
20. Ibid. p. 233 (trans., p. 224).
21. *Qasr al-Shawq*, pp. 531–2 (trans., p. 414).
22. Ibid. p. 481 (trans., p. 374).
23. *Al-Sukkariyya*, p. 30 (trans., p. 25).
24. *Qasr al-Shawq*, p. 443 (trans., p. 344).
25. *Al-Sukkariyya*, p. 292 (trans., p. 284).
26. Ibid. p. 207 (trans., p. 197).
27. El-Enany and Peled ascribe ʿAʾisha's suffering to her utility, or lack thereof, in society. El-Enany, *Pursuit of Meaning*, pp. 77–8; Matittyahu Peled, *Religion My Own: The Literary Works of Najib Mahfuz* (New Brunswick, NJ: Transaction Books, 1983), pp. 109–18.
28. *Bayn al-Qasrayn*, p. 10 (trans., p. 5).
29. Ibid. p. 24 (trans., p. 19).
30. I am using Hutchins and Kenny's translation here, which explains to the English reader what is implicitly understood in the Arabic: *wa khamsa fi ʿayn min lam yuṣalli ʿalā al-nabī*. *Bayn al-Qasrayn*, p. 309 (trans., p. 267).
31. *Bayn al-Qasrayn*, pp. 97, 120, 294 (trans., pp. 87, 104, 254); *Qasr al-Shawq*, p. 100 (trans., p. 78), the latter refers to Jalila and Zubayda both.
32. Hutchins and Kenny's translation. *Bayn al-Qasrayn*, p. 303 (trans., p. 261). *Dhikr*, lit. 'remembrance', a characteristically Sufi practice which involves repeating a name or names of God, often aloud and in groups and with musical accompaniment. See William Chittick, *Sufism: A Short Introduction* (Oxford: OneWorld, 2000), pp. 52–60.
33. *Bayn al-Qasrayn*, p. 106 (trans., p. 93).
34. *Qasr al-Shawq*, p. 110 (trans., p. 86).
35. ʿAbd al-Rahman al-Sharqawi, *Muhammad Rasul al-Hurriyya* (Cairo: Dar al-Shaʿb, 1972). Al-Sharqawi also wrote books on the Prophet's cousin and son-in-law ʿAli b. Abi Talib and other famous Islamic figures such as Ibn Taymiyya, as well as a verse drama *Al-Thaʾir: al-Husayn Shahidan*. His fiction includes *Al-Ard* (1954), *Qulub Khaliyya* (1956), *Al-Shawariʿ al-Khalifiyya* (1958) and *Al-Fallah* (1967), and two short story collections, *Ard al-Maʿraka* (1953) and *Ahlam Saghira* (1956).
36. I refer here to a 1968 edition (Cairo: Dar al-Katib al-ʿArabi li'l-Tibaʿa wa'l-

Nashr, 1968). Corresponding page references provided from Desmond Stewart's English translation, which abridges and adopts a liberal approach to the original text, *Egyptian Earth* (London: Saqi Books, 1990).

37. On the village novel, see ʿAbd al-Muhsin Taha Badr, *Al-Riwaʾi waʾl-Ard* (Cairo: al-Hayʾat al-Misriyyat al-ʿAmma liʾl-Taʾlif waʾl-Nashr, 1971); Samah Selim, *The Novel and the Rural Imaginary 1880–1985* (London and New York: Routledge. 2010). Further reading on the author and *Al-Ard* includes Sabry Hafez, *Suradiqat min Waraq: Dirasat Wadaʿiyya wa Taʿmulat fi Manaqib al-Rahilin* (Cairo: al-Haʾyat al-ʿAmma li Qusur al-Thaqafa, 1991), pp. 20–57; Mustafa ʿAbd al-Ghani, *Al-Sharqawi Mutamarridan: al-Dalala al-Dhatiyya waʾl-Ijtimaʿiyya* (Cairo: Maktabat al-Taʿawun al-Sahafiyya, 1987); Selim, ch. 5, 'The Land', pp. 159–84.
38. *Al-Ard* foregrounds the link with *Zaynab* itself. See *Al-Ard*, p. 314 (trans., pp. 220–1(. While the *fellahin* are valorised in *ʿAwdat* and *Zaynab*, the portrait is coloured with urban prejudices, and while their narrative strategy is realism both texts are romantic in their treatm+ent of love and portrait of rural Egypt.
39. See *ʿAwdat*, vol. 2, ch. 4.
40. *Al-Ard*, p. 71.
41. *Al-Ard*, p. 192 (trans., p. 143).
42. Ibid. p. 191 (trans., p. 142). The suggestion is made in jest by ʿAbd al-Hadi but the shaykh's response is telling.
43. Yusuf Idris, 'Al-Mishwar', *Arkhas Layali*, pp. 138–55.
44. *Al-Ard*, pp. 75, 76 (trans., pp. 62, 63).
45. Ibid. pp. 76, 77 (trans., pp. 63, 64–5).
46. Ibid. p. 149 (trans., p. 115).
47. Ibid. p. 158 (trans., 122).
48. Ibid. pp. 8–11, 34 (trans., pp. 5–7, 29).
49. Siddiq, *Arab Culture and the Novel*, p. 94. Siddiq further observes that 'the gratuitous incident forms part of a deliberate strategy by al-Sharqawi the "socialist" (at the time of writing) to debunk religion by debasing the space that represents it metonymically in the novel' (p. 112). He also notes a reference to the story of *Isaf* and *Naʾila*, who defiled the Kaaba according to Arab folklore (ibid.).
50. *Al-Ard*, p. 149 (trans., p. 115).
51. Ibid. pp. 298–300 (trans., pp. 210–11).
52. Yusuf Idris, 'Abuʾl-Hawl', in *Qaʿ al-Madina* (Cairo: Dar al-Katib al-ʿArabi, 1970).
53. *Al-Ard*, p. 199 (trans., p. 147).

54. e.g. 'Shuʿaʿ al-Fajr', 'ʿIndama Yurid al-Shaʿb', 'ʿIndama Tasud al-Sakina', 'Fi'l-Aghlal', 'Al-Thawra lan Tamut' and 'Raʾs al-Thaniyya', as noted by Sabry Hafez, *The Quest for Identities*, p. 248.
55. *Al-Sukkariyya*, p. 49 (trans., p. 43).
56. *Al-Ard*, p. 302 (trans., p. 213).
57. Factual in the sense that they derive from the hadith authority. The authenticity of hadith is not under scrutiny here.
58. My discussion expands on observations made by these two scholars. See Wessels, *A Modern Arabic Biography of Muhammad*, pp. 19–24; M. M. Badawi, 'Islam in Modern Egyptian Literature', *Journal of Arabic Literature*, vol. 2 (1971), pp. 172–5. Hafez records some of the commentary on *Muhammad* and its message of freedom and contemporary import in *Suradiqat*, pp. 33–6.
59. *Muhammad*, p. 5. Al-Sharqawi, in stating that there is little on Muhammad the man, ignores the efforts of Haykal and al-ʿAqqad.
60. *Muhammad*, p. 9.
61. Ibid. p. 166.
62. The full verse Q. 18:110 (Yusuf Ali translation) is: 'Say: "I am but a man like yourselves, (but) the inspiration has come to me, that your Allah is one Allah. whoever expects to meet his Lord, let him work righteousness, and, in the worship of his Lord, admit no one as partner"'. See Badawi, 'Islam in Modern Egyptian Literature', p. 172.
63. Wessels, *A Modern Arabic Biography of Muhammad*, p. 20.
64. *Muhammad*, p. 17.
65. Ibid. p. 87. Badawi, 'Islam in Modern Egyptian Literature', p. 173.
66. See e.g. *Muhammad*, pp. 106–7 and 410–12.
67. Ibid. p. 411.
68. On the benefits of labour, see also ibid. pp. 107, 148ff, 330, 341–2. Wessels also notes the prominence of the labour theme. Wessels, *A Modern Arabic Biography of Muhammad*, p. 21.
69. See Wessels, *A Modern Arabic Biography of Muhammad*, p. 22.
70. Badawi, 'Islam in Modern Egyptian Literature', p. 173; Wessels, *A Modern Arabic Biography of Muhammad*, p. 22.
71. Ibn Ishaq, *The Life of Muhammad: A Translation of Ibn Ishaq's Sirat Rasul Allah*, trans. with intro. and notes A. Guillaume (Oxford: Oxford University Press, 1957), p. 106.
72. Al-Sharqawi does the same to al-Husayn in his play *Al-Husayn Thaʾiran, al-Husayn Shahidan* (Cairo, 1969). Ballas writes: 'Al-Husayn is portrayed by al-

Sharqawi as a popular leader of the impoverished classes who preaches justice and equality and works to rid the kingdom of foreign tendencies inimical to original Islam'. Shimon Ballas, 'Nationalist and Islamic Themes in the Dramatic Works of al-Sharqawi', *Arab and African Studies*, vol. 18, no. 3 (1984), p. 277.

73. Ibn Ishaq, *The Life of Muhammad*, p. 118: 'When the apostle openly displayed Islam as God ordered him his people did not withdraw or turn against him, as far as I have heard, until he spoke disparagingly about their gods. When he did that they took great offence and resolved unanimously to treat him as an enemy, except those whom God had protected by Islam from such evil, but they were a despised minority'. Ibn Ishaq further quotes the Quraysh addressing Abu Talib: 'By God, we cannot endure that our fathers should be reviled, and our customs mocked and our gods insulted. Until you rid us of [Muhammad] we will fight the pair of you until one side perishes' (p. 119).
74. *Muhammad*, pp. 153–4.
75. Members of other social classes in Mecca do convert early on but they do not form the majority. The merchants who convert early, such as is ʿUthman b. ʿAffan, al-Zubayr b. al-ʿAwwam, ʿAbd al-Rahman b. ʿAwaf, Saʿd b. Abi Waqqas, Talha b. ʿAbdullah and of course Abu Bakr, are portrayed as exceptional, as some of the few rich merchants who 'follow a pure path in trade and reject usury and wrong-doing' (*Muhammad*, pp. 81–2).
76. *Muhammad*, pp. 79–80.
77. Ibid. pp. 101–4.
78. See the account of ʿAbdullah b. Abu Najih in Ibn Ishaq, *The Life of Muhammad*, pp. 157–8. Ibn Ishaq also relates the version with the Abyssinian woman and Fatima (see pp. 155–7).
79. Badawi, 'Islam in Modern Egyptian Literature', p. 173.
80. Al-ʿAqqad was motivated in part to write ʿ*Abqariyyat Muhammad* by Thomas Carlyle's essay 'The Hero as Prophet' and Tawfiq al-Hakim wrote his play 'Muhammad' in part as a response to Voltaire's *Mahomet* (1736).
81. *Muhammad*, p. 187.
82. Ibn Ishaq, *The Life of Muhammad*, p. 289.
83. *Muhammad*, p. 181.
84. Ibn Ishaq, *The Life of Muhammad*, pp. 286–9.
85. *Muhammad*, pp. 334, 404, 412. Ibn Ishaq, on the other hand, includes an account of poisoned meat being fed to Muhammad by a Jewish woman at Khaybar but presents Muhammad's death as the result of a choice: 'God has given one of his servants the choice between this world and that which is with

God and he has chosen the latter'. See Ibn Ishaq, *The Life of Muhammad*, p. 679. Other accounts have Muhammad dying from a fever.
86. Wessels, *A Modern Arabic Biography of Muhammad*, p. 23.
87. *Muhammad*, pp. 122, 123.
88. Ibid. p. 58.
89. Ibid. p. 218. See also p. 214 (ᶜUmar urging Muhammad to have women covered up).
90. Ibid. pp. 49–50, 169, 174–5, 219.
91. Ibid. pp. 9 and 6 respectively.
92. Ibid. p. 9. Introduction written: 15 Ramadan 1381 / 20 February 1962. The Gregorian calendar represents secular time insofar as it is used as a civil calendar and because it functions as the global time standard. Its Christian origin and BCE/CE format of course complicate the extent to which it can be called secular, but it is generally thought of as such.
93. Ibid. p. 63.
94. Ibid. p. 74.
95. Ibid. p. 62.

PART 2

4

Introduction: Religion, the Egyptian Novel and the New Literary Sensibility

With the trilogy the Arabic novel comes of age, at least within an aesthetic value system and historico-literary trajectory that assumes realism to be the principal goal and signifier of artistic maturity, and upon finishing it Mahfuz took a five-year break from writing. This was not, however, an effect of the labour expended in producing the Cairene epic, nor is the trilogy's association with Arabic novelistic maturity entirely transparent – literary values evolve and the argument for maturity might equally be made for the first works that remodel the Arabic novel on Arabic popular narrative and traditional storytelling, producing what is regarded as a more authentic and specifically Arab literary form as opposed to a domesticated Bildungsroman. In Mahfuz's account his publishing hiatus was due to seismic changes in the socio-political milieu, which effectively meant that the reality about which he had been writing hitherto no longer existed.[1] The Palace, which featured often in the discussions of Kamal and his friends and whose power struggle with the Wafd shaped 1930s and 1940s politics, was ousted by the 1952 revolution when Egypt became a republic, and the new leader, Gamal Abdel Nasser, broke with the Egyptian nationalism of the last half century, preaching Arab unity and Arab socialism instead. The following decade, with its ambitious industrialisation projects, confrontations with western superpowers, and hero-president, marked a sharp contrast for Egypt to the political wrangling and economic depression of 1940s. Under the banner of socialism Nasser instituted a programme of land reform which saw mass redistribution of land and hugely expanded the public sector. Grand schemes like the Helwan steelworks and Aswan Dam got underway and Egypt gained the upper hand over the French and British in the Suez Crisis and tripartite aggression that followed, cementing Nasser's status as an Arab hero. There is a clear sense in the history books that the national mood was optimistic in the 50s and that Egypt's newfound status in the region was welcomed by the Egyptian population. But the Nasser years also bear the hallmarks of military dictatorship, not least in the severe treatment of dissent and poor human rights record of this period, and it did not take long for doubts and discomfort to set in, especially among writers and intellectuals, society's professional critics and visionaries. In comparison to the disenfranchisement of artists under Sadat, Nasser's presidency is sometimes seen as a good time for Egyptian cultural activity. A Higher Council for Arts and Letters was established in 1956, a Ministry of Culture in 1958, and the press and publishing industry were largely nationalised, which gave writers a solid platform and ensured a steady flow of novels and short stories. But censorship, official and unofficial, curbed literary expression and government sponsorship of artistic activity, from another perspective, is simply the age-old practice of cultural and intellectual co-optation.² It is in this ambivalent atmosphere that Mahfuz published *Al-Liss wa'l-Kilab* (1961) and *Tharthara Fawq al-Nil* (1966), marking a new turn in his fiction, and that novels like Muhammad Jalal's *Harat al-Tayyib* (1961), Sunallah Ibrahim's *Tilka al-Riʾaha* (1966), Naʿim ʿAtiyyah's *Al-Mirʾah wa'l-Misbah* (1967) and Yusuf al-Qaʿid's *Al-Hidad* (1969) appeared. The early 50s produced a flurry of socialist realist works, *Al-Ard* among them, but before long novels and stories appeared articulating disillusionment, alienation and even the absurd, the latter both as a socio-cultural response and an effect of French existentialist literary influence.

The events of June 1967 confirmed the misgivings of Nasser's sceptics and profoundly shook the country. Egypt lost both its army and the Sinai and the positive trajectory onto the future evaporated. Nasser held on to power for a time but pan-Arabism and Arab socialism were discredited and a national crisis of orientation ensued. After the initial shock and recriminations, the *naksa* (setback), as it is known, led to fundamental questioning of twentieth-century Egyptian political decision-making and the *nahḍa* project more broadly. 'The 1967 defeat was the acid test of Arab modernisation',³ writes Issa Boullata. And the consensus was failure. Reflections and critiques of identity, culture, tradition, modernity, Islam and foreign influence filled books, journals and newspapers and provided the topics of debate at conferences and on television and radio. In the sphere of artistic expression the impact was also profound and from the late 1960s Egyptian literature enters a period of high experimentation, expressive of rupture and the inadequacy of conventional realism and its attendant structures to communicate this rupture and anxiety or effect change, with some of the most radical experiments taking place in the short story and avant-garde magazine *Gallery '68*. This is not to deny formal innovation in the preceding decades – some of the 50s novels mentioned above move in this direction and Arabic poetry revolted against the classical *qaṣīda* in the 1940s under the auspices of the *Apollo* magazine, another avant-garde publication – but it is fair to say that the events of 1967 and the cultural crisis that followed gave artistic experimentation a new impetus and even rendered it imperative.

Central to Egyptian and Arab literary experimentation from the early 1970s was a re-engagement with *turāth* (Arab heritage). The past was one of many items up for discussion in the post-1967 soul-searching and Arab heritage, which had played a minimal role in the early formation of the Arabic novel, came to represent a rich resource of imagination and, more critically, an avenue to authenticity (*aṣāla*) and specificity (*khuṣūṣiyya*), which were identified as missing ingredients in modern Arab identity and culture in the course of *nahḍa* critique.[4] One theme to emerge from the historical turn was the heterogeneity of Arab tradition. 'The living heritage', writes Adunis, 'is not a thread of a single colour or a voice that [only] repeats itself, but rather diverse and oppositional forces, which vary and contradict life'.[5] This represents a virtual reversal of the prior concept of tradition common among the intellectual elite as limited and limiting and opened the way to connect with it through alternative lines of enquiry, for example via marginalised figures, texts and discourses. Another significant theme was the rejection of imitation. The past must not function as a brake on change and innovation. It was open for interpretation, in fact this was urgently required in shaping an authentic and liberated future. Authenticity did not mean imitating the past but engaging with it imaginatively; creative transcendence in other words.[6] Thus Adunis writes that the Arab must 'strip the past of sanctity and regard it as a non-binding part of experience or knowledge, and consequently to believe that man's essence lies not in him being a conforming heir but an innovative creator'.[7] It is in this vein that Arab novelists began to rework traditional forms, like *sīra*, historiography and Sufi discourse, or elements therefrom, into their works, reimagining them in a contemporary context, transforming them into conduits of modern meaning, and crucially producing texts with a more indigenous feel, in a sense rewriting literary history, for the formal fusion in many instances gave the Arabic novel the impression of historical Arab roots.

The *turāthī* movement in literature emerged alongside, and in dialogue with, a modernist turn often referred to as *al-ḥassasiyya al-jadīda*, or new sensibility. Idwar al-Kharrat, who coined the phrase and was himself a pioneer of Arabic literary modernism, lists a break with conventional narrative structures and traditional values, a turn inwards, rejection of linear time, mixing of grammatical tenses, revolt against the sanctity of Arabic and linguistic norms, incorporation of dream, legend and poetry, journeys into consciousness, and use of the first person to produce inter-subjectivities, among its strategies.[8] He further identifies five currents within it, whilst allowing for plenty of cross-over: *tayyār al-tashyīʾ* (nihilism), *al-tayyār al-dākhilī* (internal current), *tayyar istihāʾ al-turāth al-ʿarabī al-taqlīdī* (inspiration from traditional Arab heritage), *al-tayyār al-wāqiʿī al-siḥrī* (magical realism), and *al-tayyār al-wāqiʿī al-jadīd* (new realism), which uses conventional forms but subverts them and ultimately dominated literary production in the 70s and 80s.[9] Abu Deeb, referring to the aesthetic revolution in its second decade and to the wider Arab context, refers to the collapse of totalising discourse and emergence of minority voices. Notions of centre, unity, cohesion and harmony gave way to multiplicity and marginalised discourses, which is in itself notably not a negative thing. Fragmentation provided the conditions for a greater inclusivity and discursive heterogeneity.[10] On this logic, one might observe that the political and cultural crisis had an aesthetically positive effect on Egyptian and Arabic literature, ushering in a period of experimentation and cultural and imaginative enrichment. In the last decade of the last century experimentalism took a further turn, or rather renewed its radicalism, as the 90s generation withdrew from collective concerns and focused more on private, isolated experiences and began to dabble in digital culture.[11]

New directions in literature naturally affected approaches to religion within the Egyptian novel. Religious traditions represent the most pervasive of grand narratives in any culture, the source (or assumed source, for unpicking religious and cultural origins is an established minefield), and storehouse of many a social ethic and cultural norm, and as such they represent an obvious target for attacks and interrogations of unitary discourse and authority of the kind that emerged in this period. Mystical texts and spiritual autobiography provided inspiration for *turāthī*-dialogues, for example in al-Ghitani's *Kitab al-Tajalliyyat* and Mahfuz's *Asdaʾ al-Sirat al-Dhatiyya*, and there is an opportune and fascinating overlap between the Sufi vision and new literary discourse and values. At the same time, beyond the realm of literature, whose custodians were markedly secular in orientation, Islam was in fact one of the grand narratives which, rather than losing credibility in the aftermath of 1967, gained momentum and consolidated its position. The liberal experiment of the first half of the twentieth century was broadly secularising, albeit with blips, and Nasserism, as a combination of socialism and Arabism, sided definitively with the secular. The public arena in the 50s and 60s was mostly purged of religious discourse and the Muslim Brotherhood, who represented the political arm of Islam in Egypt in this period, was banned in 1954, its members either imprisoned or exiled to Europe and the Gulf. Sadat (1970–81) reversed the policy and opened the floodgates to religio-political forces. The Muslim Brothers were released and their newspaper, *Al-Daʿwa* (The Summons), resumed publication. The president styled himself as an Islamic figurehead, assuming the epithet *al-raʾīs al-muʾmin* (the believer president), and declared Sharia the principal source of legislation, after decades of civil legislation in all but personal status law.[12] Free to speak and expand, the Brothers regrouped and emerged as a well-run, well-funded organisation. Its returnees had been strengthened ideologically and financially by their time abroad, especially those who went to Saudi and the Gulf, where they became versed in Wahhabism. The Brothers provided services and charitable works where the government failed (food, medical aid, etc.), for while the *Infitāḥ* (opening of the market to private investment) produced new economic opportunities from the 1970s, it also increased social disparity, tipped many public sector employees into poverty and left large segments of the population without welfare.[13] Next to the failure of Egyptian liberalism and Arab socialism, Islam came to represent an attractive alternative for many, including from the depressed middle classes, and the Islamic resurgence got underway in Egypt. Tarek Osman refers to a shift in values and tastes under Sadat towards 'a mix of consumerism and religious conservatism'.¹⁴ In the meantime, Egypt's Christians retreated from public life, having played a significant role on the path to independence in the first half of the century, and made efforts to protect their identity and interests through the Sunday School movement and focus on Christian business, media and church-building projects.

The religious resurgence went way beyond Egypt and its complex and multifarious motivations and formulations have been, and continue to be, analysed and debated in the social sciences and media. The key point for this study is the increasing encroachment of religious discourse into political space and the social sphere and concomitant marginalisation of writers and intellectuals. More so than in the 30s, when liberals were caught up in the wave of Islamic feeling and many adjusted their discourse accordingly, either out of genuine feeling or political exigency, Egyptian writers post-1967 maintained their secular orientation and for the most part did not drift into religion, though in Egyptian TV and film actors like Suhayr al-Babili, Shahira, Shams al-Barudi, ᶜAfaf Shuᶜayb and the famous singer and actress Shadiya (Fatma Ahmad Kamal Shakir) turned to Islam and withdrew from public life in the 70s and 80s.¹⁵ Instead they found themselves increasingly sidelined and under attack. Sadat effectively expelled the left and liberal elite, forcing them out of government, media and publishing posts, and leftist publications like *Al-Katib* and *Al-Taliᶜa* closed, whilst conservative voices publicly condemned and sought redress for perceived heresies, resulting in the assassination of controversial writer Faraj Fuda in 1992. Mahfuz himself was stabbed in the neck by a Muslim extremist in 1994. If a political and discursive shift is discernible in the literary establishment beyond the critical enquiry and aesthetic revolution of the 70s and 80s, which is besides in line with secular values, it is in the Egyptian intellectual's realignment with the people, or at least endeavour to do so. Among the pressing questions in the wake of 1967 was the role of the intellectual, the efficacy of his message and knowledge, and the perennial issue of to whom, and for whom, the intellectual speaks. Ayman El-Desouky describes the broad failure of modern Egyptian intellectual discourse to capture the collective imagination, as was starkly confirmed by the impotence and irrelevance of leftist writers and intellectuals to the events in Tahrir Square in 2011.¹⁶ The secular orientation of this discourse is no doubt a contributing factor here. While groups like the

Muslim Brotherhood were able to engage and mobilise the masses through emotive symbols and by manipulating religious sentiment, secular and intellectual discourse lacked symbolic capital – or *amāra*s to follow El-Desouky's argument – and oftentimes appears removed and distant. The Arabic novel may move closer to the people in the last quarter of the twentieth century by dispensing with omniscient postures and simulated objectivity, and by democratising narrative voice and incorporating popular narrative rhythms and the storyteller, but its secular orientation takes it in the other direction, away from the collective and social space insofar as these are increasingly percolated with sacred symbols and a more resonant salvation narrative. In fact the Arabic novel in the last quarter of the century remains broadly secular in both ideology and form. For not only does it display continuity in its approach to religion, that is, treating it as discourse, an object within a wider frame, a fundamentally secular position, but the aesthetic values and strategies that come to the fore at this time – pluralism, polyphony, fragmentation, minority voices, ambivalence, ambiguity, subversion – are broadly speaking secular tropes. Pluralism, polyphony and inclusion (of minorities and women, for example) are signifiers of secularity, and fragmentation, ambivalence and subversion align with the novel's sceptical attitude. Insofar as texts from this time reject fixed meaning and unitary discourse one might also discern a positive affront to the Logos, following Barthes' argument that 'to refuse to fix meaning is, in the end, to refuse God and his hypostases – reason, science, law'.[17] This is not to deny these values and strategies to religion and religious discourse, old or new, but rather to acknowledge them as an extension of novelistic vision post-1967 in this particular context. Another way of putting this would be to say that, as far as the religious/secular dialectic is concerned, literary modernism is a variation on literary realism; the method has changed due to shifting perceptions, for example of history, culture and identity, but the heterodox sceptical secular ideology of the novel persists. Religion is by no means monologic, unitary and uncritical, but its heterogeneity and scepticism are contained; the Logos is not up for negotiation.

While the Arabic novel in Egypt does not turn to religion in a spiritual or ideological sense after 1967, religion nevertheless increases its presence on its pages. Religious critique continues, and even gains momentum as it extends beyond religious representatives and institutions to address matters of doctrine and to deconstruct sacred themes. Given the taboo surrounding religious texts and in view of the attack on Mahfuz on the back of *Awlad Haratina* (1959), it is not surprising that scripture is largely excluded from experiments in textual fusion of the *turāthī*-type. These are limited to mystical texts and discourse and conducted rather loosely, using evocation more than clear signposting. But there is no shying away from religious myth as an intertext and religious tradition as a repository of productive symbols and images. As the coming chapters show, religious intertextuality and the employment of religious symbols are at the forefront of religion's role in the post-1967 novel. So too is religion as mysticism, counter-narrative and minority discourse. Sufi discourse and symbolism become a productive conduit of themes of the new literary sensibility and are fruitfully employed as counter-narrative. Meanwhile, Coptic Christianity provides opportunities to represent and explore minority discourse and marginalised identity and feminist writers take issue with sacred stereotypes and profuse religious misogyny. Most of this takes place within an experimental or neo-realist context.

Notes

1. El-Enany, *Pursuit of Meaning*, p. 25.
2. On intellectual freedom in Egypt see Richard Jacquemond, *Conscience of the Nation: Writers, State, and Society in Modern Egypt*, trans. David Tresilian (Cairo and New York: American University in Cairo Press, 2008), chs 2 and 3; Marina Stagh, *The Limits of Freedom of Speech: Prose Literature and Prose Writers in Egypt under Nasser and Sadat* (Stockholm: Almqvist and Wiksell International, 1993).
3. Issa J. Boullata, *Trends and Issues in Contemporary Arab Thought* (Albany: State University of New York Press, 1990), p. 1.
4. See Ouyang, *Poetics of Love*, pp. 15–24; Shukri ᶜAyyad, 'Mafhum al-Asala wa'l-Tajdid wa l-Thaqafa al-ᶜArabiyya al-Muᶜasira', *Al-Adab*, November 1971, pp. 2–5, and papers issued from the colloquium on 'The Crisis of Civilisational Development of the Arab Nation' (ᶜAzmat al-Tatawwur al-Hadari fi'l-Watan al-ᶜArabi), (Kuwait, 1974) in *Al-Adab* (May 1974). Related to the issue of *turāth* was the debate on modernity (*hadātha*) and its role and meaning in Arab culture, literature and language. On the latter see *Fusul*, vol. 4 nos 3 and 4 (1984), on 'Al-Hadath fi'l-Lugha wa'l-Adab'.
5. Adunis, *Zaman al-Shiᶜr* (Beirut: Dar al-ᶜAwda, 1972), p. 53.

6. '^cAzma al-Tatawwur al-Hadari fi'l-Watan al-^cArabi: Nadwa al-Kuwait 6–12 April', [collective declaration] *Al-Adab*, (Beirut) May 1974, p. 3.
7. Adunis, 'Khawatir hawl Mazahir al-Takhalluf al-Fikri fi'l-Mujtama^c al-^cArabi', p. 29. A translation of this piece, along with the declaration referred to in the note above, can be found in *Vision and Revision in Arab Society 1974, CERAM Reports 1974*, vol. 1 (Beirut: Dar al-Mashriq, 1974).
8. Idwar al-Kharrat, *Al-Hassasiyya al-Jadida: Maqalat fi'l-Zahirat al-Qisasiyya* (Beirut: Dar al-Adab, 1993), pp. 11–12.
9. Ibid. pp. 15–20. Mahmud Tarshuna revises these currents in an article in *Fusul* in 1998 as *tayyār al-wa^cy* (stream of consciousness) for al-Kharrat's *al-tayyār al-dākhilī, al-riwāya al-jadīda* (the new novel), which covers literary nihilism, *al-waqā^ciyya al-jadīda* (new realism), and *tawẓīf al-turāth aw al-tayyār al-turāthī* (employing heritage or the heritage current), of which the first three are global phenomena and the latter specific to Arabic literature. Mahmud Tarshuna, 'Madrasa Tawzif al-Turath fi'l-Riwayat al-^cArabiyya al-Mu^casira', *Fusul*, vol. 17, no. 1 (1997), p. 26.
10. Kamal Abu Deeb, 'The Collapse of Totalising Discourse and the Rise of Marginalised/Minority Discourses', in Issa J. Boullata, Kamal Abdel-Malek, Wael B. Hallaq (eds), *Tradition, Modernity and Postmodernity in Arabic Literature: Essays in Honour of Professor Issa J. Boullata* (Leiden-Boston-Koln: Brill, 2000), pp. 335–66.
11. See Sabry Hafez, 'The New Egyptian Novel: Urban Transformation and Narrative Form', *New Left Review*, vol. 64 (July–August 2010), available at <https://newleftreview.org/II/64/sabry-hafez-the-new-egyptian-novel> (last accessed 22 January 2019); Marie-Thérèse Abdel-Messih, 'Hyper Texts: Avant-Gardism in Contemporary Egyptian Narratives', *Neohelicon*, vol. 36, no. 2 (2009), pp. 515–23; Tarek El-Ariss, 'Hacking the Modern: Arabic Writing in the Virtual Age', *Comparative Literature Studies*, vol. 47, no. 4 (2010), pp. 533–48.
12. Tarek Osman, *Egypt on the Brink: From the Rise of Nasser to the Fall of Mubarak* (New Haven: Yale University Press, 2011), p. 81.
13. Ibid. p. 122.
14. Ibid. p. 86.
15. Siddiq, *Arab Culture and the Novel*, p. 104; Osman, *Egypt on the Brink*, p. 78.
16. See Ayman El-Desouky, *The Intellectual and the People in Egyptian Literature and Culture Amara and the 2011 Revolution* (London: Palgrave, 2014).
17. Roland Barthes, 'The Death of the Author', in *Image, Music, Text*, trans. Stephen Heath (London: Fontana Press, 1977), p. 147.

5

Intertextual Dialogues

Intertextuality, the presence of one text in another, is a fundamental characteristic of all writing. There is no such thing as an original work; every word is recycled, every text an arrangement of the already said, already spoken. Abdelfattah Kilito describes poetry as a 'scene of successive incarnations and subtle reincarnations'.[1] He compares the poet to a goldsmith who melts down silver and gold and refashions them into something new. Every poem has lived already, however difficult it is to unearth its past.[2] The paradigmatic structure of classical Arabic texts around a chain of authorities foregrounds this fact. Reports of the Prophet Muhammad's words and actions only made it into the hadith collections by virtue of having been passed through the discourse of numerous authorities, enough to ensure an unbroken thread to sixth-century Hijaz. The ideals of textual composition in Arab tradition, where merit lay in repetition and imitation, celebrates the relation between texts. Jahiz falsely attributed original works of his own to Ibn Muqaffa, al-Khalil and others, or to an anonymous author, since second-hand texts met a better reception than newly invented material.[3] Quotation was normal and expected. Open *Kitab al-Bukhalaʾ*, *Al-ʿIqd al-Farid* or *Tawq al-Hamama* and you will find a clearly demarcated map of intertextuality. Poetry, anecdote and citation embedded in reports embedded in stories, epistles and commentary, and so on. This feature of the Arabic textual tradition is the by-product of an attitude, prevalent up to the nineteenth century, which sees the early *umma* as a privileged time and history as degenerative therefrom. Wisdom and authority reside in the past, in the words of the Prophet and his Companions and in the writings of bygone authors. Islamic reading practice is also characteristically intertextual, a circular process which filters knowledge and discourse through the Qur'an and early sources, whereby the latecomer's value exists, broadly speaking, in its conformity to, and realisation of, scriptural norms and values.

If the classical tradition sought and prioritised textual linkage, modern Arabic literature in the first half of the twentieth century tended to eschew it as far as Arabo-Islamic tradition was concerned. The Arabic novel was a brand new form with a brand new vision in the hands of its Egyptian pioneers in the early decades of the twentieth century and its emergence was accompanied by new ideals of creativity and understandings of authorship. Traditional society is often described as backward-looking. The past is the pattern for the present, change occurs gradually and continuity is valued, while modern society embraces change and innovation, seeks to break with the past, and tradition is reinvented to justify the present rather than model it, as Hobsbawm has shown. The transformation of concepts of authorship that follow from this were coupled in the Arab and Egyptian context with a drive for modernity on a western model among liberal intellectuals which produced a rupture in the literary corpus, with the secular form of the novel forging forward with minimal regard for cultural heritage and classical ancestry. 'I gradually became aware that there were stories, storytelling and visions [in our heritage] that our present age had become cut off from', writes al-Ghitani, explaining his engagement in retrospect.[4] The Egyptian novel in its first phase was radically forward-looking and took the path of realism, one might say naïve realism, where the critical relation is between the text and the world, not other texts, where the work is seen as autonomous and authority ostensibly derives from within, through the invisible omniscient objective narrative voice. The preeminent aesthetic drive, after a romantic beginning in *Zaynab*, was a faithful representation of reality harnessed to a (secular) national agenda. The net result, for which the trilogy is the exemplar, is an Arabic novel intricately and innocently sewn onto society and, crudely speaking, a formal identikit to the Bildungsroman of Europe.

Into the 1960s the pattern of composition began to change, as described. The narrative certitude of the preceding decades gave way to suspicion of totalising discourse and new questions about art, freedom and nation. Realism persists but is interrogated as a strategy through experiments in point of view, interior monologue, compressed plots and poetic language. In this climate the autonomy of the text also came under scrutiny as writers became interested in the relations between texts and their role in meaning. Over in France Julia Kristeva and co-contributors to the avant-garde *Tel Quel* magazine in the 1960s made much of the interdependence of texts and the elusive relations between words and meanings, signs and sign systems. Writers are *bricoleurs* to borrow from Levi-Strauss. They select and arrange units of the cultural text – literary, social, historical – into a new formation. These units carry with them vast histories, or Derrida's traces, and do not stand still once appropriated but continue to gather new meanings and significances. Meaning in a text derives from a variety of sources, including the reader, who brings to it his or her own horizon of understanding, expectation and experience, therefore is not stable at any point. These discoveries had far-reaching implications in philosophy, linguistics and literary theory, overturning notions of originality and authorship and problematising meaning as a fixable, stable phenomenon, and corresponded with wider trends in twentieth-century art and literature. Literary modernism and postmodernism, movements which began in Europe but have spread through the global network of letters and were effectively assimilated to the new sensibility that emerged in Egyptian literary culture in the 1970s, take issue with authority and employ strategies designed to undermine unitary discourse and objective conclusions. They consciously foreground the instability of meaning, texts and words and tend towards self-reflexivity, signposting the mechanics of meaning production, which are characteristically masked by literary realism. *Re-écriture* dominates *écriture* in twentieth-century literature.[5] Concepts of writing and authorship have changed from original expression to reproduction and rearrangement. Whether as a response to a global literary movement or as an effect of the *turāthī* trend, recycling, which held a central position in Arabic textual tradition, has come to the fore once more, having lost some of its innocence in the meantime. While quotation, allusion and textual borrowing were forms of homage in the classical tradition, their modern counterparts, as scrupulous practices, entail irony.

Textual recycling ties in with the *turāthī* trend in the Egyptian and wider Arab context but is not the whole story. Convenient though the *naksa* is for demarcating a new movement in art, literary borrowing and self-conscious intertextuality were present in the early Arabic novel, for example in nomenclature (Ismail and Fatima in *Qindīl* is just one example of evocative naming), engagements with *Alf Layla wa Layla* (e.g. by Taha Husayn and Tawfiq al-Hakim),[6] framestory structures (e.g. *Hadith al-Qarya* by Mahmud Tahir Lashin), and of course Mahfuz's famous reimagining of monotheistic myth in *Awlad Haratina* in the late 1950s, which provoked widespread criticism from conservative quarters and led to the novel being withdrawn after its initial serialisation in *Al-Ahram*.[7] In the realm of Arabic poetry the Tammuz poets are an example of conscious and concerted intertextuality from the late 1940s, as indeed were the neoclassical poets before them. Intertextuality is here understood as any relationship uniting a text to another text, including cultural and non-verbal, 'in a manner that is not that of commentary', to quote Genette, and in this sense refers not only to structural and formal borrowing but quotation, pastiche, translation, allusion and evocation of character, setting, theme and language too.[8] Moreover, with regard to structural engagements, fostering authenticity and reconstituting literary genealogies, a critical goal of the *turāth*-oriented literary project, has limitations. Certainly, the integration of popular narrative strategies provides the Arabic novel with an authentic and viable narrative format and posits a happy continuum with Arab storytelling tradition. This kind of formal reinscription is straightforward and almost deferential; cyclical narrative is given precedence over linear plot lines and any implied criticism is directed at the conventional novel, aka European novel. But the past is also revived with irony. Egyptian novelistic dialogues with heritage are oftentimes parodic. Adunis and co., as discussed, called for creative engagement with *al-turāth*. Cultural heritage should be treated selectively, its paradigms developed and transcended. Intertextuality with past forms and the cultural text in the Egyptian novel entails transposition, which beyond the popular narrative mode becomes a subversion of conventions and values and correspondingly magnifies the difference and distance between hypo- and hypertext. For example, two works by Mahfuz which weld the biographical dictionary onto the novel, *Al-Maraya* (1972) and *Hadith al-Sabah wa'l-Masaʾ* (1987), end up exposing the selective and narrative character of the *muʿjam*, demystifying the historical intertext, while the resurrection of Ibn Battuta in *Rihlat Ibn Fattuma* (1983) casts doubt on the celebrated travelogue and character of the medieval explorer.[9] In this sense, intertextuality in the post-1967 Egyptian novel has a seditious quality which runs counter to the bridge-building theme identified by commentators and articulated by writers themselves in some instances. Jamal al-Ghitani, who is regarded as a pioneer of textual pastiche in the Arabic novel, wrote in 1984 that he was striving 'to establish a narrative form that derives its very foundations from our heritage at large, beginning with the oral, popular tradition ... all the way to the written heritage'.[10] He read deeply and extensively in order to create a new form inspired by the old but ultimately exceeding it. When it comes to religious rescripting the motivation is less about rediscovery and a quest for authenticity as exploiting the sacred intertext – as myth, figure, symbol and language – to catalyse contemporary meaning, and interrogating the values and assumptions of monotheism against a backdrop of modernity. In this sense religious intertextuality in the mature Egyptian novel continues the religious criticism that has already established itself as a feature of the form. Engaging tradition does not entail a substantive shift in novelistic attitudes to religion, though religion does find a new role in the post-1967 Arabic novel in the context of counternarrative, as the coming chapters will show. The focus of this chapter is on ironic engagements with religious narratives and figures, beginning with al-Ghitani's *Al-Zayni Barakat* as a seminal text in the story of modern Arabic literary intertextuality.[11]

Born in Sohag, Upper Egypt, in 1945 and initially seconded to a carpet-maker, Jamal al-Ghitani forged a successful career as a journalist, serving as editor-in-chief to *Akhbar al-Adab* for several years, whilst developing a literary oeuvre whose salient characteristic is the recycling of historical and religious texts.[12] *Al-Zayni Barakat* (1974) was the first of these. This work conducts a narrative experiment which has implications for both the novel and historiography, since intertextuality, as Genette reminds us, flows both ways. The subject of *Al-Zayni* is the oppressive regime of Gamal Abdel Nasser and the humiliating defeat he presided over in 1967 and which his radio news programme, *Sawt al-ʿArab*, sought to conceal initially. But instead of dramatising this in its twentieth-century context, which would no doubt have invited heavy censorship, al-Ghitani turns to the Ottoman invasion of Egypt in 1517, and the period leading up to it, as recorded in Ibn Iyas' *Badaʿiʾ al-Zuhur fi'l-Waqaʿiʾ al-Duhur*, which chronicles this dark moment in Egyptian history.[13] The selection is highly apposite, as others have noted, since Mamluk rule in Egypt had affinities with a police state, which is how many would precisely describe Nasser's regime with its heavy surveillance and internal spy network. Moreover, the Ottoman invasion resembles the *naksa* in the speed and shock of defeat and effort to conceal it from the populace.[14]

Al-Zayni presents as an historical document, consisting of the travelogue of a Venetian named Visconti Gianti, interspersed with letters, edicts, public announcements and other documents and quotations, and relates from a variety of viewpoints the intrigues of the Mamluk regime and extraordinary rise to power of the eponymous Barakat Ibn Musa, who along the way assumes the accolade al-Zayni ('he who decorates/adorns'), against a background of Ottoman imperialism. But this is no historical novel or textual imitation. As a self-consciously intertextual endeavour and metafiction, al-Ghitani reorients Ibn Iyas' content and material to serve contemporary concerns. The historiographic practice of including letters and other documents becomes in al-Ghitani's hands a mechanism for polyphony, so that no one voice dominates and instead we have a multitude of viewpoints, some in favour of Ibn Barakat, some opposed, some introspective, some commanding, and so on. The text becomes a collage whose fragmented structure reflects the fragmentation of discourse in the aftermath of the *naksa*. Transposition is about transformation – 'the passage from one signifying system to another demands a new articulation of the thetic', writes Kristeva – and it follows that Ibn Iyas' document itself undergoes revision in the process of its recycling. The structural intertextuality is self-reflexive; it draws attention to the formal fusion on the page and motivation behind it, which correspondingly foregrounds the proximity of novel and historiography, specifically the narrative quality of both. The magnification of narrative strategy in *Al-Zayni*, engendered in its unorthodox *tārīkhī* structure, reminds us that history is constructed as much as any story. It is noteworthy in this regard that the authoritative voice of the historian is elided in its modern rebirth. Any assumed objectivity in the novel, for example in the account of Visconti Gianti as detached onlooker, is undermined by the surrounding polyphonic context. The elision of the authoritative voice corrects and casts doubt on Ibn Iyas' account as either definitive or reliable.

Transformation and revaluation continues on the level of content. Barakat Ibn Musa, who represents the focal point of the novel, the character around whom the drama revolves even though he never assumes the narrative voice himself and appears only through the lens of other characters, is a marginal figure in Ibn Iyas' chronicle, no doubt selected as protagonist by al-Ghitani because his unexplained rise to power and accumulation of titles speaks to the remarkable ascent of Nasser. Thus the medieval figure assumes greater value in the hypertext, whilst other personages whose biographies are less useful to the novelist, such as Tuman Bey and the Sultan, are relocated to the peripheries and devalued. Likewise, the activity of spies and methods of surveillance, referred to but not pivotal in Ibn Iyas', take centre stage in the novel with several pages devoted to the craft of spying in order to foreground this feature of Nasser's Egypt, while the historian's poetry and sections detailing the mundane are omitted. This is not a relationship of one-on-one correspondence and decoding, however. The intertextual dialogue with Ibn Iyas' chronicle is broad and complex, an example of Genette's transposition which brings to bear a range of hypertextual strategies on different aspects of the hypotext simultaneously, as distinct from his category of imitation, which performs an essentially singular operation on a text in its entirety.[15] Al-Ghitani picks and chooses from the chronicle items which can be usefully parodied, magnified, transformed or negated to communicate his themes and messages. These have been explored in different measure in a number of studies, therefore the focus here is on the novel's intertexuality insofar as it involves religion, as character, symbol and language.

The figure of Shaykh Abu'l-Suʿud is key in this regard. From a minor character in the original, mentioned on three occasions, he becomes a central figure who has influence over many people, including al-Zayni Barakat himself as his master. Al-Ghitani modifies historical data from Ibn Iyas' account and details of the character to communicate new meaning. The original Abu'l-Suʿud was the Qadi of Mecca, an orthodox position and legal role. He is sought out by some of the emirs, according to Ibn Iyas', to persuade Tuman Bey to assume the sultanate, and he is enlisted in a dispute between al-Zayni Barakat and a tanner whom he has maltreated, which results in the shaykh having the *muḥtasib* beaten and imprisoned with the backing of the Sultan. Al-Ghitani's Abu'l-Suʿud, on the other hand, is a Sufi master, who mostly observes events from his refuge in Kum al-Jarih and exerts a soft influence on his disciples. He is, according to one enchanted follower, Saʿid al-Juhayni, virtuous, pleasant, noble, generous and learned, as well as well travelled and widely respected.[16] His house is a gathering place for Qur'an recitation and teaching and represents a peaceful refuge away from the clamour and intrigue of the city, and he has a cellar nearby in which 'the soul can soar to a valley where primeval truths are found'.[17] Abu'l-Suʿud has an almost mythical aura – some people even believe him to possess a ring with an imprint of Solomon that summons the jinn[18] – and it is in connection with Abu'l-Suʿud that we find the most colourful and evocative adjectives and language in the text. From one perspective, the shaykh functions as a counterpoint to oppressive state politics and corrupt governance, and as such represents the Sufi way as an alternative to mainstream life and material interests. But he becomes mixed up in the murk of politics when he summons al-Zayni early on and encourages him to take on the post of *muḥtasib*, which the latter has turned down for supposedly selfless reasons, for 'I do not want to see injustice and be silent about it'.[19] The substitution of al-Zayni for Tuman Bey has to do with his symbolic value as a figure for Nasser in the novel, and Abu'l-Suʿud's active endorsement of al-Zayni, which triggers a series of unfortunate events, not least the frenzied plotting of Zakariya which ultimately leads to the torture and recruitment of Abu'l-Suʿud's disciple Saʿid as a spy against his master, underscores the dire consequences of religion colluding with power and suggests the naivety of mystical types. This becomes increasingly problematic as al-Zayni thenceforth draws upon the shaykh for legitimacy. Yet Abu'l-Suʿud does not remain a supporter. When he sees that things have gone awry he summons al-Zayni once more, this time accusing him of theft, dishonesty and oppression and, like his medieval predecessor, has him beaten and imprisoned. The difference here is the nature of the crime. While Ibn Iyas' al-Zayni wrongs an individual, al-Ghitani's protagonist harms an entire people and must be brought down, a comment on the Egyptian president whom he symbolises. Abu'l-Suʿud's role in the text and encounters with al-Zayni are reworkings of the original loaded with contemporary politics.

Hutcheon's concept of parody as repetition with critical distance accounts for the deployment of space and language in the novel.[20] Setting in Ibn Iyas' chronicle is in the background and purely functional. The cities, mosques, buildings, houses, tombs, palaces, and so on, are part of the historical documenting of the period, present to root the narrative in historical space and provide a topographical record. The intertextual process opens up a critical distance so that these are no longer innocent details and artefacts but loaded signifiers. The medieval city, transposed onto the modern novel, becomes hypervisible and codified. Space in *Al-Zayni* is dominated by the mosque and pulpit (mostly al-Azhar) and Kum al-Jarih, home to Shaykh Abu'l-Suʿud, as well as the citadel, home of the administration. Several narrative segments take 'Kum al-Jarih' as their heading and the Azhar emerges as a hub of activity. In an atmosphere of reigning fear and surveillance, these holy landmarks and spaces become ironic; religious topography is mapped onto the police state in a manner which exposes the mosque and Sufi space as either useless or complicit. The same applies to religious language. Amidst the multitude of voices and registers in *Al-Zayni*, religious language features prominently, mostly in official documents. The novel is punctuated by letters and announcements beginning with religious preambles and Islamic formulae. These mimic the practice of quotation in medieval Arab historiography but the transposition from hypotext to hypertext once more opens up a critical distance which augments their visibility. The result is further irony. Many of the letters and documents deal with matters of governance and local administration, which in the regime in question tend towards dubious methods and oppression. The effect is religious pretensions juxtaposed with irreligious actions, underscoring false piety and the co-option of religion by power and politics. Al-Musawi makes a similar point when he notes that 'An avowed reliance on God is a legitimising process'.[21] A duplicitous letter from Zakariya ibn Radi to al-Zayni early on in his post as *muhtasib*, in which the former feigns loyalty even as he simultaneously distributes letters to the emirs written in invisible ink listing the latter's many infringements, begins with the oneness of God and tributes to the Prophet, justice and charity, and ends by invoking peace upon al-Zayni.[22] Thus Zakariya assumes a pious mask for underhand dealings. A treatise on spying, prepared by the same individual on the occasion of the international spy convention, a document that essentially advises on an oppressive practice that spreads fear among the people, begins with a series of divine quotations and is couched in pious rhetoric. This manner of presentation is commonplace in medieval histories and official documents and as such can be seen as merely a convention of particular types of discourse. But in the context of self-conscious intertexuality, where imitation and borrowing produce ironic distance and call for rereading, the convention becomes a conduit of meaning that points to the problematic role of religion in society and its exploitation by power and evil. This is mirrored in the pattern of religious reference in the discourse of the characters. Al-Zayni more than once claims legitimacy from his Sufi master, so that the latter's initial endorsement of him as *muḥtasib* becomes a free pass for any behaviour, and he invokes God often too. Again the juxtaposition of piety and crafty dealings and oppressive actions suggests an unhealthy relationship between religion and power. Meanwhile, a touch of humour creeps in when Zakariya, ever anxious ever scheming, draws an envious analogy between spies and the angels of death, Nakir and Nakeer, and marvels at the final judgement: 'a great system, a most splendid arrangement. Thus it grasps the whole world and no good or evil deed gets away'.[23] In Zakariya's mind, God is the ultimate spy!

While al-Ghitani's intertextuality targets specific documents and their content and form, other writers address their intertextual dialogues to myths and symbols and less bounded aspects of the cultural text. The Sufi path features prominently among these (see Chapter 7). So too does eschatology and messianic allusion. Mahfuz's *Malhamat al-Harafish* (1977) is a good example of this.[24] *Harafish* rewrites *Awlad Haratina*, which narrates human history through the lives of monotheism's major prophets ending in the modern era, when science takes over the function of God. As such *Awlad* rehearses themes of modernity such as the death of God thesis and triumph of science, even as this same novel, written nearly a decade before the cataclysmic events of 1967, contains early signs of a shift in literary sensibility and critique of modernity's certainties in its grand sweep allegorical format, a dramatic contrast to the social documenting and predominantly realist style of the 40s and 50s, and in its employment of the scribe and attempt to give voice to the Egyptian collective, as described in a paper by El-Desouky.[25] The project of *Harafish* is similarly ambitious, attempting once more to tell the story of mankind using the *ḥāra* as a microcosm and combining the construction of a political imaginary with key existential questions (time, divinity, the sources of evil) in a popular-cum-religio narrative framework, but the intertextuality is more sophisticated and the emphasis and vision has shifted somewhat. Science as a solution is significantly absent from *Harafish*. By the 1970s the idea that the future lay in science and reason, modernity on a western model, no longer held much sway. On the one occasion that science encroaches on alley space, in the form of official advice on hygiene in the event of plague, it is combined with an exhortation to prayer; there is no epistemological struggle here, only an admission of the singular inadequacy of science to ward off disaster: 'Pray and accept your destiny'.[26] El-Desouky identifies a Marxist vision in *Awlad*; history is here a cycle of revolutions in which sacred time is embedded as a way of seeing for some. It produces a continuum in the experience of popular struggles whilst sacred history is revealed as discontinuous.[27] In *Harafish* the latter returns in full force with a vision of history as distilled in moments and ruptures, or Walter Benjamin's messianic time. Between the two ʿAshurs, separated by eight generations, we have not a learning curve nor any other linear development or upward trajectory, but a cycle of misery and disappointment, broken eventually by a revolution that both revives and innovates. ʿAshur II's coup heralds a new epoch whilst simultaneously becoming, at that moment, the teleological end point of a hitherto indeterminate salvation narrative. The past, present and future are not plotted on a line but connected by significant moments and details, most critically the ascendency of a Naji champion and restoration of rights to the harafish, but also copious parallels in the biographies of the central family and, less auspiciously, the ironic circumstances of death of many of the protagonists.[28] Repetition and parallelism bind history into narrative and substitute for continuum and progression.

While the novel ends on a positive note, with the harafish mobilised around a humble leader and a system founded on justice and integrity, the narrative dismantles the equation of history as progress implied in the discourse of modernity. The emergence of ʿAshur II is more a stroke of luck for the harafish than the culmination of a process. He was preceded by generations of oppression, even if his great uncle Fath al-Bab offered temporary respite. Without the fortuitous appearance of a new champion, the alley's experience would not be intelligible as a redemption story and, more importantly, alley history would remain fragmented and flat, an endless cycle of suffering and tyranny held in place by an unholy alliance between money and power. For there is little moral progress between the two Naji champions and, although the harafish materialise as a unified and effective force in the end, they do so under the tutelage of an extraordinary leader with mystical colouring not as an organic popular movement. The positive ending is more coincidence than evolution. People power is only partially recognised in this scenario; or could this be an argument for 'inspired' action and mysticism in a postsecular, postmodern world? In the absence of a cogent, progressive, predictable political and national trajectory following 1967, alternative futures and solutions are sought, including the irrational, mystical and messianic. Though *Harafish* is usually read as the triumph of popular action and collective responsibility, such a reading forgets the sequence of action which has the hero's work precede any popular awakening. The revolution is initiated and spearheaded by an exemplary figure and visionary. What makes this more interesting and somewhat ironic is the critique of messianic myth that precedes the synchrony of popular power and prophethood in the final pages. *Harafish*'s handling of the saviour trope is consequently rather ambivalent.

With its proximity to the monastery and the obscure anthems filtering its space, the alley is overlaid with a sense of the divine, though it remains ultimately out of reach of its inhabitants. The monastery's doors are closed to the outside world and the dervishes are indifferent to the suffering beyond their enclosure. What the harafish have instead is the legend of ʿAshur al-Naji, in whom is inscribed the prophetic pattern of monotheism, inviting scrutiny of messianic myth and the cult of heroes and saints.[29] Originally an orphan, ʿAshur grows into a paradigmatic leader, strong, heroic, a champion of the poor, enamoured of the monastery and the recipient of divine messages, including one to vacate the alley at the time of plague. He is, as is customary for prophets, ignored on the latter occasion, thus when he returns with his family after six months in the open country (*khalāʾ*), he finds an empty quarter. The alley has been seemingly purged by divine decree and the way is clear for ʿAshur to start anew, in the style of Noah post-flood, and establish a God-fearing community. ʿAshur's survival of the plague, which earns him the title al-Naji (the survivor) along with his good works and spell in jail, confirm his sainthood to the harafish, thus a legend is born, corroborated by his mysterious disappearance, which excuses him the indignity of death and opens the possibility of redemptive return at a later date. In the years that follow, ʿAshur's legacy is eroded and tyranny takes over once more. His son Shams al-Din is able to hold fort for a time but his own son, Sulayman, is seduced by wealth and the harafish have to wait generations for another champion and outbreak of justice. In the meantime, the legend of ʿAshur, and by extension messianic myth, is dismantled. As the harafish suffer successive humiliations and the Najis fail to produce another worthy leader, the short-lived benefits of prophethood are exposed along with the flaw in systems that depend on the qualities of a single individual and in the face of trouble wait passively for salvation to come from elsewhere. The deferral of responsibility of the harafish becomes an ever greater problem. Prophecy is installed as intertext in order to debunk the myth and underscore the message of popular action and collective responsibility, which is fully spelled out in the concluding chapter.

If the text exposes the paralysing effects of salvation narratives and overdependence on heroes, divine or popular (for there is a dialogue with *sira* here too, which I have explored elsewhere),[30] so it reminds us that our saints are human and that sacred stories are just that – stories, open for interpretation and rewriting. ʿAshur al-Naji, for a start, is far from perfect. When he falls for Fulla, a local prostitute, he uses the legality of marriage to mask what is essentially a betrayal of his existing wife and sons. Moreover, he moves into the Bannan house and appropriates the fortune of the deceased family, inventing a new ethic to justify his actions: 'Money is forbidden when it is spent on forbidden things', implying the reverse, that the spoils are permissible if spent permissibly.[31] Worse still, when he stands accused of theft he recasts the affair as an altruistic project in the service of the poor, expunging personal gain and temptation from the story and thereby spinning his own legend. There is a hint of ʿAbd al-Jawwad here; Mahfuz has reworked an ideal to include human foibles and weakness and create a more relatable hero and even challenge black and white discourse on morality. But there is no escaping the shadow that these actions cast over ʿAshur's person and the halcyon associated with his *fatwana*. Nor are the harafish blind to the issue and as the story proceeds ʿAshur's legacy is up for debate. He is venerated as a saint but blamed too for the misfortunes of the alley. Attitudes to his rule and legacy vary according to contemporary experience and the fortunes of the Naji clan. Thus the narrative not only challenges the superiority of saints but revokes the sanctity of sacred biography. While the *sira* of Muhammad and life of Christ are beyond reproach, ʿAshur's legend is available for interpretation and revision. One could even argue that in the varying attitudes of the harafish vis-à-vis their ancestor Mahfuz has substituted sacred story for a deliberation on leadership and responsibility, misguided though the harafish's commentary on the latter is for the most part, habitually heaping it upon the Najis and effectively discounting themselves as players in their destiny.

For much of the novel the religious intertext is itself a target of criticism. A new political imaginary is posited as a correction to salvation narratives and the cult of saints and heroes. The old is overwritten with the new. Later in the text, with the arrival of ʿAshur II, sacred rescripting takes on another function, which is less deconstructive and more about augmenting the new order and signalling a trajectory onto the metaphysical in the nation-state. The prophetic evocation also becomes more specific, for it is unmistakably the messenger of Islam who we are dealing with in the final chapter. As El-Enany notes, ʿAshur II is a shepherd like Muhammad and brought up by a woman named Halima just like the Prophet (whose wet nurse was Halima al-Saʿdiyya).[32] ʿAshur II's periods of meditation in the *khalāʾ* and forced exile followed by resolute homecoming and destruction of Jalal's irreligious freestanding minaret mirrors Muhammad's forced departure from Mecca and destruction of the idols at the Kaaba. But ʿAshur II's message is significantly not tied up with love of God or the duty to serve anything other than the community. Though he is buttressed by divinity in a visionary sense, his genius lies less in foretelling natural disasters, like plague, than in educating the harafish in justice and collective responsibility. As such he can be read as a correction to Muhammad and prophetic messages centred on prayer and obedience. Yet ʿAshur's divine connection cannot be ignored, especially given the preceding critique of prophecy and sainthood. Indeed it is remarkable in the work of a writer who has long sided with reason that a divinely inspired hero should be part of the final solution. Of course revolutions always have their leaders, but while a socialist hero emerges from the people, shaped by and speaking for them, ʿAshur II thinks up his revolution away from the alley and devises the political formula by himself. In the aftermath of 1967, writers and intellectuals no longer set much store by laws of development and historical progress; a better future was possible but not assured or in process. The prophetic and mystical symbolism in the final pages is thus part of an alternative vision and search. The rescripting of Muhammad in the person of ʿAshur II sends the message that utopia is not confined to the distant past, but it also, by harnessing transcendence to the new order, subverts the idea, hitherto popular in Egyptian novelistic discourse, that the future of the nation lies in reason and secular humanism. When the dervish announces in the final paragraphs that the Grand Shaykh is coming out of seclusion, it not only signals a divine stamp of approval for ʿAshur's work but a future that makes space for the mystical and metaphysical.

Another work that takes on messianic symbolism is ʿAbd al-Hakim Qasim's short novel *Al-Mahdi*, this time to comment on the rise of Islamic fundamentalism and treatment of the Copts in Egypt. Born in al-Bandara, Lower Egypt, to a peasant family, ʿAbd al-Hakim Qasim (1935–90) studied law at Alexandria University and started writing fiction in the 1960s, becoming a key member of *jīl al-sittīnāt*.[33] *Al-Mahdi*, which was written in 1977 but not published until 1984, tells the story of the forced conversion of a Copt named ʿAwdallah in a condensed narrative format where the style is realism but without its panoramic thrust.[34] Unable to afford his rent in Tanta, ʿAwdallah takes his family into the countryside in search of work and ends up in Mahallat al-Jayad, where a local Sufi ʿAli Effendi extends him his hospitality before turning his case over to the charity of the Muslim Brotherhood, who have been gaining popularity in the village recently and who waste no time in organising a festive ceremony for the Copt's conversion, against his will. The ceremony turns into a frenzied occasion, with the crowd, believing ʿAwdallah to be the Mahdi, fighting to get close to him while the Brothers lead him to the mosque. He does not make it inside, however, for he collapses at the gate and dies in the arms of his wife as she prays and makes the sign of the cross over him.

Religion and religious difference take centre stage in this short work. The Muslim Brotherhood have long used charitable works as a means of converting rural Egypt to their cause. Qasim represents this phenomenon and underscores its sinister effects in a fictional context. The setting is an ordinary village in rural Egypt, a space where Sufism has traditionally thrived, as comes across clearly in another work by the same author, *Ayyam al-Insan al-Sabaʿa* (1968). But in recent times the Brotherhood has increased its presence in the countryside so that by the point at which the narrative opens Mahallat al-Jayad has become a site of conflict between the Sufis and Muslim Brothers, though it has not been articulated as such yet and the tension is merely simmering. In fact, the villagers display a high degree of naivety in this regard. ᶜAli Effendi describes the Brotherhood as a positive influence: 'They have turned hatred and rancour into solicitude for religion', he comments artlessly,[35] and readily entrusts them with ᶜAwdallah's well-being, thereby sealing his fate. What follows is a process of communal self-purification along the lines of René Girard's theory of sacred violence as the catastrophic outcome of unregulated mimetic desire.

'The impulse toward the object is ultimately an impulse toward the mediator', writes Girard.[36] In other words, we borrow our desires from others. This is seen in the structure of relationships in the text. ᶜAbd al-Aziz, a character who recurs in Qasim's work and who here acts as an onlooker, is drawn to the Sufi leader Shaykh Saᶜid al-Hasiri on account of the friendship and respect he enjoys from his uncle ᶜAli Effendi. Similarly and more ominously, Talᶜat and Subhi are drawn to the Muslim Brotherhood via characters they esteem or love. Talᶜat finds his way to militant Islam through his brother the Azharite, whose galvanising speeches he listens to with pleasure, while Subhi's journey to Islamic fundamentalism is mediated by school colleagues first, then Brother Saᶜid, a handsome well-turned-out Brother with whom he forms a homosexual relationship. Religion is notably the object of mediated desire in both cases, that is, secondary. When two subjects desire the same object the result is mimetic rivalry, which is when the situation becomes dangerous. This is what we encounter in the struggle between the Sufis and the Muslim Brothers over religious truth. The two groups are antithetical. The Sufis are a disorganised, democratic cluster of men who pray together, read fortunes and indulge their appetites; the Muslim Brothers are highly organised, smartly dressed and, if Talᶜat's avoidance of tea, coffee and tobacco is representative, strict and abstinent. The triangle of desire is a complex one here and encountered at an advanced stage, after the principle of contagion has taken effect. If two people desire an object, there will soon be a third, a fourth and the process will escalate, hence by the time we meet the villagers of Mahallat al-Jayad they are divided between the Muslim Brothers and the Sufis and their alternate paths to God. The spread of mimetic desire brings with it the threat of violence. This is normally held in check by taboos and prohibitions, but in abnormal circumstances these mechanisms cease to function, with catastrophic results, as is the case here. The normal order, the Sufi orientation of village life in Mahallat al-Jayad, has been upset by the missionary activities of the Muslim Brothers, who are fast gathering members. The village is thus at odds with itself. The tendency in this situation, Girard tells us, is not to suppress the crisis but to bring it to a head, generally with the help of a surrogate victim or scapegoat, who must be perceived as guilty, for '[t]he community could not be at peace with itself once more if it doubted the victim's enormous capacity for evil',[37] and an outsider, for the group 'is seeking to deflect upon a relatively indifferent victim, a "sacrificeable" victim, the violence that would otherwise be vented on its own members, the people it most desires to protect'.[38]

This pattern of self-purification is replicated in *Al-Mahdi*. From the moment ᶜAwdallah arrives in Mahallat al-Jayad events gain a momentum of their own. ᶜAli Effendi and Talᶜat, representatives of the opposing factions, work together to find a house for the Copt, whose fate is transferred to the Muslim Brothers, who in turn waste no time planning his conversion, ignoring ᶜAwdallah's deteriorating health and the fact that he has no wish to switch holy allegiance. ᶜAwdallah is the ideal surrogate, since the substitute must bear a resemblance to the object they replace – in this case the villagers – or the violent impulse would not be satisfied, yet he must still be unmistakably different or other to the group.[39] Animals make suitable sacrifices because they satisfy the need for living blood to be spilled in certain situations. As a man of faith, ᶜAwadallah resembles the Muslim villagers but is wholly other because of his Christian creed, which is regarded as aberrant and becomes an excuse for the broken community of Mahallat al-Jayad to suspend normal standards of behaviour in their treatment of him. As preparations for the ceremony proceed, the principle of contagion comes into force once more as the villagers transform into a mob. Meanwhile ᶜAwdallah's voice is ignored as the Muslim Brothers focus attention on the triumphant show they are about to stage. The events that follow do not deliver the desired purification, however, for the Sufis and other key players reject the ceremony, and when the sacrificial moment has passed the community is still disunited, indeed worse off as the potential for evil is now confirmed and recognised. When the shaykh finally names the episode for what it is, coercion, ᶜAli Effendi's protest that the victim 'found his way to God' sounds hollow indeed.[40] When the sacrificial moment has passed equilibrium has not been restored.

This conclusion is corroborated and reinforced by the sacred intertexts.

In Sunni eschatology, the Mahdi is expected to usher in a period of peace and righteousness at the end of time, at which point he will defeat the false messiah (*masīḥ al-dajjāl*) with the assistance of ʿIsa (Jesus), while the Shia have a whole doctrine surrounding the Mahdi, his occultation and reappearance as redeemer. The title of the narrative and the appellation awarded to the Copt by the characters within it – ʿAwdallah al-Mahdi – summon both of these concepts so that his demise at the end becomes a comment on the rise and fall of heroes and a deconstruction of messianic thought reminiscent of *Harafish*, though the falsity of prophetic myth more than its paralysing effects is the issue here. The words of ʿAwdallah as he approaches his end suggest Judeo-Christian tradition to be an even more productive context of interpretation. As the Copt is led through the town to the mosque he provides a disjointed narrative of events. 'Father, the hour has come', he calls out when they come to fetch him from his house.[41] 'The soldiers wove a crown of thorns and placed it on his head and dressed him in a purple robe',[42] he cries out as the Muslim Brothers dress him in a turban. 'Then the soldiers, the chief officer, the Jewish servants arrested Jesus and took him away'.[43] His commentary is not heard by anyone, nor is his fervid address to the crowd: 'Peace be with you', he says, 'his face shining with joy and fever'.[44] Nevertheless they confirm to the reader that the character is a reincarnation of Christ and that his story should be read against a backdrop of the crucifixion. The procession through Tanta is Jesus' passage through Via Dolorosa and the Brothers are the roman soldiers, a likeness elaborated in the military imagery used to portray them. The image of Fulla bent over her dead husband, praying and weeping, evokes the lamentation of Christ and the famous image of Mary cradling Jesus in her arms (*pieta*), and the crowd is the bloodthirsty mob in Jerusalem. The crucifixion intertext elaborates the narrative's moral hierarchy. ʿAli Effendi, who hands ʿAwadallah over to the Brothers, effectively betraying his trust and sealing his fate, becomes Judas Iscariot and the connection undermines any sympathy he might claim as the protagonist's initial helper and friend. Likewise, Mashriqi Bey, as the authority figure who bows to pressure and mandates the use of Fakiha bint Tarawa's house against his conscience and in full knowledge of what lays in store, is the Roman prefect Pontius Pilate. In intertextual dialogues meaning lies in points of divergence and difference, and it is significant in this regard that missing in the mayor's assent is any real struggle with the delegation that comes to his house. While Pilate sought to spare Jesus and washed his hands before the crowd to dissociate himself from the crime, the mayor cares only to be left alone to indulge himself and thus deserves none of the sympathy and reprieve granted to Pilate by history.

Another significant divergence from the Christian intertext is the absence of a trial and resurrection. In the gospel accounts Jesus is brought before the Jewish elders of the Sanhedrin, who find him guilty of blasphemy and take him to Pontius Pilate, who orders his crucifixion under pressure. Jesus' death is the result of a Jewish-Roman conspiracy, his people working with the authorities in Judaea. ʿAwdallah, on the other hand, is a man without a community when he meets the Muslims of Mahallat al-Jayad. A lone Copt, he is seized upon first by ʿAli Effendi, then Talʿat and his men. The Coptic community to which he belongs has no part in his demise, therefore the guilt resides entirely with the Muslim villagers, including the Sufis who fail to act. As Shaykh Saʿid al-Hasiri says, 'We all did this'.[45] ʿAwdallah is also denied a trial in a marked deviation from the crucifixion story. At no point is he questioned or consulted about his conversion. Instead a copy of the Qur'an is thrust into his hand, bookmarked on a verse that denies the divinity of Jesus and Mary (Q. 5:116), thereby augmenting the culpability of the Muslims and showing them to be acting outside the law, for even if Jesus was wrongfully condemned, he was given the opportunity to make representations whereas ʿAwdallah is not.

The same is true of the resurrection. In the Christian story Jesus rose from the dead on the third day and appeared to his apostles over a period of forty days before ascending into heaven, a pattern which is understood to confirm his identity as the Son of God and to signify man's salvation. *Al-Mahdi*, on the other hand, ends with ʿAwdallah's death. The community of Mahallat al-Jayad does not apparently deserve absolution. The death of its messiah does not mark a new beginning as it does in the gospel narratives, for the community remains broken. While John 23: 12 refers to newfound harmony between Herod and Pontius Pilate, the Sufis boycott the ceremony, ʿAbd al-ʿAziz returns to his village and the mayor retreats into alcohol and depression. The denial of the resurrection and the symbolism it carries with it ties in with the failure of the sacrificial process detailed above which is unsurprising since Christ's crucifixion is a particular instance of scapegoating. Egypt, as mentioned, experienced much religio-political turmoil in the years following independence. Islamic voices came to the fore as the liberal experiment waned and committed secularists were forced to make concessions, hence the shift in message of the Liberal Constitutionalists. In this climate the Copts were frequently held responsible for national and social problems in the press, a pattern which would become all too familiar to Egypt's Christians in the decades that followed. In the text too ʿAli Effendi is quick to accuse Sitt Jabuna. Just as al-Ghitani finds in Mamluk rule in fifteenth-century Egypt an analogy for Nasser's police state, so Qasim finds in first-century Judaea a means of commenting on religious tension and extremism. Qasim casts a contemporary story in the mould of the crucifixion to expose it for what it is – an exercise in ritual violence and age-old scapegoating.

Another novel that revolves around a death and draws on an eschatological intertext is *Turaf min Khabar al-Akhira* (1981).[46] This peculiar work, also by ʿAbd al-Hakim Qasim, borrows scenes from the afterlife as understood in Muslim tradition to develop its critique of society and of Islam itself. The plot is confusing, calling for a highly engaged reader to decipher the intertextuality, and unusual in its direct attack on specific items of doctrine. Sharia, revelation, the afterlife, Islamic marriage all come under fire here. While post-1967 Arabic fiction does not limit its religious criticism to institutions and representatives nor shy away from subverting core values of monotheism, explicit verbalised criticism, such as is dealt out by the angels in *Turaf*, is rare.

Turaf is set in an unnamed village in the Egyptian countryside. In real time it takes place over a few hours but through the thought excursions of two of the characters, the dead man and grandson, and an extended dream sequence, it traverses several decades and takes in several lives, or at least the fragments thereof. The narrative is divided into five chapters, whose titles follow the stages that the believer passes at the end of his life: *al-mawt* (death), *al-qabr* (the grave), *al-malakān* (the two angels), *al-ḥisāb* (the reckoning) and *al-nushūr* (resurrection). In the first chapter we learn of the death of a neighbour and this provides the excuse for the journey to the afterlife indicated in the book's title. After leaving the house of his grandfather, an old Sufi, and visiting the wife of the deceased, the grandson joins the mourners on the way to the graveyard. Qasim uses the funeral procession and burial to paint a detailed picture of the rituals and processes of death, which carries on into the second chapter and includes a description of the decomposing body. The grandson falls asleep on the tomb and the dead man's perspective takes over to portray the sensations he experiences in the grave and to fill in the story of his life and its significant events and relationships, which are the things for which he will be called to account shortly. The dead man's narrative is thus part of the grandson's dream. In the third chapter the angels of death arrive and conduct a discussion with the deceased in which they deal with the criteria upon which he is to be judged and proceed through the key moments and themes in his life. This is the content of the third and fourth chapters respectively. In the final chapter, 'Al-Nushūr', the grandson's narrative resumes again and he awakens from the dream and returns to the village. This stretch of text sees the boy renouncing his studies at the Azhar, standing up to his father and carving a role for himself in the village as a teacher and farmer.

This synopsis reveals the unusual character of *Turaf*. The plot is neither linear nor teleological and leaves several questions unanswered. What is the connection between the grandson's story and that of the dead man? What is the purpose of this text which brings together separate stories without visibly synchronising them? What are we supposed to make of the ending, which consists of a continuation more than a conclusion? Some of these problems are resolved when we turn to the intertexts, namely Islamic eschatology and dream narrative. Although the Qur'an reveals very little on what takes places between death and resurrection, during the time/space known as the *barzakh*, a commonly held picture of what to expect has grown up thanks to the work of classical scholars, who over the centuries have elaborated an account with the help of hadith and other materials.[47] According to Islamic tradition, when a person dies he is visited by angels; the angel of death, ᶜAzraʾil, who announces the fact of death, and the two recording angels, Munkar and Nakir (or Nakir and Nakeer), who interrogate the deceased about his faith and record his answers.[48] If the deceased responds truthfully and shows himself to be a believer he is given a glimpse of paradise and his time waiting for the resurrection is made pleasant. If, on the other hand, he is an infidel or sinner the wait is made wretched. The questioning by Munkar and Nakir is thus a preliminary event in anticipation of the ultimate Day of Judgement and the reward or punishment they confer on the deceased is intermediary, a taste of what is to come. There are a number of variations in the textual accounts of this episode in the afterlife. Some writers include details of the awesome sight of Munkar and Nakir, others merely suggest they are fearful to behold or ignore their physical appearance altogether. Al-Ghazali distinguishes between four categories of people who are dealt with in four different ways by the angels and has the arrival of Munkar and Nakir preceded by the angel Ruman, who instructs the deceased to write down his good and bad deeds on a record that is then hung around his neck until the Day of Resurrection.[49] There are also differences regarding the number and wording of the questions addressed to the deceased, with Sufi accounts including enquiries as to shaykh and *madhdhab* (school). But all accounts agree that the deceased's adherence to Islam and Sharia is decisive in determining his fate.

Qasim depicts this famous scene from the afterlife but predictably modifies it. The criteria of judgement have changed and the simple and direct questioning of the deceased in the traditional account becomes an extended dialogue in which his voice and grasp of the process are important factors. When they first appear the angels are portrayed as a comely sight and serene presence.[50] Rather than fearful the dead man is at ease and the conversation starts off with humorous reference to the fact that the angels are not using Aramaic, as the deceased had expected. This leads into a more serious deliberation on language and its tendency to distort truth, as a preliminary to a more wide-ranging discussion of the criteria and purpose of judgement. In Qasim's version, before judgement can begin the deceased must understand the rationale behind it, a detail which transports this episode in Islamic eschatology onto a different plain, an intellectual one, where the three actors in the scene debate with one another and the deceased is able to question his interrogators. As the discussion proceeds, it becomes apparent that the criteria upon which the dead man is to be judged are different to those posited in the traditional account. Qasim's angels are not interested in the deceased's faith or in weighing his conduct against formal principles enshrined in the Sharia. Instead they are concerned with motives, and how far actions reflect these motives, or to put it more clearly, since Qasim's angels typically talk in riddles, how far behaviour and conscience cohere. The angels' criteria call for a new set of values which makes judgement a far more subjective and flexible process and which revises the concept of correct action so that it becomes not an immutable model aspired to by all believers but one that varies from person to person. The right path becomes the most authentic path for the individual. Mitigating factors and context are also considered.⁵¹ Qasim's angels are thinking and compassionate creatures who follow guidelines rather than unbending rules and who posit an alternative morality that is closer to Freudian theory than Islamic thought. For the disjunction between motive and deed of which they disapprove is analogous to the friction between Id and Ego that Freud identifies as a vital problematic in well-being and that leads to unnatural behaviour.

The meditative approach continues in the angels' attitude towards canonical law or revelation (*al-shar͑/al-sharī͑a*), which too is subject to scrutiny. The angels reject it as a model beyond contemplation (*namūdhaj a͑lā min al-ta͑ammul*)⁵² in a clear challenge to the divine status of Sharia, and couple this with an attack on the sanctification of prophecy and religious texts. Miracles distract from the Prophet's personality and misread his genius – here again Muhammad the mortal is preferred to Muhammad the miracle-worker. Qasim repeats the prophetic concept espoused by Haykal and al-Sharqawi. Focus on the wondrous renders prophecy untouchable, while the texts that record prophecy are exploited by those in power to control the masses. Law and prophecy should be a beginning and not an end in the angels' analysis, a source of thought and not a constraint upon it.⁵³ The angels are highly critical of the co-option of sacred institutions in oppression and propose instead law as 'the expression of nature', or instinct, far away from static legal codes.⁵⁴ The discourse of the angels is poetic and abstruse, but a theme of responsibility and authentic living nevertheless shines through; man should abide by his conscience and instinct and not depend on higher causes, 'however loud the din'.⁵⁵

Once the dead man has understood the rationale and philosophy of the angels, the judgement can begin. This is fairly straightforward now that the theory is out of the way, though again the dead man is able to converse and debate with his interrogators. The judgement works through the events and relationships referred to by the dead man when he considered his life upon burial and involves social criticism. The deceased is commended for speaking out in favour of his father in the Islamic court, because he listened to his inner voice and acted on it, but he betrayed that same voice when he failed to stand up to his father later on and in his poor treatment of his stepmother, when deep down he loved her. In fact, all the dead man's relationships are cause for criticism because they involve him behaving in unnatural ways. He loved his cousin but deliberately insulted her by refusing to visit his sick uncle; he betrayed the country girl, too afraid to let a woman love him; and he humiliated his wife, as was expected of him as a prominent member of the family and in spite of the voice inside him. Discussion of these relationships provides an opportunity to scrutinise patriarchal norms in the village and the angels' contempt is clear. The hypocrisy of the protection afforded women and children as a facade for domination and sexual gratification was referred to by the angels in the previous scene.[56] Now they castigate the practice of turning women into objects. Powerful womanhood should be celebrated, not denied, and the subjugation of women is reprehensible. Moreover, while Islam upholds marriage and considers sexual relationships outside it unlawful, the angels propose love, not a legal document, as the critical factor: 'If happiness is abundant on both sides, and there are no legal obstacles, and there is a high degree of openness, then that is a legitimate and valid marriage'.[57] The final theme of the judgement relates to the dead man's religion. In a departure from the traditional account, the angels are not concerned with the nature of the deceased's faith, whether or not he is Muslim, but the motives behind him joining the Sufi brotherhood, which were not to do with authentic belief but fear and the desire to escape reality. The judgement does not end with a decision on the part of the angels. Nor is the dead man offered a glimpse of paradise or hell. Rather he dissolves into the horizon and achieves knowledge, which is an appropriate ending to an episode in which the deceased's understanding is of paramount importance but again diverges from traditional accounts.

Qasim thus transforms the familiar scene of the interrogating angels in several ways. The angels have become friendly, compassionate and contemplative; the exchange is sophisticated and includes the voice of the deceased; the criteria of judgement relate to conscience not faith and the deceased's understanding of its terms is requisite; the angels are interested in the material world and comment on it; and the process ends with knowledge, not paradise or hellfire. Several meanings emerge herein. Most obviously the alterations to the mythical scene constitute a rejection of Muslim eschatology. Qasim mocks the image of accusatory angels interrogating the deceased about belief.

The ironic distance, coupled with various instances of humour, naturally assist. The revision of the terms of judgement is a repudiation of religiosity as a moral standard, and the reward of knowledge rather than the pleasure of paradise or suffering of hellfire envisages a new value system. At the same time and on the structural level, Qasim's reimagining of the angels and the terms of the exchange transforms the mythical scene into a vehicle for social commentary. The angels, more than interrogators, are spokesmen for Qasim's messages about society and religion, corruption and female oppression. It is noteworthy that God is hardly mentioned over the course of the angelic encounter and that the resurrection that follows takes place on earth, confirming that the religious intertext has nothing to do with piety and everything to do with social and cultural concerns.

If the significance and purpose behind Qasim's use of the encounter with Nakir and Nakeer is clear, this still needs to be reconciled with the story of the grandson. After the angels depart and the dead man merges into the atmosphere, the narrative returns to the village. The boy wakes from his dream and his story resumes. The events that follow bear a resemblance to events in the life of the dead man, so that the 'resurrection' in the chapter's title comes to refer to the resurrection of the dead man in the boy. The grandson's actions and conduct in the following stretch of narrative become a kind of correction of the dead man's mistakes as laid out by the angels. For instance, his reaction against school recalls that of the deceased but he deals with it more appropriately. He attends the Azhar but does not adapt well to formal teaching and when the shaykhs despair of him he leaves. Unlike the deceased, who allowed his father's will to prevail, the boy stands up for himself with a firm proposition that will enable him to remain in the village and earn his keep. Back in the village the grandson becomes a teacher, but of an unorthodox nature, for he neglects subjects like arithmetic and dictation and instead encourages the children to do the talking and they all learn about life together. He farms land and cares for the mosque and cemetery, and follows the advice of children. He leads a peculiar life, outside the mainstream of village life, and his fellow villagers regard him as an anomaly. But what matters is that the boy lives authentically. He obeys his instinct and does not harm anyone, unlike the dead man who betrayed his conscience and brought suffering to the women in his life. He figures the eccentric as a credible and morally superior alternative to mainstream and patriarchal society. The grandson's attitude to women is a clear improvement on the dead man's. Initially in awe of them, he grows to understand them through his grandfather's companion. 'Now he knew what the words mother, sister, darling, confidant and companion meant',[58] in contrast to the deceased who could only relate to women sexually.[59] This culminates in a replay of the scene from the first chapter of the grandson visiting the dead man's wife in her room on the roof, in which she significantly refers to her liberation.[60]

There is, then, a thematic *intra-textual* link between the story of the boy and the story of the dead man. This can be appreciated more fully by turning once more to Islamic heritage, specifically Muslim oneiric tradition, which upholds the idea of interaction between the dead and the living through dreams and serves as a further intertext. On the basis of Q. 39:42, which informs believers that God takes souls at death and during sleep, and sayings by the Prophet, Islamic tradition recognises an ongoing communication between this world and the next.[61] Muslim writers and exegetes have elaborated the narrative around this phenomenon, often by way of dream anecdotes and dream analysis, while the belief grew up that information imparted in dreams is reliable because, since prophecy has ceased, 'dreams are the only transcendental source of guidance'.[62] From the Muslim sources, notably *Kitab al-Manam*, it appears that the encounter can take place in two ways; either the dreamer's soul travels to the afterworld during sleep and interacts with the souls of the dead there, or the deceased travels to this world and interacts with the living in their dreams. In the first case, the (passive) dreamer might see paradise with all its beauty or overhear a conversation or statement in heaven. In the second case he enters into a dialogue with the deceased, in which he might have information about the afterlife related to him, be informed of certain conditions he should fulfil in order to guarantee him a good place in heaven, or he may be tasked with rectifying a wrong in order to improve the situation of the deceased's soul, the latter implying the living have the ability to affect the dead through their deeds.[63] Whatever format the dream takes, the purpose is edifying; interaction between the living and dead through dreams revolves around imparting information to the dreamer which will prompt him to act in the right way.

The boy's journey into the afterlife in *Turaf* reimagines this oneiric interaction. The boy is transported in a dream into the afterlife, where he witnesses a scene of judgement. A great many lessons are imparted over the course of this judgement, which the grandson applies when he awakes. Though the encounter with the angels is presented from the point of view of the deceased, it is nevertheless clear that the grandson is its subject and beneficiary, for it is to the grandson that the narrative returns when it is over and through the grandson that its lessons are implemented. While the scene from the afterlife is evoked to communicate social and religious critique, the intertextuality here is to do with the symbolic power of the dream sequence, which serves to confirm the edifying aspect – the real-life relevance – of the judgement scene, whose purpose is not to show the fate of one individual so much as effectuate a warning for society. Qasim's dialogue with sacred myth and form, here as in *Al-Mahdi*, has an admonishing quality. He uses holy forms to chastise contemporary irreligious practices.

Notes

1. Abdelfattah Kilito, *The Author and His Doubles*, translation by Michael Cooperson of *L'Auteur et ses Doubles* (New York: Syracuse University Press, 2001 [1985]), p. 16.
2. Ibid. p. 15.
3. Ibid. pp. 68–70.
4. Jamal al-Ghitani, *Muntaha Talab ila Turath al-ʿArab: Dirasat fi'l-Turath* (Cairo: Dar al-Shuruq, 1997), p. 5.
5. Heinrich F. Plett, 'Intertextualities', in Heinrich F. Plett (ed.), *Intertextuality* (New York and Berlin: De Gruyter, 1991), p. 27.
6. Taha Husayn, *Ahlam Shahrazad* (1943), Tawfiq al-Hakim, *Shahrazad* (1934, play). Hakim and Husayn, *Al-Qasr al-Mashur* (1935, novel).
7. A selection of studies of *Awlad Haratina* include: Philip Stewart, 'Introduction', in *Children of Gebelawi* (London: Heinemann, 1981), pp. vii–xxi; Ayman El-Desouky, 'Heterologies of Revolutionary Action: On Historical Consciousness and the Sacred in Mahfouz's *Children of the Alley*', *Journal of Postcolonial Writing*, vol. 47, no. 4 (2011), pp. 428–39; Richard Jacquemond, 'Thawrat al-Takhyil wa Takhyil al-Thawra: Qiraʾa Jadida fi *Awlad Haratina*', *Alif: Journal of Comparative Poetics*, vol. 23 (2003), pp. 118–32; Nabil Matar, 'Christ and the Abrahamic Legacy in *Children of the Alley*', in Waïl Hassan and Susan Muaddi Darraj (eds), *Approaches to Teaching the Works of Naguib*

Mahfouz (New York: The Modern Language Association of America, 2012), pp. 144–55; Sasson Somekh, 'The Sad Millenarian: An Examination of *Awlad Haratina*', *Middle Eastern Studies*, vol. 7 (January 1971), pp. 49–61; George Tarabishi, *Allah fi Rihlat Najib Mahfuz al-Ramziyya* (Beirut: Dar al-Taliʿa li'l-Tibaʿa wa'l-Nashr, 1978). See also Fauzi M. Najjar, 'Islamic Fundamentalism and the Intellectual: The Case of Naguib Mahfouz', *British Journal of Middle Eastern Studies*, vol. 25 (1998), pp. 139–68.

8. Genette defines his category of hypertextuality as 'any relationship uniting a text B ... to an earlier text A ... upon which it is grafted in a manner that is not that of commentary'. Gérard Genette, *Palimpsests: Literature in the Second Degree*, trans. Channa Newman and Claude Doubinsky (Lincoln and London: University of Nebraska Press, 1997), p. 5.

9. See Ouyang, 'The Dialectic of Past and Present in *Rihlat Ibn Fattuma* by Najib Mahfuz', *Edebiyat: Journal of Middle Eastern Literatures*, vol. 14, nos 1–2 (2003), pp. 81–107.

10. Jamal al-Ghitani, 'Intertextual Dialectics', trans. Samia Mehrez, in Ferial J. Ghazoul and Barbara Harlow (eds), *The View from Within: Writers and Critics on Contemporary Arabic Literature* (Cairo: American University in Cairo Press, 1994), pp. 20–1. This essay originally appeared in *Alif*, vol. 4 (1984).

11. I refer here to the 1979 printing (Cairo: Dar al-Shuruq). Translations my own, with corresponding page numbers from the English translation by Farouk Abdel Wahab, *Zayni Barakat* (London: Penguin, 1990 [1988]). Studies on *Al-Zayni Barakat* include: ʿAbd al-Salam al-Kakili, *Al-Zaman al-Riwaʾi: Jadaliyyat al-Madi wa'l-Hadir ʿind Jamal al-Ghitani min Khilal al-Zayni Barakat wa Kitab al-Tajalliyyat* (Cairo: Madbuli, 1992); Samia Mehrez, 'Al-Zayni Barakat: Narrative as Strategy', *Arab Studies Quarterly*, vol. 8, no. 2 (Spring 1986), pp. 120–42; Ouyang, *Politics of Nostalgia in the Arabic Novel* (Edinburgh: Edinburgh University Press, 2013), pp. 202–19.

12. Examples include *Al-Zayni Barakat* (1974), *Khitat al-Ghitani* (1980), *Kitab al-Tajalliyat* (1983–6), *Hatif al-Maghrib* (1992), *Mutun al-Ahram* (1994).

13. On the historical figure of Zayni Barakat in Ibn Iyas' chronicle, see Carl Petry, *Protectors or Praetorians: The Last Mamluk Sultans and Egypt's Waning as a Great Power* (New York: State University of New York Press, 1994), pp. 145–7.

14. See e.g. Mehrez, 'Al-Zayni Barakat', pp. 124–5.

15. Genette's typology of intertextuality, which he calls transtextuality, is set out in *Palimpsests* (see note 8).

16. *Al-Zayni*, p. 25 (trans., p. 19).
17. Ibid. p. 126 (trans., p. 107).
18. Ibid. p. 80 (trans., p. 67).
19. Ibid. p. 45 (trans., p. 38).
20. Linda Hutcheon, 'The Politics of Postmodernism: Parody and History', *Cultural Critique*, no. 5: Modernity and Modernism, Postmodernity and Postmodernism (Winter 1986–7), p. 185.
21. Al-Musawi, *Islam on the Street*, p. 164. See his full analysis of the novel, pp. 155–72.
22. *Al-Zayni*, pp. 67–9 (trans., pp. 57–8).
23. Ibid. p. 96 (trans., p. 83).
24. I refer here to the Maktabat Misr 1985 printing, trans. Catherine Cobham, *The Harafish* (London and New York: Doubleday, 1993). For some studies of the novel, see Cobham, 'Enchanted to a Stone: Heroes and Leaders in *The Harafish* by Najib Mahfuz', *Middle Eastern Literatures*, vol. 9, no. 2 (2006), pp. 123–35; M. M. Badawi, 'Mamlakat al-Harafish: Dirasat fi Malhamat al-Harafish', *Fusul*, vol. 17, no. 1 (Summer 1998), pp. 97–124; Qayid Diyab, 'Al-Mas'ala al-Mitafisiqiyya fi'l-Harafish, *Fusul*, vol. 69 (Summer–Autumn), pp. 124–35; Christina Phillips, 'An Attempt to Apply Gérard Genette's Model of Hypertextuality to Najib Mahfuz's Malhamat al-Harafish', *Middle Eastern Literatures*, vol. 11, no. 3, pp. 283–300; Yahya al-Rakhawi, 'Dawrat al-Hayat wa Dalal al-Khulud: Malhamat al-Mawt wa'l-Takhalluq fi'l-Harafish', in Faruq ʿAbd al-Mu'ti (ed.), *Najib Mahfuz: Bayn al-Riwaya wa'l-Adab al-Riwaya* (Beirut: Dar al-Kutub al-ʿIlmiyya, 1994), pp. 164–235. The word 'harafish' refers to the riffraff or Cairo's urban poor in historical sources and was adopted by Mahfuz and his friends to designate their circle. See William M. Brinner, 'The Significance of the Harafish and their "Sultan"', *Journal of the Economic and Social History of the Orient*, vol. 6, no. 2 (July 1963), pp. 190–215.
25. El-Desouky, 'Heterologies of Revolutionary Action' (see note 7 for full reference).
26. *Harafish*, p. 53 (trans., p. 34).
27. El-Desouky, 'Heterologies of Revolutionary Action', p. 433.
28. See Phillips, 'An Attempt to Apply Gérard Genette's Model of Hypertextuality', pp. 288–9.
29. Al-Musawi also notes the prophetic symbolism of ʿAshur, as well as a Sufi element, and further reads the emergence of his descendent, the second ʿAshur, in terms of the Shia Mahdi tradition. See *Islam on the Street*, pp. 125–51.

30. Phillips, 'An Attempt to Apply Gérard Genette's Model of Hypertextuality' (see note 24 for full reference).
31. *Harafish*, p. 71 (trans., p. 47).
32. El-Enany notes this similarity in *Pursuit of Meaning*, p. 156, and writes that ᶜAshur's attachment to the *takiyya, khalāʾ* and admiration for female beauty are attributes that would also fit the Prophet.
33. On ᶜAbd al-Hakim Qasim and his work, see Hafez, *Suradiqat min Waraq*, pp. 70–83; Hilary Kilpatrick, 'ᶜAbd al-Hakim Qasim and the Search for Liberation', *Journal of Arabic Literature*, vol. 26 (1995), pp. 50–66; Phillips, 'ᶜAbd al-Hakim Qasim', in Majd Yaser al-Mallah (ed.), *Dictionary of Literary Biography: Twentieth Century Arabic Writers* (New York: Bruccoli Clark Layman, Inc, 2008), pp. 198–202.
34. I refer here to the text of *Al-Mahdi* printed in *Al-Riwayat al-Qasira* (Cairo: Dar al-Shuruk, 1985), pp. 8–68. Translations my own, with corresponding page numbers from the English translation by Peter Theroux, *Rites of Assent: Two Novellas* (Philadelphia: Temple University Press, 1995).
35. *Al-Mahdi*, p. 10 (trans., p. 4).
36. René Girard, *Deceit, Desire and the Novel: Self and Other in Literary Structure*, trans. Yvonne Freccero (Baltimore and London: The Johns Hopkins University Press, 1966 [1961: *Mensonge romantique et erité Romanesque*), p. 10.
37. Girard, 'Mimesis and Violence', in James G. Williams (ed.), *The Girard Reader* (New York: Crossroad Publishing Company, 1996), p. 14.
38. Girard, 'Sacrifice as Sacral Violence and Substitution', in Williams, *The Girard Reader*, p. 73.
39. Ibid. p. 81.
40. *Al-Mahdi*, p. 56 (trans., p. 50).
41. Ibid. p. 60 (trans., p. 54).
42. Ibid. p. 61 (trans., p. 56).
43. Ibid. 62 (trans., pp. 56–7).
44. Ibid. p. 62 (trans., p. 57).
45. Ibid. p. 67 (trans., p. 62).
46. I refer to a 1986 edition (Cairo: al-Haᶜyat al-Misriyya al-ᶜAmma li'l-Kitab). Translations my own with corresponding page numbers to Theroux, *Rites of Assent*.
47. Sources include Abu Hamid al-Ghazali, *Al-Durra al-Fakhira*; Jalal al-Din Suyuti, *Bushra al-Kaʾib bi Liqaʾ al-Habib*; Abu Layth al-Samarqandi, *Kitab al-Haqaʾiq wa'l-Daqaʾiq*; and an anonymous text entitled *Kitab Ahwal al-Qiyama*. See

Jane I. Smith and Yvonne Y. Haddad, *The Islamic Understanding of Death and Resurrection* (Albany: State University of New York Press, 1981), ch. 2: 'From Death to Resurrection: Classical Islam', pp. 31–61. See also Sachiko Murata and William C. Chittick, *The Vision of Islam* (London and New York: I. B. Tauris, 1994), ch. 5, 'The Return', pp. 193–235.

48. In some accounts four angels are mentioned. The names Munkar and Nakir are not Qur'anic and appear rarely in canonical traditions. Smith and Haddad, *The Islamic Understanding of Death*, p. 41.
49. Ibid. p. 43. See also Jane I. Smith, *The Precious Pearl: A Translation from the Arabic with Notes of the Kitab al-Durra al-Fakhira fi Kashf ʿUlum al-Akhira of Abu Hamid Muhammad b. Muhammad b. Muhammad al-Ghazali* (Missoula, MT: Scholars Press, 1979).
50. *Turaf*, p. 45 (trans., p. 103).
51. Ibid. p. 47. The angels are not talking about motive (*hikma*) in an abstract sense but 'the motive of a specific deed in specific circumstances'. Theroux's translation, p. 105.
52. Ibid. p. 48 (trans., p. 107).
53. Ibid. p. 60 (trans., p. 121).
54. Ibid. p. 51 (trans., p. 110).
55. Ibid. p. 62 (trans., p. 124).
56. Ibid. p. 53 (trans., p. 114).
57. Ibid. p. 81; Theroux's translation, p. 147.
58. Ibid. p. 100 (trans., p. 165).
59. 'Don't you know how to express your love for a woman other than through sexual relations with her?' Ibid. p. 74 (trans., 137).
60. Ibid. p. 107. 'She told him that she was free of her husband, she felt her soul was free and liberated' (Theroux's translation, p. 171).
61. See Leah Kinberg, 'Interaction between this World and the Afterworld in Early Islamic Tradition', *Oriens*, vol. 29 (1986), pp. 285–308. See also Jane I. Smith, 'Concourse between the Living and the Dead in Islamic Eschatological Literature', *History of Religions*, vol. 19, no. 3 (February 1980), pp. 224–36; Ibn Abi al-Dunya and Leah Kinberg, *Morality in the Guise of Dreams: A Critical Edition of Kitab al-Manam with Introduction* (Leiden and New York: Brill, 1994).
62. Kinberg, 'Interaction between this World and the Afterworld', p. 296.
63. Ibid. pp. 296ff.

6

The Coptic Theme

The story of the Copts is integral to the story of Egypt. They are the original inhabitants of the country, who converted to Christianity during the Roman period whilst preserving certain aspects of Pharoanic heritage, including an ancient language.[1] Although today the Copts make up around ten per cent of the population, they were once the majority (until the tenth century) and their contribution to Egyptian life past and present is wide and varied, ranging from a distinctive art, ancient textiles and monasteries to modern-day business and commerce, medicine, pharmaceuticals and tourism.[2] Yet it is politics and tensions with the country's Muslim majority that dominates their story in the modern era. As Islamic elements have sought to seize the agenda at various points over the past hundred years, the Coptic community has frequently found itself under attack, both verbally and physically.

The 1920s, the decade of liberal nationalism, saw Muslims and Christians uniting under the banner of 'Egypt first' and working together against British imperialism. There were Coptic ministers in the new Wafdist government and national identity trumped religious and ethnic ties for a time. The Copts opposed Britain's right to protect them, as a minority, in the 1922 treaty and many rejected the possibility of proportional representation when it was proposed. However, in the 1930s, as the Wafd failed to deliver on its promises and Egypt's economy continued to suffer from foreign exploitation, religious and semi-religious groups promoting Islam as the solution to society's problems gained momentum. The Muslim Brotherhood, whose programme of Islamic reform at the time supported the classification of Egypt's Christians as *ahl al-dhimma* (protected people), harking back to the caliphate, was successful in recruiting disillusioned Wafd supporters and instrumental in escalating tension between Muslims and Copts in the 1940s. The Brothers accused the

Wafd of hostility to Islam and, along with the Liberal Constitutionalists, who as mentioned attempted to turn the resurgence of religious feeling to their political advantage, made claims about its pro-Christian agenda. Their emotive rhetoric led to the desecration of churches, attacks on priests and sabotage of Christian funerals, weddings and religious processions in the 1940s, in particular in Upper Egypt. The Brotherhood was banned in 1948 and Nasser's presidency represented a period of relative peace for Egypt's minorities, even as pan-Arabism threatened Coptic identity. The Copts also suffered from the president's nationalisation policy, which saw a large proportion of Coptic land confiscated and redistributed to Muslims, though the intention was not to punish but coincidental – it was a socialist, not a religious, policy which applied to all large landowners in the country. The Islamic revival that followed the Arab–Israeli War of 1967 and flourished under Sadat marks the beginning of a sharp downward trajectory for the Copts which is yet to be reversed. The 1970s witnessed considerable communal strife, beginning with arson attacks in Khanka in 1972 and spreading to Cairo where riots broke out in al-Zawiya al-Hamra in June 1981 resulting in eighty-one Coptic deaths. Sadat was slow to punish the perpetrators and further provoked Egypt's Christians by sending Pope Shenuda III into exile in September 1981, after he embarrassed the president by cancelling Easter celebrations and banning Coptic pilgrimage to Jerusalem in response to Camp David. By the time Mubarak came to power, Christian–Muslim relations in Egypt had reached an all-time low. Mubarak, though he released clergymen from prison and reinstated Shenuda (January 1985), was unable to contain religious tensions resulting from the pressures of radical Islam and his presidency witnessed a number of incidents, including multiple killings in Manfalout (1990), Imbaba (1991), Manshia (1992), al Kossia (1994), Abu Qurqas (1997), Kosheh (1998), Alexandria (2005) and Nagi Hammadi (2010). The fall of Mubarak and his regime in 2011 and the Arab Spring, despite early optimism, unleashed further suffering upon Copts. Mob violence against Christians became common as the state apparatus collapsed, with numerous reports of murders and kidnappings. Notable incidents include a bombing in Alexandria (January 2011), church attacks in Imbaba (May 2011), the Maspero massacre (May 2011), mass looting and torching of churches (August 2013), incidents in the Sinai (February 2017) and suicide bombs in churches in Alexandria and Tanta with multiple fatalities (April 2017). After a century of troubles, the current situation for the Copts does not give much cause for hope.³

In view of the above it is hardly surprising that when the Coptic theme appears in the Egyptian novel it is often the relationship between Muslims and Copts that is at issue. At the turn of the twentieth century it was possible for a Muslim writer, ʿAbd al-Hamid Khidr Albu Qurqasi, to depict a Christian community in and of itself in his short embryonic novel *Al-Qisas Hayat* (1905), but by the second half of the century community tension and the contested status of the Copts could no longer be ignored.⁴ *Al-Mahdi*, as seen, explores the dangerous potential of Islamic fundamentalism and appropriately casts a Copt as its most unfortunate victim. Other novels depict friendship and cooperation between Copts and Muslims, as though to remind of the human stories behind sectarian tension and to urgently make space for Christians in the national imaginary. *Khalati Safiyya waʾl-Dayr* (1991) is one such work.⁵ Its author, Bahaʾ Tahir, was born in 1935 and published his first set of short stories, *Al-Khutuba*, in 1972. He is another key figure of *jil al-sittinat*,⁶ who tends to employ the realist mode, subverting it from within as per al-Kharrat's description of *al-tayyār al-wāqiʿī al-jadīd*.⁷ *Khalati* tells the story of a village in Upper Egypt in the period leading up to and following the Six-Day War with Israel and of a remarkable pact between a Muslim village and Christian monastery to thwart the blood vendetta of the narrator's cousin, Safiyya, against another cousin, Harbi.⁸ It is narrated in the first person by a boy who is involved in the events but only passively and whose youth and inexperience provides for a simple style of narration, which in turn creates the impression of simple village life and simpler times, though this is not without irony since events in the story run counter to the benign imagery; discourse and reality do not necessarily correspond in this short work. *Khalati* severs the link between character and milieu expressive of the *Bildungsroman*. As the narrative moves through its various episodes, so the narrator perceptibly moves through different stages of his education, but the two do not take place in dialogue with one another. The learning experience and expanding horizon of the narrator is not an expression or reflection of village or national progress, as for example in *Al-Ayyam*, but rather a parody of it. The symbolic value of the education trajectory so integral to the early Egyptian novel and its national allegory is here elided and the ideology of progress that accompanies it is subverted. *Khalati* is a late twentieth-century reimagining of the village novel, introduced by Haykal with an urban intellectual viewpoint and reoriented towards *fellāḥ*-consciousness by al-Sharqawi, with its enlightenment themes and positive national trajectory. While in *Zaynab* and *Al-Ard* the significant divisions in society are concentrated in class, and religious identity is displaced by territorial belonging and shared history, sacred affiliation is the foremost marker of identity in *Khalati* and it is precisely through this that the dialectic of nation is worked. Al-Musawi's observation that secularism has not necessarily extended to rural Egypt is well-attested here and there is little sense that religion might be relegated or superseded.[9] In this context the question becomes how to manage religious difference, not erase it; how to unite and cooperate for the common good in spite of division. Here again, the narrative moves in two directions, installing an image of cooperation whilst at the same time sabotaging it.

On the face of it *Khalati* reads as an allegory of Muslim–Coptic partnership. In the opening chapters the narrator paints a portrait of a close-knit community which has good relations with the monks of the monastery situated on its outskirts. The village has a mythical flavour, living off stories and inhabiting a realm beyond modern signs and signifiers, so that distance is measured not in kilometres but duration on foot or mount and time is marked by Coptic and Muslim feast days. It is in this primordial space, beyond politics and the metropolis, that cross-sectarian friendship can flourish. The villagers and monks exchange gifts and hospitality and work together when a family dispute threatens the rural peace. When Safiyya marries the Bey and falls pregnant, rumours circulate that Harbi plans to kill the child to protect his inheritance, as he is the Bey's nephew. The Bey grows paranoid and hunts him down, torturing him until the nephew turns the gun on his uncle. Thus a blood feud is born between Safiyya and Harbi, but forestalled by an alliance between the village's Copts and Muslims. When Harbi returns from prison he is taken by the narrator's father to live in the monastery under the protection of Miqaddis Bishay, an eccentric monk who provides him with food and shelter and who is thoroughly loyal to the village, such that he aligns himself with his Muslim neighbours over his co-religionists from abroad. He 'was proud of the story of our village as though he had participated in its creation',[10] and sees Christian visitors to Luxor as near traitors in their pagan fetishism and disregard for Christian heritage, 'crowding together and shoving one another and almost killing themselves in the heat and sun to get a glimpse at the statues of heathen idols in the temples of Luxor'.[11] As such Bishay prefers local myth to the Pharoanic heritage celebrated in the narrative of territorial nationalist and Coptic identity. The alliance is a success insofar as Harbi lives in relative peace in the monastery, receiving a stream of daily visitors, and eventually dies there from illness rather than foul play, ending the cycle of bloodshed.

As an example of late twentieth-century Egyptian fiction and response to deteriorating community relations and fragmented national imaginary, there is naturally more to *Khalati* than positive allegory. For a start, religious tolerance applies only to Muslims and Christians. When Egypt's sovereignty is under threat and Muslims and Christians unite under the banner of Mother Egypt and Arab unity, reliving the real-life events of 1967, contradictions begin to emerge. The mechanism for unity and cooperation here is a common enemy defined by its creed. The Arab–Israeli conflict is cast as a religious conflict more than a battle of nations. The enemy is the Jews, more than the Israelis, revealing incongruence in the narrative of nation and an as yet unresolved problem of religious identity. The topography and viewpoint, moreover, signal a more complicated and fragile situation than emerges from a superficial reading of the allegory. The monastery is situated at a distance from the village and surrounded by high walls. It is reached by a dirt road but the traffic between the village and monastery decreases, first because the route is disrupted by bandits and ultimately because it is unsuitable for motor vehicles, which take over as the main means of transport. In other words, the Coptic monks occupy the fringes and are increasingly cut off from the Muslim village mainstream. Outside intervention (the bandits) and modern technology (cars) create a schism; past friendship becomes future dislocation. Marginalisation also describes the textual presence of Miqqadis Bishay. The first chapter takes him as its subject and devotes some time to the character, creating a degree of expectation about his centrality to the story. But he barely features in the following long chapter ('My Aunt Safiyya') and, though he continues to be a key personage, he is marginalised to the extent that he appears only infrequently and is only ever viewed through the eyes of the

(Muslim) narrator. In other words, he is not allowed to speak for himself. And when his discourse is found to be at odds with the new monastery leadership, he is silenced completely. The irony here is that it is his own people who effect this, enlisting the help of the narrator's father who, along with the rest of the villagers, is reluctant to see Bishay go. Bishay's outsider status, which within his own group derives from the fact that he is a layman amongst the monks and an eccentric, signals the flaw in the alliance from the outset, that it is not the organic product of flourishing Muslim–Copt relations but the work of two extraordinary individuals, neither of whom fully represent their communities, for the narrator's father too stands apart from the village majority insofar as he adopts non-village practices, like educating his daughters, and is generally speaking working towards a different future, as is clear from his exchanges with his son.

Certainly as the narrative proceeds the prospect of continued Muslim–Copt unity and cooperation becomes less likely. Sometime after Harbi takes up residence in the monastery a group of bandits arrive. These men follow a strict if warped moral code and position themselves as protectors of Harbi and the monastery, and as defenders of the nation when the possibility of fighting Israel is raised. But there is dissent among their ranks and a Christian member, Hinayn, is expelled and joins forces with Safiyya and violates the monastery by attacking Harbi within its sacred precincts. The episode prompts Father Maximus, the new monastery head, to begin the process of withdrawing the monks' protection, though as it happens Harbi dies before the decision is acted upon, thereby ending the blood vendetta. Thus the title of the penultimate chapter, 'Al-Naksa', refers to the decline in Muslim–Christian relations in the village as much as to the Israeli invasion. And this *naksa* is significantly instigated by a Copt, which lays the blame for the unravelling of the pact in Christian hands. The text's symbolism corroborates this conclusion and introduces a further possibility. Hinayn is symbolically cast as Judas. Miqaddis Bishay refers to him as such and washes his wound and leg just as Jesus washed the feet of Judas at the Last Supper. If Hinayn is Judas then Bishay, kneeling at the feet of the traitor, becomes the messiah and the man betrayed, as opposed to Harbi or his group. An alternative reading of the later sections of the narrative imagines Bishay as the victim of Hinayn's actions, a prophet betrayed by one of his own.

Good relations between Muslims and Copts and the minority theme are also at issue in Ibrahim ʿAbd al-Majid's *La Ahad Yanam fi'l-Iskandariyya* (1996)[12] and Idwar al-Kharrat's *Turabuha Zaʿfaran* (1986).[13] The former, although hailed by some critics as a portrait of positive inter-religious exchange, suggests a similarly fragile situation. Like *Khalati*, it depicts a special friendship between a Muslim and a Copt, but this is set within a wider context of intercommunal tension and strife. Deborah Starr proposes that the novel represents 'not an idealised model of coexistence, but rather a cosmopolitan, pluralist nationalism forged through interethnic conflict'.[14] Siddiq arrives at a similar conclusion, noting that individual love and friendship relations emerge as 'the only viable substitutes for the atrophied civil, political, and geographic motives of unity'.[15] Written by a Copt, the shape and nuance of *Turabuha Zaʿfaran*, on the other hand, is rather different. Harmony with fellow Muslims is here merely one aspect of a broader Coptic experience that the text communicates in a manner which recalls aspects of Deleuze and Guattari's minority discourse, combining a subversive narrative strategy with affirmative identity politics.

Turabuha follows the narrator around Alexandria, and occasionally beyond, during his childhood and youth in the 1930s and 1940s, in so doing painting a rich, eclectic and nostalgic picture of a past era. The narrative has autobiographical elements but these are masked by the assignment of a fictional name, Mikhail Qaldas, to the character, as well as a prefatory statement by the author denying life-writing. Similarly, the possibility of a straightforward identity between the text and existing genre categories is subverted by the subtitle *nuṣūṣ iskandariyya*, a deliberate repudiation of the novelistic label,[16] and by its unconventional format, which satisfies reader expectations for neither novel nor autobiography. The intention is no doubt to test the limits of the reader's *Erwartungshorizon* and mark out a new space in the literary system. As a life story *Turabuha* is incomplete and uneven and as a novel it lacks a ready entry and exit point and flouts literary values like coherence, causality and closure. Instead, we have a series of nine texts (*nuṣūṣ*), which bear a superficial resemblance to chapters but are better described as literary fragments. These fragments in turn consist of smaller fragments, so that the narrative becomes a montage, an assembly of texts held together by memory and an alternative logic of continuities and discontinuities. Memory is of course a favourite device of writers attempting to break away from the causal narrative pattern, with its associations with authority and logic, and is usually combined with other forms of linkage, for to do without is to risk the text's dissolution into non-sense. The linkage is provided here by a variety of themes and motifs, which either manifest throughout the text or are operative for certain parts of it, creating a network of relations which, through a pattern of overlaps, hold the work together. For example, the image of the protagonist travelling across the city recurs and, along with a steady reference to place names, keeps the Alexandrian setting at the forefront. A fascination with script, Arabic, Greek and Coptic, expands the text's reference beyond the local and anchors it in a wider Arab, Mediterranean and ancient Egyptian tradition. Coupled with frequent allusion to European, Arabic and religious books and characters, the script motif contributes to the impression of a world of intersecting cultures. Baking is another recurrent motif and, having been linked to an age of purity in the opening pages, harks back to this time whenever it occurs, underlining the distance between the narrative past and narrating present, which are both shifting. Other motifs include death, the vine trellis and modern transport, which each carry their own meanings and associations. At the same time, themes of education, sexual awakening, love of women and politics are developed as the narrative follows the protagonist around the city and, along with the motifs, lend the narrative a degree of psychological coherence in compensation for what it lacks in the way of conventional logic.

The themes and motifs in *Turabuha* are, for the most part, particular to the narrator; they belong to his individual memory and private experience and in this sense produce a highly subjective work. But there are two areas of experience which the protagonist shares with other characters and which, by subsuming the individual into the larger community, transform his story into a collective enunciation.[17] The first of these is the experience of being a Copt in a predominantly Muslim country.

The Coptic theme is introduced early in the first *naṣṣ* where difference between the narrator's Christian mother and Muslim neighbour is balanced by shared affection for Jesus and a close friendship. From this moment, the Coptic identity of the protagonist and his family and the idea of inter-religious friendship and tolerance are foregrounded. The boy attends a Coptic school, receives special religious instruction and spends his holidays at Bible camp. His mother swears by Christ and the cross frequently and his father barely utters a sentence that does not include divine reference. The parents' speech patterns leave the reader in little doubt about their Christian worldview. And if the parents see the world through the eyes of scripture, so too does the son. The protagonist feels an intimate connection with St Mikhail the Archangel, whose name he bears, and views his life as a reliving of Christ's. The strategic positioning of the Bible in the opening pages, the first book mentioned in the text, and the narrator's confession of the profound effect the Passion of Christ had on him at a young age, establishes its formative role in the character's intellectual and emotional development and sets the tone.[18] From this point on scripture functions as an intertext against which the narrator reads his life. The crucifixion becomes a reference point for his romantic suffering and the resurrection an alternative vision of death. On three separate occasions he pictures himself wounded in his side by a lance, just as Christ's side was pierced as he hung on the cross.[19] Two of these are coupled with an image of death. But the narrator's death is a conscious one; cognition extends beyond annihilation – 'he knew he had been killed'.[20] Elsewhere he pictures his namesake St Mikhail rolling back the stone from Christ's tomb, augmenting the gospel account, for an angel is mentioned only in Mark and John and neither specifies the angel's identity.[21] Could the narrator be using the connection between the character and archangel to suggest a different end for the protagonist, a re-entry into the world facilitated by his guardian angel? Do we have here an expression of faith in an afterlife to mitigate the abrupt endings of some of the characters? Are the extraordinary attributes implied by this and the St Mikhail connection part of the portrait of an artist? The intertextuality is ultimately unresolved, and there is a degree of thematic nihilism here, a deliberate thwarting of meaning with no discernible intent, but at the very least the intertextuality conveys the extent to which the protagonist is immersed in Christian theology and foregrounds the spiritual heritage of the Copts, the alternative history of Egypt's Christian minority.

Temporal and topographical reference is another conduit of the Coptic theme. Narrative time is for the most part Coptic time, represented either by the Coptic calendar or in the form of Coptic feasts and celebrations. Many scenes and episodes revolve around events in the Coptic calendar. The memorable trip to the oil press and Uncle Hanna's house, which provides an extended insight into the child's sensual world as well as the life of the family, is really a recollection of the preparation and celebration of the Feast of the Archangel St Mikhail. The effect is to subsume the narrative into a Coptic temporality, even if secular or political time retains a background presence. Similarly, references to Christian landmarks like St. Catherine's Church, the Greek Orthodox Church, the red stone Evangelical Church, Shatbi cemetery, and al-Karma Orthodox Coptic Kindergarten and Primary School create an alternative topography based on religious sites and accentuates the Coptic heritage of Alexandria.

Meanwhile a theme of religious tolerance is developed. Alexandria is portrayed as a cosmopolitan city, where people from every denomination and background mix with each other on a daily basis, and an image of cooperation and good will between Christians and Muslims is drawn.[22] At the Abbasiyya Secondary School, where there is a Muslim majority, food is offered on Christian feast days as well as Ramadan. Mikhail's mother and her Muslim neighbours exchange pastries and other dishes on Easter, Ashura, Eid al-Adha, Christmas and other religious festivals. The narrator recalls how Copts and Muslims would go around together on the nights of Ramadan, carrying lanterns and singing.[23] The Qur'an even functions as an instrument of reconciliation between Mikhail and his bullies at primary school, when he explains the meaning of a *sūra* to the boys who have been teasing him.[24] The portrait of religious tolerance is no doubt idealistic, for the frequency with which it is repeated implies that the status quo is not a given. The act of repetition betrays a degree of anxiety and confirms that the object or idea is not in the order of things and must therefore be constantly inscribed and reiterated. The recent history of the Copts of course leads to the same conclusion. Nor should it be assumed that the protagonist's Coptic identity is unproblematic. Apart from the impression made on the boy by the Bible and stories about St Mikhail, we have little information about the character's faith, and what we do have suggests that it is uncertain. As he enters young adulthood he is caught between sexual urges and puritanical tendencies, the latter based more on habit and upbringing than on religious belief: 'I was eighteen, uncertain about faith, strong in piety, drowning in my body but puritanical, and I'd never been with a woman'.[25] The absence of conviction perhaps explains his anger and depression at the sight of the Muslim workers at the Navy Depot spreading out their prayer mats at dawn.[26] He is also displeased at being separated from the Muslim boys for religious instruction, since he is himself drawn to the music of the Qur'an.[27] The Qur'an has an artistic appeal that transcends religious division and the narrator's Christianity is evidently more a cultural than a spiritual identity, a social more than a religious reality, even if the Passion of Christ and narrative of St Mikhail have a profound effect on him *as story*. If the protagonist is ideologically committed to anything it is the Egyptian struggle for independence, as is clear from his clandestine political activities, membership of a revolutionary group and willingness to undergo incarceration for these convictions, a detail which becomes even more apparent in *Ya Banat Iskandariyya* (1990), which reads as a kind of sequel to *Turabuha*.

Commitment to Egypt's future accounts for and compliments some of the Coptic theme in *Turabuha*. Behind the Coptic narrative – the Christian scriptural reference and Coptic level of experience – is the story of the nation. References are indirect and subtly integrated into the personal story, but a nationalist theme is nevertheless developed alongside the Coptic and other themes, represented in overheard political discussions, the character's political activism, and the event of the Second World War, which affects Christians and Muslims alike. The latter becomes a signifier of common experience and purpose when, following an air raid, both faiths come together to mourn the victims and interpret the survival of Abu'l-Dardar's tomb as a divine miracle. It is also noteworthy that World War II is one of the few events provided with a date outside of the Coptic calendar. The wider nation narrative in the background frames the Coptic narrative and explains some of its features.

In the preceding chapters we saw a good deal of criticism directed at religious institutions and traditions on the part of Egyptian authors of Muslim background. *Turabuha*, on the other hand, is not interested in religious critique. The Coptic headmaster may have a mean side in the boy's eyes, but on the whole the Church is portrayed as a supporting force, as the case of Uncle Maqar demonstrates.[28] Religious rituals and institutions are brought in not to be criticised but as a means of detailing and asserting an alternative experience within the wider life of the nation. In other words, the positive portrayal of the Christian Church, alongside the assertion of Coptic religion as a cultural identity, is an effect of the narrator and author's minority status within a broadly Muslim society. Religious criticism is easy from a dominant subject position, but when speaking from the margins reform and critique come second to recognition and survival, for within the discourse of the nation the minority voice must assert itself or risk assimilation.

The issue of minority status is pertinent to narrative strategy. *Turabuha* sits at the more extreme end of post-1967 literary experimentation and the author's long-standing commitment to aesthetic radicalism, after many 60s generation writers reverted to more conventional themes or limited their experimentation to post-realism, may well be to do with his Coptic identity. Jacquemond notes a readiness among Coptic artists to adopt styles outside the realist mainstream, with Yusuf al-Sharuni (b. 1924), Naʿim ʿAtiya (b. 1927) and Nabil Naʿum (b. 1944) as other examples within the realm of prose.[29] Less able to gain status as major intellectuals, this group has tended towards cosmopolitanism in art and literature, though al-Kharrat himself has not struggled for literary status.[30] There is also a notable correlation between *Turabuha* and Deleuze and Guattari's concept of minor literature as a textual strategy that 'produces an active solidarity in spite of skepticism'.[31] *Turabuha* exceeds the destructive tendency of *al-ḥassasiyya al-jadida* as an avant-garde movement in its positive expression of Coptic identity. While Kendall writes that the new literary sensibility partakes in a 'culture of negation',[32] *Turabuha* is as concerned with creating new spaces as it is with upturning the status quo. A minor literature, in Deleuze and Guattari's analysis, is a special kind of writing that works within a major language, subverting it or making it its own: 'We might as well say that minor no longer designates specific literatures but the revolutionary conditions for every literature within the heart of what is called great (or established) literature'.[33] In other words, it is a matter of positionality and involves the writer adopting a particular stance with respect to the mainstream, challenging notions of genre, canon, value, language, and so on. So far this sounds very much like *al-ḥassasiyya al-jadida* as described by al-Kharrat himself. But what is distinctive about minor literature is that its challenge is effected with a view to opening new spaces and mapping new realities – and this is what we see in *Turabuha*. The text revolts against conventional narrative and the discourse of the nation but it also consciously creates new possibilities and spaces. Its subtitle and structure, along with its blend of fiction and autobiography, confounds the existing genres of *riwāya* and *sīrat dhatiyya*, and its highly sensual and highly subjective language, which includes colloquial in places, is a rejection of formal literary language and expectations surrounding it; it is an individualised, *minor* use of Arabic. The use of the first person and role of memory in governing the content and arrangement of the text challenges objective narrative voices and unitary discourse, and the subject's identity as a Copt and locus as Alexandria confronts accounts of the Egyptian nation, which are happy to acknowledge Pharoanic heritage but habitually ignore Egypt's Christian history and which tend to be Cairo-centric. A comparison with the trilogy is instructive. Mahfuz's magnum opus tells the story of modern Egypt from a dominant subject position and, conventionally structured and narrated, purports to speak for everyone. Its one Coptic representative, Riyad Qaldas, is a secondary character on the fringes of the action whilst its protagonist Kamal, whose journey of self-discovery represents that of a whole generation, exchanges religious identity and sympathies for a secular worldview. *Turabuha* repositions this story in a Coptic Alexandrian trajectory whilst foregrounding the subjective nature of discourse – there is no omniscience here. Moreover, religious identity is not shed but preserved and reimagined as a cultural experience and signifier. The latter detail exemplifies the constructive thrust of the text, that is, the reterritorialisation that accompanies its iconoclastic endeavour. Similarly, the subversion of existing genres referred to above is twinned with the creation of a new one – *nuṣūṣ iskandariyya* – and the challenge to dominant discourse and mainstream accounts of the nation and its history is compensated by the creation of a new space wherein emerges the voice of the Copt and individual. As an example of minor literature, the text negates to create.

The minority element has significance beyond *Turabuha* and becomes a critical trope in the post-1967 post-realist context, when national history and Egyptian identity are up for debate once more and grand narratives are readily attacked and deconstructed. The minority character of the Copts, which has historically involved their marginalisation, not least because the history of Egypt and the caliphate has been written for the most part by Arabs and Muslims, makes them an attractive subject for writers who may not themselves be Copts but who find in them a useful means for challenging mainstream discourse and authority. Abu Deeb, as discussed, identifies a gravitation towards minority voices in Arabic literature in the later decades of the twentieth century as the ideologies and identities that held sway in the 1950s and 1960s – Arab, socialist, anti-imperialist, secular – lost credibility.[34] Hutcheon speaks of the same phenomenon in postmodernism, which is another way of thinking about the post-1967 Egyptian novel.[35] She writes that 'The local, the regional, the non-totalising are reasserted as the center becomes a fiction'.[36] The Copts, with their minority status and history of persecution, represent an ideal symbol of marginalised discourse for writers seeking to expose totalising narratives, including the narrative of nation. *Al-Bashmuri* (1998, 2002) by Salwa Bakr (b. 1949) is an example of this.[37]

Al-Bashmuri, the author's fifth novel, is the story of a Copt named Budayr whose accidental involvement with the Bashmuri uprising of 830–2 CE[38] results in him embarking on a journey of self-discovery that takes him around the centres of medieval Islam and Christianity. The story is told in the first person and filtered through Budayr, whose antihero quality and, in particular, his historical obscurity offer a fresh perspective on this period, as well as a radical rereading of the Muslim conquest of Egypt. The text begins in the Coptic realm, at the Church of Qasr al-Sham in Cairo, where Budayr serves as a sexton. In the early part of the novel we are told how he came to this position, having fled from scandal and heartbreak, and are given a good idea of his piety and the piety of the priests around him. Coptic ritual is described in minute detail – the kneading of the Eucharist bread, the ritual washing of baking utensils in pure water, the recitation of psalms, the ceremonial greeting to the archdeacon and deacons, the cleaning and arrangement of instruments on the alter, the various ecclesiastical vestments worn by the clergy, the order of prayer and mass, ritual ablutions, and so on. And the narrative, as the author states, is written 'with a Coptic tint',[39] which further authenticates the medieval Coptic experience enshrined in the text and indicates its peculiarity. This Coptic experience is situated in an historical trajectory that runs back to Pharaonic Egypt via the Old and New Testament, as suggested by various references, including in the dialogue of Thawna, who as a pagan-turned-Christian brings together the old and the new and represents the cultural and civilisational mix of the Egyptian Copt, whilst at the same time embodying the ancestral line that links the Copts to the ancient Egyptians. For example, his style of drawing he describes as 'one of the ancient methods inherited by Coptic artists',[40] and it is him who alerts Budayr to the architectural debt of the Coptic Church and indeed Islam to ancient Egypt.[41] The narrative is also situated in a concrete geographical and social context, with place names and the presence of other communities properly detailed, further corroborating a national symbolism.

The Coptic perspective dominates for the first half of the text, which is set in Egypt. The protagonist-narrator is naïve and inexperienced, which serves as a good excuse for him to record every observation he makes on his journey and for the inclusion of much theological and historical exposition, often related second-hand from his mentor Thawna. He travels as Thawna's translator to Bashmur, his original home, to try and convince Mina b. Baqira to halt the uprising that he is leading in the area. Their submissions to Mina, who is significantly portrayed as a brave and noble leader of an oppressed Coptic community, are rejected and when the caliph's army arrives to end the rebellion, Budayr finds himself amongst the caliph's prisoners. He is transported to Antioch, where is abused by a priest, and eventually finds himself in Baghdad, where he is employed in the caliph's kitchen before he is granted his freedom. In Baghdad, Budayr makes friends with Husayn b. Falih, who teaches him Arabic and the Qur'an. As he learns more about the faith he becomes enamoured with it and converts, opting for asceticism in the Sufi mould. Thus in the second half of the narrative Budayr continues his voyage of self-discovery within an Islamic-Sufi framework.

Budayr does not forget his origins, however. Egypt continues to exercise a hold over him and he resolves to return home, albeit only after circumstances have altered such as to necessitate departure and with a digression via Jerusalem. He is particularly concerned to see Thawna again and invite him to Islam. He is also keen to visit the church at Qasr al-Sham, though he never considers turning back to Christianity. Rather he brings his Islam with him to Egypt, just as the Arabs did, in this respect making him a symbol of the wider Islamisation of Egypt in the nineth century and foil to Thawna, who represents its Christianisation. Thawna rejects Budayr's invitation when they are eventually reunited, offering instead a message of religious pluralism: 'Don't you think, Budayr, that God will encompass them in his affection and benevolence irrespective of whether they are Muslims or Copts?'[42] A similar observation is made by Budayr at the time of his conversion:

> I concluded in the end that God is the Lord of all of humanity and that the essence of every religion is simply to guide mankind and encourage him to the path of peace and serenity, and raise his primitive senses to sublime human levels.[43]

Budayr thus departs the monastery with a new equilibrium, the oneness of religion confirmed. The moment is marked by an experience of ecstasy which evokes the moment of complete knowledge at the end of the Sufi path and as such symbolises the completion of his moral and metaphysical quest.

The Coptic theme here, as in *Khalati* and *Turabuha*, has a conciliatory aspect. As the author hopes in her preface to the English translation, the novel underlines 'the profound commonalities shared by Muslims and Copts in Egypt'.[44] There is also, as in *Khalati*, an attempt to portray Muslims and Christians as equally culpable, so that neither occupies the moral high ground.[45] The Christian Copts are represented as persecuted by the Arab Muslims. They are subjected to excessive government levies, 'punished so severely that they have sold their children for land tax (*kharāj*)'.[46] They are forbidden from riding horses by government decree and branded with tattoos for the purposes of taxation.[47] Arab soldiers raid their villages, steal their crops, murder the innocent and kidnap their women and children, all without reaction from the governor.[48] Not even their places of worship are off-bounds. Rather they represent an easy source of revenue for the overlord: 'there is not a single church (*bīʿa*) between Damietta and Rashid ... that has not had its significant effects looted, including chorus symbols and alter vessels ...'.[49] Yet the Copts are no saints. They are guilty of beating and killing pagans and their church is a mainspring of corruption and competition.[50] Apart from the gossip among monks at Qasr al-Sham, they are portrayed as motivated in many instances, including the Bashmuri episode, by hatred of the Melkites, so that internal tensions in the church override wider community interests.[51] At the same time, there are positive Muslim characters to counter the injustice and brutality of the caliph's men, for example the Muslim commander in Egypt who lends Budayr and Thawna his guards, and Husayn b. Falih, Shihab al-Hallaj and Yashkuri in Baghdad. There are also unfavourable Christians to balance the idea of Coptic victimhood, such as Father Michael in Antioch.

Like *Khalati*, *Al-Bashmuri* is no easy allegory of pluralism and tolerance. The narrative may portray close friendships between Muslims and Copts and allude to instances of cooperation and mutual concern, including Muslim involvement in the Bashmur uprising,[52] but on the level of ideology the narrative prioritises Islam, for the very fact of the protagonist's conversion presents Islam, intentionally or not, as a correction to Christianity. Moreover, the nature of Christian teaching leads to suffering in the character, in contrast to the peace he derives from Islam. As Budayr explains to Thawna:

> Every day I lived before I became a Muslim I would wake up anxious, my thoughts and ideas confused, my soul tormented by memories of my teens and early youth …
>
> Before I became a Muslim I had confessed in church several times but confession did not banish my pain nor make me forget my feeling of sin and fault. However, when I took the path of a seeker and committed myself to the spiritual way, I arrived at 'There is no he but He (*lā huwa illā huwa*)' and I forgot 'was' (*kāna*) and stuck firmly with 'is' (*yakūn*), my pain disappeared and the distance increased between me and everything perishable save the face of God. The Revealing Light has come to me and my soul is tranquil, and my worry and suffering have vanished.[53]

It is also the case that, away from exceptions and aspirations, tolerance is not the experience of the majority of Coptic characters in the novel and, rather, constitutes one of the fictions that the narrative seeks to undo. In traditional accounts, the conquest of Egypt by the Arabs was achieved with minimal bloodshed. The scholarly consensus is that the Copts viewed the Arab Muslim invaders as preferable to the Byzantine Christians, whose Patriarch at the time, Cyrus (al-Muqawqas in Arabic sources), persecuted them in an attempt to wipe out the monophysite doctrine to which they subscribed, as distinct from the dyophysite or Melkite doctrine of the wider Church focused on Constantinople.[54] Some even suggest that the Copts not only favoured but aided the Muslims in their takeover of Egypt.[55] And following a relatively peaceful takeover, history tells us that Muslim rule was characterised by tolerance, in accordance with the Qur'an's endorsement of Christians and the Prophet's instruction to ʿUmar b. al-Khattab to take good care of the Copts, as well as expediency, for the local population was needed for its expertise and administration.⁵⁶ Meinardus writes that

> from the very beginning of the Arab conquest, the Islamic government in Egypt offered its protection to the Copts, thus creating an atmosphere of sufferance, which to the Copts was a welcome change from the oppressive policies of the Byzantine rulers.⁵⁷

This view is stated often, and even appears in the novel. Thawna, whilst referring to the oppression of the Copts, says that 'At the beginning of [the Muslims'] time in our country, their governors treated the people well'.⁵⁸ And Father Thomas, in the context of rebuffing a Byzantine priest, states that 'tolerance (*al-musāmaḥa*) has been the practice [of the Muslims] since they took control of the country'.⁵⁹ Yet the novel also alerts us to the fact that there is another side to the story. The scenes in Bashmur draw attention to the bloodshed and violence involved in the process of Islamisation, while references to various uprisings, and the Bashmuri revolt itself, remind us that the Arab invasion was certainly not welcomed by all. Together these destabilise the discourse of peaceful takeover and tolerance. In the narrative we see a courageous but essentially weak Coptic community crushed by the caliph's army. Many Copts perish and those who survive are shipped to Iraq to be sold as slaves or similar. This is not the impression created by Meinardus and others. While *Al-Bashmuri* does not deny that there were pacifist and tolerant elements in early Islamic Egypt, it rejects this as a general rule.

The destabilising movement carries over to other areas of the text. *Al-Bashmuri* presents as an historical novel, a genre which in its traditional form has to do with communicating the experience of the past. The historical novel runs alongside historiography, borrowing the outline but filling in the gaps that historians, with their scientific approach and reliance on verifiable evidence, necessarily leave behind. As Herbert Butterfield argued in 1924, in the historical novel we find the *sentiment* of history and a *feeling* for the past.⁶⁰ Historians provide a chart of facts but omit human experience, which is where fiction writers come in. The historical novel is not normally concerned with the events depicted, except insofar as they affect the character/s: 'What matters', writes Lukacs, 'is not the retelling of great historical events, but the poetic awakening of the people who figured in those events'.⁶¹ Consequently, the historical novel prefers characters who are marginal to the events in question, sidestepping issues of veracity, but who are at once individual and emblematic, so that 'they really concentrate in themselves the salient positive and negative sides of the movement concerned'.[62] *Al-Bashmuri*, by contrast, takes on history. The narrative does not complement history so much as intervene in it. It does not illustrate history as we know it so much as reconstruct it. The protagonist functions as a symbol of the Islamisation of Egypt insofar as he converts to Islam over the course of the narrative, in this sense fulfilling one of the form's generic criteria, but he is far from a 'type', a synthesis of the general and the particular. He is eccentric; a naïve and impressionable individual who finds in the abandonment of his Christian faith and conversion to Islam the opportunity to break with a past that troubles him. His function in the novel is not to convey historical process but to rectify the marginalisation of a voice such as his own, the Coptic peasant, and to foreground the role of the Bashmuri revolts in Egyptian and wider Islamic history. In mainstream histories of Islam and the caliphate, the uprising in Bashmur constitutes a minor episode, a rebellion on the periphery of empire that was easily quashed. Even books focused on the Copts often pass over it. Bakr's novel, by taking this uprising as its starting point, challenges the revolt's marginal status – in the author's words, 'viewing it as the most significant link in the evolution of Egypt's cultural-civilisation history'.[63] Similarly by taking Egypt as its departure point it situates that country at the centre of the medieval world, instead of on the margins as represented by histories of the caliphate centred on Baghdad or the Hijaz.

The latter detail should not be taken as a constant, however. The position of Egypt in the narrative, like the portrayal of tolerance, is characterised by variation. Egypt is installed as a centre in the early part of the narrative and holds a special place in the protagonist's psyche, functioning as a reference point for him through the text. But Budayr does not remain in Egypt and once abroad develops a strong affinity with the places he visits, with the exception of Antioch, due to abuse suffered there. He describes Baghdad as the capital of the world[64] and is reluctant to leave it, and he speaks of how Jerusalem captivated him as no city had before: 'I became unable to leave. It was as though my soul knew nowhere else on earth where it could find repose and be tranquil as it could here'.[65] In other words, Egypt is not the sole point of orientation. True he eventually returns to Egypt and his homecoming marks a high point, but his travels introduce Antioch, Baghdad and Jerusalem as alternative loci. The narrative installs Egypt as a centre only to undermine it with a concept of multiple centres, in a move that recalls postmodernism's impulse towards double or contradictory stances.[66] The shifting locus of the protagonist exposes the subjectivity inherent in the dichotomy of centre and periphery. Meanwhile, Budayr's plural affinities point to the multiple streams that feed into Egyptian identity (Coptic, Greek, Arab, Christian, Muslim, ancient Egyptian) demystifying the notion of cultural purity upon which nationalisms are often constructed. This is further conveyed in the pluri-lingual nature of the text. Though written in Arabic, ancient Egyptian, Coptic, Syriac, Greek and Farsi are worked into the narrative. In fact it is not just Egypt that is portrayed as a boiling pot for a variety of identities. The medieval Near East in general is portrayed as a great mix of people and ideas. Against this historical trajectory, the nation-state as a constant and the notions of cultural and linguistic purity that accompany it are on shaky ground.

Thus *Al-Bashmuri* moves in two different directions. On the one hand, it conveys a message of religious tolerance and pluralism, with the Coptic angle functioning to redress the historical marginalisation of the Copts – 'No one thinks of the Copts', Yashkuri says to Budayr[67] – and rescue the Christian foundations of modern Egypt. On the other hand, it takes issue with the grand narratives of Islam, Egypt and the caliphate, challenging concepts of nation and culture and revealing the relativity of centre and periphery, self and other. This kind of contradictory movement is at the heart of another novel that employs a Coptic subject to interrogate entrenched positions with recourse to history: Yusuf Zaydan's ʿ*Azazil* (2008).[68] ʿ*Azazil* and *Al-Bashmuri* have much in common. They both focus on a Coptic protagonist-narrator on a journey of self-discovery around the Near East several centuries ago. The protagonists both have roles in the Church of their day, linking their experiences to that institution, and they are both notably naïve and inexperienced, which facilitates plenty of description and exposition of the historical and cultural setting in the respective texts. The self-discovery in both cases involves a move away from formal religion and, against a background of sectarian strife and beneath a good deal of religious critique, both novels convey a message of tolerance and portrait of religious violence. Other shared details include the presence of a mentor with a structuring role,[69] theological questioning on the part of the protagonist, and an interest in medieval medicine and herbs. ʿAzazil, however, is a more radical text. It goes further in its religious criticism, to the point of questioning the existence of God, and adopts a self-reflexive textual strategy to conduct its intervention into history and historiography. It also has an intertextual theme that is not present in Bakr's novel.

ʿAzazil, the second of university professor Zaydan's five novels to date,[70] assumes the form of a translation. In the opening pages we are told that what follows is the author's rendering of an old Syriac manuscript dating to the fifth century, which has been recently discovered at ruins near Aleppo. The following text is divided into chapters of varying length that correspond with the manuscript scrolls and are labelled as such, so that the reader is reminded of the nature of the text at regular intervals. The device of presenting a fictional work as an historical document and foregrounding the enunciative situation aligns the text with Hutcheon's historiographic metafiction: 'novels which are both intensively self-reflexive and yet paradoxically also lay claim to historical events and personages'.[71] ʿAzazil borrows the conventions of historical writing but their transposition into a fictional context is a subversion enacted to underline the similarity between fiction and history, that is their fundamental constructedness as a product of their dependence on narrative. On the other hand, the textual theme – the description of the imaginary physical manuscript and numbering of the scrolls – draws attention to history as text, the fact that 'the past arrives in the form of texts and textualised remainders – memories, reports, published writings, archives, monuments, and so forth'.[72] The presence of first person narration, first as fictional translator and then as fictional protagonist, foregrounding the authorial role, underlines the subjective nature of history and historiography, a detail which also applies to *Al-Bashmuri* as a work assuming an historiographical form, while the naïve and eccentric character of the protagonist-narrator casts doubt on his account in a general sense. His narrative is limited, provisional and highly subjective. The fact that the text is presented as a translation adds another dimension to this, for what remains is a report by a dubious narrator related second-hand by a translator several centuries later. The text is thus doubly mediated and the possibility of it conveying anything other than a subjective second-hand truth is wholly undermined.

Provisionality established, the narrative of the manuscript opens in September 431 CE, or Thout 147 of the Coptic calendar, defined as 'the inauspicious year in which the revered Bishop Nestorius was excommunicated and dismissed',[73] and the recollection begins with the author's first encounter with Nestorius, thereby signalling the importance of this character to the story, or rather stories, for *ʿAzazil* is the tale both of a Copt named Hypa's journey of self-discovery and of the internecine strife of the early Christian Church, brought together by the person of Nestorius, who is central to the monk's life as confidant and mentor and to early Church history as the figure who brought to a head in the first half of the fifth century the theological ferment surrounding the question of hypostasis.

Both Hypa and the Church suffer crises over the course of the novel. Hypa leaves his village of Najʿ Hammadi as a young man, having witnessed the murder of his pagan father by Christians and the collusion of his mother with his father's killers. His stated mission is to master medicine and theology then return to his village to lead a monastic life and confirm the existence of God through treating people, a statement which reveals his naivety early on.[74] His first port of call, Alexandria, is not what he expects – he finds a city of man more than a city of God[75] – and he suffers his first identity crisis here. Soon after arriving he meets Octavia, a pagan, who takes him into her house, and introduces him to physical pleasure, which is new to him as a monk of extreme austerity. For Octavia, Hypa is the fulfilment of a prophecy of a pagan priestess and she dedicates herself to him without hesitation. For Hypa, Octavia is the key to happiness that he cannot appreciate because he is riddled with guilt having bought into a Christian notion that pleasure is inherently evil. He repeatedly resolves to end the affair and resume his spiritual mission but lacks the moral strength. In the end, Octavia throws him out of the house in a scene that evokes Adam's expulsion from Eden, after Hypa admits that he is a Christian monk and therefore of the people whom she despises for killing her late husband. Hypa's next stop, the church of St Mark, where he takes up residence with the monks of Alexandria and leads a quiet life for a time, also ends suddenly. As relations deteriorate between Bishop Cyril and the governor Orestes and tensions increase between the city's Christian and pagan populations, Cyril pronounces war on pagans and Hypa's secret hero, Hypatia, the Savante of the Ages, accused of plotting against the bishop, is brutally murdered, skinned and burned by the mob. Hypa's erstwhile lover Octavia also falls victim to the mob as she rushes to Hypatia's rescue. The episode shakes Hypa to his core and prompts a second identity crisis. He tears off his cross and sets out into the desert. The Alexandrian sojourn thus ends in calamity, whilst at the same time marking out the shape of events to come with respect to the coincidence of drama in the public and private spheres.

Hypa's onward journey takes him to Sinai, the Dead Sea, Jerusalem and the environs of Aleppo, where he settles in a monastery and serves as physician to the local population whilst pursuing books and learning in the monastery's library. His spiritual quest is frequently challenged during this period, mostly through his own theological questions – 'Does [God] only punish believers?'[76] 'Why did God want man to remain ignorant to begin with?',[77] 'Why will God on the Day of Judgement take us back and hold us to account for what we did a long time ago, as though we have lived a singular life and not changed during it?'[78] – but he manages to remain steadfast in his belief and, whilst residing in the monasteries in Jerusalem and near Aleppo, finds a kind of peace. This ends with the arrival of Martha, a singer sent to him by the abbot. Hypa immediately falls in love whilst struggling with guilt once more and doubting her morality as a woman, the latter pointing to a deep-seated gender bias in Christian thought and tradition. A relationship ensues but Hypa's mission and belief system are too deep-seated to permit a happy ending to their story and when Martha asks for his hand he cites Matthew's gospel on marriage after divorce (Matt. 19: 9).[79] Thus Hypa loses the second woman he loves and second chance of happiness in the world. Recognition of this leads to a mental and physical breakdown, which those around him interpret as fever but which the reader knows is an effect of psychological stress arising from the opposing forces within him, physical and spiritual.

Meanwhile the Church to which Hypa belongs suffers a crisis. Throughout the text reference is made to a theological rift in the Christian Church, namely the polarisation of belief over the nature of Christ's divinity in the early fifth century, which culminated in the excommunication of Nestorius, then Archbishop of Constantinople, and his supporters in 431 CE. As the latter explains to Hypa, Christ is 'a man through whom God appeared for us'.[80] He was not born a divinity therefore the appellation *theotokos* for the Virgin Mary is theologically flawed. The issue simmers in the background, referred to at various points and elaborated not only by Nestorius but by Pharisee, another friend of the protagonist. Cyril of Alexandria escalates the crisis by formally accusing Nestorius of heresy and condemning him at the Council of Ephesus (431 CE), which he convenes in the absence of Nestorius and the Emperor and Pope of Rome.[81] In the narrative, as in the history books, Nestorius and his supporters respond by holding another council and passing a resolution excommunicating Cyril. The emperor then arrives and, angered by preceding events, excommunicates both men but later reinstates Cyril, in order to maintain good relations with Alexandria. These events are, for the most part, related second-hand; we do not follow Nestorius and Cyril to Ephesus but learn of developments via the abbot and other reporters. The internecine strife both reflects and feeds into Hypa's own crisis, for Hypa is implicated in the events around him. He is summoned to verify the translation of documents exchanged between Nestorius and Cyril so is privy to them. Moreover, the tension mounting around Nestorius and the sense of impending doom has an effect on him, for he grows increasingly anxious on his friend's behalf and the anxiety contributes to his breakdown. Hypa, however, emerges from his personal breakdown in a better state than the Church from its internal breakdown. The depths of despair to which Hypa sinks and his journey away from God, represented in the narrative as submission to ʿAzazil (Satan), results in liberation – liberation to write, to express himself, and to be himself. At the end of the narrative he buries the manuscript. 'With it I will bury all the fears I inherited and old illusions', he says. 'Then I will set out with the sunrise, free'.[82] Thus Hypa puts the past behind him. He has submitted to ʿAzazil and in so doing gained his freedom.

Satan has long inspired the literary imagination. Maximilian J. Rudwin writes that 'The fair angels – all frankness and goodness – are beyond our comprehension, but the fallen angels, with all their faults and sufferings, are kin to us'.[83] The Devil has featured often in the literary canon, called upon to symbolise pure evil, victimhood, heroic rebellion and more. Dante's *Divine Comedy*, Milton's *Paradise Lost*, Goethe's *Faust*, Byron's *Cain*, Bulghakov's *The Master and Margarita* are some of the better-known titles in the western canon. In modern Arabic fiction Tawfiq al-Hakim, Nawal Saʿdawi and Najib Mahfuz are three major names who have engaged Satan as character.[84] The European Romantics found in Satan a perfect articulation of dissatisfaction with terrestrial affairs,[85] whereas into the twentieth century the character of the Devil has evolved to reflect modernity's relativity of thought, hence Satan is no longer 'a villain of the deepest dye' but functions more as satirist and mischief maker.[86] Zaydan's Satan unsurprisingly belongs to the latter category. From the beginning of the narrative he appears to Hypa encouraging him to write his story and taunting him about his beliefs and fears. His role is not to do evil or even to incite evil, although the protagonist may interpret it as such, but to give voice to the thoughts and impulses that Hypa dare not express. In fact, as ʿAzazil suggests on more than one occasion, he is himself one of these impulses. He is not an independent entity but a presence summoned by the monk. 'Hypa, I have told you repeatedly that I do not come and go. It is you who summons me when you want to. I come to you from you, through you and within you'.[87] ʿAzazil represents Hypa's inner voice, his conscience, his will to creativity, freedom and selfhood. It is significant that freedom and the Devil are linked here, for it implies that God, Satan's opposite number, is the enemy of freedom and the self. God and religion are in *ʿAzazil* forces at odds with the ego.

Other features of Satan as represented in the text reflect onto God. Satan is presented as a construct, a means of articulating and justifying evil. To this end, the choice of ʿAzazil as the name for Satan in the novel is significant, for of the various diabolic appellations, *ʿAzazil* is particularly connected with the idea of scapegoat, following Leviticus 16: 8: 'And Aaron shall cast lots upon the two goats; one lot for the Lord, and the other lot for the scapegoat (*ʿAzazil*, Hebrew: עֲזָאזֵל)'. Thus the idea of evil assigned, heaped onto the scapegoat, as opposed to perpetrated, is foregrounded, which casts Satan as a victim and ties in with the notion of Satan as invention: 'I am the justification of evil … It is [evil] that causes me', announces ʿAzazil in the novel.[88] And if Satan is a construct, then so too is God. If Satan is invented to justify and bear the burden of evil in mankind, then God is invented to embody man's aspirations and provide a moral framework. As ʿAzazil explains: 'in every age mankind creates a god for his convenience, and his god is always his visions, impossible dreams and desires'.[89]

The novel, then, takes a dim view of God and religion. God is a construct, at least inasmuch as He is beyond human grasp and we end up inventing Him,[90] and the discourse that surrounds Him is the antithesis of freedom and creativity. The choice of historical timeframe, the early decades of the fifth century AD and the internecine discord surrounding hypostasis, is convenient in this regard for it provides a window onto man's hand in the formulation of faith. The early Christian Church harboured a variety of theological positions and possibilities that were either channelled into a uniform system of belief or anathemised. Today the doctrine of hypostatic union is taken for granted in the Catholic Church (which of course no longer equates with the Christian Church) but it was not always thus. Zaydan's focus on the period leading up to the Council of Ephesus reminds us of this fact. Moreover, the sympathetic treatment of Nestorius casts him as a victim, wronged by the Church and by history. He is portrayed as a thoughtful and pious monk, his questionable actions as Archbishop of Constantinople referred to in passing and deemed to be misconstrued, at least by our dubious narrator. Meanwhile Cyril of Alexandria, who is today celebrated as a saint, embodies all that is wrong in religion. His hypocrisy is neatly summed up by a comparison the narrator draws between the bishop and a statue of Jesus situated behind him during a sermon:

> Jesus' clothes were shabby rags torn from the chest and most of the limbs, while the clothes of the bishop were decorated with gold thread all over so that his face was only just visible. Jesus' hands were free from the vanities of the world, while in the hands of the bishop was a sceptre which [Hypa] presumed was made of pure gold on the basis of its bright shine. On his head Jesus had the excruciating crown of thorns, while on the bishop's head was a lustrous golden episcopal crown. Jesus seemed to [Hypa] submissive as he met his sacrifice on the cross of redemption, while Cyril seemed to [Hypa] to be intent on clasping the limits of heaven and earth.[91]

Worse than hypocrisy is Cyril's character as oppressor, seen in his persecution of the Jews of Alexandria, his pronouncement of war on the pagans, resulting in the killing of Hypatia and Octavia, and his cursory condemnation of Nestorius without a proper hearing. Zaydan reverses the historical dynamic between Nestorius and Cyril whereby the former is heretic and troublemaker and the latter defender of the faith, and in so doing exposes the mechanics of faith construction. Dogma and doctrine are portrayed as the work of man and the prerogative of the powerful. Good relations with Alexandria are of paramount importance to the emperor so Cyril is granted authority over Christian discourse in the debate on hypostasis.

Further religious criticism is expressed through the violence perpetrated under the banner of religion. The narrative highlights the relationship between the two, which has a long history in Christianity as in other global religions. Lloyd Steffen, writing about Christianity, identifies three arenas in which its adherents have been involved in violence: (1) internally: violence against fellow believers, (2) externally: violence against people of other faiths, and (3) state violence: when Christian spiritual authority has been called on to legitimate political violence.[92] Examples of all three are seen in the novel. In the context of internecine violence (first category), Nestorius orders the destruction of churches and is himself stripped of his rights when he is excommunicated. The latter, though it does not result in physical or material injury, is violence nonetheless, since as Mary Jackman argues, violent acts may be corporal, written or verbal and the injuries may be corporal, psychological, material or social.[93] With respect to violence against other faiths, Steffen's second category, the murders of Hypatia and Octavia offer the most stark example and are related in some detail, but Hypa's father and Octavia's husband are also killed for paganism and reference is made to the destruction of pagan temples by Christians and accompanying killing by monks.[94] The murders of Hypatia and Octavia, which are in the novel sanctioned by Cyril of Alexandria with appeal to the Christian faith,[95] also fall into Steffen's third category of state violence, as does the persecution of the Jews of Alexandria. Nestorius, the main exponent of theology in the text, downplays the religious underpinnings of these acts (his pacifist interpretation is of course ironic in the context of his own actions as Archbishop of Antioch). He argues that monks do not kill and reminds Hypa that 'Killing people in the name of religion does not make it religious'.[96] In so doing he echoes the commonly held opinion that religions are forces for love, peace and harmony in the world: 'Adherents of most religious traditions almost universally regard their own faith as pacifist', write Juergensmeyer, Kitts and Jerryson.[97] The narrative, however, rejects any easy sidestepping of the association between religion and violence, instead pointing to scripture's sanctioning of it. Cyril cites

Matthew 10: 34: 'I came not to send peace, but a sword'.[98] It may be possible to blame the character here, but there is no escaping the troublesome gospel citation. The novel intimates an inherent connection between Christianity and violence.

Another kind of violence produced by religion but not included in Steffen's limited typology is psychological. Hypa's faith, not unlike Budayr's in *Al-Bashmuri*, brings him endless suffering in the form of guilt. He twice forgoes happiness on account of his faith and as far as possible lives a mundane ascetic life, which as noted denies him freedom and individuality. He is not alone in this. Christianity as a whole is portrayed as a religion that precludes pleasure in life. Christians 'fill life with gloom and austerity', remarks Octavia.[99] ʿ*Azazil*, in addition to implying the dubiousness of God's existence and theorising a deep connection between Christianity and violence, exposes the negative effects of religion on the individual. The portrait is not only grim but undeniably confrontational. There is no escaping the anti-Christian theme in ʿ*Azazil*, which is why it provoked outrage in the form of press releases, protests, a lawsuit and a book-length response by a Coptic bishop when it was first published.[100] Zaydan's response to his critics is that the book is not against Christianity but violence, especially violence in the name of religion, and he disputes the idea that the Christian history of Egypt is the private property of the Coptic Church.[101]

The choice of historical setting on this logic is part of an attempt to rescue and reconstruct a sometimes forgotten period of Egyptian history. By situating the narrative in Christian Egypt, before the coming of Islam and therefore without any mention of it, Zaydan draws attention to the important role that Christianity played in Egyptian history and identity, and vice-versa. To this can be added references to the strong monastic tradition in Egypt, which the narrative reminds us originated there.[102] There is also the reported presence of Christian personages, specifically Christ and the Virgin Mary, in the country at different times, even if the legend is dubious.[103] These details develop an Egyptian theme and serve to place Egypt at the centre of the early Christian Near East. The move is provisional, however, for, as in *Al-Bashmuri*, the concept of centre and periphery is challenged and replaced by a concept of multiple centres when the protagonist takes up residence in, and develops attachments to, other places on his travels. Other meanings that emerge from the traveller trope in *Al-Bashmuri* also apply here – the challenge to notions of cultural and linguistic purity and autonomy of the nation-state, the portrayal of Egypt and the Near East as fluid in terms of identity and ethnicity, the relativity of self and other.

One detail that does not appear in *Al-Bashmuri* and which aligns *ʿAzazil* more with *Turabuha* is biblical intertextuality. Hypa lives his life against a background of Christian scripture. His suffering at the loss of his father is likened to Mary's suffering at losing Jesus and his journey into the desert is compared to the exile of the Jews in Sinai. The allusions confirm and elaborate the character's theocentric worldview and at times carry further meanings. For example, Hypa's sojourn with Octavia is framed by an intertextual dialogue with the biblical story of original sin, established by explicit reference to paradise and other recognisable symbols. Hypa becomes Adam, the servant of God tempted into sin by Eve/Octavia. He is seduced by her and significantly eats an apple with her encouragement.[104] The latter act is immediately followed by a series of questions about God, as though eating the forbidden fruit has opened Hypa's mind to doubt just as Adam became aware of his nakedness after eating from the tree of knowledge. Hypa is then expelled from the house, mirroring Adam's expulsion from Eden. The connection with the biblical story casts the relationship with Octavia as a lapse in morality on the part of Hypa, which is how he views it himself, and as a turning point in his life, as though the pre-Octavia period is a time of innocence as contrasted to the period that comes after. The idea of a lapse in morality is echoed later on in an allusion to Peter the Apostle's denial of Christ when Hypa recalls that Peter denied Jesus three times in one night while 'I denied myself for three days before Octavia'.[105] On the other hand, after his expulsion Hypa compares his loss of Octavia to that of the apostles' loss of Christ, which casts her as his saviour, perhaps in the sense of a route out of the path of denial which he and the Church have determined for him:

> My emptiness and loneliness were painful. I fell into a slumber, like that which prevailed on Jesus' apostles on the evening of the Last Supper, after he told them that he would leave them soon to his Father in heaven.[106]

The scriptural reference in *ʿAzazil* thus both accentuates and complicates meaning.

Notes

1. The Coptic language derives from ancient Egyptian and is one of the oldest recorded languages. Its alphabet is an adaptation of the Greek with a handful of letters from Demotic. It comprises several dialects, most prominent among them Sahidi and Bohairi, of which the latter is used in liturgy. As a spoken language Coptic was used until the end of the seventeenth century, when it was overtaken by Arabic, though a handful of speakers remain.
2. Christian Cannuyer, *Coptic Egypt: The Christians of the Nile* (London: Thames and Hudson, 2001), p. 110.
3. Sources for the modern history of the Copts upon which this information is based are as follows: Cannuyer, *Coptic Egypt*, pp. 93–111; S. S. Hasan, *Christians versus Muslims in Modern Egypt: The Century-Long Struggle for Coptic Equality* (Oxford: Oxford University Press, 2003); Samuel Tadros, *Motherland Lost: The Egyptian and Coptic Quest for Modernity* (Stanford, CA: Hoover Institution Press, 2013).
4. I have not had access to this work myself and am relying on Matti Moosa's account of the text in *The Origins of Modern Arabic Fiction*, pp. 254–5. See also Sayyid Hamid Nassaj, *Banurama al-Riwaya al-ᶜArabiyya al-Haditha*, 2nd edn (Cairo: Maktaba Gharib, 1985), pp. 53–6.
5. Bahaʾ Tahir, *Khalati Safiyya wa'l-Dayr* (Cairo: Dar al-Hilal, 1991), trans. Barbara Romaine, *Aunt Safiyya and the Monastery* (Berkley, LA: University of California Press, 1996). Translations my own. Studies of the novel and the author's other stories include Mahmud Amin al-ᶜAlim, 'La Yazal al-Suʾal Qaʾiman … Qiraʾa li-Riwaya "Khalati Safiyya wa'l-Dayr" li-Bahaʾ Tahir', *Arbaᶜun ᶜAm min al-Naqd al-Tatbiqi* (Beirut: Dar al-Mustaqbal al-ᶜArabi, 1994), pp. 237–43; Shakir ᶜAbd al-Hamid, 'Al-Mawt wa'l-Hilm fi ᶜAlam Bahaʾ Tahir', *Fusul*, vol. 12, no. 2 (1993), pp. 180–203; El-Enany, *Arab Representations of the Occident*, pp. 135–41.
6. The term *jīl al-sittīnāt* is used to designate a group associated with literary innovation, most of whom began writing in the 1960s. Aside from al-Kharrat, prominent writers include Jamal al-Ghitani, Muhammad al-Bisati, ᶜAbd al-Hakim Qasim, Bahaʾ Tahir, Yahya Tahir ᶜAbdullah, Ibrahim Aslan, Radwa ᶜAshur and others. See Elisabeth Kendall, *Literature, Journalism and the Avant-Garde: Intersection in Egypt* (New York: Routledge, 2006); al-Kharrat, *Al-Hassasiyya al-Jadida*; Ghali Shukri, *Al-ᶜAnqa al-Jadida: Sirat al-Ajyal fi'l-Adab al-Muᶜasir* (Beirut: Dar al-Taliᶜa li'l-Tibaᶜa wa'l-Nashr, 1977); Yasmine

Ramadan, 'The Emergence of the Sixties Generation in Egypt and the Anxiety over Categorisation', *Journal of Arabic Literature,* vol. 43, nos 2–3 (2012), pp. 409–30.
7. Kharrat, *Al-Hassasiyya al-Jadida,* pp. 19–20. Works by Baha˒ Tahir include: *Al-Khutuba* (short stories collection, 1972); *Bi'l-Amsi Halamtu Biki* (short stories collection, 1980); *Sharq al-Nakhil* (novel, 1985); *Qalat Duha* (novel, 1986); *Ana al-Malik Ji˒tu* (short stories collection, 1987).
8. Safiyya is referred to as *khalati* (my aunt) by the narrator and his sisters but is a maternal cousin.
9. Al-Musawi, *Islam on the Street,* p. xiii.
10. *Khalati,* p. 37 (trans., p. 26).
11. Ibid. p. 41 (trans., p. 31).
12. Ibrahim ᶜAbd al-Majid, *La Ahad Yanam fi'l-Iskandariyya* (Cairo: Dar al-Hilal, 1996), trans. Farouk Abdel Wahab, *No One Sleeps in Alexandria* (Cairo: American University in Cairo Press, 1999).
13. Idwar al-Kharrat, *Turabuha Zaᶜfaran: Nusus Iskandariyya* (Cairo: Dar al-Mustaqbal al-ᶜArabi, 1986), trans. France Liardet as Edwar al-Kharrat, *City of Saffron* (London and New York: Quartet Books, 1989). Translations my own. Critical discussions of this novel include Muhammad Siddiq, *Arab Culture and the Novel,* pp. 67–77; Mona Mikha'il, 'Al-Rajl wa'l-Bahr: Jawanib min al-Tanass fi Riwayat Idwar al-Kharrat "Turabuha Zaᶜfaran"', *Fusul,* vol. 15, no. 4, pp. 25–32; Magda al-Nowaihi, 'Memory and Imagination in Edwar al-Kharrat's *Turabuha Zaᶜfaran*', *Journal of Arabic Literature,* vol. 15 (1994), pp. 34–57; Iᶜtadal ᶜUthman, 'Tashkil Fada˒ al-Nass fi "Turabuha Zaᶜfaran"', *Fusul,* vol. 6, no. 3 (1987), pp. 162–9.
14. Deborah Starr, *Remembering Cosmopolitan Egypt: Literature, Culture, and Empire* (New York and Oxford: Routledge, 2009), p. 60.
15. Siddiq, *Arab Culture and the Novel,* p. 79.
16. Al-Nowaihi, who also sees the subtitle as a deliberate rejection of existing literary category, notes that 'Edwar al-Kharrat has always been a rebel against "the pre-ordained order of narration" and was an advocate of "the dismantling of the classical plot" long before this became fashionable'. Al-Nowaihi, 'Memory and Imagination in Edwar al-Kharrat's *Turabuha Zaᶜfaran*', p. 34, n. 1.
17. Deleuze and Guattari's term (Gilles Deleuze and Felix Guattari, *Kafka: Toward a Minor Literature,* trans. Dana Polan (Minneapolis and London: University of Minnesota Press, 1986), p. 18).
18. *Turabuha,* p. 15 (trans., p. 6).

19. Ibid. pp. 23 (trans., p.13), 148–9 (trans., p. 129), 200 (trans., pp. 173–4).
20. Ibid. p. 149 (trans., p. 129).
21. Ibid. p. 129 (trans., p. 110).
22. The same effect is produced in ʿAbd al-Majid's *La Ahad Yanam*. See Starr, *Remembering Cosmopolitan Egypt*, ch. 4.
23. *Turabuha*, p. 140 (trans., pp. 120–1). See also pp. 88 (trans., p. 69) and 107 (trans., p. 87).
24. Ibid. p. 68 (trans., p. 52).
25. Ibid. p. 113 (trans., p. 93).
26. Ibid. p. 118 (trans., pp. 98–9).
27. Ibid. p. 73 (trans., p. 57).
28. Ibid. p. 138 (trans., p. 118). The Church takes in Maqar, who has no family, and arranges work for him and facilitates his marriage to the narrator's aunt Hanuna.
29. Also noteworthy are Bishr Faris (1906–63) and Raʾfat al-Duwayri in drama, the surrealist works of Georges Henein (1914–73) and Ramses Yunan (1913–66), and free verse of Luwis Awad's *Plutoland* (1947). See Jacquemond, *Conscience of a Nation*, pp. 97–8.
30. Jacquemond, *Conscience of a Nation*, p. 97.
31. Deleuze and Guattari, *Kafka: Towards a Minor Literature*, p. 17.
32. Kendall, *Literature, Journalism and the Avant-Garde*, p. 106.
33. Deleuze and Guattari, *Kafka: Towards a Minor Literature*, p. 18.
34. Abu Deeb, 'The Collapse of Totalising Discourse and the Rise of Marginalised/Minority Discourses'.
35. For a discussion of Arab postmodernism, see Faysal Darraj, 'Ma Baʿda al-Hadatha fi ʿAlam bi-la Hadatha', *Al-Karmal*, vol. 51 (1997), pp. 64–90; Stefan Meyer, *The Experimental Arabic Novel Postcolonial Literary Modernism in the Levant* (New York: University of New York State Press, 2000).
36. Linda Hutcheon, *The Poetics of Postmodernism* (London: Routledge, 2004 [1988]), p. 58. Hutcheon devotes a whole chapter to 'Decentering the Postmodern: the Ex-centric' (ch. 4), pp. 57–73.
37. The first part of the novel was published in 1998 by Dar al-Hilal, Cairo. The second part was then published along with the first in 2002 by al-Majlis al-ʿAla li'l-Thaqafa, Cairo. I refer to the 2005 combined publication (Cairo: Makataba Madbuli), trans. Nancy Roberts, *The Man from Bashmour* (Cairo and New York: American University in Cairo Press, 2007). Translations my own unless stated. Caroline Seymour-Jorn discusses the novel in her chapter 'Salwa Bakr:

The Poetics of Marginalisation', in *Cultural Criticism in Egyptian Women's Writing* (New York: Syracuse University Press, 2011), pp. 17–55.
38. This is the dating suggested by evidence in the text, namely the letter from Coptic Patriarch Yuᶜsab (830–49), to the Bashmuris urging them to end their revolt and the subsequent quashing of the revolt by the caliphal army and deportation of prisoners to Iraq via Antioch.
39. Salwa Bakr, *The Man from Bashmour*, p. ix (preface).
40. *Bashmuri*, p. 18 (trans., p. 12).
41. Ibid. p. 67 (trans., p. 52).
42. Ibid. p. 368 (trans., p. 294).
43. Ibid. p. 286 (trans., p. 227).
44. *Man from Bashmour*, p. vii.
45. This is seen in *Khalati* in the fact that evil acts are performed on both sides – by Hinayn, a Christian, and the Bey, a Muslim.
46. *Bashmuri*, p. 25 (trans., p. 18).
47. Ibid. pp. 24, 40–1, 54 (trans., pp. 18, 31, 42).
48. Ibid. pp. 25, 55, 101 (trans., pp. 18, 42, 78).
49. Ibid. p. 166 (trans., p. 131).
50. Cf. the murder of Thawna's pagan teacher Dalluka; also *Bashmuri*, pp. 148, 233 (trans., pp. 117, 183–4).
51. Melkites: Chalcedonian Christians, i.e. those who accepted the 451 CE Council of Chalcedon which acknowledged the subsistence of two natures, divine and human, in Christ, which come together in one person and one hypostasis. The non-Chalcedonians, which included the Coptic Church of Egypt, rejected the creed of Chalcedon, understanding divinity and humanity to be united in one nature in Christ. Hence non-Chalcedonians are sometimes referred to as monophysites and Chalcedonians as dyophysites.
52. *Bashmuri*, p. 130 (trans., p. 102).
53. *Bashmuri*, p. 373 (trans., pp. 297–8).
54. The persecution of the Copts by Cyrus is detailed in Alfred J. Butler, *The Arab Conquest of Egypt and the Last Thirty Years of the Roman Dominion*, 2nd edn (Oxford: Clarendon Press, 1978), pp. 168–93, which remains an important authority on this episode in Egyptian history despite its age (first edn: 1902).
55. See e.g. Kennedy citing Ibn ᶜAbd al-Hakam's *Futuh Misr* and other sources. The Copts are portrayed as playing a supporting role though not actually fighting. Hugh Kennedy, *The Great Arab Conquests: How the Spread of Islam Changed the World We Live In* (London: Weidenfeld and Nicolson, 2007),

pp. 155, 167–8. Kennedy in the end concludes that the Coptic response to Muslim invasion likely varied.
56. *Sūra*s 2 and 5 maintain that all believers in God will be rewarded (Q. 2:62; 5: 69). The Prophet said to ʿUmar b. al-Khattab, 'Allah will open Egypt to you after my death. So take good care of the Copts in that country, for they are your kinsmen and under your protection' (*EI2*, 'ḳibṭ', p. 90). References to Arab tolerance are found in many histories of the Arab conquest and of Egypt. To cite just a few: Otto F. A. Meinardus, *Christians in Egypt: Orthodox, Catholic and Protestant Communities Past and Present* (Cairo and New York: American University in Cairo Press, 2006), p. 28; P. J. Vatikiotis, *The History of Modern Egypt*, 4th edn (London: Weidenfeld and Nicolson, 1991); Kennedy, *The Great Arab Conquests*, pp. 148–9. A notable exception is E. L. Butcher, *The Story of the Church of Egypt* (London: Smith, Elder & Co., 1898).
57. Meinardus, *Christians in Egypt*, p. 28.
58. *Bashmuri*, p. 159 (trans., pp. 126–7).
59. Ibid. p. 251 (trans., p. 198).
60. Herbert Butterfield, *The Historical Novel: An Essay* [1924] (Cambridge: Cambridge University Press, 2011), p. 3.
61. Georg Lukacs, *The Historical Novel*, trans. Hannah and Stanley Mitchell (London: Merlin, 1962), p. 42.
62. Ibid. p. 40. Lukacs is talking about Scott's *Waverley* here.
63. *Man from Bashmour*, p. ix (preface).
64. *Bashmuri*, p. 300 (trans., p. 237).
65. Ibid. p. 341 (trans., p. 272).
66. See Linda Hutcheon, *The Politics of Postmodernism* (New York: Routledge, 1989).
67. *Bashmuri*, p. 347 (trans., p. 276).
68. Yusuf Zaydan, *ʿAzazil* (Cairo: Dar al-Shuruq, 2008), trans. Jonathon Wright as: Youssef Ziedan, *Azazeel* (London: Atlantic Books, 2012). Translations my own. *Al-Nabati* (2010) by the same author also has a Coptic protagonist (Maria) but focuses on the period prior to the coming of Islam.
69. Budayr's journey starts and ends with Thawna in *Al-Bashmuri*; Hypa begins his story with his first encounter with Nestorius and it ends with Nestorius' excommunication in *ʿAzazil*.
70. Yusuf Zaydan's publications include several scholarly works, plus fiction: *Zill al-Afʿa*, *ʿAzazil* (2008), *Al-Nabati* (2005), *Muhal* (2013), *Guantanamo* (2013) and *Hall wa Tarhal* (2014, short story collection).
71. Hutcheon, *Poetics of Postmodernism*, p. 5.

72. Dominick LaCapra, *History and Criticism* (Ithaca, NY: Cornell University Press, 1985), p. 128. Cited from Hutcheon, *Poetics of Postmodernism*, p. 129.
73. ʿ*Azazil*, p. 15 (trans., pp. 6–7).
74. Ibid. p. 97 (trans., pp. 75–6).
75. Ibid. p. 70 (trans., p. 52).
76. Ibid. p. 97 (trans., p. 75).
77. Ibid. p. 120 (trans., p. 95).
78. Ibid. p. 107 (trans., p. 84).
79. See ibid. p. 336 (trans., p. 279).
80. Ibid. p. 47 (trans., p. 33).
81. Theodosius II (r. 408–50 CE) and Pope Celestine I (r. 422–32 CE).
82. ʿ*Azazil*, p. 368 (trans., p. 307).
83. Maximiliam J. Rudwin, *Devil Stories: An Anthology* (New York: Alfred A. Knopf, 1921), p. xi.
84. See Tawfiq al-Hakim's 'The Martyr' (Al-Shahid), in the collection *Arini Allah* (Cairo: Maktabat al-Adab, 1953), pp. 13–29, and 'Era of Satan' (ʿAhd al-Shaytan; play) (Cairo: Maktabat al-Adab, 1938); Najib Mahfuz, *Awlad Haratina* (the character of Idris) (Beirut: Dar al-Adab, 1967) and some of the short stories in his collection *Al-Shaytan Yaʿiz* (1979); Nawal Saʿdawi, *Jannat wa Iblis* (see Chapter 8 of this study). The Devil has also been taken up in modern Arabic drama, for example by Muhammad Farid Abu Hadid, 'The Devil's Servant' (ʿAbd al-Shaytan), and Ali Ahmad Bakathir, 'The New Faust' (Fawst al-Jadid). See Mustafa Mahir, 'Fawst fi'l-Adab al-ʿArabi al-Muʿasir', *Fusul*, vol. 3, no. 4 (1983), pp. 237–48 and ʿIsam Bahiyya, 'Al-Shaytan fi Thalath Masrahiyyat', *Fusul*, vol. 3, no. 4 (1983), pp. 248–64.
85. Rudwin, *Devil Stories*, p. xv.
86. Ibid. p. xvii.
87. ʿ*Azazil*, p. 100 (trans., p. 78). There is an ironic echo here, perhaps unintentional, of the conclusion to the Eucharistic prayer: 'Through him, with him, in him, in the unity of the Holy Spirit …'.
88. Ibid. p. 350 (trans., p. 292).
89. Ibid. p. 348 (trans., p. 290).
90. This is the gist of Pharisee's monologue on the conundrum of God's unknowability in which he predicts a time when 'everyone will have his own private doctrine different to that of others'. See ʿ*Azazil*, pp. 329–30 (trans., 274).
91. ʿ*Azazil*, p. 146 (trans., p. 117).
92. Lloyd Steffen, 'Religion and Violence in Christian Traditions', in Juergensmeyer

et al. (eds), *The Oxford Handbook of Religion and Violence* (Oxford: Oxford University Press, 2013), p. 101.
93. Mary Jackman, 'License to kill: Violence and Legitimacy in Expropriative Social Relations', in John T. Jost and Brenda Major (eds), *The Psychology of Legitimacy: Emerging Perspectives on Ideology, Justice, and Intergroup Relations* (New York: Cambridge University Press, 2001), p. 443.
94. ʿ*Azazil*, p. 122 (trans., p. 97).
95. See Cyril's speech: ʿ*Azazil*, pp. 151–2 (trans., pp. 122–3).
96. ʿ*Azazil*, p. 185 (trans., p. 151).
97. Mark Juergensmeyer, Margo Kitts and Michael Jerryson, 'Introduction: The Enduring Relationship of Religion and Violence', in Juergensmeyer et al., *Oxford Handbook of Religion and Violence*, p. 2.
98. ʿ*Azazil*, p. 152 (trans., p. 123). Cyril repeats the quotation twice in close succession. King James full citation: 'Think not that I am come to send peace on earth: I came not to send peace, but a sword'.
99. ʿ*Azazil*, p. 111 (trans., p. 88).
100. While not banned by the state or officially condemned by the Coptic Church, the novel sparked press releases, protests and Zaydan had a lawsuit filed against him by a Christian group. A book-length response by Coptic Bishop Bishoy has also been published (ʿ*Azazil: al-Radd ʿala al-Buhtan fi Riwayat Yusuf Zaydan*, Cairo: Dar Antun, 2009).
101. Khaled Diab, 'So what if Egypt's Copts find a book insulting?', *Guardian*, 12 May 2010, available at <https://www.theguardian.com/commmentisfree/belief/2010/may/12/egypt-coptics-book-insulting>; Mike Collette-White, 'Egypt author wins Arab fiction prize for Beelzebub', Reuters, 16 March 2010, available at <https://af.reuters.com/article/egyptnews/idAFLG58593520090316>. See too Zaydan's detailed response to Coptic Bishop Bishoy: 'Duktur Yusuf Zayden Yakub: Buhtan al-Buhtan fi-ma Yatawahhamuh al-Mutran', Al-Masry al-Yawm, 26 July–9 September 2009. See too Saba Mahmoud, 'ʿ*Azazeel* and the Politics of Historical Fiction in Egypt', *Comparative Literature*, vol. 65, no. 3 (Summer 2013), pp. 265–84.
102. ʿ*Azazil*, pp. 34, 187, 217 (trans., pp. 22, 153, 179).
103. See ibid. p. 61 (trans., p. 44).
104. Ibid. p. 120 (trans., p. 95).
105. Ibid. p. 195 (trans., p. 160). At the same time Hypa regrets denying Hypatia in the face of her killers.
106. Ibid. p. 127 (trans., p. 101).

7

Mystical Dimensions

Sufism, the mystical tradition in Islam, has played a role in the Egyptian novel from its inception. In many instances, and in particular to begin with, this is bound up with the realistic depiction of life in Egypt and critique of traditional culture and superstition. Writers in the early decades of the twentieth century, concerned with matters of nation and identity and with nurturing a new narrative discourse, found in the Sufis an authentic Egyptian type and expression of what was wrong in national life. Taha Husayn found much to criticise in local Sufi shaykhs and sects, painting them as corrupt and dangerously ignorant in *Al-Ayyam*, and Haykal's Shaykh Masʿud is a charlatan. Mahmud Taymur portrays the dark aspects of popular religion in *Rajab Effendi* (1928) and is critical of local shaykhs in his short stories.[1] On the other hand, the profile of Shaykh ʿUsfur in Tawfiq al-Hakim's *Yawmiyyat Naʾib fi'l-Aryaf* (1937) is more nuanced. An eccentric figure who both aids and thwarts the murder investigation around which the drama revolves, the shaykh is sympathetically portrayed, thanks in part to the author's comic handling of the character. There is also a strong suggestion in the fictional diary that the shaykh possesses extraordinary knowledge, in contrast to the ignorance associated with Sufis in *Zaynab* and *Al-Ayyam*, and looks forward to the mystics of Mahfuz's stories in decades to come. Taha Husayn, it might be noted, was not uncompromisingly critical and presented a kinder portrait of the local Sufi shaykh in *Shajarat al-Buʾs* (1944).[2]

Aside from the Sufi character as authentic type and conduit of cultural criticism, there emerges, already in the pre-war period, a sense of Sufism as a spiritual counterpoint to modern life and alternative route to truth. Taymur's novel *Nidaʾ al-Majhul* (1939) depicts a character (Miss Evans) who abandons urban life and seeks refuge in the countryside and mysticism,[3] and Mahfuz's

Zuqaq al-Midaq (1947) includes two Sufi characters who represent the spiritual other to modernity. Radwan al-Husayni is a saintly individual who bears the alley's suffering but enjoys a tranquillity unknown to ordinary folk, and Shaykh Darwish appears mad but utters prophetic statements from time to time. The Sufi voice in *Zuqaq* marks the beginning of an engagement with Sufi themes and characters that would be sustained throughout Mahfuz's writing career and, as counter-narrative, foreshadows a critical function of Sufism in post-1967 Egyptian fiction.[4] In the cultural climate that prevailed from the early 1970s, with the emergence of a new literary sensibility that rejected unitary discourse and revelled in unconventional narrative and experimentation, Sufism took on new life and significance. Its problematic relationship with orthodox Islam, which derives from its unconventional readings of scripture, rejection of *kalām* (Islamic intellectual discourse) and emphasis on the unmediated encounter with God via *qalb* (heart) and *khayāl* (imagination), made it a pertinent symbol of marginalised and dissenting discourse, that is, the kind of discourse that came to the fore in this period. Moreover, its association with popular culture and the masses, for the local shrine and shaykh constitute a focal point for everyday Islam, made it attractive to writers in this period, who, as al-Musawi and others have shown, were concerned with reconnecting with the populace, having hitherto focused on *nahḍa* paradigms and ignored religion as 'a reality that also informs structures and currents of feeling'.[5] Elmarsafy, referring to the wider Arabic novel from 1980, understands Sufi themes and voices as an effect of the altered reality and a testimony to a selfhood under siege. Applying the logic of Michel de Certeau and Wittgenstein, who identify a gravitation towards mysticism in times of social and existential confusion, Elmarsafy proposes that

> what is surprising is not the appearance of Sufism but the fact that it is not more prevalent, that there are not more saints cropping up every minute to propagate something like an idea of order – personal and public – amidst the chaos of history.[6]

The characteristically metaphorical language and pluralistic vision of the Sufis also dovetails with aspects of the post-1967 literary sensibility, as comes across in two of Mahfuz's less studied works, *Hikayat Haratina* (1975) and *Asdaʾ al-Sirat al-Dhatiyya* (1994). Before exploring these two novels in detail it is worth revisiting the trilogy and dwelling for a moment on the author's symbolic forays into Sufism in the early 60s, which confirm doubts about the *nahḍa* project prior to the cataclysmic events of 1967 and confirm Mahfuz as a pioneer of this theme.

Kamal's infatuation with ʿAyda in *Qasr al-Shawq*, of which there are still remnants in *Al-Sukkariyya*, mirrors the Sufi's love affair with God. Love is central to Sufi doctrine. The Qur'an teaches that God loves mankind (5: 54) and that His love for man grows as he strives in God's way (3: 31). Love is the mainspring of the Sufi path. The Sufi aspirant is a lover striving to please God, or the Beloved. ʿAyda in *Qasr al-Shawq* is referred to by Kamal, through whose eyes we encounter her, as *al-maʿbūd* (the adored), recalling the Sufi phrase *ʿishq Allāh, maʿbūd Allāh* and occasionally *al-maḥbūb* (the beloved), and, as El-Enany notes, he uses words and phrases imbued with religious association in connection with her. For example, upon hearing her utter his name for the first time he feels like crying out 'Zammiluni, Daththiruni!', recalling the Prophet's exhortation to Khadija after encountering the angel Gabriel for the first time.[7] Moreover, his descriptions of her emphasise her sacred character. Her hair is a black halo and her face is angelic.[8] She is beautiful, fascinating and captivating but also omnipotent[9] and for Kamal belongs to a realm beyond the human and mundane: 'How my soul wishes to touch her hand, but it seems that you will journey through this world before you experience her touch'.[10] Hence he is somewhat uneasy at the sight of her eating at the Pyramids[11] and deeply disturbed when a wily Hasan Salim confirms not only ʿAyda's engagement but also her receptivity to ordinary emotions, like desire and affection, a revelation he significantly compares to the Copernican revolution, which dealt a major blow to religious authority in the sixteenth century.[12] Like the Sufi devotee, Kamal stands before ʿAyda as a humble believer. 'Bow in praise and thanksgiving', he tells himself as he gets into a car with her.[13] Her name is too holy for him to utter even in secret, which may contradict the Sufi practice of *dhikr* but certainly conveys the degree of mystery surrounding her. Moreover, her presence has an overwhelming effect on him.

> Kamal felt held in place by an overpowering magnetic force. He was in a state between sleeping and waking, conscious only of a sense of gratitude and a pulsing ecstasy.[14]

The state of sleeping and waking and image of pulsing ecstasy are Sufi tropes. To these evocative images we can add the theme of drunkenness. The encounter with God, when after a long struggle on the path of self-purification the seeker is finally opened up to effusions of divine love, mercy and knowledge, is likened in Sufi discourse to a state of intoxication.[15] The Sufi aspirant becomes drunk in the embrace of the Lord. He loses consciousness of his self, dissolving in the divine presence and experiencing the state of *fanā'* (annihilation).[16]

The language of intoxication is employed frequently in *Qasr al-Shawq* to portray the effect that ʿAyda has on Kamal. Her angelic voice sends him into an inebriated ecstasy and the mention of her voice leaves him feeling intoxicated.[17] The mystical character of Kamal and ʿAyda's relationship is corroborated by the kind of love that Kamal feels for her and the kind of union that he envisages. At no point does he express physical longing for ʿAyda, nor does he aspire to marriage in the future.[18] His love is of the purest kind, divine rather than human, and will not be consummated through conventional methods. 'All the evidence indicates that there is no connection to the adored (*al-maʿbūd*) except through chanting and insanity. So chant or go insane'.[19] In other words, Kamal pictures an encounter with ʿAyda in terms of the kind of *dhikr* ritual for which the Sufis are famous, whilst the reference to madness here is another Sufi signifier. In spatial terms, it is noteworthy that the Shaddad mansion, where ʿAyda lives with her family, is portrayed as a shrine in *Qasr al-Shawq* and becomes Kamal's new site of pilgrimage, after the mosque of al-Husayn in *Bayn al-Qasrayn*. Its 'aloofness and introversion seemed to symbolise the power, purity, refusal and obscurity of the beloved (*al-maḥbūb*)'.[20]

Kamal is of course disappointed in love. ʿAyda turns out to be a cruel goddess and he is left with a broken heart. But the Sufi symbolism does not end here. It continues into *Al-Sukkariyya* with truth as the new object of the quest. For the greater part of the third volume Kamal is committed to discovering truth via rational and scientific methods. However his goal is elusive and grants him only limited satisfaction.[21] Thus he turns to alcohol and prostitutes for pleasure and relief. Alcohol provides an escape from his barren world, his 'key to happy release (*miftāḥ al-faraj*)'.[22] Intoxication (*sukr*), as noted, describes the state of ecstasy which the Sufi experiences in God's presence. The irony here is that Kamal achieves this ecstasy without faith or a divine presence, either literal or metaphorical. Does this mean that the quest for God is over by the third volume? Is intoxication now merely a physical state with no spiritual content? Kamal abandoned his religious faith at the end of *Qasr al-Shawq* at the same time as he lost ʿAyda and the perfect image of his father. Yet he did not abandon God altogether. He insists that he is not an atheist (*kāfir*)[23] and regards his search for truth as synonymous with the quest for God, for 'by liberating himself from religion he will become closer to God.'[24] In his revised quest he is playing out another theme of the Sufi path, since the Sufis strive for knowledge as well as love. Indeed celebrated Sufi poet Rumi suggests understanding the former to be a condition of the latter:

> Love makes kings into slaves –
> But this love results from knowledge.
> When did a fool sit on this throne?
> How can faulty knowledge give birth to love?[25]

This knowledge sought by the Sufis is of a special kind, intuitive rather than rational.[26] It cannot be found in books but comes instead from opening up the heart to God (2: 282), which in turn requires self-purification. Kamal's quest for truth is an intellectual one, but the image of purifying the self is the same. If this is not enough to establish the Sufi path as an intertext for Kamal's quest in *Al-Sukkariyya*, we are told explicitly in this volume that 'his soul is fighting with two extremes: the abode of carnal appetites and Sufism (*taṣawwuf*)'.[27] We are even told that he has experimented with modern spiritualism (*al-rūḥiyya al-ḥadītha*),[28] though no detail is provided in respect of this. In this reading, Kamal's refusal to marry is an expression of worldly rejection and signifier of Sufi asceticism. The decision is surely a religious one, even if Kamal admits this only indirectly: 'he would look up [to the sky] and imagine that marriage would cause him to lower his gaze'.[29] His turn to alcohol in *Al-Sukkariyya*, more than a marker of a newfound scorn towards religious prohibitions, is an expression of spiritual yearning, an activity undertaken in order to achieve the state of annihilation (*fanāʾ*) that the Sufi experiences in God's presence. He explains the symbolism himself towards the end of *Qasr al-Shawq* on the occasion of his first drink. Alcohol is merely a precursor and the real question is how to achieve perpetual intoxication without resort to alcohol.[30]

In the end, the Sufi path leads nowhere. Kamal does not connect in any significant way with the beloved in *Qasr al-Shawq* and he does not discover the truth for which he is searching in *Al-Sukkariyya*, perhaps because his method is flawed – knowledge of God, the Sufis will tell us, is communicated to the heart, and Kamal's heart remains closed. Human love is a route to divine love in Sufi discourse but Kamal rejects marriage and his love for ʿAyda is platonic. The nobleman in Yahya Haqqi's 'Al-Qiddis la Yuhar'[31] suffers a similar failing in Elmarsafy's reading. The character's rejection of love and dance in this short story is an obstacle on the path to God.[32] In the end Kamal's nephew Ahmad guides him to perpetual revolution and he realises that doubt is simply another form of escape, like Sufism and passive belief in science.[33] The Sufi theme does not, in the end, take us much further with respect to the question of God than what is communicated on the surface of the plot. What it does is deepen the protagonist's quest, developing the metaphysical theme on a subterranean level, and introduce the symbolic potential of Sufism in Egyptian narrative discourse. In the years following the trilogy the author built on this potential. In *Al-Tariq* (1964), published seven years later, whose title alludes to both the Sufi path and the Sufi orders, a paternal search becomes a metaphor for a profound mystical quest. The absent father, like the God of the Sufis, is mysterious, elusive and the key to his son's happiness, and its protagonist's journey recalls the Sufi way inasmuch as, like the Sufi aspirant, Sabir cuts ties with the world he knows and goes in search of an elusive entity.[34] *Al-Shahhadh* (1965), published a year later, uses a character's personal crisis to explore the path of the mystic. ʿUmar is overcome by lethargy and a sense of futility. After attempting to overcome his ennui through extra-marital activities, he renounces everything – family, friends, work, women – in the hope of finding truth and happiness in solitude, in a manner reminiscent of the Sufi.[35] Both searches fail. Sabir catches sight of his father but only when it is too late, after he has sealed his fate through murder, and ʿUmar experiences a state of ecstasy and intoxication but the moment is fleeting and he acquires from it no lasting knowledge or understanding. The story ends with its protagonist dragged rudely back into the world, caught up in the arrest of a former friend and political activist. Meanwhile his quest is condemned as selfish and self-serving: 'When we are conscious of our responsibility towards the millions the search for personal meaning becomes meaningless'.[36] A similar criticism of the Sufi way is developed in *Al-Liss wa'l-Kilab* (1961), where Shaykh al-Junaydi's spiritual counsel and transcendental escapism, to borrow from El-Enany, is irrelevant to the very pressing problems faced by its protagonist Saʿid Mahran.[37]

These works reveal a critical flaw in Sufism from the point of view of an artist concerned with social and existential problems. The individualistic nature of the path, the fact that it is taken alone and involves renunciation of the world, means that it is necessarily limited. Characters who achieve spiritual tranquillity, like Radwan al-Husayni and Shaykh al-Junaydi, are of no practical help to those around them, while ordinary folk who strive in the path of Sufism either fail ('Zaʿbalawi') or achieve glimpses that serve no enduring purpose (*Al-Shahhadh, Al-Tariq*).[38] At the same time the author has doubts about the benevolence and existence of God. This is suggested in the person of Jabalawi in *Awlad Haratina* and another allegorical novel, *Qalb al-Layl* (1975), which also deals with man's spiritual evolution but envisages the journey away from God as one of freedom and discovery.[39] Stories like 'Al-Zalam' (1967) and 'Dunya Allah' (1963) challenge the equation of divinity and goodness. The former portrays a group of people at the mercy of a cruel old man whose omniscience and omnipotence make him a symbol for God and whose betrayal of his followers hints at divine malevolence, and in the latter the character Ibrahim gestures to God's neglect.[40]

Given the author's doubts about God, the question arises as to why he should continue to engage with Sufism beyond the 1960s, by which point its limitations have been amply revealed in his stories and its goal more or less rejected. The answer lies in the possibilities Sufism offered to him as an artist and to the new literary sensibility, whose rejection of unitary meaning, reason and orthodoxy and tendency towards symbol, allusion, polyphony and fragmentation found echoes in Sufi discourse. In the 1970s and 1980s Mahfuz's engagements with Sufism focus on its symbolic value and potential as counter-narrative. Shaykh ʿAbdullah al-Balkhi's function in *Layali Alf Layla* (1980), Mahfuz's tour de force reimagining of *1001 Nights* which combines political allegory, spiritual quest, multi-layered intertextuality and superlative storytelling, and cleverly begins where the original tale left off, with Shahrazad's pardon, thus becoming in part a study of the *Nights*' resolution and model of kingship (its autocratic character being a metaphor for contemporary Egypt), is to cast doubt on the appearance of things, as al-Musawi has shown in his chapter on the novel.[41] Shaykh ᶜAbdullah al-Balkhi, like Shaykh al-Junaydi in *Al-Liss waʾl-Kilab*, stands for spirituality and moral perfection and where characters stand in relation to him is a good indication of their integrity or state of mind at a given moment in the text. For example, ᶜAlaʾ al-Din alternates between the shaykh's house and fountain as his social conscience and spiritual yearning vie with one another. But more significantly, ᶜAbdullah al-Balkhi's subdued response to the news of Shahrayar's change of heart, which brings the slaughter of the kingdom's virgins to an end and occasions widespread jubilation in the quarter, signals that something is amiss, namely that this single act of mercy does not necessarily mean that the king has ceased to be a menace to his subjects. The shaykh also intuitively grasps ᶜAbdullah the Porter's secret and that Sinbad is hiding something: 'To him discourse is not necessarily identical with the story'.[42] The Sufi theme in *Rihlat Ibn Fattuma* (1983) serves a similar purpose, undermining the quest for political utopia undertaken by the protagonist on the surface of the plot. For while on one level the text reads as a reimagining of the travelogue of famous twelfth-century Moroccan traveller Ibn Battuta as a journey through ideological time in search of a perfect society, references in the opening lines, such as to the dreaming and wakefulness and the perplexed soul passing through different stations, invite a Sufi reading of the text and suggest the goal to be rather more transcendental than socio-political, as Ouyang has shown.[43] The disruptive elements and symbolic potential of Sufism were also taken advantage of by other Egyptian writers in this period. ᶜAbd al-Hakim Qasim in *Ayyam al-Insan al-Sabᶜa* (1969) employs the framework of a Sufi festival to problematise the protagonist's journey from childhood bliss and ignorance to adult cognisance. The Sufi sensibility that pervades the text, even after the protagonist rejects it, exposes the tensions in modern life and rational discourse.[44] Salwa Bakr in *Maqam ᶜAtiyya* (1986) combines popular aspects of Sufism with fragmentation, polyphony and myth to challenge patriarchal ideology and the discourse of the nation.[45] Jamal al-Ghitani in his *Kitab al-*

Tajalliyyat (1983) conducts an intertextual dialogue with Ibn ʿArabi's work of the same name and draws on Sufi language and idiom to explore themes of selfhood and survival, among other things.[46] The contributions of these and other writers post-1967 are what critics are referring to when they speak of the turn to Sufism in modern Arabic literature. Its potential as a counterpoint to modernity and source of meaning, and the commonalities between its language and vision and the new literary sensibility, ensured a place for Sufism in Egyptian fiction of this period.[47] The remainder of this chapter will use the short novels *Hikayat Haratina* (1975) and *Asdaʾ al-Sirat al-Dhatiyya* (1995) by Mahfuz to further explore this mystical–literary coalescence.

Hikayat Haratina takes the form of a fictional memoir. The seventy-eight tales that make up the text combine to tell not one but three stories, two of which have the theme of transition at the centre. The most basic of these concerns a child's induction into the world. The narrator begins by recalling a series of formative episodes in his young life, like his circumcision and first encounter with pain, romance, death and separation (tales 2–11), then moves on to reminisce more generally. This reminiscing, broadly speaking, proceeds from tales relating to the 1919 revolution to accounts of local figures and events, including a cluster presenting clan chiefs in different lights (tales 50–57). The last part of the text presents a series of peculiar and rather disturbing tales, which underline the ironies of time and fate. The boy's maturing process is thus traced indirectly; it is implied in the sequence of material, in the transition from private recollection to public observation as opposed to through conventional diegesis, as well as reflected in the language, which is at its most poetic in the childhood section. The second story is that of the *ḥāra*. Over the course of the text, the narrator paints a vivid picture of his local habitat, which could be any one of the quarters of old Cairo in the early years of the twentieth century (students of Mahfuz will naturally read it as Jamaliyya). As the reader follows the boy's journey towards maturity he/she follows Egypt's journey through a particularly turbulent period in its history – the decades in which the battle for independence was fought and won but with a heavy price, as evidenced by the martyrs in the text. The connection between the child's journey and that of the nation means that the latter too is cast in the role of initiate: Egypt, like the child, is travelling from an age of innocence to one of enlightenment and sophistication, so that on the face of it the narrative rehearses the master narrative of modernity. The ousting of the *futuwwa* system in Tale 57 corroborates this, as an event driven by the people and demonstrative of a growing consciousness of popular power and self-determination. The path to nationhood, here as in the novels discussed in Part 1, involves the displacement of religion, as suggested by the fate of Shaykh Labib, who finds himself cast into oblivion as Egypt embraces modernity: 'frequent visitors to him become rare until they cease or as good as cease'.[48] Yet modernity and self-determination do not solve society's problems. The impression is rather that the alley simply moves from one dark age into another, for the abolishment of the *futuwwa* is followed by a scene of pandemonium (Tale 58) and a number of disturbing, at times surreal tales, summed up by Anwar Jalal's hysterical outburst in the penultimate *ḥikāya*. With progress, which apart from the ousting of the *futuwwa* is represented by the introduction of electricity, come chaos and moral degeneration. The sight of Nuʾnuʾ and One-Eye (al-Aʿwar) stumbling around in the dark in Tale 74 implies that progress is illusory; the waiter recalls 'watching the two of them as they circled around each other under the illusion that they were making progress'.[49] The most critical moment in the *ḥāra* story comes in Tale 76 when an urban renewal project threatens the existence of the *takiyya*, another indicator of the incongruity of religion with modern life. On this occasion the *takiyya* survives, amidst protests from the locals and pleas for constraint: 'Isn't there more than one way north?'[50] But the impression is that its days are numbered and that religion is losing ground. In this respect it is noteworthy that the role of prophet is taken over by the geography teacher. It is now a representative of science who foretells the storm and flood.[51]

The third story is that of the Sufi striving to achieve divine union and requires an allegorical and intertextual reading. In other works written during this period, Mahfuz creates structural relationships with past texts or genres to establish the interpretative context. *Hikayat*, on the other hand, depends on a system of Sufi references and symbols to signal another level of meaning, which in fact moves in the opposite direction to the *ḥāra* story: towards religion rather than away from it, thus countering and problematising the surface movement of the plot.

The Sufi connection is established on the first page. The narrator opens the text with the words 'I like playing in the square between the arch and the *takiyya*'[52] and goes on to introduce the Grand Shaykh, who is pictured in a green cape and chanting a line of Persian poetry: 'My nightingale, *khūn dalī khurd wakullī ḥāṣal kurd*' before tossing the boy a mulberry.[53] The *takiyya* and its serene inhabitants stand for the *ṭarīqa* tradition, that is, the Sufi orders that proliferated from the twelfth century and found their natural home in private hostels where they could celebrate God away from the world. The Grand Shaykh, with the allusion to green clothing, apart from a Sufi leader is an allusion to al-Khidr, the legendary companion of Moses (cf. *Surat al-Kahf*) and patron saint of travellers, who in Sufi tradition may invest a *murīd* (Sufi aspirant) with the *khirqa* (inauguratory cloak) and initiate him into the way in place of an earthly mentor. His peculiar indirect address to the boy followed by silence recalls the difficult first stages of initiation, which Schimmel notes may involve days of waiting at the Sufi master's door and other methods of humiliation.[54] The lines in Persian bring in the historical role played by this region in mystical Islam, for Iran produced some of Sufism's most important figures and the Persian language has also left its distinct mark on Arabic's mystical vocabulary. The nightingale and mulberry tree are significant too. The former symbolises the lover of beauty in Rumi's verse and in mystical poetry is usually mentioned in connection with the rose and represents the soul's yearning for union with God,[55] while the mulberry tree has mythological and religious connotations and is associated with certain Sufi orders.[56]

References continue throughout the text. *Sukr* (intoxication)[57] is repeatedly evoked by expressions of drunkenness, either metaphorical or literal. Saniyya in Tale 24 becomes 'melodiously drunk'[58] and ʿAbbas Jahsh's heart is filled with the intoxicating nectar of love.[59] The boy is attracted to a girl significantly named Darwisha at the *kuttāb* in Tale 6 and after their encounter claims to have known drunkenness (*sukr*) before touching wine (*al-khamr*).[60] These combine to form a Sufi code which, together with poetic language in the early part of the text, suggests a deep level of symbolism and calls for a Sufi reading.

Such a reading renders the first tale anew. The Grand Shaykh becomes, more than a reference to Khidr or leader of a *ṭarīqa*, a symbol of the Divine. He is a magnificent sight – 'I become drunk from his light, his spectacle fills the universe'.[61] The transcendence of human imagination and encompassment of the universe indicated here represents the indescribability of God at the heart of Sufi discourse and *tawḥīd*, while the boy's intoxication once more summons the state of *sukr*. The whole episode recalls *fanāʾ*, the moment the Sufi achieves divine union. The experience is transitory, for the mulberry tossed by the Grand Shaykh and the Grand Shaykh himself vanish almost immediately. According to Sufism, through *fanāʾ* the mystic develops perfect selfhood and returns, inspired, to the world. But the experience leaves the boy confused and alone, unable to convince his own father of what he has seen. From this point on the narrative becomes an attempt to retrieve, or at least understand, the mesmerising episode, to answer the question posed at the end of Tale 1: 'Did I really see the Shaykh or pretend I did to get attention then come to believe it myself?'[62] Presenting *fanāʾ* at the outset, positioning the destination of the Sufi at the beginning as opposed to the end of the text, inverts the Sufi path. The rest of the text becomes a sequel to divine union, an exploration of what comes after and an attempt to retrieve that elusive moment of bliss and cognition. The father's suggestion that his son keep his experience quiet further recalls the subversive element of mysticism. Direct communion with the Divine threatens the authority of the *ʿulamāʾ*, Islamic law and even scripture, which is why Sufis have been persecuted historically.

The first two stories of *Hikayat*, while their start and end points are arbitrary, progress in a more or less linear fashion; the innocence and ignorance of the boy and his country are gradually replaced by a more enlightened consciousness and scepticism. The third story, the attempt to retrieve God, on the other hand, reproduces the traditional strategy of accruing tales which persuade through their repetition.[63] Once the rupture (the loss of the Grand Shaykh) is introduced in the first tale, the narrator of *Hikayat* falls back on Sufi references and language (the Sufi code) to keep the mystical tradition in the reader's consciousness and goes on to amass memories, the sum total of which imparts the message that the sublime experience will not be repeated; the Sufi path is flawed, no doubt on account of the transitory and exclusive nature of divine union. The first tale shows us that the intoxication and ecstasy lasts only a moment, while the text in its entirety is evidence that it has no lasting benefits for either the recipient or wider society. Time and again evil, injustice and tragedy beset the alley's inhabitants as the boy stands by as spectator. If he has known God it has certainly not equipped him to live or understand life any differently. When all this is confirmed in the final tale it does not perceptibly follow on from events in the tales that immediately precede it, but nor does it come as a surprise, for the pattern of the *ḥikāyāt* – the cycle of misery, tragedy and confusion – prepares the reader for a disappointing ending.

The Sufi theme in *Hikayat* does not, then, resolve any metaphysical questions and merely rehearses the author's familiar criticisms of the mystical path. What it does do is serve as a counter-narrative to the story of individual and national becoming and as a counterpoint to modernity and its assumptions. The quest for God signified in the Sufi reading moves in the opposite direction to the surface plot – away from God and religion – and points to a lacuna in modernity and the ideology of nation. The Sufi references draw attention to another realm or possibility, a spiritual alternative to modern life, secular ideology and science. The *takiyya* is the spatial representation of this. Located on the fringes of the alley, prominent yet impenetrable, it signifies the alluring presence of the mystical and irrational suppressed by the discourse of modernity and nation. The character of Shaykh ʿUmar Fikri in the final tale is significant in this respect. A retired law clerk, ʿUmar's attempt to meet the Grand Shaykh years earlier involved interrogating the wise and pious and gathering data on the *takiyya*'s endowment, the particular *ṭarīqa* of its inhabitants and the dervish responsible for collecting the income from the Bureau of *Waqf* (endowments) but to no avail. ʿUmar's profession, method and surname, Fikri (intellectual), align him with the Muslim theologians, that is, the Sufis' ideological opponents. The Bureau stands for Islamic science and learning and the wise and pious evoke religious authorities. ʿUmar's failure to gain access to the Grand Shaykh exposes the limitations of reason and rational methods and makes space for the mystical, irrational and unscientific.

The criticism of reason and its accompanying values – logic, causality, unitary discourse – implied by ʿUmar's tale is developed on the level of form, where again it is helped along by the Sufi connection. *Hikayat* employs fragmentation as a narrative strategy. The memoir is inconsistent in terms of material and patchy in terms of content; character profiles are mixed with recollections of events and scenes, symbolism and allegory are found next to realism and virtual surrealism, language oscillates between evocative prose and near reportage, and large segments of the child's life remain unaccounted for. Longer tales are broken down into sections separated on the printed page by asterixes and empty space so that they are visually fragmented. The pretext for fragmentation here is of course memory, which follows its own pattern of association and overrides chronology and totality, but it also represents a challenge to unitary discourse. Life, reality and meaning do not form a singular cohesive thread, therefore the kind of causal relations and tidy beginnings and endings found in conventional narrative and life-writing are false. The text communicates this by flouting the rules of conventional storytelling and presenting itself in a supposedly random and episodic form. This sentiment has echoes in the Sufi vision of God and the world. Sufis reject the kind of thinking that forces everything into a single authoritative discourse. They believe that every visible thing (*ẓāhir*) has an inner aspect (*bāṭin*), and their vision of God as all-encompassing, transcendent yet imminent, allows space for paradoxes and plural meanings. The fragmented, discontinuous shape of *Hikayat* enacts this semiotic multiplicity and celebration of incongruence, while the multi-layered plot and inverted mystical quest mirror Sufism's dualistic vision (*ẓāhir/bāṭin*).

Time in the narrative further aligns with Sufi concepts, or can be seen as such in a text in which mysticism is consistently referenced. Like *Al-Maraya* and to an extent *Hadith al-Sabah wa'l-Masaʾ*, *Hikayat* operates a complex hierarchy of temporal schemes. At the top is the present tense narrator as he delivers his account (story-time). To this is subordinated the private time of the narrator, public time, the private times of the characters profiled, alley time – a mythical time distinct from public time in the wider world – and fate. At different points different time schemes dominate but they never form a unity or continuity. Instead, time is simultaneity, which coincides with the Sufi concept of time compressed in a moment and the synchronicity of everything. In the context of the memoir this has the added significance of destablising conventional historiography. Man is not on an upward trajectory of progress, as the absence of answers to key questions at the end of the text demonstrates. Rather, the coexistence of different time currents leads to tension. Tradition and local custom prevail on the alley majority while modernity, innovation and foreign ideals – the ingredients of time beyond the alley confines – threaten to upset its harmony. When representatives of the latter intrude or when alley inhabitants embrace the time of the other, the result is conflict, as Tawhida, Patrick al-Hamawi and the geography teacher all discover.

The convergence of post-1967 narrative strategies and the Sufi themes and concepts is also a feature in *Asdaʾ al-Sirat al-Dhatiyya*, another fragmented text that presents itself as life-writing. Indeed the personal element is stronger here insofar as the subject is now the individual self, not its environment as in *Hikayat* as fictional memoir. But it would be wrong to assume a correlation between the personal experience recounted in the text and its author, not least because of his attitude to the form of autobiography. In an interview for *Al-Musawwar* in 1990 (four years before *Asdaʾ* appeared) Mahfuz articulated a distaste for the genre, which in his view should be reserved for politicians and military officials to communicate previously unknown facts of public interest.[64] Moreover, the text includes details which contradict the author's life story, including the protagonist's incarceration and initiation into a Sufi brotherhood. Indeed El-Enany remarks that there is more of Mahfuz's personal life in other works of his which make no claim to biography.[65] The focus of attention in reading *Asdaʾ* should not, then, be what it reveals about the author's life but what the author seeks to achieve by presenting it in the form of an autobiography. This is partly a play on genre expectations, or internalised notions of literary form. It also signals confessional literature, or spiritual autobiography, to be a context of interpretation, for the title refers to echoes (*aṣdāʾ*) of *al-sīrat al-dhātiyya*, that is, the genre of autobiography, not 'echoes of *an* autobiography', as the title of the published English translation has it.

The practice of writing an account of one's spiritual development in Arabic goes back as far as al-Muhasibi (d. 857) and al-Tirmidhi (d. 898) and reached a high point with al-Ghazali's (d. 1111) *Al-Munqidh min al-Dalal* (Rescuer from Error). It continued to flourish in the centuries that followed in works by al-Simnani (d. 1336), Zarruq (d. 1493), al-Shaʿrani (d. 1565), al-Yusi (d. 1691) and Ibn ʿAjiba (d. 1809) and there are examples of continuity in modern times in ʿAbd al-Halim Mahmud's *Al-Hamdu li'Llah Hadhihi Hayati* (*This is My Life, Praise God*), Mikhaʾil Nuʿayma's *Sabʿun* (*Seventy*) and Ahmad Amin's *Hayati* (*My Life*), to name but a few.[66] The purpose of the form is to describe one's path to God as a model for others to follow. Al-Ghazali offers an erudite account of an existential crisis that compelled him to set out in search of Truth, which he eventually found in Sufism. Al-Samawʾal al-Maghribi (d. 1174) describes his conversion from Judaism to Islam in *Ifham al-Yahud* (Silencing the Jews) and Fray Anselmo Turmeda (d.c. 1432) outlines the road that brought him from Christianity to Islam. Spiritual autobiography thus cuts across the religious spectrum. It is the Sufi version, more specifically its goal (the discovery of Truth) and basic premise (the idea that by emulating the author's example the reader too will find God), that are at issue here.

The title only tentatively points the reader towards this body of work – *sīra dhātiyya* is after all a modern coinage, as Tetz Rooke lays out in his study of Arabic autobiography,[67] and it is sometime before the Sufi intertext is properly established in *Asdaʾ*. The narrative begins with a child confronting history. Aged six he one day finds school closed and lessons cancelled due to demonstrations and is so delighted that he prays the revolution, which can be read as the popular Egyptian uprising of 1919, will last forever.[68] The text is divided into short segments that range from dramatic scenes, episodes and character sketches, to dream narratives, allegories, poetic lines and moments of sheer absurdity. Some of these consist of no more than a sentence or two, especially towards the end of the text. Thus it is no longer possible to speak in terms of tales (*ḥikāyāt*); rather this is a medley of narrative events held together by the narrator and governed by his unpredictable mind. The effect is of course fragmentation, with all the implications this has for the representation of time, space, character and event. And on this occasion the very brevity of the individual excerpts heightens the visual effect on the page. Textual fragmentation is once again a reflection of the narrator's mind and an embodiment of social and ideological breakdown. In the latter quarter of the twentieth century tidy and logical plot sequences were out of step with experience. As the narrative progresses it becomes increasingly clear that the scenes and characters glimpsed, only ever for a moment, are more important for what they signify than for what they are. The title raises certain expectations; it establishes the autobiographical pact and instructs the reader to adopt a certain set of interpretative strategies.[69] But these expectations are not met as he/she is deprived of basic information like the subject's name, family, time and place. Instead information is imparted indirectly, the emphasis rarely on the event described. In the third segment, 'Dayn Qadim' (An Old Debt), the nature of the boy's illness is not revealed, only the resolution to apply himself following the experience. Following this, in 'Al-Haraka al-

Qadima' (The Next Move), the details of the posting are omitted and the reader is left guessing the meaning of the words exchanged, which are obviously symbolic. In the segment after that, 'Muftaraq al-Turuq' (Crossroads), the recollection of various visitors to the house draws attention to destiny, the fact that some people grow rich while others remain poor, and to the boy's inquisitive nature, but gives little away about the persons involved, not even their names and professions. The pattern of omitting or obscuring information continues throughout the text and produces two effects. On the one hand it blurs the lines between the novel and the historiographical form of autobiography, drawing attention to the constructedness of the past by challenging expectations and foregrounding the narrator's role in narrative. On the level of the individual segments, on the other hand, it encourages the reader to concentrate on their meaning, what lies beneath the surface.

The first half of the text can be described as a trip down memory lane fueled by questions the narrator finds particularly troublesome. Time, as ever with Mahfuz, is a consuming issue. The suffering it occasions is introduced early with the death of the boy's grandmother in the second excerpt, 'Ritha'' (Lamentation), and it does not take long for the reader to realise that in the bewildering and chaotic world of the narrator death is the only certainty, 'the firmly established truth (al-ḥaqīqa al-rāsikha)'.[70] The narrator's deliberations on the ageing process and the transient nature of joy and beauty also remind us why the relation of time and man is for Mahfuz a tragic one. The passage of time is certainly not something the narrator cherishes. Moreover, unlike in *Hadith al-Sabah wa'l-Masa'*, where the disintegration of traditional institutions and values and a way of life treasured by the writer is balanced by positive developments, like education, female emancipation, new economic opportunities and increased social mobility, there is nothing to compensate the narrator when he returns to his childhood quarter in 'Al-Saʿada' (Happiness): 'No trace of its golden form to speak of'.[71] Memories of love, romance and feminine beauty stir regret and nostalgia for days past, for instance in 'Al-Marah' (Joy)[72] and 'Hayhata' (Vainly!).[73] The act of recollection naturally turns the narrator's thoughts to the question of memory. Can it be trusted? Did all those people really live?[74] Apart from what it betrays about the narrator's personal apprehensions, constant allusion to memory, either explicit or implicit, draws the reader's attention to what he is dealing with; namely that every segment of the narrative has its origins in a subjective phenomenon and can only ever represent one truth among many.

Time, the passage of time, love and memory thus emerge as key themes in the first half of the text.[75] Two thirds through the narrative, the narrator meets Shaykh ʿAbd Rabbihi al-Taʾih[76] and is initiated into a Sufi brotherhood. The event and narrator's decisive statement that 'I am almost fed up with the world and wish to flee from it',[77] though sudden, hardly comes as a shock, for by this point the reader has a good idea of the character, his anxieties and the incoherent world he inhabits, of an individual ill at ease in his environment. Instead it makes sense of the Sufi references that proliferate in the preceding text and confirms that this is a story of religious conversion, that the biography of the self (*sīra dhātiyya*) in the title refers not to Mahfuz the man but a fictionalised Sufi convert. Midway through *Asdaʾ* the reader is finally equipped with the necessary reading apparatus with which to decipher the text. If Sufi references early on had led him/her to suspect mystical Islam to have a role in *Asdaʾ*, then the initiation into the brotherhood along with certain developments in structure and mode in the second half of the text provide the confirmation. The event is not only marked by a spatial shift, the cave now the predominant setting, and the emergence of a new storyteller in the person of Shaykh ʿAbd Rabbihi al-Taʾih and relegation of the narrator to the status of transmitter, but there is also a shift in form. The fragmentary and elusive portrayal of characters and scenes gradually gives way to sermonettes, adages, admonitions, and question and answer excerpts reminiscent of Sufi writing on a range of topics, many of which echo themes raised in the first half of the text, and to an even greater poeticism, which makes greater demands on the reader's imagination.

The final segment of *Asdaʾ* finds the shaykh's disciples assembled in the cave eagerly awaiting 'Al-Faraj' (Release) as indicated in its title. On the shaykh's instructions they fix their gaze upon the door of the cave and at the appropriate moment the reader is informed that 'In our apprehension the inner vision (*baṣīra*) saw it and the soul (*sarīra*) heard it'.[78] After a period of preparation under the tutorship of ʿAbd Rabbihi al-Taʾih the narrator and his companions succeed in their mission (the inner vision parallels Ibn ʿArabi's esoteric eye, *ʿayn al-baṣīra*) and we have another reference to *fanāʾ*. With this the narrative trails off, leaving the reader wondering what exactly was seen and heard, what exactly the shaykh meant when he predicted moments earlier: 'Happy is he who has fulfilled his task in the market or who has defied grief.'[79] As was the case with the narrator's initiation into the brotherhood, the reader is once again not surprised that he should not be privy to the sublime experience afforded the narrator, for he has already become quite distanced from the speaking voice. The first half of the text is presented in the first person with the narrator addressing his reader. When he meets ʿAbd Rabbihi al-Taʾih this changes. The reader follows him into the cave but from this point on the narrator is absorbed by the shaykh and his inner life. His gaze focused on the sublime, the narrator loses interest in the exoteric world to which the reader belongs. The shaykh assumes control of the narrative and from now on most of the segments are related in the third person and begin: '*Qāla al-Shaykh ʿAbd Rabbihi al-Taʾih …*' Moreover, the narrator makes no attempt to unravel his master's ambiguous utterances or mediate for the reader, who is consequently marginalised. That the reader is denied the ultimate epiphany shows that divine union, and the insight derived forthwith, are exclusive and private. Mahfuz draws the reader into the life of the narrator only to separate them at the critical moment. The point to note here is the way in which the message is assimilated. Rather than spelling it out explicitly, the reader is made to experience himself the limitations or exclusivity of the Sufi path.

A Sufi code is developed from the beginning in *Asdaʾ*. The first half of the text, as mentioned, contains a number of Sufi references whose significance the reader only fully appreciates when ʿAbd Rabbihi al-Taʾih emerges onto the scene. For example, as in *Hikayat*, there are several references to intoxication and drunkenness. The nightingale is evoked once more, this time pictured as a group of birds singing above a golden tomb upon which are engraved the cryptic words 'Salubrious is he whose upbringing was in the crucible of abandonment', which one can easily imagine in a Sufi text.[80] Excerpt titles like 'Al-Rihla' (The Journey) and 'Al-Bahth' (The Search) allude to the Sufi path, while another, 'Al-Mutasawwil' evokes the Sufi figure of the beggar. A man is overcome by depression and ennui and takes himself off to wander on the seashore, calling to mind the Sufi metaphor of the ocean, which symbolises the vastness of being.[81] In this context, the narrative's female contingent assumes a symbolic role. Just as Sufi poetics conflates profane love and divine love, so some of the women in *Asdaʾ* take on divine attributes and evoke the Beloved. A woman of exquisite beauty emerges from the Nile, filling the narrator with fear. She invites him to follow her and he advances with magical power, his eyes locked on her countenance.[82] The narrator dreams that a beautiful woman invites him to meet her but he is so distracted by the slave-girl that he enters the meeting in a state of unreadiness, 'defeated and rusted'.[83] In an excerpt significantly entitled 'Al-Tarab' (Rapture), a reference to Sufi ecstasy, 'a beautiful woman is created in a state of rapture and loved by pure hearts',[84] then leaves no trace except in the world of rapture (*dunyā al-ṭarab*), recalling the Sufi idea that God is glimpsed only in traces and reflections. On the next page the narrator finds himself on a shore and notices a 'woman standing neither far away nor close by'.[85] As he approaches the distance does not lessen and she does not turn around despite his repeated calls. These encounters and others in the text are not simply lyrical accounts of exoteric events; the language they employ and the emotions and states (*aḥwāl*) they engender – fear, rapture, intoxication, confusion, serenity – point to a deeper symbolism.

With the first part of the text geared towards everyday experience, the world and the manifest and the second towards spiritual experience, the metaphysical and the veiled the text's structure embodies the dualism that characterises the Sufis' way of viewing the world. The first half corresponds with *ẓāhir*, the second with *bāṭin*. This idea also informs the deployment of space, for the drama is divided between two main spaces; the realm of daily life – the alley with the market as its focal point (exoteric space), and the realm of spiritual life – the cave where the shaykh and his disciples convene and where dervish jamborees and ecstatic worship take place (esoteric space). That the cave is located away from the city and is not open to everyone, as suggested in 'Al-Taʿarruf' (Becoming Acquainted), implies that transferring to esoteric reality is not simple.[86]

The most obvious Sufi reference of course comes in the character of ʿAbd Rabbihi al-Taʾih and it is not insignificant that the cave he inhabits is known as the tavern. As the leader of a brotherhood and spiritual guide to the narrator, he is a reincarnation of the traditional Sufi master. His typically obscure utterances and anecdotes, apart from reflecting the linguistic norms of mystical discourse, call to mind characters like ʿAbdullah al-Balkhi and al-Junaydi, but unlike them he does not reject the world, at least not in his discourse (his positioning in the cave tells a different story). Love of the world is a guiding principle for him and something of a refrain. When the shaykh enquires about the narrator's motivations the narrator cites escape and the shaykh replies: 'Love of the world is the pivot of our path and our enemy is escape'.[87] When questioned on his ideal the shaykh recalls a man who devoted his life to serving other people and God and who celebrated his hundredth birthday with wine and song and married a young virgin. He was then visited by angels, confirming God and the shaykh's approval.[88] When the shaykh's love of women, food, poetry, knowledge and singing is questioned he attributes it to God, and he seems to excuse rather than endorse his brethren's disparagement of the world ('They find fault with the corruption that prevails in it').[89] The Sufi shaykh of *Asdaʾ* is a correction to the aesthetic recluse who abandons the world altogether, though there is a conflict between action and words here, for the shaykh is hardly a practical actor himself, but this can perhaps be attributed to the narrow lens onto this character, whom we meet only in his capacity as dispenser of wisdom.

The symbolic character of *Asdaʾ*, the fact that the segments are more important for what they signify than for what they are, and the intertextual dialogue with spiritual autobiography and Sufism, points once more to plural readings and meaning and a convergence of mystical discourse and post-1967 literary sensibilities. The marriage is further embodied in the text's employment of surrealism, paradox and poetic language. Many scenes and events break with familiar experience and enter the realm of dream and fantasy. For example, the scene of the man in a cafe who claims to prefer playing billiards alone in front of a crowd but is surrounded by sleeping customers breaks with realism,[90] as does the following excerpt, which relates how the narrator dreamed of a gift of a pearl and woke to find one on his pillow.[91] A few pages later the narrator meets 'an enormous person with a stomach the size of the ocean and a mouth that could swallow an elephant', who claims to be forgetfulness (*nisyān*).[92] The narrator dreams he is in a spacious room resolving to carry out an unspecified task when his companion disappears and reappears as a face in his coffee cup.[93] In the following excerpt, another dream sequence, he finds himself in a room with no doors or windows unable to find a way out and ignored by the people around him, when suddenly a face appears through a peephole and teaches him a tune which is 'the cure for every worry and affliction'.[94] The fantastic and surreal elements in these excerpts break open an alternative order of reference that goes beyond verifiable reality. In some instances the symbolic register provides answers – for example the pearl referred to above may stand for an idea of the divine to which the narrator clings ('I have not yet found anyone who will believe me. Yet despair has not found its way to my heart')[95] and the predicament described in 'Al-Lahn' (The Tune) may be an expression of the narrator's artistic and spiritual disconnection with his surroundings. Other times the symbolism is not easily deciphered. Either way the illogical scenes and surreal moments have a disorienting effect on the reader. The same is true of the paradoxical statements which abound in the text. 'The power of memory manifests itself in remembrance just as it manifests in oblivion', the wise friend tells the narrator.[96] The same individual states that 'He who possesses life and will possesses everything, and the poorest living being possesses life and will'.[97] When the narrator recounts the favours of the Bestower, the wise friend tells him 'All this good fortune is the fruit of [the world] shunning you'.[98] In the later sections of the text ᶜAbd Rabbihi al-Taᵓih is found making similarly contradictory observations.

The text's surreal moments and paradoxical statements, and their bewildering effect, tie in with the Sufi theme and intertext. With its rejection of reason and intellect and understanding of God as the Ultimate Reality who consists of everything and its opposite – transcendence and immanence, presence and absence, mercy and wrath, etc. – Sufi discourse is characterised by unconventional images, interpretations and paradoxes. The latter, writes Chittick, 'help break down the insistence of the rational mind that everything can be explained and grasped'.[99] Statements like *huwa lā huwa*, which represents a fundamental contradiction, and Ibn ᶜArabi's interpretation of the Qur'anic story of Noah (Q. 71), which envisages the flood as a blessing rather than a punishment and inverts the story to mean almost its precise opposite, not only point to truths that lie beyond reason but produce a state of perplexity (*ḥayra*), which scholars have noted is a positive value in Sufism. Whereas philosophy and Islamic thought regard confusion as failure, Ibn ᶜArabi and his cohort regard it as a 'more honest possibility of truth'.[100] Inability to perceive is perception itself, according to one Sufi saying traced to companion of the Prophet and first Muslim caliph Abu Bakr.[101] Mustafa Tahrali and Ian Almond see the paradoxes and contradictions in *Fusus* as a strategy deliberately intended to confuse: 'by literally arousing a state of perplexity in the reader, the *Fusus* begins the long process of detaching the reader from his/her reliance on rationality and logic',[102] which prepares the way to a 'more divine perplexity'.[103] The unreal moments and bewildering effects of *Asdaʾ* thus recall a strategy of Sufi writing and one of its critical states.

The poetic language of *Asdaʾ* represents another meeting point of post-1967 artistic sensibilities and Sufi themes. The fact that God cannot be described in finite language means that the Sufis tend to speak in symbols and images and poetry is their favoured means of expression. As a text in dialogue with Sufism, *Asdaʾ* also tends towards poetic expression, which has the effect of shifting attention from material events to symbolic dimensions and tests the boundaries of the novel. In the opening excerpt, the short account of school closure due to political demonstrations becomes the tale of a child's sensory experience and bursting emotion as his daily routine is cancelled. He is cast as someone led off to prison, 'In my hand was a notebook, in my eyes was dejection, in my heart a longing for chaos',[104] and pictured swept away by waves of joy to shores of happiness. The structure and rhythm of the sentence quoted, constructed of three clauses which mirror one another, point to a poetry and lyricism which grows more pronounced over the course of the text so that in the final section, where the voice of ʿAbd Rabbihi dominates, many excerpts consist of one or two evocative sentences which come very close to poetry. In the context of post-1967 writing, the fusion of prose and poetry can be understood as an experiment in form and deliberate blurring of genres. Writers in this period tested the limits of the novel, which in its conventional form represented ideologies and systems that were now discredited. They were also interested in drawing the reader into the creative process by producing *writerly* texts (*scriptable*), and *Asdaʾ* is a good example of this. The narrative is characterised by gaps and ambiguity. Basic information is withheld and scenes are communicated in a manner that requires the reader to supply much of the meaning. Where does the narrator travel to in 'Al-Rihla' (Journey)? Who are 'the good-hearted' he refers to in this excerpt and what is the path to which they refer? Is the beautiful garden in which enchanted women are swaying a symbol of paradise or a real-life scene? Do the 'gardens of the north' refer to a spiritual abode? What is the significance of the 'bloody jungle' and 'crushing battle'?[105] The reader must decide these things for him/herself.

Also part of the narrative's poeticism, writerly strategy and dialogue with Sufism is *Asdaʾ*'s high dependence on imagery. Like the poet and mystic who uses figurative language to arouse the senses and create new meaning and connections, so *Asdaʾ* employs image and metaphor to produce a reading that reaches beyond material experience and ignites the reader's imagination. Death pays the narrator a visit in the second segment and is described as a giant, 'its breath coming and going in all the rooms'. The image turns death from a moment or state into a dynamic living force to be feared. When the singer's voice rings out in the eighth segment, 'the blurred shapes of women would appear behind the chinks in the windows, while men's eyes would emit sparks of disapproval', which captures the mystery that women represent for the child. The juxtaposition here of blurred shapes, with their nebulous rounded edges, and sparks, with their linear clarity, presents male and female as opposites. Memories reigning above the funeral cortege and earth trembling beneath the tread of the old, lost men in 'Al-Talqin' (Instruction) transforms a mundane scene into a reflection of time and death. Evocative images and metaphors abound and, together with the narrative's lyricism and system of Sufi reference, evoke the poetic language of Islamic mysticism. Here again Mahfuz fuses elements of Sufi discourse with post-1967 narrative strategies, communicating contemporary themes through authentic historical channels.

Notes

1. See 'Al-Shaykh Jumʿa' (1925), 'ʿAmm Mitwalli' (1925) and 'Al-Shaykh Sayyid al-ʿAbit' (1926).
2. See Ali B. Jad, *Form and Technique in the Egyptian Novel 1912–1971* (London and Oxford: Ithaca Press, 1983), pp. 33–5.
3. Mahmud Taymur, *Nidaʾ al-Majhul* (Beirut: Dar al-Makshuf, 1939). See Jad, *Form and Technique*, pp. 98–100. On Taymur's life and works see Sabry Hafez, *Genesis*, pp. 199–214; Nazih al-Hakim, *Mahmud Taymur, Raʾid al-Qisa al-ʿArabiyya* (Cairo, 1944); Anwar al-Jundi, *Qissat Mahmud Taymur* (Cairo, 1951).

4. By contrast Muhammad Hasan ᶜAbdullah sees a spiritual tendency in Mahfuz's early historical novels, which was suppressed in his early realistic tendency (*Al-Islamiyya wa'l-Ruhiyya fi Adab Najib Mahfuz* (Cairo: Dar Qibaʾ li'l-Tibaᶜa wa'l-Nashr wa'l-Tawziᶜ, 2001), p. 15), while Hamdi Sakkut delays signs of spirituality to the later volumes of the trilogy and understands Shaykh Darwish from *Zuqaq* and Shaykh Mitwalli ᶜAbd al-Samad from *Bayn al-Qasrayn* as simply part of drawing a comprehensive portrait of the popular quarter in the realist novel. Sakkut, 'Najib Mahfuz wa'l-Hal al-Sufi', *Alif: Journal of Comparative Poetics*, vol. 5 (Spring 1985), p. 40.
5. Al-Musawi, *Islam on the Street*, p. xix.
6. Elmarsafy, *Sufism in the Arabic Novel*, p. 6.
7. See El-Enany, *Pursuit of Meaning*, p. 87, esp. n. 23.
8. *Qasr al-Shawq*, pp. 325, 212 (trans., pp. 250, 165). With regard to the relation of love and mysticism in an Arabic literary context, Sabry Hafez notes that the love theme in the short story can assume a mystical aspect, as for example in some of Saᶜd Makkawi's stories (e.g. 'Qiddisa min Bab al-Shaʾariyya', in *Rahiba min al-Zamalik*, 1995, pp. 7–27). See Hafez, *Quest for Identities*, p. 224, for further examples.
9. *Qasr al-Shawq*, p. 263 (trans., p. 203).
10. Ibid. p. 232 (trans., p. 181).
11. Ibid. p. 249 (trans., p. 192).
12. Ibid. pp. 273, 276 (trans., pp. 211, 213).
13. Ibid. p. 224 (trans., p. 175).
14. Ibid. p. 223 (trans., p. 174). Hutchins' et al. translation (*Palace of Desire*).
15. See e.g. *Al-Khamriyya* (The Wine Song) of ᶜUmar Ibn al-Farid. Intoxication is juxtaposed with the concept of sobriety, which comes after intoxication and corresponds with the stage of *baqāʾ* (subsistence), when the Sufi returns to the world after mystical union.
16. The terms *fanāʾ* and *baqāʾ* come from the Qur'anic passage: 'Everything upon the earth is undergoing annihilation, but there subsists the face of your Lord, Possessor of Majesty and Generous Giving' (55: 26–7), Chittick, *Sufism*, p. 36. See also Fazlur Rahman, 'Baḳāʾ wa-Fanāʾ', *EI2*, vol. 1, p. 951.
17. *Qasr al-Shawq*, pp. 225, 257 (trans., pp. 176, 198).
18. 'Doesn't he know that I don't even aspire for her to return my love?' *Qasr al-Shawq*, p. 273 (trans., p. 210).
19. *Qasr al-Shawq*, p. 233 (trans., p. 181).
20. Ibid. p. 183 (trans., p. 142).

21. On the volatility of truth: 'truth is a lover, just like a human lover in terms of coquetry, rejection and mind games ...' *Al-Sukkariyya*, p. 15 (trans., p. 11).
22. *Al-Sukkariyya*, p. 206 (trans., p. 197).
23. *Qasr al-Shawq*, p. 433 (trans., p. 336).
24. Ibid. p. 437 (trans., p. 339).
25. Rumi, cited from Chittick, *Sufism*, p. 68. Ma'rifa is even another name for Sufism.
26. On this point, Sufi thought intersects with Henri Bergson's understanding of morality as deriving from two sources: intelligence and intuition. For the latter's influence on Mahfuz, see El-Enany, *Pursuit of Meaning*, pp. 14–15.
27. *Al-Sukkariyya*, p. 186 (trans., p. 177).
28. Ibid. p. 101 (trans., p. 95).
29. Ibid. p. 30 (trans., p. 25).
30. *Qasr al-Shawq*, pp. 455–6 (trans., p. 354).
31. The story is published alongside Qindil Umm Hashim. See Haqqi, *Qindil Umm Hashim*, pp. 99–113.
32. Yahya Haqqi, 'Al-Qiddis La Yuhar', in *Qindil Umm Hashim*, pp. 99–113. See Elmarsafy, *Sufism in the Contemporary Arabic Novel*, pp. 16–17.
33. *Al-Sukkariyya*, p. 318 (trans., p. 308).
34. Hala Fu'ad has written a book on *Al-Tariq* including its Sufi connection. See Hala Fu'ad, *Tariq Najib Mahfuz bayn al-Ustura wa'l-Tasawwuf* (Cairo: Dar al-'Ayn li'l-Nashr, 2006).
35. *Al-Shahhadh* (Cairo: Maktabat Misr, 1966), trans. Kristin Walker Henry and Nariman Khales Naili al-Warraki, *The Beggar* (Cairo: American University in Cairo Press, 1986). On this novel see El-Enany, *Pursuit of Meaning*, pp. 107–10; 'Abdullah, *Al-Islamiyya wa'l-Ruhiyya*, pp. 199–204.
36. *Al-Shahhadh*, p. 161 (trans., p. 118). See also p. 110 (trans., p. 83): 'This question [of the meaning of life] only pesters us when our hearts are empty'.
37. El-Enany, *Pursuit of Meaning*, p. 103. See *Al-Liss wa'l-Kilab* (Cairo: Maktabat Misr, 1961), trans. Trevor Le Gassick and M. M. Badawi, *The Thief and the Dogs* (Cairo: American University in Cairo Press, 1984). On *Al-Liss*, see Mohamed Mahmoud, 'The Unchanging Hero in a Changing World: Najib Mahfuz's *Al-Liss wa'l-Kilab (The Thief and the Dogs)*', in Trevor le Gassick (ed.), *Critical Perspectives on Naguib Mahfouz* (Washington, DC: Three Continents Press, 1991), pp. 115–30; Sa'id Shawqi Muhammad Sulayman, *Tawzif al-Turath fi Riwayat Najib Mahfuz* (Cairo: Itrak li'l-Nashr wa'l-Tawzi', 2000), pp. 148–50. The latter study has sections on Sufi characters and Sufi language

in Mahfuz's fiction. See also ʿAbdullah, *Al-Islamiyya wa'l-Ruhiyya*, pp. 187–98.
38. See Ami Elad, 'Mahfuz's Zaʿbalawi: Six Stations of a Quest', *International Journal of Middle East Studies*, vol. 26 (1994), pp. 631–44; Sasson Somekh, 'Zaʿbalawi: Author, Theme and Technique', *Journal of Arabic Literature*, vol. 1 (1970), pp. 24–36.
39. El-Enany, *Pursuit of Meaning*, pp. 119–24; Roger Allen, 'Some Recent Works of Najib Mahfuz: A Critical Analysis', *Journal of the American Research Center in Egypt*, vol. 14 (1977), pp. 101–10.
40. *Dunya Allah* (story collection) (Cairo: Maktabat Misr, 1963), trans. Roger Allen and Akef Abadir, *God's World: An Anthology of Short Stories* (Minneapolis: Bibliotheca Islamica, 1973).
41. Al-Musawi, *The Postcolonial Arabic Novel*, pp. 316–19 and his chapter on the novel, 'Scheherazade's Gifts: Mahfuz's Narrative Strategies in *Layali Alf Layla*', ch. 10, pp. 375–87. See also al-Musawi, *Islam on the Street*, pp. 72–87; Ferial Ghazoul, 'Naguib Mahfouz's Arabian Nights and Days: A Political Allegory', in *Nocturnal Poetics: The Arabian Nights in Comparative Context* (Cairo: American University in Cairo Press, 1996), pp. 159–76; Sabry Hafez, 'Jadaliyat al-Binya al-Sardiyya al-Murakkaba fi Layali Shahrazad wa Najib Mahfuz', *Fusul*, vol. 13, no. 2 (1994), pp. 20–70.
42. Al-Musawi, *The Postcolonial Arabic Novel*, p. 386.
43. See Ouyang, 'The Dialectic of Past and Present in *Rihlat Ibn Fattuma* by Najib Mahfuz'.
44. On *Ayyam al-Insan al-Sabʿa*, see Elmarsafy, *Sufism in the Contemporary Arabic Novel*, pp. 18–22; Richard Leuvan, 'The Journey in Two Arabic Novels', in Robin Ostle (ed.), *Sensibilities of the Islamic Mediterranean: Self-expression in a Muslim Culture from Post-classical Times to the Present Day* (New York and London: I. B. Tauris, 2008), pp. 133–40; al-Musawi, *Islam on the Street*, pp. 110–25; Selim, *The Novel and the Rural Imaginary in Egypt*, pp. 188–205.
45. On Salwa Bakr and *Maqam ʿAtiyya*, see al-Musawi, *Islam on the Street*, pp. 195–202; El-Enany, 'The Madness of Non-Conformity: Women versus Society in the Fiction of Salwa Bakr', *Journal of Arabic Literature*, vol. 37, no. 3 (2006), pp. 376–415. As a journalistic investigation into a multidimensional and somewhat mythical figure, *Maqam ʿAtiyya* and Mahfuz's *Al-ʿAʾish fi'l-Haqiqa* (1985) have themes in common.
46. On *Kitab al-Tajalliyyat*, see Elmarsafy, *Sufism in the Contemporary Arabic Novel*, pp. 78–106; al-Kakili, *Al-Zaman al-Riwaʾi*.
47. Sufism is viewed as overlapping with other modern movements, including

deconstruction (see Ian Almond, *Sufism and Deconstruction*, London and New York: Routledge, 2004) and surrealism (Adunis, *Al-Sufiyya wa'l-Suryaliyya*, London: Saqi Books, 1992, trans. Judith Cumberbatch, *Sufism and Surrealism*, London: Saqi Books, 2005).
48. Lit. trans. 'until it almost ceases'. *Hikayat*, p. 158 (trans., p. 101).
49. *Hikayat*, p. 180 (trans., pp. 112–13).
50. Ibid. p. 182 (trans., p. 114).
51. Tale 55.
52. *Hikayat*, p. 3 (trans., p. 11).
53. 'My nightingale has suffered much but gained much too' (*Hikayat*, 4; trans., p. 12).
54. Schimmel, *Mystical Dimensions*, p. 101.
55. See Layla S. Diba, 'Gol o bolbol' (Rose & Nightingale), *Encyclopaedia Iranica*, available at <http://www.iranicaonline.org> (last accessed 7 February 2019); Anne-Marie Schimmel, *Mystical Dimensions of Islam* (Chapel Hill: University of North Carolina Press, 2011 [1972]), pp. 287–434.
56. See Jane Hathaway, 'The Mulberry Tree in the Origin Myths', ch. 8 in *A Tale of Two Factions: Myth, Memory, and Identity in Ottoman Egypt and Yemen* (Albany: State University of New York Press, 2003), pp. 135–42. The mulberry tree reappears two years later as an evocative Sufi symbol, associated with the *takiyya*, in *Harafish*.
57. On sobriety/intoxication see Javad Nurbakhsh, *Sufism: Fear and Hope, Contraction and Expansion, Gathering and Dispersion, Intoxication and Sobriety, Annihilation and Subsistence* (New York: Khaniqah-i Nimatullahi, 1982).
58. *Hikayat*, p. 51 (trans., p. 36).
59. Ibid. p. 134 (trans., p. 79).
60. Ibid. p. 16 (trans., p. 18).
61. Ibid. p. 4 (trans., p. 12).
62. Ibid. p. 5 (trans., p. 12).
63. See Ghazoul, *Nocturnal Poetics*, p. 93.
64. *Al-Musawwar* (19 October 1990). Cited from Milson, *Novelist-Philosopher*, p. 24.
65. El-Enany, *Najib Mahfuz: Qiraʾa Ma Bayn al-Sutur* (Beirut: Dar al-Taliʿa li'l-Tibaʿa wa'l-Nashr, 1995), p. 155. El-Enany also discusses *Asdaʾ* in *Naguib Mahfouz: Egypt's Nobel Laureate* (London: Haus, 2007), pp. 150–3.
66. See Rooke, *In My Childhood*, pp. 102–3.

67. Ibid. pp. 65–72.
68. Ibid.
69. In Lejeune's analysis, the reader expects the characters and events in a novel to be fictional and tries to connect them to real life and experience while in an autobiography the reverse is true. Lejeune, *Le Pacte autobiographique*, p. 26. Cited from Rooke, *In My Childhood*, p. 50.
70. *Asdaʾ*, p. 108 (trans., p. 81).
71. Ibid. p. 12 (trans., p. 8).
72. Ibid. p. 24 (trans., pp. 9–10).
73. Ibid. p. 48 (trans., p. 18).
74. Ibid. p. 99 (trans., p. 75).
75. See El-Enany, *Najib Mahfuz: Qiraʾa Bayn al-Sutur*, ch. 15 'Asdaʾ al-Sirat al-Dhatiyya: Qiraʾa fi Khulasat al-Fikr al-Mahfuzi', pp. 153–62.
76. The first reference to the shaykh in the narrative may be in 'al-Nasiha' (Advice): 'We had a neighbor who was a Sufi aspirant. He would invite his shaykh every Thursday for *dhikr* and recitation'. *Asdaʾ*, pp. 45–6; trans., p. 35.
77. *Asdaʾ*, p. 104 (trans., p. 79).
78. Ibid. p. 156 (trans., p. 118).
79. Ibid.
80. Ibid. p. 41 (trans., p. 32).
81. Ibid. pp. 43–4 (trans., pp. 33–4).
82. Ibid. p. 20 (trans., p. 15).
83. Ibid. p. 23 (trans., p. 17).
84. Ibid. p. 64 (trans., p. 49).
85. Ibid. p. 65 (trans., p. 50).
86. Ibid. pp. 102–3 (trans., p. 78). The narrator is introduced to the shaykh by a friend. The shaykh seems to ignore him, which the narrator takes as a rejection but the friend says: 'He has accepted your friendship. If he had refused you he would have dismissed you with a hand gesture'.
87. Ibid. p. 104 (trans., p. 79).
88. Ibid. p. 124 (trans., p. 93).
89. Ibid. p. 114 (trans., p. 85).
90. Ibid. p. 57 (trans., p. 45).
91. Ibid. pp. 57–8 (trans., p. 45).
92. Ibid. p. 61 (trans., p. 48).
93. Ibid. pp. 51–2 (trans., pp. 40–1).
94. Ibid. p. 53 (trans., p. 42).

95. Ibid. p. 58 (trans., p. 45).
96. Ibid. p. 14 (trans., p. 10). The English translation compounds the paradox by translating this as 'The cruelty of the memory manifests itself in remembering what is dispelled in forgetfulness'.
97. Ibid. p. 16 (trans., p. 12).
98. Ibid. p. 38 (trans., p. 29).
99. Chittick, *Sufism*, p. 34.
100. Almond, *Sufism and Deconstruction*, p. 39.
101. 'Incapacity to perceive' is perception – see Chittick, *Sufism*, p. 35.
102. Almond, *Sufism and Deconstruction*, p. 42; Mustafa Tahrali, 'The Polarity of Expression in the *Fusus al-Hikam*', in S. Hirtenstein and M. Tierman (eds), *Muhyiddin Ibn ʿArabi: A Commemorative Volume* (Dorset: Element, 1993), pp. 351–8.
103. Almond, *Sufism and Deconstruction*, p. 42.
104. *Asdaʾ*, p. 4 (trans., p. 1).
105. Ibid. p. 70 (trans., p. 54).

8

Feminist Perspectives

The feminist movement in Egypt has engaged with religion from the beginning, not least because several of the norms it sought to abolish or reform – veiling, segregation, marriage, divorce laws, inheritance – are linked to particular interpretations of scripture. Arab and Egyptian feminists from the nineteenth century to the present have referenced and engaged with Islam, and at times the other monotheistic religions, either for criticism or a solution to oppression, and some of the most heated controversies have centred on religious symbols, foremost among them the veil. Leila Ahmed identifies two streams in the Egyptian feminist moment: a secularising, westernising tendency that has tended to be hostile towards religion and which dominated the feminist movement to the end of the 1960s, and an Islamic reformist trend that seeks to improve the lot of women from within, through reinterpretation of founding texts and critical examination of cultural norms, and which, though present from the outset in the work of Zaynab al-Fawwaz (c. 1850–1914), ʿAʾisha Taymur (1840–1902) and Malak Hifni Nassif (1886–1918), has become more prominent since the 1970s as part of a wider shift towards religious and local paradigms.[1] This is not to say that the secular strand has retreated. Nor should the binary categorisation imply that the experience of women in Egypt is determined by religion. It is simply that the secular and the religious once more represent a critical polarity and frame of reference.

In its early stages the Egyptian feminist movement can be linked to the colonial encounter and rise of national consciousness. The beginnings of female education in the second half of the nineteenth century, although modest, meant that by the 1890s there were enough literate women in Egypt to begin making their voice heard in the press, and the influx of Europeans and European ideas under Khedive Ismail introduced changes into Egyptian society which opened avenues for women to engage in activities beyond the home. Women from the upper classes began writing articles and essays for women's journals and general newspapers and founded organisations and societies, such as the Society for the Advancement of Women (est. 1908) and the Intellectual Association of Egyptian Women (est. 1914).[2] They also set up dispensaries, nursery schools and charities, making them key players in social welfare. These initiatives helped foster a female consciousness that would become vocal in the early decades of the twentieth century. Meanwhile Egyptian men returning from study periods in Europe recognised the benefits of educated wives and mothers, and reformers from both traditionalist and modernist quarters began to see the impoverished status of women in Egyptian society as a sign of cultural backwardness and obstacle in the way of modernity and nationhood. Muhammad Abduh, whilst defending Islam and insisting on its enlightened attitude to women, argued for an end to polygamy and reform of divorce laws. Qasim Amin published *Tahrir al-Marʾa* in 1899 in which he called for girls' education up to primary school and an end to segregation and veiling. While it is incorrect, as has sometimes been the case, to regard these men as the progenitors of Egyptian feminism, they gave it momentum and helped bring the issue of women into the mainstream. As Egypt worked towards independence, women like Huda Shaʿrawi looked for ways to secure a voice and rights for women in the new system. Shaʿrawi founded the Egyptian Feminist Union in 1923 and together with Nabawiyya Musa and other activists campaigned for suffrage, women's education, reform in marriage and divorce laws, and an end to restrictions on women's dress and behaviour. Their efforts bore fruit in certain areas. The minimum age of marriage was raised to sixteen for girls and eighteen for boys in 1923, the first women were admitted into Cairo University in the late 1920s, women were granted the right to vote in the 1956 constitution, and by the 1980s women were visible in significant numbers in all areas of Egyptian life and work – as doctors, educators, engineers, scientists, academics, politicians, and so on. However, polygamy is still legal in Egypt and gender inequality and female oppression persists, especially in the home, where levels of domestic violence are reportedly high and FGM is still widely practised, even after it was banned (as late as 2008). At the same time, the Islamic resurgence of recent decades has brought widespread re-veiling, huge numbers of young women adopting the veil as a signifier of religious commitment or cultural symbol.

The last quarter of the twentieth century also saw the emergence of women as a powerful voice in the Egyptian novel, which itself serves as a measure of women's lib both in terms of how women are portrayed in its pages and the exclusion/inclusion of women in the canon. Bouthaina Shaaban describes how Arab women have been marginalised by a predominantly male critical establishment. A perception has lingered that women's writing is narrow in focus, such that many Arab women writers reject 'women's literature' as a category, and key texts by women have been forgotten or sidelined, such as Zaynab Fawwaz's *Husn al-ᶜAwaqib wa Ghada al-Zahira* (1899), Labiba Hashim's *Qalb al-Rajul* (1904) and other early forays into fiction.[3] At the same time the roles assigned to women in the Egyptian novel, in the early period in particular, reveal gender biases that speak for the environment in which they were written. Progressive female characters are in short supply in male-authored texts before the 60s; instead women often feature as symbols and types – the prostitute, temptress, honourable wife, devoted mother, romantic ideal, symbol of the nation, etc.[4] – leading Nawal Saᶜdawi to argue in the 1970s that the portrayal of Arab women in modern Arabic literature had not progressed much on premodern gender stereotypes.[5] Haykal's novel may take the name of a female character as its title but Hamid is the only character with real depth. Women are peripheral to the first two volumes of *Al-Ayyam*. Saniyya in *ᶜAwdat al-Ruh* and Suzy Dupont in *ᶜUsfur min al-Sharq* are more important for their symbolic value and contribution to Muhsin's learning journey than any independent interest. Amina in the trilogy is intellectually inferior and submissive, and ᶜAyda in *Qasr al-Shawq* manifests several negative stereotypical female traits and her role in the story is dependent upon her relation to the protagonist. Neither attains the psychological complexity of Kamal or Ahmad ᶜAbd al-Jawwad. Even the prostitutes in the trilogy, who may seem sexually liberated insofar as they have chosen a path outside the social mainstream, merely reinforce the patriarchal order; their social exclusion reinforces definitions of ideal womanhood in patriarchy. These writers, whilst developing progressive views on society and nation do little to challenge embedded structures of patriarchy.[6] Into the 1960s and beyond the improved status of women in Egyptian society is reflected on the pages of the novel. *Al-Maraya* by Mahfuz, a collection of character sketches which was serialised in the magazine *Al-Idhaʿa wa'l-Television* a year before it was published in novel form in 1972, has women populating government offices, cafes, the university and other public spaces, and well-drawn female characters are no longer a rarity in Egyptian fiction. But it remains the case that the feminist cause in the Egyptian novel has been championed in the main by women. *Al-Maraya* may inadvertently expose the injustices suffered by women, and male writers have at times addressed themselves specifically to the violence inflicted upon women by society, and even linked this to religion as Yusuf Idris does in 'Bayt min Lahm' (1971), but it is unsurprisingly primarily Arab women writers who have championed Arab women's issues in fiction. Campaigners like Nawal al-Saʿdawi and Latifa al-Zayyat have employed fiction as one of a variety of mediums through which to develop a feminist discourse. Others like Radwa Ashur, Miral al-Tahawy, Ahdaf Soueif and Salwa Bakr have explored feminist themes as part of a broader literary or intellectual project. Both approaches have involved an engagement with religion in its myriad forms – as myth, symbol, law, discourse, language. The most strident voice in this mix is undoubtedly al-Saʿdawi, physician, psychiatrist, campaigner and author of a long list of short stories, novels and critical works, many of which have caused controversy and been banned. *Suqut al-Imam* (1987) is one such work.[7]

The plot of *Suqut* is difficult to follow, for instead of a story arc we have two events, the deaths of Bint Allah and the Imam, repeated over and over and interspersed with stories of characters close to them and other tangential episodes, including state celebrations, journeys to the West and to heaven, scenes from the battle front, and excursions into *Alf Layla*. None of these are related in a coherent manner; rather details of the narrative often contradict one another. What is not in doubt is the nightmarish world that the characters inhabit, especially if they happen to be women or simply outside the ruling circle. The world of *Suqut* consists of a degraded society ruled by a power-obsessed and paranoid dictator, the Imam, flanked by his Chief of Security, the Great Writer and Leader of the Opposition, who each stand for different aspects of totalitarianism. The Chief of Security, who recalls the aide to the Mayor in an earlier work by Saʿdawi also attacking religion and power, *Mawt al-Rajul al-Wahid* (1974),[8] represents the culture of surveillance and killing in authoritarian regimes. The Great Writer, who is intelligent but has let his brain go to sleep, represents the co-optation of the intelligentsia and control over discourse, and the Leader of the Opposition and his puppet party, Hizb al-Shaytan, which was created by the Imam to breed fear – since 'if there is no Satan among the people, there would be no fear'[9] – stands for the speciousness of political process in authoritarian regimes. The Imam derives his power from God, indeed is understood to be divinely inspired by his subjects, and governance is carried out in the name of Islam. What we are dealing with here is in effect a religious dystopia, the Islamic ideal gone wrong.[10] Many at the time of writing and since have dreamed of a nation founded upon traditional Islam; Saʿdawi shows us where this dream leads in the wrong hands whilst simultaneously targeting gender biases at the heart of monotheism, for Christianity as much as Islam is in the firing line here, and the disturbing character of the patriarchal systems they spawn.

The Abrahamic religions, as feminists and anthropologists of religion know well, are intrinsically patriarchal; 'they are built upon the subordination of woman to man, as also man to God, through the gendered nature of their hierarchical structure'.[11] God is conceived of as a man, and as the transcendental signifier in subject position sets in motion a hierarchical dichotomy that routinely works against woman. If God is gendered male, then the other is gendered female. If God is transcendence, gnosis and goodness, then woman as other is baseness, ignorance and an accomplice of Satan. Moreover, the oppositional thinking that emerges from this binary system denies women independent identity, since she is always defined in relation to man, as deficiency, and her reality is always pre-scribed, as she is condemned to object position on the logic of Hegel's master/slave relation. God is the model of male perfection, onto which men project themselves, and woman is everything else. Saʿdawi brings this phallic ordering into focus in *Suqut*. Women in the text are base, and it is a baseness sanctioned by religion. Her face is shameful and should be hidden, a directive predictably referred back to God.[12] 'She was created from a twisted rib (*ḍilʿ aʿwaj*)',[13] and she is associated with the origin of evil: 'woman is the snake (*al-ḥayya*) and devil even if she wraps a veil around herself and enters the Party of God (*ḥizb al-raḥmān*)'.[14] Yusuf Idris highlights the same connection as his character Shaykh ʿAbd al-ʿAl repeatedly equates Lili with Satan in 'AKana La Budd Ya

Lili an Tudi'i al-Nur?'.[15] Men can behave with impunity, for 'the treachery of men is allowable by God's decree',[16] whereas women are inspired by Satan and sex is sinful for them. Only men may enter paradise and only men may have a relationship with the Divine, since 'God does not visit women nor does He reveal Himself to them'.[17] The religious framing of these statements and themes draws a clear line between religion and female oppression. The symbolic value of the characters is also significant in this regard. God is present in the text in the form of the Imam, who is divinely inspired and virtually merged with Allah at times in the text, rendering his involvement in the rape and killing of Bint Allah and her mother all the more scandalous. He is also named as Bint Allah's father, a man who has denied and cast her out. Installing God as a semi-character in the text, albeit on a symbolic level, elides the distance that normally separates God and the plight of women and that ordinarily masks religion's role in female subjugation. (One might also note the same as an unintentional effect of 'Abd al-Jawwad's symbolism in the trilogy.) *Suqut* closes the gap between God and mankind to reveal an unholy alliance between religion and patriarchy. This alliance is alternatively highlighted in a suggestive scene referencing the story of Abraham, that founding myth of monotheism in which is embedded a starkly authoritarian model of patriarchal rule and submission.[18] The sacrificial son here, as signalled by Baba's stick 'shining like a knife' coming to rest on his neck,[19] is Fadl Allah, the protagonist's half-brother, and he is no hero. He does not embrace his fate as Ismail/Isaac did but squeezes up against his sister and wets himself. The reworking of filial response points to fallacy in the myth whilst the episode in its totality in *Suqut* provides the opportunity to spell out the religio-patriarchal hierarchy: 'A father does not question God, and a son does not question the father. Obedience to God is incumbent, and obedience to God means obeying the father and husband'.[20]

As indicated in this scene patriarchal religion is not harmful to women alone. The paradigms of masculinity enshrined in scripture and myth, and the binary system engendered by the transcendental signifier, cast men too as deficient and disrupt productive bonds and relations within and across gender. The men of *Suqut*, though mostly installed in positions of authority and privileged by virtue of biology, are portrayed as disturbed and insecure. Fadl Allah is the exception here, but his fate is in fact worse, as he is sent to die in the Imam's war. The Imam suffers from an inferiority complex, which goes back to childhood and colours his relationships such that they are all expressions of power and devoid of emotional connection. His aides are essentially rivals and his wives and mistresses are conquests and possessions. There is no brotherhood in this atmosphere of fear and competition, only specious friendship and covert contest. The Imam's henchmen vie with one another when stoning Bint Allah's mother, for he who strikes her most in the womb will be rewarded by the Imam.[21] The state apparatus is anti-fraternity even in its oppression of women. Fatma Mernissi argues that the Muslim system is opposed to the heterosexual unit, for an 'all-encompassing love satisfying sexual, emotional and intellectual requirements of both partners ... constitutes a direct threat to man's allegiance to Allah, which requires the unconditional investment of all his energies, thoughts and feelings in his God'.[22] The same applies in the hellscape of *Suqut*, where there is an absence of productive love relations and equal exchange between the sexes. Instead we are reminded of the hadith 'When a man and woman are alone together outside of Sharia, Satan is the third one present'.[23] The discovery of Fadl Allah and Bint Allah in the trench, wrapped in an embrace, is met with hysteria, an affront to a system which cannot tolerate cross-gender relations. Yet the Great Philosopher longs for love and yearning for the mother is a recurrent theme among the text's men. The French feminists, drawing on psychoanalysis, conceive of man as depleted and restless, 'forever searching for a completion which has been lost and which the mother represents'.[24] The path to manhood in religio-patriarchy demands severance from the womb, hence Sarah/Hagar must die in Abrahamic myth, 'so that Isaac [or Ishmael] could leave the world of women and enter the world of men'.[25] The Imam and the Great Writer return to their mothers after extended absences. For all their power and privilege, they are restless and in need of the lost maternal. In the case of the latter, maternal reunion offers the opportunity to reflect upon women's role in sustaining patriarchy and to provide some psychology for the male character, so that the Great Writer becomes merely another victim of the system, trapped in a prescribed model of masculinity:

> If you had resisted injustice just once, if you had defended your rights, then maybe I would have known justice, and if I'd known justice I would

have known God. But mother, you were unable to defend your rights. And if you were unable to defend yourself, how could you defend others? ... You were unable to defend my rights. You saw my father oppress me and you were silent. In every struggle between me and him you stood still and watched.[26]

The Great Writer's mother is not the only woman complicit in perpetuating male hegemony. The wives of the powerful ignore their husbands' adultery and by failing, for the most part, to read the newspapers and classical texts, they exclude themselves from political, intellectual and cultural discourse. Just like the Great Writer, in the absence of an alternative model, they fall into the existing ideology. As Simone de Beauvoir said, with 'no virile myth in which their projects are reflected; they have no religion or poetry of their own: they still dream through the dreams of men. Gods made by males are the gods they worship'.[27]

Saʿdawi has written extensively about religion and women in her non-fiction. Here she has argued that religion itself is not the problem, that gender inequality is rooted in political and economic realities and religion is merely co-opted to serve these. In particular, looking back into history, she argues that the emergence of feudal systems and private ownership, which divided society into different classes, is responsible for the rise of patriarchy: 'The old structures [matrilineal family/communal ownership] were replaced by systems based on exploitation and women were relegated to the bottom orders of society'.[28] But this is not the angle adopted in *Suqut*, where monotheism is portrayed as a root cause. It is true that the Imam's dictatorship highlights the co-optation of religion as an instrument of state and that distortion of scripture is a theme in the text, but the deliberate subversion of core principles of monotheistic belief posits the latter as a fundamental problem. Bint Allah's mother 'became pregnant like the Virgin Mary',[29] and her virginity becomes a recurrent motif. Likewise Bint Allah speaks of carrying Jesus in her womb and insists upon her own virginity through the text. The claim is of course false in both cases, for Bint Allah's mother was a prostitute and Bint Allah is assaulted by the judge and probably Baba, who rapes all the orphans. However, the point is not to replicate a miracle but to challenge the rationale of immaculate conception. Was Mary really a virgin and why should she be? Why is sex sinful for women and not men? These questions point to the hypocrisy that underlies the image of the ideal woman in Christian tradition. The figure of the Virgin Mary is problematic for feminists insofar as her mythical status is contingent upon servility and celibacy. The murder of Bint Allah and her mother in this respect becomes not only an attempt by the text's men to crush the lone heroine, but the symbolic destruction of a problematic idol.

On the other hand, Bint Allah reads as a reimagining of Christ. Her name, which translates as Daughter of God, mirrors Christ's epithet, Son of God. She is allegedly the product of a virgin birth and references to her heart continuing to beat for three days in the grave recalls Christ's death and period in the tomb. The repetition of her murder, after which she always reappears, casts her tale as a story of resurrection, and her mission is not unlike that of a messiah: 'I must either save myself or I must die for my sisters'.[30] The specific mention of sisters here turns Bint Allah's mission into a feminist correction of Christ's ministry, whilst the juxtaposition of Bint Allah and Christ highlights gender politics in the Christian story. That God should have a son and not a daughter constitutes a bias at the core of Christian belief, which the narrative deliberately reverses. The name Bint Allah, as Malti Douglas notes, is a subversive construction that parodies a common pattern of naming in Arabic and, from an Islamic point of view, violates the unity and transcendence of God by assigning Him offspring.[31] Christian tradition as much as Islam is under attack here. It is Saʿdawi's contention that the monotheistic religions are not only inextricably linked but equally culpable in the oppression of women.[32] In the preface to the English edition of *The Hidden Face of Eve* she describes the 'western view' of Arab women as oppressed by Islam as a form of imperialism and cultural blindness and elsewhere details the maltreatment of women in Christianity and Judaism in a comparative context that at times reads as an Islamic apology.[33] Thus polygamy becomes a less hypocritical version of the sexual promiscuity rife in all societies. 'As a matter of fact, the oppression of women exercised by the temple and the church has been even more ferocious than that in the case of Islam'.[34] This relativising approach no doubt accounts for the narrative excursion into a non-specific western society, which it portrays as no less morally depraved, a soulless existence where babies are born from test-tubes.

The system in *Suqut* is not without its weaknesses, however, and as a feminist novel it is only right that resistance should constitute a theme. The Imam's paranoia and the anxiety and the restlessness of his men reveal instability at the heart of government. At the same time their insistent and repeated derision of women points to psychological vulnerability in the men of authority. Their power is not in the order of things therefore they must constantly reaffirm it. Bint Allah's ongoing presence, the fact that she rises every time she is killed and remains defiant, testifies to the strength of the female spirit; 'even if part of her fell off the rest would remain'.[35] She faces her oppressors, who prefer to conceal themselves and attack from behind, and points to incongruities in religious teaching and practice: 'God visited the Virgin Mary and she was a woman', she retorts when told that God appears only to men.[36] The hysteria that accompanies the transgressions of this lone girl testifies to a deep-seated fear of women, which Freud and others, including Saʿdawi herself, have written about. Likewise, the effort to prevent her from rejoining her mother – for women in the text yearn for the maternal too – betrays a fear of sisterhood. The text is critical of women's role in sustaining the status quo, as noted. But women also represent the solution and there are hints of change towards the end, for example in the behaviour of the Great Writer's wife, who no longer obeys her husband and has begun to argue religious points with him,[37] and the encounter of the Imam's legal wife, mistress and illegitimate daughter at the leader's wake in one of the final scenes. As they embrace over his dead body,

> The smile on his lips disappeared and his facial features vanished, so the fact no longer resembled that of the Imam, nor the Great Writer, Chief of Security, Leader of the Legal Opposition or any man from Hizb Allah or Hizb al-Shaytan.[38]

In this moment of solidarity the Imam and his unit cease to represent a threat.

Resistance is not only a theme in *Suqut* but a strategy. As Roller writes, '[t]he formal elements of the feminist novel are central to its meanings because its stylistic features convey its ideology, its politics, and its values'.[39] *Suqut*'s structure and techniques radically flout literary convention, associated as it is with the system and patriarchy. The narrative is cyclical, featuring a selection of repeated events and motifs – the killing of protagonists, God appearing in dreams, return to the mother, and so on. But within the interstices of the cyclical movement the story moves gradually forward, so that by the end of the text we have moved beyond the leader's assassination to the wake and its aftermath, a small step admittedly but one that facilitates the coming together of the Imam's women and shows that the narrative is not without a future. Many of the scenes and storylines woven between the recurrent events take place in the past; indeed the narrative's flitting back and forth between an inconstant present and various points in the past is an expression of experiential chaos, recreating in the reader some of the disorientation felt by the inhabitants of this irrational universe. But the progress portrayed in the final scenes and their chronological advance on the opening drama suggest a gradual forward movement. The impression is of a cycle of tyranny in which the potential for change is present.[40]

The plot of *Suqut* includes confusing and contradictory details. It is not clear if it is the Imam or his Bodyguard who takes the bullet and Bint Allah is killed one minute by gunshots, the next by a knife. The discrepancy between the Great Writer's blind devotion and intellectual paralysis and the critical faculties and self-consciousness he displays when speaking in the first person is also problematic, and the nature of the relationship between Bint Allah and Fadl Allah is unclear. Multiple viewpoint is employed and ensures that no one character dominates, and the narrative alternates between first and third person voices. It is also the case that symbols are fragmented and fluid, thus Jesus represents variously a saviour, western culture, a counterpoint to the Imam and villain, while the Imam's Christian wife is both an enemy of women and a potential champion (the latter on the basis of the bedside scene). In terms of chronotope, the story is suspended in time, with only a few references to newspapers, nuclear radiation and modern transport to situate it in modern times, and space, made up of abstract locations, is a symbolic code more than a means of grounding events in recognisable experience. The merging of characters – Imam/Bodyguard, Bint Allah/her mother, Jesus/the Imam, etc. – subverts the concept of character as coherent and unique and in this context conveys a commonality of experience that translates roughly to male power vs female victimhood, even if men also suffer as noted. The employment of fantasy and hyperbole in the scenes that rewrite *Alf Layla* are also subversive in relation to both conventional narrative and to the style of

Suqut itself. For the most part the text consists of believable events portrayed in a distorted and disjointed manner, creating a nightmarish feel, but in the chapter 'Ihyaʾ al-Turath' it tips over into the fantastic, with the Imam transformed into a sheep by Bint Allah, contravening the norms it has developed up to this point.

Such strategies and devices are relevant to *Suqut*'s feminist agenda. Realism is a deceptive mode, since it can conceal social difference and gender inequality. Realist novels, with their projected objectivity and invisible perspective, trick the reader into accepting the story presented as truth; the world of the text is the only possible world.[41] There is no suggestion that events might be more complicated than they appear or might have a different meaning than the one proposed, that characters are not knowable, that there might be an irreconcilable gap between language and object. A passive reading is all that is required, which is why Barthes finds realistic writing so unfulfilling. From a feminist point of view, realism is dangerous because it reinforces patriarchal modes of thought. Male and female ideals underlie creative choices and are reflected back to the reader as natural, inevitable. By rejecting the strategies of realistic narrative, Saʿdawi rejects the notion of a coherent world and avoids presenting religio-patriarchal order as natural. Instead it appears dystopic, thoroughly unnatural.

Another exploration of the collusion of religion and patriarchy in a dystopic frame is undertaken in *Jannat wa Iblis*, published five years later and described by Malti-Douglas as Saʿdawi's 'tour de force novelistic foray into theology'.[42] The text has much in common with *Suqut*, including a dystopic texture, deconstructive dialogue with monotheism and subversive narrative strategy. However, the framework has shifted. While *Suqut* evokes the figure of the Virgin Mary and takes issue with the religio-patriarchal hypocrisy surrounding female sexuality, *Jannat* turns to the figure of Eve to highlight the theological connection between women and evil. The God–Satan relation is in the foreground once more, but this time dismantled in a manner which sees Satan rehabilitated and Eve forgiven. *Jannat* is set in a mental asylum, known as *al-sarāy* (palace),[43] and revolves around a group of patients – Jannat, Nafisa, Iblis and God (*al-rabb*)[44] – and the head nurse Narjis. The asylum provides the perfect setting for the dystopian themes developed in the text and has an ironic twist, for its inmates are not mentally unwell but rebels and thinkers. The impression is that, prior to sectioning and the sedated state in which we encounter them, the patients were fully functioning individuals whose critical faculties rendered them a threat to the system: 'Only fools go to prison. Intelligent people enter the asylum with us'.[45] The setting is thus a comment on authoritarian rule and aggressively unitary systems and their inability to tolerate dissent and difference. As such it speaks to modern theories of madness and the asylum, which show them to be responses to, and symptoms of, prevailing social perceptions of moral, behavioural and sexual norms. The inmates of the asylum are kept under tight controls and injections are administered to subdue them. They wear belts indicating the nature of their illness and any transgression invites a session of electric shock treatment. Women are particularly persecuted in this setting, punished more than the men, prohibited from laughing and kept in a separate area. Nor is their persecution confined to the asylum; narrative excursions into the past and beyond the walls of the enclosure reveal that sexual oppression and subservience are normal female experiences in *Jannat*. All the women in the text suffer. Jannat's grandmother is forced to convert by a cruel philandering husband and eventually sets fire to herself.[46] Jannat's great-aunt drowns herself after giving birth to an illegitimate child.[47] Nafisa's mother is stoned for protesting the loss of her son after he is taken for national service and martyred.[48] Jannat is abused by her school master, Nafisa by hers and by the character who calls himself God, and Head Nurse Narjis is seduced by her boss, the Director of the Asylum. The drastic actions of Jannat's aunt and grandmother epitomise the desperate situation of women and point to a world in which the female has no voice or autonomy. Suicide, write Grubar and Gilbert, along with self-starvation and self-harm, 'form a complex of psychoneurotic symptoms that is almost classically associated with female feelings of powerlessness and rage'.[49] There is also an enunciative aspect to self-murder in the sense of personal or political protest. The suicides of the women in the text are not only means of escape but means of reclaiming control over themselves and speaking out, using their bodies as signs, and as such follow in a long tradition of female self-mutilation and immolation, including early Arab feminist and writer Mayy Ziyada (1886–1941).

The pretext for female oppression is once more religious. Women in *Jannat* are sinners on account of their gender. They are 'accomplices of the Devil (*ḫalīfāt al-shayṭān*)'⁵⁰ and their bodies testimony to the evil they harbour in their souls. Thus Narjis starves herself to ward off the evils of her maturing flesh, an action which also reflects on the alienation of body and soul engendered in monotheism, in particular Christianity. Menstruation is a sign of impurity. It is bad blood and the cause of great shame: 'As she walked down the road to school she could feel the towel between her legs. It rolled itself up like a swelling, like a sin hanging down under her belly'.⁵¹ This discourse of intrinsic baseness is interwoven with references to Eve and the serpent, so that the originary myth of monotheism becomes a vital intertext. Women are daughters of Eve and the blood running down Narjis' leg during the menses is the tail of a snake.⁵² As in *Suqut* women are complicit in the system. Head Nurse Narjis is the right arm of the Director, working with the guards to restrain and punish inmates. But more significant is Jannat's grandmother who, even as she despises her husband and oppressor, is quick to recount the story of Adam and Eve to deter Jannat from learning to write, and significantly misquotes Genesis 3:14–15 such that God's curse on the serpent becomes a curse on Eve: 'You shall crawl upon your belly for eternity, and your longing will be for your husband and he shall rule over you'.⁵³ Much has been written on the temptation of Eve and her relative guilt. Hélène Cixous argues that the threat of death has no meaning in a paradise that pre-exists death and that partaking of the apple is a measure of openness to another found in female subjectivity alone. Miriam Oren and Anda Amir portray Eve positively in their poetry, the latter seeing Eve's actions as bringing sexual knowledge and pleasure to the world.⁵⁴ Some excuse Eve on the basis that she was naïve, while Phyllis Trible and others, including the author, refer to Eve's superior intelligence and character, for she alone grasped that God was hiding something when He placed a prohibition on fruit from the tree of knowledge and took steps to gain knowledge.⁵⁵ The contribution of *Jannat* to the debate is to remind of the serpent's role in all of this and highlight a wrongful conflation of woman and snake in cultural memory.

The grandmother's misquotation feeds into a linguistic theme. Feminist scholars have long commented on the patriarchal language of scripture and theology. The Hebrew and Greek Bibles tend to use masculine nouns and pronouns in a gender inclusive sense and God is gendered male in the holy books. In the Qur'an, Allah is signified by the masculine singular and the Arabic language enforces a patriarchal order in its structure, formality and androcentricity. The masculine takes precedence over the feminine in sentences in classical Arabic, for example *rajulun wa imraʿ*, *ṭiflun wa ṭifla*.[56] Ibn al-ᶜAnbari (d. 940), whose grammatical explanations epitomise the patriarchal bias of classical linguistics, notes that feminine markers are additional, and therefore secondary, for example *qāʾim* for standing (m.) and *qāʾim-a* (f.).[57] Having targeted the gender bias in Christian myth in *Suqut*, Saᶜdawi draws attention to linguistic bias in the Qur'an in *Jannat* and indicates the instability of a hegemony reliant upon points of grammar and orthography. Jannat recalls her grandfather's anger when his wife pronounces his name, ᶜAbdil Illah, with a final *t*, rendering God in the feminine.[58] 'Turning the world upside down because of two dots', the grandmother scoffs.[59] In school Jannat makes the same mistake. She tries to write the letter *hāʾ* but her pen leaks and two dots of ink fall onto the page turning the letter into a *tāʾ*, prompting a similar outburst of rage from Shaykh Basyuni. The hysterical reaction of these two men reveals their dependency on the conception of a male God and fear of female divinity. As Malti-Douglas suggests, the 'distinction between male and female deities becomes as arbitrary, in the Saussaurian sense of the arbitrariness of the sign, as the presence or absence of dots on a consonant'.[60] Elsewhere Narjis' father insists that Adam partook of the apple but God forgave him, and only him, using grammatical evidence to back up his argument.

> The verse came down [from God] in the singular not the dual. In the verse on disobedience, God used the dual not the singular. God is knowledgeable of language and the rules of grammar. It's impossible that He would use the singular or dual in the wrong context.[61]

Similarly the absence of *sāqiṭ* in the Qur'an, as a masculine equivalent to the feminine active participle *sāqiṭa*, proves to the text's men that only women can be *fallen*: 'Adam wasn't "fallen". Men do not fall except in elections, or in battle, or as a pupil in school exams'.[62] These episodes highlight the collusion between religious language and patriarchy. Yet just as the English book, and the Bible in particular, is an ambivalent emblem of power in the colonial context, ever capable to co-opt to the other side, as Homi Bhabha has shown, so scripture can be used against men in *Jannat*.[63] Narjis turns the sacred logic against the Director by pointing out that lesbian love is not mentioned in God's book. If women are condemned because the Qur'an uses the masculine singular and Eve is therefore not expressly forgiven, then they are also excused the punishment of Lot's people, since the Qur'anic verse refers only to men.

The system once more has its weaknesses but exposure and revelation are not enough here. The text portrays three women who come into conflict with the system. Jannat, whose period in the asylum frames the narrative and whose name is an ironic reference to Eden (*janna* – paradise; pl. *jannāt*), is an extraordinary individual whose special attributes render her a threat to patriarchy. She was born with her eyes wide open and her memory stretches back to the Garden of Eden 'when the serpent whispered to Iblis, and when Iblis was still a virtuous angel who knew nothing of corruption and evil'.[64] As such, she has the potential to expose as a lie the logic that is used to subordinate women in the text and is imprisoned in the asylum and her memory forcibly erased. Narjis, who begins the text as an agent of patriarchy, eventually regains her memory and self-awareness and stands up to the Director, though ironically this occurs at precisely the moment when Jannat's memory is finally expunged. The third woman, Nafisa, is a pathetic version of Jannat. As with Narjis her rebellion comes late and she throws a stone at the Head Guard and a shoe at a driver who attempts to assault her. None of these women survive the narrative; they achieve small victories which tend towards exposure but nothing on the scale required to reform the system. This can only be achieved by dismantling the alliance between God and the Devil, or what Miriam Cooke calls the God–Satan dichotomy.[65] Saʿdawi attempts to do just this at the end of the novel. As Jannat is carried out of the asylum, Iblis looks on in despair at the woman he loved, the only one amongst the slaves who refused to kneel before him and said no.[66] He tries to follow but fatally injures himself scaling the fence. At that same moment al-Rabb begins to lose respect and authority. 'You made the world so rich for me, Iblis',[67] he laments, confirming the interdependence of God and Satan. The shock prompts a confession; he was the one who insisted that Iblis tempt people into sin and he pronounces the innocence of the Devil and is found dead shortly afterwards.

Given the association of women and evil developed in the text, the pronouncement of the Devil's innocence in the final pages amounts to no less than the absolution of women, for to be accomplices of the Devil no longer carries any weight. In the warped world of *Jannat*, God finally bestows upon women the forgiveness that he denied to Eve in Eden. The characterisation of Satan in the novel is significant in this respect. Far from the maligned figure of scripture, Iblis is here portrayed as a victim, a reluctant trouble-maker who would rather sleep than sow evil. His role is dictated to him by the character who calls himself God:

> Get up and whisper in people's ears, boy!
> What will happen if I don't whisper? Why not let everyone go to heaven?
> Then who did I create Hell for, you ass?
> You can roast sheep in it, brother …?[68]

Thus Iblis is a figure misunderstood, and his role assigned to him from outside. The mistreatment of Satan again reflects on women; like Iblis in the narrative they are victims. The God-character, on the other hand, is negatively portrayed, a self-appointed divinity and oppressor. Placing God in a social setting once again closes the gap and shows how He functions society, as an excuse to oppress women. In this sense, the God-character's rape of Nafisa becomes a striking metaphor. He is also portrayed as a misogynist: 'Deep down inside him was a revulsion for the other sex'.[69] The only mitigating factor here is that God is a persona adopted by the character – only he, and occasionally Iblis under duress, use the name. It is an identity he cultivated for himself. Following an approach characteristic of her critical discourse, Saʿdawi condemns here not God but the misappropriation of divinity and religion by society.

Few women have achieved mythical status in monotheism. Saʿdawi takes on the Eve and the Virgin Mary in subversive fashion and the negative concepts of womanhood built around them. The third most notable figure in theological discourse on women is Zulaykha, or Potiphar's wife, whose seduction of Yusuf (Joseph), recounted in the Bible and Qur'an and which has given rise to a literature of its own, has played a significant role in defining female artifice through the ages. 'Indeed your guile is great', ʿAziz Misr (Potiphar) famously exclaims in the Qur'anic *sūra*, applying his wife's crime to the whole of womankind through use of the feminine plural: *inna kaydahunna ʿaẓīm* (Q. 12:28). Salwa Bakr, another champion of women's issues, transposes the story of Yusuf and Zulaykha onto a modern setting in her first novel, *Wasf al-Bulbul* (1993), in a manner which restores Zulaykha's reputation. The story revolves around Hajir, a widow in her forties who has renounced men after a miserable marriage in her youth, and Yusuf, a philosophy student and hotel waiter. Far from the self-assured beautiful temptress of Islamic myth, Hajir in Bakr's novel is modest and timid, and severely contained by social mores and taboos, constantly worrying about the opinions of others. In fact, the story can be read as a journey of awakening in which the protagonist discovers her dormant sexuality and takes control of her destiny. Hajir falls hopelessly in love with Yusuf, but this is no one-sided seduction. The two are brought together more or less by accident and it is Yusuf who drives the romance. The role reversal recasts the scandalous episode of religious tradition, in which a wily woman seeks to corrupt an honourable young man, as a story of mutual love struggling to reach fruition in a stiflingly conservative context. Meanwhile Hajir's retiring character and backstory, which includes adolescent marriage to a terminally ill older man, betrayal and widowhood, repaints Zulaykha as a victim of patriarchal society and to an extent rehabilitates her. As such Bakr's novel can be read as a feminist correction of a scriptural event that has fostered an injurious concept of female perfidy.[70] But from a feminist point of view the novel is also unsatisfactory, for Hajir is no rebel or heroine. She is overly romantic and plays a minor role in driving the action. The exception to this is in the final chapter when she resolves to stay behind when her son and travel companions return home at the end of the holiday, so that she can realise her love and future with Yusuf and 'escape from the cocoon (*sharnaqa*)', a recurrent theme in her lover's discourse. But even at this moment Hajir is essentially giving herself to a man who is early on established as her intellectual superior. With no obvious means of her own or practical plan, the reader does not look at Hajir's future with much optimism.

More satisfying from both a feminist and artistic point of view is Bakr's next novel, *Al-ᶜAraba al-Dhahabiyya la Tasᶜad ila al-Samaʾ* (1991), which critiques religion and patriarchy in a satirical mode.[71] *Al-ᶜAraba* focuses on the inmates of a women's prison located on the outskirts of Cairo and like *Suqut* and *Jannat* employs a subversive strategy in the service of its feminist theme. Multiple narrators replace the authorial voice of realistic fiction and linear narrative gives way to a story-within-a-story structure, in which ʿAziza and her fantasy of transporting deserving inmates to heaven in a golden chariot constitutes the frame story, and the individual tales of the inmates she selects to join her make up the enframed stories. The literary device allows to speak a set of voices seldom heard in the public domain, namely those of women prisoners, who represent a doubly marginalised group insofar as they are both female and social outcasts, without attempting to weave them into a unitary narrative nor to integrate them into an historical process. The text is thus thoroughly polyphonic, more so than *Suqut* and *Jannat* where there is not in the end that much variety between the different voices; Bint Allah, Niʿmat Allah and her mother speak as one, Nafisa and Narjis' discourse is subsumed into Jannat's.[72] There is no dominant feminine discourse countering patriarchal logic here, a feature that would in the end merely replace like for like. The narrative structure is designed specifically to preserve the individual voice. The prison enclosure, cut off from the outside world, effectively severs the link between the individual and society at the centre of *Bildungsroman* ideology whilst neatly suggesting the extreme marginalisation of Egyptian women, especially in their domestic capacity, and opens up a new universe, or *third space* to borrow again from Bhabha, where an alternative morality and ethics come into play. In other works Bakr achieves similar by limiting the drama to claustrophobic suspended loci, such as the house in 'Kayd al-Rijal' (The Wiles of Men), where the co-wives' plot to murder the husband becomes a not unreasonable strategy for survival in context.[73] The title of this story, incidentally, as El-Enany has pointed out, is an ironic and highly symbolic reversal of Q. 12:28, while its protagonist's divine gratitude in the opening paragraphs is revealing of religion's role in female oppression insofar as it encourages false consciousness.[74] Other devices that contribute to the transgressive texture of *Al-ʿAraba* include a colloquialised use of Arabic and shifting registers, emphasis on orality and high instance of repetition, which together lean away from the authority of the written word and closer to popular discourse, with its democratic character, indeterminacy and basis in oral tradition. Magda al-Nowaihi describes the book as 'a communal performance in which many voices chime in' and draws attention to the chapter titles as further evidence of the text's oral quality.[75] Taking into account theories of language that link the written word to authority, the oral emphasis is surely pertinent to the text's feminist agenda, a prioritising of the semiotic over the symbolic. The repetitive character of the narrative, which consists in systematic reference to the golden chariot at the end of chapters and recurring events – such as forced marriage, mariticide, scapegoating, suicide, etc. – produces a circular effect that further underscores a lack of change and impossibility of escape.

With respect to the third space opened up by the choice of setting, although Bhabha theorises this locality with postcolonial identity and expression in mind, it can be understood more generally as an ambivalent site, intrinsically opposed to essentialist positions – in this case on gender as well as identity and culture – where new meanings and possibilities are able to emerge.[76] Thus, in a reversal of conventional understandings of crime, punishment and culpability, the inmates in *Al-ʿAraba* refuse to bear any guilt, even when confessing their crimes. In their alternative reality they view the murders and abuses they commit not as heinous crimes but examples of justice and paths to liberation. ʿAziza's recollections of murdering her stepfather 'did not make her regret what she did because she only killed to preserve these pure sweet, beautiful memories'.[77] There is a further ethical twist here, for the memories ʿAziza cherishes are of incest and violation; she alternatively loves and despises her lover/oppressor. Hinna experiences happiness for the first time since killing her husband when she is placed on the ward for the weak with other older women. Their removal from public space and entry into prison in effect liberates them from misery and serfdom in a reimagining of freedom and emancipation. Incarceration may even signify victory in this alternative universe. Zaynab sees her sentence as victory not defeat.[78] At least imprisonment is a fate which she chose for herself. Another possibility opened up by the prison space is the forging of horizontal gender relations.[79] The women inmates, away from their husbands, fathers, brothers and lovers, are for the first time able to develop ties with other women based on love, trust and reciprocity, which is something they were denied in the outside world, where patriarchal norms preclude productive female relations and there is a conspicuous absence of sisterhood. ʿAziza's mother, who puts everything in the hands of fate and amulets and whose physical blindness is a metaphor for her inability to see the paedophilia practised by her husband upon her daughter, provides for ʿAziza not a model of strength and agency but of domesticity and servitude, rendering it all the more difficult for ᶜAziza to rise above her situation. She exemplifies de Beauvoir's point that the mother 'saddles her child with her own destiny: a way of proudly laying claim to her own femininity and also a way of revenging herself for it'.[80] The latter, a subconscious drive for vengeance, perhaps explains the harsh treatment of Muna by her mother in 'The Sorrows of Desdemona'. This woman, who follows her husband from room to room like a dog, consistently sides with her husband and son against Muna as the daughter's horizons are broadened and she covertly gravitates towards her liberated drama teacher.[81] The other woman in ᶜAziza's life, Nadira, an uninhibited modernised type, assumes a superior posture and represents a threat to ᶜAziza's cherished though warped existence and becomes a rival in love. Neither woman does anything to attenuate ᶜAziza's situation and the relationships between them are wholly unproductive from a feminist point of view. The three women's focus on the stepfather precludes sisterhood. In a similar vein, we are told that Umm al-Khayr sends her daughters back to their husbands when they complain and ᶜAyda's mother blames her daughter for her husband's cruelty and forces her to take the blame for the murder committed by her brother, repeating an age-old pattern of belief in the superiority of male offspring in patriarchal society on the pretext of stemming a vendetta. She also, along with other mothers in the narrative, helps to arrange a marriage for her daughter, denying her a say in her future. Beyond the prison walls, disharmony frames female relations, which the text, echoing de Beauvoir again, acknowledges 'is natural and the result of long years of [women] being unable to exist in their own right in a world where they depend on men'.[82] This dependency, and the power structure it holds in place, collapses in the alternative world of the women's prison, where the inmates are able to come into their own. The irony is of course that this can only happen in the third space of the prison, cut off from society and public time.

Women like ᶜAziza's mother evoke the angel in the house, that meek and submissive type 'who has no existence outside the context of her home and whose sole window on the world is her husband',[83] and the manner in which the narrative zooms in on her, juxtaposing her servitude, ignorance and deference to fate and superstition with the positive action of her daughter, highlights her passivity and complicity in patriarchy, condemning her in a manner of which Virginia Woolf, who famously called for killing the angel, would approve.[84] Nadira's character, on the other hand, recalls the *femme fatale* who has recurred in Arabic literature from Zulaykha in the Qur'an and classical texts to Jaziya in *Sirat Bani Hilal* to Zahira and Zaynat in *Harafish*. However, the framework in which she is presented here, that is, from the point of view of one of her lover's victims and among a series of vignettes of abused women, means that it is not the seductive, ensnaring, dangerous attribute of this trope that we see so much as the tragic element, the fact that she is simply another victim of ʿAziza's stepfather and of a society which fails to protect its women. The underlying irony destabilises the familiar stereotype and replaces the portrait of wily seductress with one of naivety and victimhood, not unlike the change Hajir effects on Zulaykha in *Wasf*. ʿAziza, Hinna, ʿAzima and many of the other women prisoners of course represent the angel's double, the monster woman, or rebellious female who upsets the system, breaks taboos and inspires fear in men. This familiar character, whose presence in Victorian fiction has been explored by Gilbert and Grubar but who also finds expression in the Arabic novel, not least in *Bint Allah* and *Jannat*, is again laid bare by the setting and narrative viewpoint.[85] By enabling these women to speak with their own voice, which tends to bring in a backstory, it becomes apparent that they are not so much freaks of nature as victims of an oppressive society, and what is represented as insanity and irrationality in patriarchal discourse becomes a function of their maltreatment and the absence of options within a male hegemony. The representation of insanity thus differs slightly from *Jannat*. Whereas Jannat's madness is assigned to her by a patriarchal system that cannot cope with insubordinate women and views violations of its narrow understanding of femininity as evidence of insanity, *Al-ʿAraba* takes this further by representing madness as a disease of maladjustment.[86] ʿAziza is not only seen as mad because of behaviour that contravenes patriarchal logic, but is driven to madness by a system that silences her and denies her selfhood. Madness, writes Shoshana Felman, 'is the impasse confronting those whom cultural conditioning has deprived of the very means of protest and self-affirmation'.[87] ʿAziza's insanity is the outcome of alienation and repression, as well as an expression of the senseless and preposterous world she inhabits, where myths of love, marriage, happiness and family have turned out to be false and injustice and oppression rule. At the same time, as Dinah Manisty suggests, madness is here a strategy that permits the elaboration of the chariot fantasy without losing the real-world connection and challenges the dividing lines between natural/unnatural, sane/insane, moral/immoral.[88]

Religion is once more implicated in the horror. The text presents several examples of female subjugation justified with reference to God and religion. Hinna's husband insists that it is his religious right that she indulge his every sexual desire and refusal to do so will lead her to hellfire, 'where she would experience painful torment for not obeying him as God prescribed'.[89] Her resort to religious arguments and suggestion that he focus on God in old age is rounded on her in a scene that confirms that the power of discourse belongs to men. ᶜAzima's wily lover exhorts God and feigns the role of humble believer in order to avoid marrying her, and the scene in which ᶜAyda's fate is sealed by recitation of the *fātiḥa* at a betrothal ritual held in her absence underscores the complicity of scripture in denying young girls a say in their future. The narrative also cites the hadith 'Marry a woman for four reasons: her money, her beauty, her standing and her piety', a selection no doubt intended to underscore the misogyny embedded in Islamic theology.[90] As in *Suqut, Jannat, Al-Mahdi* and *ᶜAzazil*, religion is associated with violence. The surgeon who performs the castration on Hussein the flautist under ᶜAzima's orders does so whilst professing his faith and Shafiqa's sister's relationship with a Christian leads to her death, highlighting the danger and wastage of religious intolerance. At the same time, religion as faith and belief is represented as a form of false consciousness and impediment to individual agency and social change. References to fate are plentiful and make it clear that the characters believe human life to be pre-determined. ᶜAziza asks herself 'why is it ordained that a beautiful young girl like [Jamalat] should bear all this ugliness', as though Jamalat's predicament is the will of God rather than a function of patriarchy.[91] Hinna's mother repeats for her daughter the religious dictum that everyone's fate is inscribed on a tablet in heaven, which negates any effort by the individual to control his/her own destiny. And Hinna herself believes that 'her husband met his foreordained end (*nihāyatuh al-maktūba*)', ignoring her own part in his demise.[92] Faith and belief serve as a blinker in *Al-ᶜAraba*, preventing characters from seeing the world as it is.

This naturally gives rise to a good deal of irony which, along with its close cousin parody, abounds in the text, constituting perhaps its most effective mode of criticism where religion is concerned, especially when combined with humour. Under the guise of the latter, writes al-Nowaihi, 'Bakr is constantly pushing her readers to rethink almost all their categories of thought and speech: political, literary, and religious, among others',[93] and further to see the author's humour as a sign that she 'has not given up on the nation, and still deeply cares'.[94] Characters like ʿAzima and Bahija, the latter despite her education and successful career, yearn for marriage with no appreciation of it as a curb on their freedom and individualism. The prison symbolism is of course ironic, for the combined effect of the women's individual stories is to dismantle any equation between freedom and the outside world. Shafiqa's sister's adoption of the veil to deflect attention has the opposite effect with regard to her bothersome relative. Movement for these women is simply from one enclosure to another, as Dinah Manisty has noted.[95] ʿAziza's mother's blindness produces a stark example of a character's viewpoint conflicting with the reader's understanding of the situation, especially when we see her thanking God for her husband's interest in her daughter.[96] But dramatic irony is common among the text's believing women. Umm al-Khayr praises God when her son is spared a long prison sentence for drug offences, forgetting that it was her own actions, namely her false confession, that enabled him to escape prosecution, and ignoring the suffering and loss of freedom this means for her. Mahrusa's statement that 'God rewards everyone according to their good deeds',[97] in the context of a work that highlights injustice and is concerned with vindicating many of the crimes portrayed in its pages, makes a mockery of the well-known proverb. The same character endures her husband's cruelty in the belief that she is fulfilling a divine obligation, when in reality all she is doing is facilitating her mistreatment and demonstrating the depth of her ignorance and naivety and the role of religion in the dispossession of its female followers. ʿAziza views her stepfather and oppressor in godly terms; he is 'no less than a worshipped deity, whose requests and orders could not be refused'.[98] The chasm between the character's viewpoint and reality here redoubles the tragedy. At the same time the vocabulary of divinity surrounding the stepfather not only creates a highly suggestive association between God and sexual abuse reminiscent of *Suqut* but mocks and subverts religious language, by using it to produce non-religious meaning. Further subversion is found in the snake symbolism in ʿAziza's story. Although her devotion to her stepfather is for the most part absolute, she is on one occasion distracted by a jeweller on a trip to the souq. The flirtation between them is acted out around a gold snake necklace, evoking the temptation in Eden. The irony here is that the jeweller and his necklace represent a potential route out of evil, which ʿAziza in her obsession with her oppressor ignores. The conventional symbolism is thus subverted in an ironic twist that underscores the character's blindness whilst challenging traditional understandings of the serpent; was Eve really wrong to submit to the snake and eat the forbidden fruit? As Mieke Bal has argued, in so doing did she not grant to mankind the gift of knowledge and ensure the continuance of the species?[99] Is ʿAziza spurning knowledge and enlightenment out of distorted logic and misplaced attachment? From a strictly feminist point of view, to pursue the jeweller would hardly bring liberation but merely reposition her in relation to another man, and in this sense the episode merely highlights a lack of options for women.

Parody is also in wide supply in its classical sense of ridiculing imitation. References to Qur'anic recitation and the exhortations of a shaykh on the radio in the opening paragraphs introduce a religious setting so that the scene of ʿAziza washing herself that immediately follows takes on the symbolism of religious ablution (*wuḍūʾ*), which Muslims perform before prayer and which, in wider monotheistic tradition, signifies the washing away of impurity and sin. But ʿAziza's ablution is incomplete, for she washes only some of the body parts stipulated in *wuḍūʾ* and she does not follow it with prayer. Moreover, as the reader soon discovers, the character has no intention of purifying herself, for her alternative moral system justifies the murder of her lover and idol. The reference to recitation and sound of the shaykh in the background evokes a spiritual setting only to subvert it with an act of profane washing. The parodic pattern here, by subverting and emptying a religious ritual of its spiritual significance, mocks religion. Further parody is found in the story of ʿAzima, whose unusual height precludes marriage through the traditional route so that she ends up first as a mourner and eventually as singer at religious festivals. Mention of eulogists and Sufi poets from the Middle Ages in the course of ʿAzima's story installs this group as the backdrop against which is read the character, who turns funerals and religious events into a business and ultimately ends up a criminal, having orchestrated a shocking castration plot. ʿAzima thus becomes a subversive incarnation of this respected group, which in turn develops two lines of meaning. On the one hand, the fact that she is a woman brings into focus, and serves as a correction to, the predominantly male character of this class. At the same time, her seemingly indulgent lifestyle, financial gain and criminal act cast a shadow over the Sufi poets and eulogists in whose footsteps she supposedly follows and underscores the money-making function of religion, which is also seen in the sale and purchase of amulets in the text. The latter are in turn parodied in the analogy which the narrator draws between them and the lingerie and accessories purchased by the stepfather for ʿAziza, 'charms (*tamāʾim*) with which the stepfather bewitched his young lover'.[100] There is also a sense that the flautist parodies the grandson of the Prophet, for the narrative deliberately draws attention to their shared name, which blights the sacred image of Husayn the saint.

The most significant employment of parody in the narrative lies in the golden chariot, which frames the text both structurally and dramatically. The main character, ʿAziza, plans to travel to heaven in a golden chariot and the stories included in the text, which ends with its departure pictured by ʿAziza as she breathes her last, belong to the women whom she has selected to accompany her on this celestial journey. The chariot features in the text as a product of ʿAziza's insanity and hallucinations and she is the only person for whom it has any meaning (indeed most of the characters are unaware of its existence). Nevertheless its symbolic and parodic value is far-reaching. For a start, as a symbol of escape the chariot represents the desperation of ʿAziza and the tragedy of her and the other prisoners' predicament. There is no prospect of social reintegration or positive change for the women in *Al-ʿAraba*, so escape is the only way out, a theme also developed in the suicides, and attempted suicides, in the text. The fact that the destination of the chariot, heaven, is a place visited after death signals an absence of faith in life, that extinction is preferable to continued female suffering, and even casts the present of these women as a form of death or non-existence. On the other hand, the sublime but fanciful descriptions of the chariot ascending to the sky with winged white horses and enveloped in billowing clouds parodies the luxuriant portrait of the afterlife found in religious texts and the hyperbolic tendency of religious language, and the chariot's association with the madwoman ʿAziza pokes fun at the whole concept of a journey to heaven embedded in monotheistic belief. This is further developed in the mundane details and practical considerations that ʿAziza refers to in her decision-making and departure plan. She thinks about where passengers should sit and what clothes should be worn. The pettiness of these considerations invokes amusement, which of course augments the suggestion of religious pettiness. This is strengthened by the mixing of the profane and religious. The spiritual aspect of the chariot, and by extension the journey to heaven, is dismantled by its involvement with the profane and trivial and its fantastical frame.[101] The fact that it is supposedly criminal women who are awarded a place on the journey confirms the innocence of these women and their commendable qualities – 'for they were really angels without wings, who had lost their way to heaven and come to this depressing, desolate place'[102] – and challenges the conventional criteria used to assess an individual's worthiness, a challenge already posed in the discourse with the angels in *Turaf* as they replace the traditional criteria of judgement at the Reckoning, namely faith and adherence to Sharia, with authentic action and individual conscience.[103] The fact that the chariot does not actually take off, for its path is blocked by the prison governor and his men, recalls a theme highlighted by Saʿdawi in *Suqut*; that heaven is mostly closed to women in Islam.[104]

Religion and religious myth are thus satirised in *Al-ʿAraba* and heavily implicated in patriarchal oppression. But unlike in Saʿdawi's work, where it is equated with evil in all of its manifestations, there are occasions in *Al-ʿAraba* where religion can be empowering for women and even, in its popular or ancient form, threaten the patriarchal order. ʿAzima, for example, finds a voice and degree of public presence and recognition through her role as official neighbourhood mourner and as a performer at religious festivals, and Umm ʿAbd al-ʿAziz is respected and achieves a certain status in prison from her piety, religious knowledge and apparent ability to interpret dreams. These two women are able to turn religion to their advantage, albeit in limited spheres, which points to an instability within the power structure, again on the logic of Bhabha's English book; that which empowers one party may be usurped by the other party and used against it. Further signs of this are found in Zaynab's *zār* ceremonies and references to ancient Egyptian divinities.

The former, which are represented as diametrically opposed to the masculine rationality of Zaynab's brother-in-law and oppressor and portrayed as frenzied events to which women of all classes flock, are seized on as evidence of the woman's insanity. Although they do not directly challenge the patriarchal order, they represent a degree of threat, as suggested by the brother-in-law's efforts to negate and marginalise them as abnormal and his lawyer's attempt to use them as evidence of infirmity in the custody case. Popular religion, as seen in the Sufi chapter, has a subversive potential, and its association with women in the text compounds this and necessitates its marginalisation. The narrative mentions that women of all classes flock to Zaynab's ceremonies, so it is only to be expected that the ceremonies are decried by patriarchal orthodoxy. References to ancient Egyptian goddesses further draw attention to a link between women and divinity severed in the era of monotheism. With her mystery, charm and poetic aura, ʿAziza's mother is compared to 'the queen from an ancient mythical world' and an analogy is drawn between goddess of fertility Hathur and prison inmate Umm al-Khayr.[105] The latter possesses a strong maternal instinct and, for all ʿAziza can see, has a supernatural relationship with the prison cat, which also puts her on the side of matriarchal earth religions. These associations remind us of a spiritual world beyond monotheism and the era of female deities and goddesses, which cropped up already in Bakr's novella *Maqam ʿAtiyya* (1978).

Far more intent on suggesting the empowering potential of religion for women are writers like Alifa Rifʿat who, although more focused on the short story, merits brief mention here as representative of another strand of feminist literary discourse on religion in Egypt. Rifʿat deals with the plight of women with reference to religion but without attacking it. In Rifʿat's world, it is not Islam that is at fault but the misdeeds of men and a widespread patriarchal conspiracy in Egyptian and Arab society.[106] The impression from reading her stories is that more attention to the Qur'an would improve the lot of women, a message which is diametrically opposed to the iconoclasm of Nawal Saʿdawi in *Suqut* and *Jannat* and satirical approach of Salwa Bakr in *Al-ʿAraba*. Her well-known short story 'Manzar Baʿid li-Miʾdhana' (Distant View of a Minaret) addresses the disavowal of female sexuality.[107] The story depicts a woman whose husband habitually deprives her of sexual gratification and represents this as an injustice wrought by man and a contravention of Islam.

In 'Bahiyya's Eyes', the narrator specifically excuses God of the tragedies she has suffered – 'I'm not crying now because I'm fed up or regret that the Lord created me a woman', but because society has prevented her from fulfilling this role.[108] Instead the story points to the irony that 'Allah the Sublime had in this manner given the female the task of continuing His creation', yet woman is habitually maltreated and subordinate.[109] In another story, 'Hadhihi laylati' (My Wedding Night), Rifᶜat turns the depressing image of an arranged marriage into a hopeful one as the couple discover common ground and as the reluctant bride has a change of heart and embraces the occasion of her wedding night.[110] In 'The Kite', the widow accepts a marriage proposal in order to regain access to religion and prayer.[111] After initial reluctance, she pictures herself standing behind her suitor following his movements and performing the prayers, as she has been unable to do since her husband died, and is filled with contentment. The ready acceptance of male lead here, and the absence of radical action by women across Rifᶜat's work, does not fit in with the usual trajectory of feminist fiction, which likes to see shackles broken and freedom realised. From an artistic point of view, the presence of religious belief in a modern narrative context is also problematic, its unitary discourse conflicting with the heterodox ideology of modern narrative forms. Rifᶜat's subtle treatment of religion, which exists in hints and intimations rather than strongly articulated messages and images, enables her to get away with it, to secure a place in the secular canon in spite of transcendent commitment, but remains exceptional.

Notes

1. Leila Ahmed, *Women and Gender in Islam* (New Haven and London: Yale University Press, 1992). See also Margot Badran, *Feminists, Islam and Nation: Gender and the Making of Modern Egypt* (Princeton: Princeton University Press, 1995); Beth Baron, *The Women's Awakening in Egypt* (New Haven and London: Yale University Press, 1994).
2. See Ahmed, *Women and Gender*, 'The First Feminists', pp. 169–88. Journals established by women include: *Al-Fatah* (1892–1894), *Anis al-Jalis* (1898–1908), *Fatat al-Sharq* (1906–39), *Al-Jins al-Latif* (1908–24), *Al-ᶜAfaf* (1910–22), *Fatat al-Nil* (1913–15). Ahmed, *Women and Gender*, p. 172.
3. See Shaaban, *Voices Revealed*, chs 1 and 2 on 'The Marginalisation of Women's Writing' and 'The Beginnings' (i.e. of women's novel-writing).

4. On the representation of women and feminist themes in modern Arabic literature, see Evelyne Accad, *Sexuality and War: Literary Masks of the Middle East* (New York: New York University Press, 1992); Nadje al-Ali, *Gender Writing/ Writing Gender: The Representation of Women in a Selection of Modern Egyptian Literature* (Cairo: American University in Cairo Press, 1994); Roger Allen, Hilary Kilpatrick and Ed de Moor (eds), *Love and Sexuality in Modern Arabic Literature* (London: Saqi Books, 1995); Sawsan Naji, *Al-Mar'a fi'l-Mir'at: Dirasa Naqdiyya li'l-Riwaya al-Nisa'iyya fi Misr 1888–1985* (Cairo: al-ᶜArabi li'l-Nashr wa'l-Tawziᶜ, 1989); Shaaban, *Voices Revealed*; George Tarabishi, *Sharq wa Gharb, Rujula wa Unutha: Dirasat fi ᶜAzmat al-Jins wa'l-Hadara fi'l-Riwaya al-ᶜArabiyya* (Beirut: Dar al-Taliᶜa, 1997 [1977]); Anastasia Valassopoulos, *Contemporary Arab Women Writers: Cultural Expression in Context* (London and New York: Routledge, 2009).
5. Nawal Saᶜdawi, 'Al-Mar'a fi'l-Adab al-ᶜArabi', in *Al-Wajh al-ᶜAri li'l-Mar'a al-ᶜArabiyya* (Beirut: al-Muʾassasat al-ᶜArabiyya li'l-Dirasat wa'l-Nashr, 1977), pp. 75–81 and ff.
6. Daphne Grace makes a similar observation of Mahfuz, with particular reference to *Bayn al-Qasrayn*. D. Grace, *The Woman in the Muslin Mask: Veiling and Identity in Postcolonial Literature* (London: Pluto Press, 2004), pp. 80–2.
7. I refer here to the Saqi Books edition (London, 2000), trans. Sherif Hetata, *The Fall of the Imam* (London: Saqi Books, 2002). Translations my own unless stated.
8. See Alamin M. Mazrui and Judith I. Abala, 'Sex and Patriarchy: Gender Relations in "Mawt al-Rajul al-Wahid ᶜala al-Ard (God Dies by the Nile)"', *Research in African Literatures*, vol. 28, no. 3: Arabic Writing in Africa (Autumn 1997), pp. 17–32.
9. *Suqut*, p. 39 (trans., p. 49).
10. On the dystopic element, note Fedwa Malti-Douglas' comparison to western dystopic fiction, which projects the dystopia into the future, as a vision of what could be, and Saᶜdawi's world of *Suqut*, which is a comment on the present. *Men, Women, and God(s): Nawal El Saadawi and Arab Feminist Poetics* (Berkley, LA, and London: University of California Press, 1995), pp. 101–2.
11. Daphne Hampson, 'The Sacred, the Feminine and French Feminist Theory', in G. Pollock and V. Turvey Sauron (eds), *The Sacred and the Feminine: Imagination and Difference* (London and New York: I. B. Tauris, 2007), pp. 73–4.

12. *Suqut*, pp. 16, 30 (trans., pp. 19, 36).
13. Ibid. p. 39 (trans., p. 50).
14. Ibid. p. 41 (trans., p. 52).
15. Yusuf Idris, in 'AKana La Budd Ya Lili an Tudi͑i al-Nur?' (Did You Have to Turn the Light on Lili) in *Qa͑ al-Madina* (Cairo, 1959).
16. *Suqut*, p. 59 (trans., p. 75).
17. Hetata's translation. *Suqut*, p. 30 (trans., p. 36).
18. Dalya Cohen-Mor, *Fathers and Sons in the Middle East* (Basingstoke: Palgrave Macmillan, 2013), pp. 1–3. See also Najat Rahman, 'The Trial of Heritage and the Legacy of Abraham', in Lahouzine Ouzgane (ed.), *Islamic Masculinities* (London: Zed, 2006), pp. 72–85.
19. *Suqut*, p. 28 (trans., p. 33).
20. Ibid. p. 28 (trans., p. 34).
21. Ibid. p. 20 (trans., p. 23). Or the sense could be stomach here.
22. Fatma Mernissi, *Beyond the Veil: Male–Female Dynamics in Modern Muslim Society* (London: Saqi Books, 1983), p. 8.
23. *Suqut*, p. 123 (trans., 160).
24. Hampson, 'The Sacred, the Feminine and French Feminist Theory', p. 64.
25. Cohen-Mor, *Fathers and Sons*, p. 2.
26. *Suqut*, p. 82 (trans., p. 107).
27. Simone de Beauvoir, *The Second Sex*, trans. H. M. Parshley (London: Vintage, 1997 [1949]), p. 174.
28. Sa͑dawi, 'The Thirteenth Rib of Adam', in *The Hidden Face of Eve: Women in the Arab World*, trans. Sherif Hetata (London: Zed Press, 1980), p. 94.
29. Visited by God in a dream. *Suqut*, p. 24 (trans., p. 28).
30. Hetata's translation. *Suqut*, p. 106 (trans., 139).
31. Malti-Douglas, *Men, Women, and God(s)*, p. 95. See p. 94 for further analysis of naming in the text.
32. Sa͑dawi, *Al-Wajh al-͑Ari li'l-Mar᾿a al-͑Arabiyya*, pp. 20 and ff.
33. See Sa͑dawi, *Hidden Face of Eve*, 'Preface' (pp. i–xvi) and 'The Thirteenth Rib of Adam', pp. 91–101.
34. *The Nawal Sa͑dawi Reader* (London and New York: Zed Books, 1997), p. 86. Also *Al-Wajh al-͑Ari li'l-Mar᾿a al-͑Arabiyya*, pp. 30ff.
35. *Suqut*, p. 156 (trans., p. 200).
36. Ibid. p. 30 (trans., p. 36).
37. Ibid. p. 115 (trans., p. 151).
38. Ibid. p. 151 (trans., p. 193).

39. Judi M. Roller, *The Politics of the Feminist Novel* (New York and London: Greenwood Press, 1986), pp. 7–8.
40. This incidentally conflicts with Malti-Douglas' conclusion, when comparing Shahrazad and Bint Allah, that the struggle simply goes on (*Men, Women, and God(s)*, p. 107). It may be the case that Saʿdawi's text 'shows no resolution' but the final scenes plant the seed of hope. Elsewhere Malti-Douglas notes that the pessimistic vision engendered in the repeated killing of Bint Allah is matched by an optimistic vision of her repeatedly rising up (p. 102).
41. See also Roller's discussion of fragmentation and unity in *The Politics of the Feminist Novel*, pp. 67ff.
42. *Jannat wa Iblis* (Beirut: Dar al-Adab, 1992). Translations my own unless stated. Trans. Sherif Hetata, *The Innocence of the Devil* (London: Methuen, 1994). Malti-Douglas, *Men, Women, and God(s)*, p. 119.
43. *Al-Sarāyat al-ṣafrāʾ*, lit. yellow palace = mental asylum in Egyptian Arabic.
44. The narrative, through its flashbacks, indicates the character is named Zakaria and is Jannat's brother, but he is referred to as God/Lord (*al-rabb*) in the text.
45. *Jannat*, p. 64 (trans., p. 81).
46. Ibid. p. 132 (trans., 169).
47. Ibid. p. 19 (trans., p. 21).
48. Ibid. pp. 61–2 (trans., p. 78).
49. Sandra M. Gilbert and Susan Gubar, *The Madwoman in the Attic: The Woman Writer and the Nineteenth-Century Literary Imagination*, 2nd edn (New Haven: Yale University Press, 2000 [1979]), p. 284.
50. *Jannat*, p. 130 (trans., p. 167).
51. Ibid. p. 94 (trans., p. 120).
52. *Dhayl al-siḥliya*. *Siḥliya* also translates as 'lizard'. Hetata's translation also renders *siḥliya* as snake. *Jannat*, p. 94 (trans., p. 120).
53. *Jannat*, p. 73 (trans., p. 92).
54. See Sally Frank, 'Eve was Right to Eat the "Apple": The Importance of Narrative in the Art of Law-Making', *Yale Journal of Law and Feminism*, vol. 8, no. 1 (1995), pp. 94–5.
55. Phyllis Trible writes that 'Throughout the myth she is the more intelligent one, the more aggressive one, and the one with greater sensibilities'. Trible, 'Eve and Adam: Genesis 2-3 Reread', in Judith Plaskow and Carol P. Christ (eds), *Womanspirit Rising: A Feminist Reader in Religion* (San Francisco: Harper and Row, 1979), p. 79; Saʿdawi, *The Hidden Face of Eve*, p. 103 ('Yet in the story Eve is more intelligent than Adam, able to understand what Adam fails

to grasp, and to realise that the forbidden tree bears the most delicious and exhilarating of all fruits – knowledge, and with knowledge the capacity to differentiate between good and evil'). On feminist rereadings of Eve, see Alice Ogden Bellis, 'The Story of Eve', in *Helpmates, Harlots, and Heroes: Women's Stories in the Hebrew Bible* (Louisville, KY: John Knox Press, 1994), pp. 45–66.

56. Fatima Sadiqi, 'Language and Gender', in Lutz Edzard and Rudolf de Jong (eds), *Encyclopaedia of Arabic Language and Linguistics*, online edn (Brill, online).
57. Ibid.
58. Malti-Douglas discusses this effect in detail in *Men, Women, and God(s)*, ch. 6, pp. 124–5.
59. *Jannat*, p. 157 (trans., 201).
60. Malti-Douglas, *Men, Women, and God(s)*, p. 125.
61. *Jannat*, pp. 91–2 (trans., 116–17).
62. Ibid. p. 47 (trans., p. 58).
63. See Homi Bhabha, 'Signs Taken for Wonders: Questions of Ambivalence and Authority under a Tree Outside Delhi, May 1817', *Critical Inquiry*, vol. 12, no. 1 (Autumn 1985), pp. 144–65.
64. *Jannat*, p. 166 (trans., pp. 211–12).
65. Miriam Cooke, *Women Claim Islam: Creating Islamic Feminism through Literature* (London and New York: Routledge, 2001), p. 76.
66. *Jannat*, p. 170 (trans., p. 216).
67. Hetata's translation. *Jannat*, p. 181 (trans., p. 229).
68. *Jannat*, p. 52 (trans., p. 65).
69. Ibid. p. 43 (trans., p. 53).
70. El-Enany also reads an intertextual dialogue with the story of Hajar and Abraham. See El-Enany, 'The Madness of Non-Conformity', for this and further discussion of the novel, including the Yusuf/Zulaykha story.
71. Cairo: Dar Sina li'l-Nashr, 1991, trans. Dinah Manisty, *The Golden Chariot* (Reading: Garnet, 1995). Studies of the novel include: Magda al-Nowaihi, 'Reenvisioning National Community in Salwa Bakr's "The Golden Chariot Does Not Ascend to Heaven"', in *The Arab Studies Journal*, vols 7–8, nos 1–2 (Fall 1999/Spring 2000), pp. 8–24; Manisty, 'Madness as Textual Strategy in the Narratives of Three Egyptian Women Writers', *Alif: Journal of Comparative Studies*, no. 14 (1994), pp. 154–74; Caroline Seymour-Jorn, 'A New Language: Salwa Bakr on Depicting Egyptian Women's Worlds', *Critique: Critical Middle Eastern Studies*, vol. 11, no. 2 (Fall 2002), pp. 151–76; Latifa al-Zayyat, 'Qiraʾa

fi Riwayat Salwa Bakr *Al-ʿAraba al-Dhahabiyya La Tasʿad Ila al-Samaʾ*', *Fusul*, vol. 11, no. 1 (1992), pp. 273–7.
72. Sabry Hafez makes a similar point with reference to *Suqut* as part of a highly critical review of some works by Saʿdawi. Hafez, 'Intentions and Realisation in the Narratives of Nawal El-Saadawi', *Third World Quarterly*, vol. 11, no. 3 (July 1989), p. 192.
73. Salwa Bakr, 'Kayd al-Rijal', in *Maqam ʿAtiyya: Riwaya wa Qisas Qasira* (Cairo: Dar al-Fikr li'l-Dirasat wa'l-Nashr wa'l-Tawziʿ, 1986), pp. 97–109.
74. El-Enany comments on the significance of the title of the story in his piece 'The Madness of Non-Conformity', pp. 385–6.
75. Al-Nowaihi, 'Reenvisioning National Community', p. 14.
76. Ibid.
77. *Al-ʿAraba*, p. 11 (trans., pp. 7–8).
78. Ibid. p. 181 (trans., p. 157).
79. See also al-Nowaihi ('Reenvisioning National Community', p. 17), who refers to an 'alternative familial model' that flourishes among the women in prison, away from societal impositions and regulations.
80. de Beauvoir, *The Second Sex*, p. 309.
81. Trans. Denys Johnson-Davies in *The Wiles of Men and Other Stories* (London: Quartet, 1992).
82. *Al-ʿAraba*, p. 27 (trans., p. 20).
83. Elaine Hartnell, '"Nothing but Sweet and Womanly": A Hagiography of Patmore's Angel', *Victorian Poetry*, vol. 34, no. 4: 'Coventry Patmore: 1823–1896. In Memoriam' (Winter 1996), p. 460.
84. Woolf introduced her take on the angel of the house, a trope she borrowed from Coventry Patmore's poem of that name, in her 1931 address to the Women's Services League. The speech, 'Professions for Women', was published posthumously in *The Death of a Moth and Other Essays* (London: Hogarth Press, 1942).
85. Gilbert and Gubar, *The Madwoman in the Attic*. See note 49 for publication details.
86. Gilbert and Gubar's phrase, referring to nervous disorders among women. *The Madwoman in the Attic*, p. 53.
87. Shoshana Felman, 'Women and Madness: The Critical Phallacy', *Diacritics*, vol. 5, no. 4 (Winter 1975), p. 2.
88. Manisty, 'Changing Limitations: A Study of the Woman's Novel in Egypt (1960–1991)' (unpublished PhD thesis, SOAS, 1993), p. 242.

89. *Al-ʿAraba*, p. 56 (trans., p. 45).
90. Ibid. p. 170 (trans., p. 148).
91. Ibid. p. 127 (trans., p. 109).
92. Ibid. p. 47 (trans., p. 38).
93. Al-Nowaihi, 'Reenvisioning National Community', p. 11.
94. Ibid. p. 22.
95. Manisty, 'Changing Limitations', p. 239.
96. *Al-ʿAraba*, p. 17 (trans., p. 12).
97. Ibid. p. 132 (trans., p. 114).
98. Ibid. p. 15 (trans., p. 11).
99. Bellis, *Helpmates, Harlots, and Heroes*, p. 51.
100. *Al-ʿAraba*, p. 17 (trans., p. 13).
101. See also a similar argument made by al-Nowaihi, 'Reenvisioning National Community', pp. 11–12. Al-Nowaihi writes that 'it is precisely the otherworldliness of the dream that Bakr is attempting to undermine, and instead to doggedly insist that the focus of desire must be "to achieve 'justice and mercy on earth'"'.
102. *Al-ʿAraba*, p. 32 (trans., p. 24).
103. See pp. 141–8 of this study.
104. *Suqut*, p. 57 (trans., p. 73): 'There are no legal wives in paradise'.
105. *Al-ʿAraba*, p. 16 (trans., p. 11).
106. Ramzi Salti, 'Feminism and Religion in Alifa Rifaat's Short Stories', *The International Fiction Review*, vol. 18, no. 2 (1991), p. 108.
107. In *Fi Layl al-Shitaʾ al-Tawil* (Cairo: Matbaʿat al-ʿAsima, 1985), pp. 54–60.
108. Alifa Rifʿat, *Distant View from a Minaret and Other Stories*, trans. Denys Johnson-Davies (Oxford: Heinemann, 1983), p. 11. I have not been able to locate the original Arabic text of this story.
109. Ibid. p. 9.
110. In *Man Yakun al-Rajul* (Cairo: Al-Hayʾat al-Misriyya al-ʿAmma liʾl-Kitab, 1981), pp. 2–12, trans. 'My Wedding Night', pp. 120–6.
111. In Johnson-Davies (trans.), *Distant View from a Minaret*, pp. 107–12. Again, I have not been able to locate the original Arabic text and am relying on the translation.

Conclusion

The story of religion and the Egyptian novel is one of ambivalent coalescence. While the characteristic vision of the novel is antithetical to religion on one level (sceptical, rational, immanent, humanist, secular), the relationship between religion and the Egyptian novel is long and enduring. The early Egyptian novel, as it self-consciously fashioned itself as a new national literature and radically broke with the recent past, could not but engage with religion in its traditional form, as a discourse in need of repositioning in the context of the nation-state, and as a perceived obstacle in the way of modernity. High doses of religious institutional criticism characterise the Egyptian novel in the early period, as well as much valorising of nation and its implied substitution of sacred affiliation with civic bonds. Yet as religion is reconstituted as the other to the national self and secular aesthetic of the novel, so its embeddedness in cultural consciousness and indispensability to secular articulations of nation, novel and self are revealed. This period sees the emergence of the literary shaykh as a comic yet dangerous type, the epitome of what is wrong with traditional culture, and an association between faith and ignorance developed. Disenchantment characterises protagonists' journeys and other levels of narrative, as religious knowledge, Sufi masters, the Azhar, and other Islamic signifiers and representatives are demystified and even discredited. Yet alongside the negative discourse on orthodox Islam and formal religion a theme of spiritual yearning and nostalgia for sacred forms and theological certainty emerges and sacred patterns of expression, behaviour and ethics persist. At the same time, slips and incongruities in the discourse of secular characters and narrative voice, and the persistent return to religion which in itself bespeaks dependency, consistently problematises the novel's secular aesthetic. The novel's secularity is always compromised, religion is constitutive of its existence.

As the Egyptian novel matures, discursive slips and incongruities largely disappear but religion maintains a presence as theme, image, symbol, metanarrative, spirituality and target of criticism. In fact religion increases its presence insofar as it suffuses multiple layers of narrative and as its critique extends beyond institutions and representatives to matters of doctrine and deconstruction of sacred themes and tropes. Religion in the mature Egyptian novel also habitually extends beyond Islamic orthodoxy and Sufism to take in Coptic tradition, Christian imagery and mysticism more broadly. What is remarkable as one surveys the Egyptian novel of the last forty years is that the Islamic resurgence, which has had a transformative effect on Egyptian politics and society, has left the Egyptian novel formally and ideologically virtually untouched. There are no novels of faith in the modern Egyptian literary canon. Occasionally an author writing from a position of faith can break through, as is the case with some of Alifa Rifʿat's short stories, but to do so requires such a delicate balance of religious and aesthetic values, easier to achieve in the short story than novel, thanks to its brevity and fragmentary character, that such works are the exception and likely to remain so. The secular aesthetic of the novel, in particular its immanence and contingency, is evidently highly pervasive, even against a rising tide of religiosity. ʿAlaʾ al-Aswani's famous ʿImarat Yaʿqubiyyan (2002), one of the most successful novels of the last twenty years and a realistic portrait of late twentieth-century Egyptian life, represents the religious revival whilst remaining loyal to the secular spirit of the novel.[1]

It is worth pausing for a moment on Yaʿqubiyyan, as a Cairene saga published almost fifty years after Mahfuz's trilogy, to summarise some areas of change and continuity and briefly revisit the question of literary secularism. Here again we have a national allegory set in downtown Cairo using the strategy of realism. But instead of a family, the cast of characters is made up of unrelated individuals and instead of a journey away from religion (Kamal) we have a journey further into religion (Taha). Furthermore, a common faith in nation among the characters in the trilogy, regardless of political leaning, has fallen by the wayside; in Yaʿqubiyyan, set in the early 90s, there is no common ambition or shared vision of the future. The nation is important only to the older generation (Zaki Desuki and Hajj ʿAzzam), and it is now only Islamism that is able to spur a character to action. Of the younger generation, besides its Islamist recruit Taha, Busayna is indifferent to politics and nation and Hatim is wholly absorbed in sexual pursuits. The picture that emerges is of betrayed national dreams, a corrupt dictatorial government, and a disaffected and alienated populace. In this context, it is notable that the theological questions and ethical dilemmas of the trilogy persist. Prostitution, extra-marital sex and homosexuality continue to elicit inventive justifications in the context of sacred law by the characters, while polygamy, which Mahfuz's ʿAbd al-Jawwad rejected in favour of bought sex so as not to dilute his children's inheritance, is here enacted with disastrous consequences. Indeed, Hajj ʿAzzam's marriage to Suʿad throws up a variety of moral and religious conundrums and exemplifies the severe conflict between this Islamic practice and contemporary life and well-being. Dogma and human nature are still at odds and religion still pervades individual conscience and social ethics. In the meantime, religion and religiosity are on the rise. *Yaʿqubiyyan* contrasts, with evident nostalgia, the liberal environment of the recent past when few women donned headscarves and alcohol was widely available, with the shift to modest dress, assisted by such campaigns as the 'Approval and Light' stores (*maḥallāt al-riḍā wa'l-nur*), and closure of bars throughout the city. Individual characters may wear their religion lightly but public space is increasingly populated by religion and its signifiers.

All of this is viewed from a critical distance. Religious language is plentiful in *Yaʿqubiyyan*, if not as testimony to the religious commitment of the characters then as a symptom of the religious patterns of Arabic, but it is contained in the discourse and consciousness of the characters, and though a good part of the narrative is taken up with Taha's conversion from pious Muslim to Islamic activist, the image is not especially sympathetic and, more importantly, is highly psychologised. The youth is rejected on grounds of class by the police academy, in spite of good grades, and when this drives him to join the Islamists at university he is tortured and raped in police custody. His journey to Islamic activism becomes an effect of the massive failing of the system, which precludes social mobility and relentlessly humiliates the poor, and the advances of a charismatic shaykh and his group. Taha is first and foremost a victim, and his path to jihad is a rational response to oppression and humiliation. The spiritual dimension is limited to the character's internal monologue, and even there it is mixed with resolutions of vengeance, and his eventual death is rather flat. In other words, religiosity, religious activism and martyrdom are viewed through a secular lens. As religion encroaches further into political, social and cultural arena in the later decades of the twentieth century, the novel's secular aesthetic holds fast.

But religion and secularity, as the previous chapters have demonstrated, are never pure forms. Beyond the slips and contradictions that inevitably mark the early period, the Egyptian novel persistently reveals the difficulty of separating the two and illustrates areas of fusion and cross-contamination. On the one hand, there is the matter of interdependence and power struggle, which is especially evident in novels in which there is a conscious attempt to nurture national consciousness and articulate nationhood and modernity, and which, as we have seen, can be explained in terms of a self/other relation. On the other hand, beyond mutual definition and power struggle, religious and secular discourse coalesce in the Egyptian novel to the point of extreme blurring. For example, religious language in the form of divine invocation and transcendent ascription signals piety and theocentric thinking in some instances but is equally a cultural norm and an effect of a long and inextricable relation between Arabic and Islam. Busayna in *Yaʿqubiyyan* readily references God as prime agent but there is no doubt in her mind that her predicament is socially determined and that individual action is what will shape her future. Divine invocation in her speech is neither wholly sacred nor wholly profane.[2] The same is true of religious expression in the speech and internal monologue of many characters encountered. The Egyptian novel, as it captures and reproduces this feature of Arabic and everyday speech patterns in Egypt, complicates the religious/secular binary. A similar effect is produced, broadly speaking, by sacred tropes and images, religious intertexts and scriptural patterns in Egyptian literary space. As these are incorporated into the secular space of the novel, they retain their sacred trace even as they are secularised, in the sense of communicating non-religious meaning. As they are transferred to a new register they are de-sanctified but they do not become wholly temporal, since their spiritual significance becomes part of the new meaning and because they carry their past lives with them. ʿAbd al-Hakim Qasim's scene of the angels, though it is put to the service of contemporary messages and social critique, is a dialogue with divine themes as much as social commentary. Islamic eschatology here is no longer a path unto salvation but nor is it entirely temporal debris. The Egyptian novel, as it integrates sacred images, intertexts and patterns into literary space, demonstrates the interpenetration and cross-contamination of sacred and profane, religious and temporal. The conditions of belief remain secular – the novel is evidently not yet ready to surrender its deep-held ideological scepticism and intellectual pluralism – but secularity itself is problematised in its pages.

Much has been written on postsecularity in recent years. Postsecular thought stems from recognition of the moral failure of modernity and persistent return of religious belief, both as radical fundamentalism and new forms of spirituality, and of the falsity of the religious/secular binary. In other words, it critiques, though not necessarily rejects, secularity. Scholars and intellectuals in the spheres of sociology, religion, political theory and art have observed that modernity's characteristic disenchantment has turned in on itself and have sought to move beyond the oppositional language surrounding religion and secularity and to better understand the ideological and cultural dimensions of these discourses and their cross-fertilisation. The Egyptian novel contributes to the debate with its persistent problematisation of the religious/secular dialectic and rejection of the secularisation thesis, which has found little support in this literary space at any point in its history. On the other hand, postsecularity as an attitude opens another vista onto religion in the modern Egyptian novel. While I have argued that the Egyptian novel of the last forty years, in its canonical form, has been untouched by the religious resurgence,[3] this is perhaps to foster too narrow an understanding of religious return. Certainly religious authority and dogma are shunned by novelistic discourse and a religious aesthetic is yet to pervade Egyptian literary canonical space. But insofar as the turn to religion in the last quarter of the last century, which is not confined to Islam and the Middle East, emerges out of a sense of modernity's failure and limitations and a desire to seek alternatives, including irrational ones, then the Egyptian novel does perhaps have something to say. John A. McClure identifies 'partial returns' and dramatic disruptions of secular structures of the real as indicative of a postsecular aesthetic.[4] Partial conversions lead not back to formal bodies of faith but to alternative modes of spirituality or ideologically mixed and confusing middle zones.⁵ The spiritual searches of Mahfuz's *Hikayat*, and *Asdaʾ*, Salwa Bakr's *Al-Bashmuri* and Yusuf Zaydan's *ʿAzazil* testify to an ongoing need for transcendence and metaphysics in modernity, though they have little sympathy for orthodox religion. The poetic language and structures, fragmentation and surrealism of Kharrat's *Turabuha*, *Hikayat* and *Asdaʾ* suggest the inadequacy of rational narrative structures to capture experience and, further, create a sense of the ethereal. These works, and others like them, carve out a space, albeit small, for the other-worldly within the secular landscape of the novel. Similarly, as an indictment on the secular nation-state and in its search of alternatives, Mahfuz's *Harafish* reintroduces the sacred into the political community. While these narrative gestures do not amount to a change in Weltanschauung as such, they represent the interstices where the mythical and sublime can seep into novelistic terrain and a newfound openness to a sphere beyond the empirical. Whether the mystical and unorthodox can pervade Egyptian novelistic space such as to drown out its rational secular underpinnings remains an open question.

Notes

1. ʿAlaʾ al-Aswani, *ʿImarat Yaʿqubiyyan* (Cairo: Matbaʿ at Madbuli, 2006 [2002]), trans. Humphrey Davies, *The Yacoubian Building* (Cairo and New York: American University in Cairo Press, 2004).
2. Magdalena Mączyńska makes a similar point in regard to Zadie Smith's representation of Jewish ritual gestures in *Autograph Man*: 'In Smith's novel, ritual gestures, both verbal and non-verbal, are neither entirely profane nor entirely sacred; they are not channels of transcendence connecting the believer to a state of ontological fullness, but neither are they the debris of a bygone era floating through the spiritual void of a godless modernity'. See 'Toward a Postsecular Literary Criticism: Examining Ritual Gestures in Zadie Smith's "Autograph Man"', *Religion and Literature*, vol. 41 (Autumn 2009), p. 78.
3. This is in contrast to the faith-inspired strand of popular Arabic fiction, *al-adab al-islāmī*, comprising of *al-riwāya al-islāmiyya* (Islamic novel) and other Islamic genres, which springs from Muslim sentiment and commitment but whose weak aesthetic has so far prevented it from entering the canon or literary mainstream.
4. John A. McClure, *Partial Faiths: Postsecular Fiction in the Age of Pynchon and Morrison* (Athens, GA: Universty of Georgia Press, 2008).
5. Ibid. p. 4.

Works Cited

ᶜAbd al-Dayim, Sabir, *Al-Adab al-Islami Bayn al-Nazariyya wa'l-Tatbiq* (Zaqaziq: Dar al-Arqam, 1990).

ᶜAbd al-Hamid, Shakir, 'Al-Mawt wa'l-Hilm fi ᶜAlam Bahaʾ Tahir', *Fusul*, vol. 12, no. 2 (1993), pp. 180–203.

ᶜAbd al-Ghani, Mustafa, *Al-Sharqawi Mutamarridan: al-Dalala al-Dhatiyya wa'l-Ijtimaᶜiyya* (Cairo: Maktabat al-Taᶜawun al-Sahafiyya, 1997).

ᶜAbd al-Majid, Ibrahim, *La Ahad Yanam fi'l-Iskandariyya* (Cairo: Dar al-Hilal, 1996), trans. Farouk Abdel Wahab, *No One Sleeps in Alexandria* (Cairo: American University in Cairo Press, 1999).

Abdel-Messih, Marie-Thérèse, 'Hyper Texts: Avant-Gardism in Contemporary Egyptian Narratives', *Neohelicon*, vol. 36, no. 2 (2009), pp. 515–23.

ᶜAbdullah, Muhammad Hasan, *Al-Islamiyya wa'l-Ruhiyya fi Adab Najib Mahfuz* (Cairo: Dar Qibaᶜ li'l-Tibaᶜa wa'l-Nashr wa'l-Tawziᶜ, 2001).

Abu Deeb, Kamal, 'The Collapse of Totalising Discourse and the Rise of Marginalised/Minority Discourses', in Issa J. Boullata, Kamal Abdel-Malek, Wael B. Hallaq (eds), *Tradition, Modernity and Postmodernity in Arabic Literature: Essays in Honour of Professor Issa J. Boullata* (Leiden, Boston and Koln: Brill, 2000), pp. 335–66.

Abu Rabi, Ibrahim M., 'The Concept of the "Other" in Modern Arab Thought: From Muhammad Abduh to Abdullah Laroui', *Islam and Christian–Muslim Relations*, vol. 8, no. 1 (2007), pp. 85–97.

Accad, Evelyne, *Sexuality and War: Literary Masks of the Middle East* (New York: New York University Press, 1992).

Adunis (ᶜAli Ahmad Saᶜid), *Zamar al-Shiᶜr* (Beirut: Dar al-ᶜAwda, 1972).

Adunis (ᶜAli Ahmad Saᶜid), 'Khawatir hawl Mazahir al-Takhalluf al-Fikri fi'l-Mujtamaᶜ al-ᶜArabi', *Al-Adab* (Beirut), May 1974, pp. 27–9.

Adunis (ᶜAli Ahmad Saᶜid), *Al-Sufiyya wa'l-Suryaliyya* (London: Saqi Books, 1992), trans. Judith Cumberbatch, *Sufism and Surrealism* (London: Saqi Books, 2005).

Ahmed, Leila, *Women and Gender in Islam* (New Haven and London: Yale University Press, 1992).

Ahmed, Sara, *Strange Encounters: Embodied Others in Post-Coloniality* (London and New York: Routledge, 2000).

Ajjan-Boutrad, Bacima, *Le Sentiment religieux dans l'oeuvre de Naguib Mahfouz* (Paris: Sindbad, 2008).

al-Ali, Nadje, *Gender Writing/Writing Gender: The Representation of Women in a Selection of Modern Egyptian Literature* (Cairo: American University in Cairo Press, 1994).

al-ʿAlim, Mahmud Amin, 'La Yazal al-Suʾal Qaʾiman … Qiraʾa li-Riwaya "Khalati Safiyya waʾl-Dayr" li-Bahaʾ Tahir', *Arbaʿun ʿAm min al-Naqd al-Tatbiqi* (Beirut: Dar al-Mustaqbal al-ʿArabi, 1994), pp. 237–43.

Allen, Michael, *In the Shadow of World Literature: Sites of Reading in Colonial Egypt* (Princeton and Oxford: Princeton University Press, 2016).

Allen, Roger, 'Some Recent Works of Najib Mahfuz: A Critical Analysis', *Journal of the American Research Center in Egypt*, vol. 14 (1977), pp. 101–10.

Allen, Roger, Hilary Kilpatrick and Ed de Moor (eds), *Love and Sexuality in Modern Arabic Literature* (London: Saqi Books, 1995).

Almond, Ian, *Sufism and Deconstruction* (London and New York: Routledge, 2004).

Asad, Talal, *Formations of the Secular: Christianity, Islam, Modernity* (Stanford: Stanford University Press, 2003).

ʿAsfur, Jabir, *Zaman al-Riwaya* (Damascus: al-Mada, 1999).

al-Aswani, ʿAlaʾ, *ʿImarat Yaʿqubiyyan* (Cairo: Matbaʿat Madbuli, 2006 [2002]), trans. Humphrey Davies, *The Yacoubian Building* (Cairo and New York: American University in Cairo Press, 2004).

Awad, Louis, *The Literature of Ideas in Egypt* (Atlanta, GA: Scholars Press, 1986).

ʿAyyad, Shukri, 'Mafhum al-Asala waʾl-Tajdid waʾl-Thaqafa al-ʿArabiyya al-Muʿasira', *Al-Adab*, November 1971, pp. 2–5.

Badawi, M. M., 'The Lamp of Umm Hashim, the Egyptian Intellectual Between East and West', *Journal of Arabic Literature*, vol. 1 (1970), pp. 145–61.

Badawi, M. M., 'Islam in Modern Egyptian Literature', *Journal of Arabic Literature* vol. 2 (1971), pp. 154–77.

Badawi, M. M., 'Mamlakat al-Harafish: Dirasat fi Malhamat al-Harafish', *Fusul*, vol. 17, no. 1 (Summer 1998), pp. 97–124.

Badr, ʿAbd al-Muhsin, *Tatawwur al-Riwayat al-ʿArabiyya al-Hadith fi Misr* (Cairo: Maktabat al-Dirasat al-ʿArabiyya, 1963).

Badr, ʿAbd al-Muhsin, *Al-Riwaʾi waʾl-Ard* (Cairo: al-Hayʾat al-Misriyyat al-ʿAmma liʾl-Taʾlif waʾl-Nashr, 1971).

Badran, Margot, *Feminists, Islam and Nation: Gender and the Making of Modern Egypt* (Princeton: Princeton University Press, 1994).

Bahiyya, ʿIsam, 'Al-Shaytan fi Thalath Masrahiyyat', *Fusul*, vol. 3, no. 4 (1983), pp. 248–64.

Bakr, Salwa, *Maqam ʿAtiyya: Riwaya wa Qisas Qasira* (Cairo: Dar al-Fikr liʾl-Dirasat waʾl-Nashr waʾl-Tawziʿ, 1986).

Bakr, Salwa, *Al-ʿAraba al-Dhahabiyya la Tasʿad ila al-Samaʾ* (Cairo: Dar Sina liʾl-Nashr, 1991), trans. Dinah Manisty, *The Golden Chariot* (Reading: Garnet, 1995).

Bakr, Salwa, *The Wiles of Men and Other Stories*, trans. Denys Johnson-Davies (London: Quartet, 1992).

Bakr, Salwa, *Al-Bashmuri* (Cairo: Dar al-Hilal, 2005 [1998–2002]), trans. Nancy Roberts, *The Man from Bashmour* (Cairo and New York: American University in Cairo Press, 2007).

Ballas, Shimon, 'Nationalist and Islamic Themes in the Dramatic Works of al-Sharqawi', *Arab and African Studies*, vol. 18., no. 3 (1984), pp. 271–81.

Baron, Beth, *The Women's Awakening in Egypt* (New Haven and London: Yale University Press, 1994).

Barthes, Roland, 'The Death of the Author', in *Image, Music, Text*, trans. Stephen Heath (London: Fontana Press, 1977), pp. 142–8.

de Beauvoir, Simon, *The Second Sex*, trans. H. M. Parshley (London: Vintage, 1997 [1949]).

Bellis, Alice Ogden, 'The Story of Eve', in *Helpmates, Harlots, and Heroes: Women's Stories in the Hebrew Bible* (Louisville, KY: John Knox Press, 1994).

Bhabha, Homi, 'Signs Taken for Wonders: Questions of Ambivalence and Authority under a Tree Outside Delhi, May 1817', *Critical Inquiry*, vol. 12, no. 1 (Autumn 1985), pp. 144–65.

Bhabha, Homi, 'The Other Question: Stereotype, Discrimination and the Discourse of Colonialism', in *The Location of Culture* (New York and London: Routledge, 2004 [1994]), pp. 94–120.

Bishop Bishoy, *ʿAzazil: al-Radd ʿala al-Buhtan fi Riwaya Yusuf Zaydan* (Cairo: Dar Antun, 2009).

Black, Max, *Models and Metaphors* (Ithaca, NY: Cornell University Press, 1962).

Boullata, Issa J., *Trends and Issues in Contemporary Arab Thought* (Albany: State University of New York Press, 1990).

Boullata, Issa J. (ed.), *Literary Structures of Religious Meaning in the Qur'an* (Abingdon: Routledge, 2000).

Brinner, William M., 'The Significance of the Harafish and their "Sultan"', *Journal of the Economic and Social History of the Orient*, vol. 6, no. 2 (July 1963), pp. 190–215.

Brubaker, Rogers, 'Religion and Nationalism: Four Approaches', *Nations and Nationalism*, vol. 18, no. 1 (January 2012), pp. 2–20.

Burayghash, Muhammad Hasan, *Nahw Adab Islami: al-Qissa al-Islamiyya al-Muʿasira* (Amman: Dar al-Bashir, 1992).

Burayghash, Muhammad Hasan, *Fi'l-Adab al-Islami al-Muʿasir: Dirasa wa-Tatbiq* (Beirut: Muʾassasat al-Risala, 1998).

Butcher, E. L., *The Story of the Church of Egypt* (London: Smith, Elder & Co., 1898).

Butler, Alfred J., *The Arab Conquest of Egypt and the Last Thirty Years of the Roman Dominion*, 2nd edn (Oxford: Clarendon Press, 1978).

Butterfield, Herbert, *The Historical Novel: An Essay* (Cambridge: Cambridge University Press, 2011 [1924]).

Cachia, Pierre, *Taha Husayn: His Place in the Egyptian Literary Renaissance* (London: Luzac and Company Ltd, 1956).

Cannuyer, Christian, *Coptic Egypt: The Christians of the Nile* (London: Thames and Hudson, 2001).

Chittick, William, *Sufism: A Short Introduction* (Oxford: OneWorld, 2000).

Cobham, Catherine, 'Enchanted to a Stone: Heroes and Leaders in *The Harafish* by Najib Mahfuz', *Middle Eastern Literatures*, vol. 9, no. 2 (2006), pp. 123–35.

Cohen-Mor, Dalya, *Fathers and Sons in the Middle East* (Basingstoke: Palgrave Macmillan, 2013).

Cooke, Miriam, *Women Claim Islam: Creating Islamic Feminism through Literature* (London and New York: Routledge, 2001).

Crites, Stephen, 'The Narrative Quality of Experience', *Journal of the American Academy of Religion*, vol. 39, no. 3 (September 1971), pp. 291–311.

Darraj, Faysal, 'Ma Baʿda al-Hadatha fi ʿAlam bi-la Hadatha', *Al-Karmal*, vol. 51 (1997), pp. 64–90.

Deleuze, Gilles and Felix Guattari, *Kafka: Toward a Minor Literature*, trans. Dana Polan (Minneapolis and London: University of Minnesota Press, 1986).

Diba, Layla S., 'Gol o bolbol' (Rose & Nightingale), *Encyclopaedia Iranica*, <http://www.iranicaonline.org> (last accessed 7 February 2019).

Diyab, Qayid, 'Al-Masʾala al-Mitafisiqiyya fi'l-Harafish', *Fusul*, vol. 69 (Summer–Autumn), pp. 124–35.
Edwards, Michael, *Towards a Christian Poetics* (London: Macmillan, 1984).
Elad, Ami, 'Mahfuz's Zaʿbalawi: Six Stations of a Quest', *International Journal of Middle East Studies*, vol. 26 (1994), pp. 631–44.
El-Ariss, Tarek, 'Hacking the Modern: Arabic Writing in the Virtual Age', *Comparative Literature Studies*, vol. 47, no. 4 (2010), pp. 533–48.
El-Desouky, Ayman, 'Heterologies of Revolutionary Action: On Historical Consciousness and the Sacred in Mahfouz's *Children of the Alley*', *Journal of Postcolonial Writing*, vol. 47, no. 4 (2011), pp. 428–39.
El-Desouky, Ayman, *The Intellectual and the People in Egyptian Literature and Culture Amara and the 2011 Revolution* (London: Palgrave, 2014).
El-Enany, Rasheed, 'Religion in the Novels of Naguib Mahfouz', *Bulletin of the British Society for Middle Eastern Studies*, vol. 15, nos 1–2 (1988), pp. 21–7.
El-Enany, Rasheed, *Naguib Mahfouz: The Pursuit of Meaning* (London and New York: Routledge. 1993).
El-Enany, Rasheed, *Najib Mahfuz: Qiraʾa Ma Bayn al-Sutur* (Beirut: Dar al-Taliʿa li'l-Tibaʿa wa'l-Nashr, 1995).
El-Enany, Rasheed, 'The Madness of Non-Conformity: Woman versus Society in the Fiction of Salwa Bakr', *Journal of Arabic Literature*, vol. 37, no. 3 (2006), pp. 376–415.
El-Enany, Rasheed, *Naguib Mahfouz: Egypt's Nobel Laureate* (London: Haus, 2007).
El-Enany, Rasheed, *Arab Representations of the Occident: East–West Encounters in Arabic Fiction* (London and New York: Routledge, 2011 [2006]).
Elmessiri, Abdelwahab, *Al-ʿAlmaniyyat al-Juzʾiyya wa'l-ʿAlamaniyyat al-Shamila*, 2 vols (Cairo: Dar al-Shuruq, 2002).
Elmessiri, Abdelwahab, 'Secularism, Immanence and Deconstruction', in Azzam Tamimi and John L. Esposito (eds), *Islam and Secularism in the Middle East* (London: Hurst and Company, 2002), pp. 52–80.
Elsadda, Hoda, *Gender, Nation, and the Arabic Novel: Egypt 1892–2008* (Edinburgh: Edinburgh University Press, 2012).
Faraj, Nabil (ed.), *Muhammad Husayn Haykal fi ʿUyun Muʿasirihi* (Cairo: Matbaʿat Dar al-Kutub al-Misriyya, 1996).
Felman, Shoshana, 'Women and Madness: The Critical Phallacy', *Diacritics*, vol. 5, no. 4 (Winter 1975), pp. 2–10.
Ferreter, Luke, *Towards a Christian Literary Theory* (London and New York: Palgrave Macmillan, 2003).

Frank, Sally, 'Eve was Right to Eat the "Apple": The Importance of Narrative in the Art of Law-Making', *Yale Journal of Law and Feminism*, vol. 8, no. 1 (1995), pp. 79–118.

Frye, Northop, *The Great Code: The Bible and Literature* (New York: Harcourt, 1982).

Fuʾad, Hala, *Tariq Najib Mahfuz bayn al-Ustura waʾl-Tasawwuf* (Cairo: Dar al-ʿAyn liʾl-Nashr, 2006).

Geer, Benjamin, 'The Priesthood of Nationalism in Egypt: Duty, Authority, Autonomy' (unpublished PhD thesis, SOAS, 2011).

Genette, Gerard, *Palimpsests: Literature in the Second Degree* (*Palimpsestes: La littérature au second degré*, 1982), trans. Channa Newman and Claude Doubinksy (Lincoln and London: University of Nebraska Press, 1997).

Gershoni, Israel and James P. Jankowski, *Egypt, Islam, and the Arabs: The Search for Egyptian Nationhood, 1900–1930* (New York and Oxford: Oxford University Press, 1986).

Ghazoul, Ferial, 'Naguib Mahfouz's Arabian Nights and Days: A Political Allegory', in *Nocturnal Poetics: The Arabian Nights in Comparative Context* (Cairo: American University in Cairo Press, 1996), pp. 159–76.

al-Ghitani, Jamal, *Al-Zayni Barakat* (Cairo: Dar al-Shuruq, 1979 [1971]), trans. Farouk Abdel Wahab, *Zayni Barakat* (London: Penguin, 1990).

al-Ghitani, Jamal, 'Intertextual Dialectics', trans. Samia Mehrez, in Ferial J. Ghazoul and Barbara Harlow (eds), *The View from Within: Writers and Critics on Contemporary Arabic Literature* (Cairo: American University in Cairo Press, 1994), pp. 17–26.

al-Ghitani, Jamal, *Muntaha Talab ila Turath al-ʿArab: Dirasat fiʾl-Turath* (Cairo: Dar al-Shuruq, 1997).

Gilbert, Sandra M. and Susan Gubar, *The Madwoman in the Attic: The Woman Writer and the Nineteenth-Century Literary Imagination* (New Haven: Yale University Press, 2000 [1979]).

Girard, René, *Deceit, Desire and the Novel: Self and Other in Literary Structure* (*Mensonge romantique et vérité Romanesque*, 1961), trans. Yvonne Freccero (Baltimore and London: The Johns Hopkins University Press, 1966).

Girard, René, 'Mimesis and Violence', in James G. Williams (ed.), *The Girard Reader* (New York: Crossroad Publishing Company, 1996), pp. 9–99.

Girard, René, 'Sacrifice as Sacral Violence and Substitution', in James G. Williams (ed.), *The Girard Reader* (New York: Crossroad Publishing Company, 1996), pp. 69–88.

Goldberg, Michael, 'Exodus 1:13–14', *Interpretation: A Journal of the Bible and Theology*, vol. 37, no. 4 (1983), pp. 389–91.

Grace, Daphne, *The Woman in the Muslin Mask: Veiling and Identity in Postcolonial Literature* (London: Pluto Press, 2004).

Hafez, Sabry, 'Intentions and Realisation in the Narratives of Nawal El-Saadawi', *Third World Quarterly*, vol. 11, no. 3 (July 1989), pp. 188–98.

Hafez, Sabry, *Suradiqat min Waraq: Dirasat Wadaʿiyya wa Taʿmulat fi Manaqib al-Rahilin* (Cairo: al-Haʾyat al-ʿAmma li-Qusur al-Thaqafa, 1991).

Hafez, Sabry, *The Genesis of Arabic Narrative Discourse: A Study in the Sociology of Modern Arabic Literature* (London: Saqi Books, 1993).

Hafez, Sabry, 'Jadaliyyat al-Binya al-Sardiyya al-Murakkaba fi Layali Shahrazad wa Najib Mahfuz', *Fusul*, vol. 13, no. 2 (1994), pp. 20–70.

Hafez, Sabry, *The Quest for Identities: The Development of the Modern Arabic Short Story* (London, San Francisco and Beirut: Saqi Books, 2007).

Hafez, Sabry, 'The New Egyptian Novel: Urban Transformation and Narrative Form', *New Left Review*, vol. 64 (July–August 2010), <https://newleftreview.org/II/64/sabry-hafez-the-new-egyptian-novel> (last accessed 22 January 2019).

Hafez, Sabry (ed.), *Najib Mahfuz: Atahaddath Ilaykum* (Beirut: Dar al-ʿAwda, 1977 [1975]).

Hafez, Sabry and Catherine Cobham (eds), *A Reader of Modern Arabic Short Stories* (London: Saqi Books, 1988).

al-Hakim, Nazih, *Mahmud Taymur, Raʾid al-Qisa al-ʿArabiyya* (Cairo, 1944).

al-Hakim, Tawfiq, *ʿAwdat al-Ruh*, 2 vols (Cairo: Maktabat Misr, 1988 [1933]), trans. William M. Hutchins, *Return of the Spirit: Tawfiq al-Hakim's Classic Novel of the 1919 Revolution* (Washington, DC: Three Continents Press, 1990).

al-Hakim, Tawfiq, *ʿUsfur min al-Sharq* (Cairo: Maktabat Misr, 1988 [1938]), trans. R. Bayly Winder, *Bird of the East* (Beirut: Khayyats, 1966).

al-Hakim, Tawfiq, *Arini Allah* (Cairo: Maktabat al-Adab, 1953).

Hampson, Daphne, 'The Sacred, the Feminine and French Feminist Theory', in G. Pollock and V. Turvey Sauron (eds), *The Sacred and the Feminine: Imagination and Difference* (London and New York: I. B. Tauris, 2007), pp. 61–74.

Haqqi, Yahya, *Qindil Umm Hashim* (Cairo: Dar al-Maʿarif, 1984 [1944]).

Hartnell, Elaine, '"Nothing but Sweet and Womanly": A Hagiography of Patmore's Angel', *Victorian Poetry*, vol. 34, no. 4: 'Coventry Patmore: 1823–1896. In Memoriam' (Winter 1996), pp. 457–76.

Hasan, S. S., *Christians versus Muslims in Modern Egypt: The Century-Long Struggle for Coptic Equality* (Oxford: Oxford University Press, 2003).

Hathaway, Jane, 'The Mulberry Tree in the Origin Myths', in *A Tale of Two Factions: Myth, Memory, and Identity in Ottoman Egypt and Yemen* (Albany: State University of New York Press, 2003), pp. 135–42.

al-Hawari, Ahmad Ibrahim, *Naqd al-Mujtamaᶜ fi Hadith ᶜIsa ibn Hisham* (Cairo: Dar al-Maᶜarif, 1986).

Hayes, Carlton J. H., 'Nationalism as a Religion', in *Essays on Nationalism* (New York: The Macmillan Company, 1926), pp. 93–125.

Haykal, Muhammad Husayn, *Zaynab: Manazir wa Akhlaq Rifiyya* (Cairo: Dar al-Maᶜarif, 1983 [1914]), trans. John Mohammad Grinstead, *Zainab: The First Egyptian Novel* (London: Darf, 1989).

Haykal, Muhammad Husayn, 'Al-Adab al-Qawmi', in *Fi Awqat al-Faragh* (Cairo: Maktabat al-Nahda al-Misriyya, 1968 [1925]), pp. 350–6.

Haykal, Muhammad Husayn, 'Al-Din wa'l-ᶜIlm', in *Al-Iman wa'l-Maᶜrifa*, ed. Ahmad Haykal (Cairo: Dar al-Maᶜarif, 1964 [1926]), pp. 11–40.

Haykal, Muhammad Husayn, *Thawrat al-Adab* (Cairo: Dar al-Maᶜarif, 1978 [1933]).

Haykal, Muhammad Husayn, *The Life of Muhammad* (*Hayat Muhammad*), 8th edn, trans. Ismail Ragi A. al-Faruqi, *The Life of Muhammad* (London: Shorouk International, 1983 [1935]).

Haykal, Muhammad Husayn, *Mudhakkirat al-Shabab* (Cairo: al-Majlis al-Aᶜla li'l-Thaqafa, 1996).

Hegel, G. W. F., *Phenomenology of the Spirit*, trans. A. V. Miller (Oxford: Clarendon Press, 1977).

Hoffmann, Thomas, *The Poetic Qur'an: Studies on Qur'anic Poeticity* (Wiesbaden: Harrassowitz, 2007).

Hourani, Albert, *Arabic Thought in the Liberal Age, 1798–1939* (Cambridge: Cambridge University Press, 1983).

Husayn, Taha, *Mustaqbal al-Thaqafa fi Misr* (Cairo: Matbaᶜat al-Maᶜarif, 1938).

Husayn, Taha, *Al-Ayyam*, vols 1 and 2 (Cairo: Dar al-Maᶜarif, 1996 [1929, 1933]), trans. E. H. Paxton, Hilary Wayment and Kenneth Cragg, *The Days: Taha Hussein, His Autobiography in Three Parts* (Cairo: American University in Cairo Press, 1997).

Husayn, Taha, *ᶜAla Hamish al-Sira* (Cairo: Dar al-Maᶜarif, 1962 [1933–8]).

Hutcheon, Linda, 'The Politics of Postmodernism: Parody and History', *Cultural Critique*, no. 5: Modernity and Modernism, Postmodernity and Postmodernism (Winter 1986–7), pp. 179–207.

Hutcheon, Linda, *The Poetics of Postmodernism* (London: Routledge, 2004 [1988]).

Hutcheon, Linda, *The Politics of Postmodernism* (New York: Routledge, 1989).

Ibn Abi al-Dunya and Leah Kinberg, *Morality in the Guise of Dreams: A Critical Edition of Kitab al-Manam with Introduction* (Leiden and New York: Brill, 1994).

Ibn Ishaq, *The Life of Muhammad: A Translation of Ibn Ishaq's Sirat Rasul Allah*, trans. with intro. and notes A. Guillaume (Oxford: Oxford University Press, 1957).

Idris, Yusuf, *Arkhas Layali* (Cairo: Nahdat Misr, 2009 [1954]).

Idris, Yusuf, 'Abu'l-Hawl', in *Qaᶜ al-Madina* (Cairo: Dar al-Katib al-ᶜArabi, 1970).

Jackman, Mary, 'License to kill: Violence and Legitimacy in Expropriative Social Relations', in John T. Jost and Brenda Major (eds), *The Psychology of Legitimacy: Emerging Perspectives on Ideology, Justice, and Intergroup Relations* (New York: Cambridge University Press, 2001, pp. 437–67).

Jacquemond, Richard, 'Thawrat al-Takhyil wa Takhyil al-Thawra: Qiraʾa Jadida fi Awlad Haratina', *Alif: Journal of Comparative Poetics*, vol. 23 (2003), pp. 118–32.

Jacquemond, Richard, *Conscience of the Nation: Writers, State, and Society in Modern Egypt*, trans. David Tresilian (Cairo and New York: American University in Cairo Press, 2008).

Jad, Ali B., *Form and Technique in the Egyptian Novel 1912–1971* (London and Oxford: Ithaca Press, 1983).

Juergensmeyer, Mark, Margo Kitts and Michael Jerryson, 'Introduction: The Enduring Relationship of Religion and Violence', in Mark Juergensmeyer, Margo Kitts and Michael Jerryson (eds), *The Oxford Handbook of Religion and Violence* (Oxford: Oxford University Press, 2013), pp. 1–12.

al-Jundi, Anwar, *Qissat Mahmud Taymur* (Cairo, 1951).

al-Kakili, ᶜAbd al-Salam, *Al-Zaman al-Riwaʾi: Jadaliyyat al-Madi wa'l-Hadir ᶜind Jamal al-Ghitani min Khilal al-Zayni Barakat wa Kitab al-Tajalliyyat* (Cairo: Madbuli, 1992).

Kendall, Elisabeth, *Literature, Journalism and the Avant-Garde: Intersection in Egypt*, Routledge Studies in Middle Eastern Literatures (New York: Routledge, 2006).

Kennedy, Hugh, *The Great Arab Conquests: How the Spread of Islam Changed the World We Live In* (London: Weidenfeld and Nicolson, 2007).

al-Kharrat, Idwar, *Turabuha Zaᶜfaran: Nusus Iskandariyya* (Cairo: Dar al-Mustaqbal al-ᶜArabi, 1986), trans. France Liardet, *City of Saffron* (London and New York: Quartet Books, 1989).

al-Kharrat, Idwar, *Al-Hassasiyya al-Jadida: Maqalat fi'l-Zahirat al-Qisasiyya* (Beirut: Dar al-Adab, 1993).

Khulayf, Yusuf, *Al-Adab wa'l-Haya al-Misryya: Muhammad Husayn Haykal* (Cairo: Dar al-Hilal, 1993).

al-Kilani, Najib, *Al-Islamiyya wa'l-Madhahib al-Adabiyya* (Beirut: Muʾassasat al-Risala, 1983).

al-Kilani, Najib, *Afaq al-Adab al-Islami* (Beirut: Muʾassasat al-Risala, 1985).

Kilito, Abdelfattah, *The Author and His Doubles* (*L'Auteur et ses Doubles* 1985), trans. Michael Cooperson (New York: Syracuse University Press, 2001).

Kilpatrick, Hilary, ''Abd al-Hakim Qasim and the Search for Liberation', *Journal of Arabic Literature*, vol. 26 (1995), pp. 50–66.

Kinberg, Leah, 'Interaction between this World and the Afterworld in Early Islamic Tradition', *Oriens*, vol. 29 (1986), pp. 285–308.

LaCapra, Dominick, *History and Criticism* (Ithaca, NY: Cornell University Press, 1985).

Lashin, Mahmud Taha, 'Hadith al-Qarya', in Sabry Hafez and Caherine Cobham (eds), *A Reader of Modern Arabic Short Stories* (London: Saqi Books, 1988 [orig. pub. in *Yukha Anna*, Cairo, 1929]), pp. 136–44.

Levinas, Emmanuel, *Totality and Infinity: An Essay on Exteriority*, trans. Alphonso Lingis (Pittsburgh: Duquesne University Press, 1969).

Levinas, Emmanuel, *Otherwise than Being: or Beyond Essence*, trans. Alphonso Lingis (Pittsburgh: Duquesne University Press, 1998).

Lukacs, Georg, *The Historical Novel*, trans. Hannah and Stanley Mitchell (London: Merlin, 1962).

Mączyńska, Magdalena, 'Toward a Postsecular Literary Criticism: Examining Ritual Gestures in Zadie Smith's "Autograph Man"', *Religion and Literature*, vol. 41 (Autumn 2009), pp. 73–82.

Mahfuz, Najib, *Bayn al-Qasrayn* (Cairo: Dar al-Shuruq, 2009 [1956]), trans. W.M. Hutchins and O. E. Kenny, *Palace Walk* (New York and London: Doubleday, 1990).

Mahfuz, Najib, *Qasr al-Shawq* (Cairo: Dar al-Shuruq, 2006 [1957]), trans. W. M. Hutchins, L. M. Kenny and O. E. Kenny, *Palace of Desire* (New York and London: Doubleday, 1991).

Mahfuz, Najib, *Al-Sukkariyya* (Cairo: Maktabat Misr, 1961 [1957]), trans. W. M. Maynard and A. B. Samaan, *Sugar Street* (London and New York: Doubleday, 1992).

Mahfuz, Najib, *Al-Liss wa'l-Kilab* (Cairo: Maktabat Misr, 1961), trans. Trevor Le Gassick and M. M. Badawi, *The Thief and the Dogs* (Cairo: American University in Cairo Press, 1984).

Mahfuz, Najib, *Dunya Allah* (Cairo: Maktabat Misr, 1963), trans. Roger Allen and Akef Abadir, *God's World: An Anthology of Short Stories* (Minneapolis: Bibliotheca Islamica, 1973).

Mahfuz, Najib, *Al-Shahhadh* (Cairo: Maktabat Misr, 1966), trans. Kristin Walker Henry and Nariman Khales Naili al-Warraki, *The Beggar* (Cairo: American University in Cairo Press, 1986).

Mahfuz, Najib, *Malhamat al-Harafish* (Cairo: Maktabat Misr, 1985 [1977]), trans. Catherine Cobham, *The Harafish* (London and New York: Doubleday, 1993).

Mahfuz, Najib, *On Literature and Philosophy: The Non-Fiction Writing of Naguib Mahfouz*, trans. Arab Byrne with intro. by Rasheed El-Enany (London: Gingko Library, 2016).

Mahir, Mustafa, 'Fawst fi'l-Adab al-ᶜArabi al-Maᶜasir', *Fusul*, vol. 3, no. 4 (1983), pp. 237–48.

Mahmoud, Mohamed, 'The Unchanging Hero in a Changing World: Najib Mahfuz's *Al-Liss wa'l-Kilab (The Thief and the Dogs)*', in Trevor le Gassick (ed.), *Critical Perspectives on Naguib Mahfouz* (Washington, DC: Three Continents Press, 1991), pp. 115–30.

Mahmoud, Saba, '*Azazeel* and the Politics of Historical Fiction in Egypt', *Comparative Literature*, vol. 65, no. 3 (Summer 2013), pp. 265–84.

Malti-Douglas, Fedwa, *Blindness and Autobiography: Al-Ayyam of Taha Husayn* (Princeton: Princeton University Press, 1988).

Malti-Douglas, Fedwa, *Men, Women, and God(s): Nawal El Saadawi and Arab Feminist Poetics* (Berkley, LA, and London: University of California Press, 1995).

Malti-Douglas, Fedwa, *Medicines of the Soul: Female Bodies and Sacred Geographies in a Translational Islam* (Berkley, LA, and London: University of California Press, 2001).

Manisty, Dinah, 'Changing Limitations: A Study of the Woman's Novel in Egypt (1960–1991)' (unpublished PhD thesis, SOAS, 1993).

Manisty, Dinah, 'Madness as Textual Strategy in the Narratives of Three Egyptian Women Writers', *Alif: Journal of Comparative Studies*, vol. 14 (1994), pp. 154–74.

Matar, Nabil, 'Christ and the Abrahamic Legacy in *Children of the Alley*', in Waïl Hassan and Susan Muaddi Darraj (eds), *Approaches to Teaching the Works of Naguib Mahfouz* (New York: The Modern Language Association of America, 2012), pp. 144–55.

Mazrui, Alamin M. and Judith I. Abala, 'Sex and Patriarchy: Gender Relations in "Mawt al-Rajul al-Wahid ᶜala al-Ard (God Dies by the Nile)"', *Research in*

African Literatures, vol. 28, no. 3: Arabic Writing in Africa (Autumn 1997), pp. 17–32.

McClure, John A., *Partial Faiths: Postsecular Fiction in the Age of Pynchon and Morrison* (Athens, GA: Universty of Georgia Press, 2008).

Mehrez, Samia, 'Al-Zayni Barakat: Narrative as Strategy', *Arab Studies Quarterly*, vol. 8, no. 2 (Spring 1986), pp. 120–42.

Meinardus, Otto F. A., *Christians in Egypt: Orthodox, Catholic and Protestant Communities Past and Present* (Cairo and New York: American University in Cairo Press, 2006).

Mernissi, Fatma, *Beyond the Veil: Male–Female Dynamics in Modern Muslim Society* (London: Saqi Books, 1983).

Meyer, Stefan, *The Experimental Arabic Novel Postcolonial Literary Modernism in the Levant* (New York: University of New York State Press, 2000).

Mikhaʾil, Mona, 'Al-Rajl wa'l-Bahr: Jawanib min al-Tanass fi Riwayat Idwar al-Kharrat "Turabuha Zaʿfaran"', *Fusul*, vol. 15, no. 4, pp. 25–32.

Milson, Menahem, *Najib Mahfuz: The Novelist-Philosopher of Cairo* (Jerusalem and New York: St Martin's Press and Magness Press, 1998).

Mir, Mustansir, 'The Qur'an as Literature', *Religion and Literature*, vol. 20, no. 1 (1988), pp. 49–64.

Moosa, Matti, *The Origins of Modern Arabic Fiction*, 2nd edn (Boulder, CO: Lynne Rienner Publishers, 1997).

Murata, Sachiko and William C. Chittick, *The Vision of Islam* (London and New York: I. B. Tauris, 1994).

Musa, Salama, *Yawm wa'l-Ghad*, in *Al-Muʾalifat al-Kamila* (Beirut: Maktabat al-Maʿarif, 1998 [1928]), pp. 523–675.

Musa, Salama, 'Al-Wataniyya wa'l-ʿAlamiyya', *Al-Majalla al-Jadida* (March 1930).

al-Musawi, Muhsin, *The Postcolonial Arabic Novel: Debating Ambivalence* (Leiden: Brill, 2003).

al-Musawi, Muhsin, *Islam in the Street: Religion in Modern Arabic Literature* (Lanham, Boulder, New York, Toronto and Plymouth: Rowman and Littlefield Publishers Inc., 2009).

al-Muwaylihi, Muhammad, *Hadith ʿIsa Ibn Hisham* (Cairo: Matbaʿat al-Saʿada 1923 [1911]), trans. Roger Allen, *A Period of Time: A Study of Muhammad al-Muwaylihi's Hadith ʿIsa Ibn Hisham* (Reading: Ithaca, 1992); revised translation, Roger Allen, *What ʿIsa Ibn Hisham Told Us* (New York and London: New York University Press, 2015).

Naji, Sawsan, *Al-Marʾa fi'l-Mirʾat: Dirasa Naqdiyya li'l-Riwaya al-Nisaʾiyya fi Misr 1888–1985* (Cairo: al-ᶜArabi li'l-Nashr wa'l-Tawziᶜ, 1989).

Najjar, Fauzi M., 'Islamic Fundamentalism and the Intellectual: The Case of Naguib Mahfouz', *British Journal of Middle Eastern Studies*, vol. 25 (1998), pp. 139–68.

Nassaj, Sayyid Hamid, *Banurama al-Riwaya al-ᶜArabiyya al-Haditha*, 2nd edn (Cairo: Maktaba Gharib, 1985).

al-Nowaihi, Magda, 'Memory and Imagination in Edwar al-Kharrat's Turabuha Zaᶜfaran', *Journal of Arabic Literature*, vol. 15 (1994), pp. 34–57.

al-Nowaihi, Magda, 'Reenvisioning National Community in Salwa Bakr's "The Golden Chariot Does Not Ascend to Heaven"', *The Arab Studies Journal*, vols 7–8, nos 1–2 (Fall 1999/Spring 2000), pp. 8–24.

Nurbakhsh, Javad, *Sufism: Fear and Hope, Contraction and Expansion, Gathering and Dispersion, Intoxication and Sobriety, Annihilation and Subsistence* (New York: Khaniqah-i Nimatullahi, 1982).

O'Connor, Frank, *The Lonely Voice: A Study of the Short Story* (Cork: Cork City Council, 2003 [1962]).

Osman, Tarek, *Egypt on the Brink: From the Rise of Nasser to the Fall of Mubarak* (New Haven: Yale University Press, 2011).

Ouyang, Wen-Chin, 'The Dialectic of Past and Present in *Rihlat Ibn Fattuma* by Najib Mahfuz', *Edebiyat: Journal of Middle Eastern Literatures*, vol. 14, nos 1–2 (2003), pp. 81–107.

Ouyang, Wen-Chin, *Poetics of Love in the Arabic Novel: Nation-State, Modernity and Tradition* (Edinburgh: Edinburgh University Press, 2012).

Ouyang, Wen-Chin, *Politics of Nostalgia in the Arabic Novel* (Edinburgh: Edinburgh University Press, 2013).

Peled, Matittyahu, *Religion My Own: The Literary Works of Najib Mahfuz* (New Brunswick, NJ: Transaction Books, 1983).

Petry, Carl, *Protectors or Praetorians: The Last Mamluk Sultans and Egypt's Waning as a Great Power* (New York: State University of New York Press, 1994).

Phillips, Christina, 'ᶜAbd al-Hakim Qasim', in Majd Yaser al-Mallah (ed.), *Dictionary of Literary Biography: Twentieth Century Arabic Writers* (New York: Bruccoli Clark Layman, Inc, 2008), pp. 198–202.

Phillips, Christina, 'An Attempt to Apply Gérard Genette's Model of Hypertextuality to Najib Mahfuz's *Malhamat al-Harafish*', *Middle Eastern Literatures*, vol. 11, no. 3 (2008) pp. 283–300.

Plett, Heinrich F., 'Intertextualities', in Heinrich F. Plett (ed.), *Intertextuality* (New York and Berlin: De Gruyter, 1991), pp. 3–29.

Qasim, ʿAbd al-Hakim, *Al-Mahdi*, in *Al-Riwayat al-Qasira* (Cairo: Dar al-Shuruk, 1985 [1984]), trans. Peter Theroux, *Rites of Assent: Two Novellas* (Philadelphia: Temple University Press, 1995).

Qasim, ʿAbd al-Hakim, *Turaf min Khabar al-Akhira* (Cairo: al-Haʾyat al-Misriyya al-ʿAmma li'l-Kitab, 1986 [1981]), trans. Peter Theroux, *Rites of Assent: Two Novellas* (Philadelphia: Temple University Press, 1995).

Qutb, Muhammad, *Manhaj al-Fann al-Islami* (Beirut and Cairo: Dar al-Shuruq, 1982).

Rahman, Najat, 'The Trial of Heritage and the Legacy of Abraham', in Lahouzine Ouzgane (ed.), *Islamic Masculinities* (London: Zed, 2006), pp. 72–85.

al-Raʿi, ʿAli, *Dirasat fi'l-Riwaya al-Misriyya* (Cairo: al-Dar al-Misriyya li'l-Taliʿa, 1965).

al-Rakhawi, Yahya, 'Dawrat al-Hayat wa Dalal al-Khulud: Malhamat al-Mawt wa'l-Takhalluq fi'l-Harafish', in Faruq ʿAbd al-Muʿti (ed.), *Najib Mahfuz: Bayn al-Riwaya wa'l-Adab al-Riwaya* (Beirut: Dar al-Kutub al-ʿIlmiyya, 1994), pp. 164–235.

Ramadan, Yasmine, 'The Emergence of the Sixties Generation in Egypt and the Anxiety over Categorisation', *Journal of Arabic Literature*, vol. 43, nos 2–3 (2012), pp. 409–30.

Ricoeur, Paul, *History and Truth*, trans. Charles A. Kelbley (Evanston: Northwestern University Press, 1965 [1955]).

Ricoeur, Paul, *Oneself as Another*, trans. Kathleen Blamey (Chicago and London: University of Chicago Press, 1990).

Ricoeur, Paul, *Figuring the Sacred: Religion, Narrative, and Imagination*, trans. David Pellauer (Minneapolis: Fortress Press, 1995).

Rifʿat, Alifa, 'Hadhihi Laylati', in *Man Yakun al-Rajul* (Cairo: Al-Hayʾat al-Misriyya al-ʿAma li'l-Kitab, 1981), pp. 2–12, trans. Denys Johnson-Davies, 'My Wedding Night', in *Distant View from a Minaret and Other Stories* (Oxford: Heinemann, 1983), pp. 120–6.

Rifʿat, Alifa, *Fi Layl al-Shitaʾ al-Tawil* (Cairo: Matbaʿ at al-ʿAsima al-Qahira, 1985), pp. 54–60.

Rifʿat, Alifa, 'Bahiya's Eyes', in *Distant View from a Minaret and Other Stories*, trans. Denys Johnson-Davies (Oxford: Heinemann, 1983), pp. 5–12.

Roller, Judi M., *The Politics of the Feminist Novel* (New York and London: Greenwood Press, 1986).

Rooke, Tetz, *In My Childhood: A Study of Arabic Autobiography* (Stockholm: Almqvist and Wiksel, 1997).

Rudwin, Maximiliam J., *Devil Stories: An Anthology* (New York: Alfred A. Knopf, 1921).

al-Rumi, Jalal al-Din, *The Essential Rumi*, trans. Coleman Barks and John Moyne (London: Penguin, 1995).

Saʿdawi, Nawal, 'Al-Marʾa fi'l-Adab al-ʿArabi', in *Al-Wajh al-ʿAri li'l-Marʾa al-Arabiyya* (Beirut: al-Muʾassasat al-ʿArabiyya li'l-Dirasat wa'l-Nashr, 1977).

Saʿdawi, Nawal, 'The Thirteenth Rib of Adam', in *The Hidden Face of Eve: Women in the Arab World*, trans. Sherif Hetata (London: Zed Press, 1980).

Saʿdawi, Nawal, *Jannat wa Iblis* (Beirut: Dar al-Adab, 1992), trans. Sherif Hetata, *The Innocence of the Devil* (London: Methuen, 1994).

Saʿdawi, Nawal, *The Nawal Saadawi Reader* (London and New York: Zed Books, 1997).

Saʿdawi, Nawal, *Suqut al-Imam* (London: Saqi Books, 2000 [1987]), trans. Sherif Hetata, *The Fall of the Imam* (London: Saqi Books, 2002).

Sadiqi, Fatima, 'Language and Gender', in Lutz Edzard and Rudolf de Jong (eds), *Encyclopaedia of Arabic Language and Linguistics* (Brill, online).

Safran, Nadav, *Egypt in Search of Political Community* (Cambridge, MA: Harvard University Press, 1961).

Saʿi, Ahmad Bassam, *Al-Waqaʿiyya al-Islamiyya fi'l-Adab wa'l-Naqd* (Jedda: Dar al-Manara li'l-Nashr, 1985).

Said, Edward, *Orientalism* (New York: Vintage, 1979).

Said, Edward, *The World, the Text, and the Critic* (Cambridge, MA: Harvard University Press, 1983).

Sakkut, Hamdi, 'Najib Mahfuz wa'l-Hal al-Sufi', *Alif: Journal of Comparative Poetics*, vol. 5 (Spring 1985), pp. 39–48.

Salti, Ramzi, 'Feminism and Religion in Alifa Rifaat's Short Stories', *The International Fiction Review*, vol. 18, no. 2 (1991), pp. 108–12.

Sartre, Jean-Paul, *Being and Nothingness*, trans. Hazel E. Barnes (London: Routledge, 1996).

Schimmel, Anne-Marie, *Mystical Dimensions of Islam* (Chapel Hill: University of North Carolina Press, 2011 [1975]).

Selim, Semah, *The Novel and the Rural Imaginary 1880–1985* (London and New York: Routledge, 2010).

Semah, David, *Four Egyptian Critics* (Leiden: Brill, 1974).

Seymour-Jorn, Caroline, 'A New Language: Salwa Bakr on Depicting Egyptian Women's Worlds', *Critique: Critical Middle Eastern Studies*, vol. 11, no. 2 (Fall 2002), pp. 151–76.

Seymour-Jorn, Caroline, 'Salwa Bakr: The Poetics of Marginalisation', in *Cultural Criticism in Egyptian Women's Writing* (New York: Syracuse University Press, 2011), pp. 17–55.

Shaaban, Bouthaina, *Voices Revealed: Arab Women Novelists, 1898–2000* (Boulder, CO: Lynne Rienner Publishers, 2009).

Shalan, Jeff, 'Writing the Nation: The Emergence of Egypt in the Modern Arabic Novel', *Journal of Arabic Literature*, vol. 33, no. 3 (2002), pp. 211–47.

al-Sharqawi, ᶜAbd al-Rahman, *Al-Ard* (Cairo: Dar al-Katib al-ᶜArabi li'l-Tibaᶜa wa'l-Nashr, 1968 [1952]), trans. and abridged Desmond Stewart, *Egyptian Earth* (London: Saqi Books, 1990).

al-Sharqawi, ᶜAbd al-Rahman, *Muhammad Rasul al-Hurriyya* (Cairo: Dar al-Shaᶜb, 1972 [1962]).

al-Shidyaq, Faris, *Kitab al-Saq ᶜala al-Saq fi ma huwa al-Fariyaq*, ed. and trans. Humphrey Davies (Arabic & English combined edition), *Leg over Leg of The Turtle in the Tree Concerning The Fariyaq, What Manner of Creature Might He Be* (New York and London: New York University Press, 2006).

Shukri, Ghali, *Al-Muntama: Dirasat fi Adab Najib Mahfuz* (Cairo: Dar al-Maᶜarif, 1969).

Shukri, Ghali, *Thawrat al-Muᶜtazil: Dirasat fi Adab Tawfiq al-Hakim* (Beirut: Dar Ibn Khaldun, 1973).

Shukri, Ghali, *Al-ᶜAnqa al-Jadida: Sirat al-Ajyal fi'l-Adab al-Muᶜasir* (Beirut: Dar al-Taliᶜa li'l-Tibaᶜa wa'l-Nashr, 1977).

Shukri, Ghali, *Tawfiq al-Hakim: Al-Jil wa'l-Tabaqa wa'l-Ruʾya* (Beirut: Dar al-Farabi, 1993).

Siddiq, Muhammad, 'Deconstructing "The Saint's Lamp"', *Journal of Arabic Literature*, vol. 17 (1986), pp. 126–45.

Siddiq, Muhammad, *Arab Culture and the Novel: Genre, Identity and Agency in Egyptian Fiction* (London: Routledge, 2007).

Singh, Amardeep, *Literary Secularism: Religion and Modernity in Twentieth-Century Fiction* (Newcastle: Cambridge Scholars Press, 2006).

Smart, Ninian, 'Religion, Myth, and Nationalism', in Peter H. Merkl and Ninian Smart (eds), *Religion and Politics in the Modern World* (New York: New York University Press, 1983).

Smith, Anthony D., *Chosen Peoples: Sacred Sources of National Identity* (Oxford: Oxford University Press, 2003).

Smith, Charles D., 'The "Crisis of Orientation": The Shift of Egyptian Intellectuals to Islamic Subjects in the 1930's', *International Journal of Middle East Studies*, vol. 4, no. 4 (October 1973), pp. 396–7.

Smith, Charles D., *Islam and the Search for Social Order in Modern Egypt: A Biography of Muhammad Husayn Haykal* (Albany: State University of New York Press, 1983).

Smith, Jane I., *The Precious Pearl: A Translation from the Arabic with Notes of the Kitab al-Durra al-Fakhira fi Kashf ʿUlum al-Akhira of Abu Hamid Muhammad b. Muhammad b. Muhammad al-Ghazali* (Missoula, MT: Scholars Press, 1979).

Smith, Jane I., 'Concourse between the Living and the Dead in Islamic Eschatological Literature', *History of Religions*, vol. 19, no. 3 (February 1980), pp. 224–36.

Smith, Jane I. and Yvonne Y. Haddad, *The Islamic Understanding of Death and Resurrection* (Albany: State University of New York Press, 1981).

Snir, Reuven, *Religion, Mysticism and Modern Arabic Literature* (Weisbaden: Harrassowitz Verlag, 2006).

Somekh, Sasson, 'Zaʿbalawi: Author, Theme and Technique', *Journal of Arabic Literature*, vol. 1 (1970), pp. 24–36.

Somekh, Sasson, 'The Sad Millenarian: An Examination of *Awlad Haratina*', *Middle Eastern Studies*, vol. 7 (January 1971), pp. 49–61.

Soskice, Janet Martin, *Metaphor and Religious Language* (Oxford: Clarendon Press, 1985).

Stagh, Marina, *The Limits of Freedom of Speech: Prose Literature and Prose Writers in Egypt under Nasser and Sadat* (Stockholm: Almqvist and Wiksell International, 1993).

Starkey, Paul, *From the Ivory Tower: A Critical Study of Tawfiq al-Hakim* (London: Ithaca, 1987).

Starr, Deborah, *Remembering Cosmopolitan Egypt: Literature, Culture, and Empire* (New York and Oxford: Routledge, 2009).

Steffen, Lloyd, 'Religion and Violence in Christian Traditions', in Mark Juergensmeyer, Margo Kitts and Michael Jerryson (eds), *The Oxford Handbook of Religion and Violence* (Oxford: Oxford University Press, 2003), pp. 100–25.

Stevens, David, 'Nationalism as Religion', *Studies: An Irish Quarterly Review*, vol. 86, no. 343 (Autumn 1997), pp. 248–58.

Stewart, Philip, 'Introduction', in *Children of Gebelawi* (London: Heinemann, 1981), pp. vii–xxi.

Sulayman, Saʿid Shawqi Muhammad, *Tawzif al-Turath fi Riwayat Najib Mahfuz* (Cairo: Itrak li'l-Nashr wa'l-Tawziʿ, 2000).

Szyska, Christian, "'Illa al-Ladhina Amanu wa ʿAmilu al-Salihat wa Dhakaru Allah

Kathiran": Hawla Mafhum "al-Adab al-Multazim" ᶜinda Udaba al-Harakat al-Islamiyya', *Al-Karmil: Abhath fi'l-Lugha wa'l-Adab*, vol. 20 (1999), pp. 33–62.

Tadros, Samuel, *Motherland Lost: The Egyptian and Coptic Quest for Modernity* (Stanford, CA: Hoover Institution Press, 2013).

Tahir, Bahaʾ, *Khalati Safiyya wa'l-Dayr* (Cairo: Dar al-Hilal, 1991), trans. Barbara Romaine, *Aunt Safiyya and the Monastery* (Berkley, LA: University of California Press, 1996).

Tahrali, Mustafa, 'The Polarity of Expression in the *Fusus al-Hikam*', in S. Hirtenstein and M. Tierman (eds), *Muhyiddin Ibn ᶜArabi: A Commemorative Volume* (Dorset: Element, 1993), pp. 351–8.

Tamimi, Azzam, 'The Origins of Arab Secularism', in Azzam Tamimi and John L. Esposito (eds), *Islam and Secularism in the Middle East* (London: Hurst and Company, 2002), pp. 13–28.

Tarabishi, George, *Sharq wa Gharb, Rujula wa Unutha: Dirasat fi ᶜAzmat al-Jins wa'l-Hadara fi'l-Riwaya al-ᶜArabiyya* (Beirut: Dar al-Taliᶜa, 1997 [1977]).

Tarabishi, George, *Allah fi Rihlat Najib Mahfuz al-Ramziyya* (Beirut: Dar al-Taliᶜa li'l-Tibaᶜa wa'l-Nashr, 1978).

Tarshuna, Mahmud, 'Madrasa Tawzif al-Turath fi'l-Riwaya al-ᶜArabiyya al-Muᶜasira', *Fusul*, vol. 17, no. 1 (1997), pp. 27–39.

Taylor, Charles, 'Modes of Secularism', in Rajeev Bhargava (ed.), *Secularism and Its Critics* (Oxford and Delhi: Oxford University Press, 1998), pp. 31–53.

Taylor, Charles, *A Secular Age* (Cambridge, MA, and London: Belknap Press of Harvard University, 2007).

Taymur, Mahmud, *Nidaʾ al-Majhul* (Beirut: Dar al-Makshuf, 1939).

Toorawa, Shawkat, 'Modern Arabic Literature and the Qur'an: Creativity, Inimitability … Incompatibilities?', in Glenda Abramson and Hilary Kilpatrick (eds), *Religious Perspectives in Modern Muslim and Jewish Literatures* (London: RoutledgeCurzon, 2005), pp. 239–57.

Toorawa, Shawkat, 'Hapless Hapaxes and Luckless Rhymes: The Qur'an as Literature', *Religion and Literature*, vol. 41, no. 2 (Summer 2009), pp. 221–7.

Trible, Phyllis, 'Eve and Adam: Genesis 2-3 Reread', in Judith Plaskow and Carol P. Christ (eds), *Womanspirit Rising: A Feminist Reader in Religion* (San Francisco: Harper and Row, 1979), pp. 74–83.

ᶜUthman, Iᶜtadal, 'Tashkil Fadaʾ al-Nass fi "Turabuha Zaᶜfaran"', *Fusul*, vol. 6, no. 3 (1987), pp. 162–9.

Valassopoulos, Anastasia, *Contemporary Arab Women Writers: Cultural Expression in Context* (London and New York: Routledge, 2009).

van Leeuwan, Richard, 'The Journey in Two Arabic Novels', in Robin Ostle (ed.), *Sensibilities of the Islamic Mediterranean: Self-expression in a Muslim Culture from Post-classical Times to the Present Day* (New York and London: I. B. Tauris, 2008), pp. 133–40.

Vatikiotis, P. J., *The History of Modern Egypt*, 4th edn (London: Weidenfeld and Nicolson, 1991).

Watt, Ian, *Rise of the Novel: Studies in Defoe, Richardson and Fielding* (London: Chatto and Windus, 1957).

Wessels, Antonie, *A Modern Arabic Biography of Muhammad: A Critical Study of Muhammad Husayn Haykal's Hayat Muhammad* (Leiden: Brill, 1972).

Wild, Stefan, 'The Koran as Subtext in Modern Arabic Poetry', in Gert Borg and Ed de Moor (eds), *Representations of the Divine in Arabic Poetry* (Amsterdam and Atlanta: Rodopi, 2001), pp. 139–60.

Wood, James, *The Broken Estate: Essays in Literature and Belief* (London: Pimlico, 1999).

Woolf, Virginia, *The Death of a Moth and Other Essays* (London: Hogarth Press, 1942).

Wright, T. R., *Theology and Literature* (Oxford: Basil Blackwell, 1988).

Yared, Nazik Saba, *Secularism and the Arab World (1850–1939)* (London: Saqi Books, 2002).

Young, Robert J. C., 'Postcolonial Remains', *New Literary History*, vol. 43, no. 1 (Winter 2012), pp. 19–42.

Zaydan, Yusuf, ᶜ*Azazil* (Cairo: Dar al-Shuruq, 2008), trans. Jonathon Wright, *Azazeel* (London: Atlantic Books, 2012).

Zaydan, Yusuf, 'Doktur Yusuf Saydan Yaktub: Buttan al-Buhtan fi-ma Yatawahhamuh al-Mutran', *Al-Masry al-Yawm* (29 July–9 September 2009).

al-Zayyat, Latifa, 'Qiraʾa fi Riwayat Salwa Bakr *Al-ᶜAraba al-Dhahabiyya La Tasᶜad Ila al-Samaʾ*', *Fusul*, vol. 11, no. 1 (1992), pp. 273–7.

Zubaidi, A. M., 'The Impact of the Qur'an and Hadith of Medieval Arabic Literature', in A. F. L. Beeston, T. M. Johnstone, R. B. Serjeant and G. R. Smith (eds), *Arabic Literature to the End of the Umayyad Period* (Cambridge: Cambridge University Press, 1983), pp. 322–43.

Index

ʿAbd al-Majid, Ibrahim, 26, 159
ʿAbd al-Raziq, ʿAli, 13, 54
Abdel Nasser, Gamal, 13, 78, 98, 113, 114, 126, 128, 129, 141, 154
Abduh, Muhammad, 12, 35, 52, 53, 56, 220
al-adab al-islāmī, 8–10, 27
al-adab al-qawmī, 22; *see also* national literature
Adam, 40, 43, 66–7, 174, 181, 232, 233
Adunis (ʿAli Ahmad Saʿid), 3, 115, 125
al-Afghani, Jamal al-Din, 12, 35
afterlife, 5, 24, 141, 143, 147, 148, 161, 244
ahl al-dhimma, 153
alcohol, 35, 83, 93, 99, 103, 140, 192–4, 256; *see also sukr* (intoxication)
Alf Layla wa Layla, 5, 50–1, 65, 125, 222, 229
alterity, 16, 17, 90, 96; *see also* the other
Amin, Qasim, 13, 36, 220
angel/s, 43, 61, 66, 67, 176, 191, 209, 234, 245
  of death (Munkar and Nakir; Nakir and Nakeer), 24, 131, 141–6, 148, 257
  in the house, 239–40
  St Mikhail the Archangel, 161, 162
al-ʿAqqad, Abbas Mahmud, 18, 56, 91, 102
Asad, Talal, 13, 15
atheism/atheist, 14, 55, 81, 85, 86, 193
autobiography, 24, 47, 52, 89, 117, 159, 165, 203–5, 209
Azhar, 35, 48, 49, 50, 51, 52–4, 55, 83, 130, 142, 146, 254
Azharite/s, 48, 52, 63, 137

Bakr, Salwa, 24, 25, 166, 171, 173, 196, 222, 235, 236, 237, 242, 246, 259

al-ʿAraba al-Dhahabiyya la Tasʿad ila al-Samaʾ, 25, 236–46
al-Bashmuri, 24, 166–73
Maqam ʿAtiyya, 196, 246
Wasf al-Bulbul, 25, 236, 240
beloved, the, 191, 192, 194, 208
Bhabha, Homi, 18, 54, 233, 237, 238, 245
Bible, 3, 7, 59, 161, 162, 232, 233, 235
Bildungsroman, 113, 123, 155, 237

Christ, 7, 24, 134, 139, 140, 161, 163, 175, 176, 180, 181, 227; *see also* Jesus
Christian/s, 12, 24, 55, 118, 141, 153, 154, 155, 157, 158, 160, 163, 166, 168, 169, 174, 179, 180, 229, 241
  community, 155; *see also* Christians; Copts
  heritage/history, 12, 157, 165, 175, 180
  intertext, 140; *see also* ʿAzazil; Qasim, ʿAbd al-Hakim; Turabuha min Zaʿfaran
  tradition, 139, 227
Christian Church, 12, 34, 35, 36, 64, 163, 169, 172, 174, 175, 176, 178, 181; *see also* Coptic Church
Christian–Muslim relations, 26, 55–6, 153–5, 157, 158, 162, 168; *see also* Coptic–Muslim relations; Coptic Christianity
Christianity, 6, 7, 34, 62, 63, 90, 153, 163, 166, 167, 169, 179, 180, 204, 223, 227, 227, 232; *see also* Coptic Christianity
colonial
  context, 233
  discourse, 16, 18–19, 54
  Egypt, 9
  encounter, 219
  struggle, 103

conversion, 8, 57, 58, 63, 100, 136, 138, 140, 167, 169, 171, 203, 206, 256, 258
Copt/s 21, 83, 136, 141, 153ff
  Coptic calendar, 161–2, 163, 174
  Coptic character/s, 24, 82, 90, 136, 138–40, 155, 158, 159, 160, 163, 165, 166, 169, 172, 174
  Coptic Christianity, 120
  Coptic Church, 21, 167, 180
  Coptic experience, 159, 163, 166
  Coptic history/heritage, 26, 161, 162, 165, 166
  Coptic identity *see* identity, Coptic
Coptic–Muslim relations, 153–5, 156–7, 168; *see also* Christian–Muslim relations
Cyril of Alexandria, 174–5, 176, 178–9

Deleuze and Guattari, 24, 159, 164
Devil, 40, 176–7, 223, 231, 234–5; *see also* ʿAzazil; Jannat wa Iblis; Satan
dhikr, 90, 99, 191, 192
displacement (of religion/ideology), 17, 18, 23, 44, 51–2, 53, 57, 58, 60, 61, 80, 81, 83, 85, 91, 94, 96, 100, 101, 103, 156, 198
Divine, the, 3, 7, 53, 60, 64, 67, 133, 199, 200, 210, 224
  divine inspiration, 98, 135, 223, 224
  divine intervention, 11, 64
  divine love, 192, 194, 208
  divine reference, 15, 53, 86, 161
  divine symbolism, 80, 81, 199–200
  divine union, 198, 200, 207
dystopia, 25, 223

Eden, 66, 174, 181, 234, 235, 243
education, 15, 22, 36, 38, 48, 52, 59, 77, 90, 155, 160, 205, 219, 220, 242
Elmarsafy, Ziad, 25, 190, 194
Eve 40, 43, 230, 232, 234, 235, 243
experimentation (literary), 115–16, 120, 123ff, 164, 190, 211; *see also* intertextuality; literary modernism

Fall, the, 66, 80
fanaʾ, 192, 193, 200, 206
fellāḥ, pl. fellāḥīn, 21, 38, 42–3, 44, 58–9, 91–2, 94, 96, 156
Frye, Northrop, 6, 8, 11, 51, 97
fundamentalism (religious), 9, 258; *see also* Islamic fundamentalism

al-Ghitani, Jamal, 24, 25, 26, 117, 123, 126, 127, 128, 129, 131, 141, 196
  Kitab al-Tajalliyyat, 25, 117, 196–7
  Al-Zayni Barakat, 24, 126–31
Girard, René, 24, 137, 138
gospel, 140, 161, 175, 180

hajj, 87, 99; *see also* pilgrimage
al-Hakim, Tawfiq, 13, 19, 23, 45, 57, 59, 61, 64, 102, 125, 177, 189
  ʿ*Awdat al-Ruh*, 13, 21, 23, 45, 57–60, 78, 85, 89, 92, 221
  ʿ*Usfur min al-Sharq*, 23, 61–8, 91, 221
  Yawmiyyat Naʾib fiʾl-Aryaf, 91, 189
Haqqi, Yahya, 57, 95, 194
  Qindil Umm Hashim, 17, 95, 124
al-ḥassasiyya al-jadida, 116, 164
Haykal, Muhammad Husayn, 11, 13, 18, 19, 20, 22, 23, 34, 36–7, 41, 45, 54–6, 91, 96, 97, 98, 144, 156, 189, 221
  Fi Manziil al-Wahy, 55, 56
  Hayat Muhammad, 55, 56
  Zaynab, 11, 21, 23, 27, 34, 36, 37–47, 49, 57, 59, 64, 80, 85, 89, 91, 92, 93, 123, 156, 189
heaven, 41, 43, 61, 65–7, 68, 80, 82, 140, 147, 178, 181, 222, 235, 237, 241, 244, 245
Hegel, 16, 83, 223
heteroglossia, 14, 37, 45
al-Husayn, 82, 86, 244
Husayn, Taha 13, 18, 20, 21, 23, 47, 50, 51, 54–5, 56, 91, 125, 189
  ʿ*Ala Hamish al-Sira*, 55
  Al-Ayyam, 23, 47–54, 57, 59, 60, 79, 80, 83, 84, 92, 136, 155, 189, 221
  Fiʾl-Shiʿr al-Jahili, 54, 55
  Mustaqbal al-Thaqafa fi Misr, 21

Ibn ʿArabi, 60, 197, 206, 210
Ibn ʿIyas, 24, 126, 127, 128, 129
identity, 7, 8, 15, 19, 51, 83, 92, 114, 115, 118, 119, 120, 156, 159, 163, 174, 175, 181, 189, 223, 235, 238
  colonial, 18
  Coptic, 24, 154, 157, 160, 162, 164, 165, 172
  Egyptian, 21, 34, 51, 54, 103, 165, 172, 180
  Islamic/Muslim, 21, 103
  national, 51, 83, 91, 153

postcolonial, 16, 18, 238
religious, 79, 83, 91, 156, 157, 163, 165
ideology, 13, 23, 28, 79, 156, 169, 196, 226
  of modernity, 77
  nationalist/of nation, 13, 60, 79, 201
  secular, 78, 79, 89, 119, 201
  of the text, 28, 44, 58, 101, 228, 237, 247
Idris, Yusuf, 77, 93, 95, 222, 223
imagination, 4–5, 97, 199
  collective, 118
  khayal, 190
  literary, 51, 115, 176
  reader's, 206, 212
intersubjectivity, 16, 17, 23, 83
intertextuality, 3, 15, 24, 120, 122ff, 161, 173, 181, 193, 196, 197, 198, 204, 209, 210, 232, 257, 258
invocation (religious), 18, 36, 53, 85, 86, 90, 257
Islamic
  activism, 256
  discourse, 40, 190
  eschatology, 24, 131, 139, 141, 142, 143, 145, 258
  ethic, 86–8
  fundamentalism, 81, 136, 137, 155
  heritage/tradition, 12, 21, 35, 90, 91, 103, 123, 142, 147
  history, 99, 171
  Islamic see *identity*
  Law, 83–4, 144, 200, 220; see also Sharia
  literature see *al-adab al-islāmī*
  mysticism, 24, 212; see also Sufism
  reform, 12–13, 35, 100, 103, 153, 219, 220
  resurgence/revival, 78, 81, 117, 154, 220, 255
  thought, 144, 210

Jameson, Frederic, 11
Jesus, 139, 140, 158, 160, 178, 181, 226, 229; see also Christ
Jews, 157, 181
  portrayal of, 102, 103
  of Alexandria, 178, 179
  of Medina, 99, 100
jihad, 81, 99, 256
jīl al-sittināt, 136, 155
Joseph (Yusuf), 7, 40, 235–6
Judaism, 203, 227
Judas, 139, 158
Judgement, final, 24, 131, 143–6, 148, 245

Judgement Day, 87, 142, 175
individual (*ijtihad*), 84

al-Kharrat, Idwar, 24, 116, 155, 159, 164, 259
  Turabuha Zaʿfaran, 24, 159–65, 168, 181, 259
  Ya Banat Iskandariyya, 163

Lacan, Jacques, 17
Lashin, Mahmud Taha, 64, 95, 125
Liberal Constitutionalists, 55–6, 141, 154
liberal nationalism, 11, 13, 21, 36, 37, 38, 41, 55, 153
Lukacs, Georg, 10, 88, 170

Mahfuz, Najib, 4, 13, 17, 23, 24, 25, 26, 43, 78, 79, 84, 93, 113, 114, 117, 118, 120, 125, 131, 134, 165, 177, 189, 190, 191, 195, 197, 198, 203, 205, 206, 207, 212, 222, 255, 256, 259
  Asdaʾ al-Sirat al-Dhatiyya, 24, 117, 190, 197, 203–12
  Awlad Haratina, 120, 125, 131, 132, 195
  Bayn al-Qasrayn, 13, 78, 79, 89, 192; see also trilogy
  Hadith al-Sabah waʾl-Masaʾ, 125, 202, 205
  Hikayat Haratina, 24, 190, 197–203, 207
  Layali Alf Layla, 195
  Malhamat al-Harafish, 5, 24, 131–6, 139, 240, 259
  Al-Maraya, 125, 202, 222
  Qasr al-Shawq, 78, 191–2, 193, 194, 221; see also trilogy
  Rihlat Ibn Fattuma, 125, 196
  Al-Sukkariyya, 78, 81, 95, 191, 192–4; see also trilogy
  trilogy, the, 23, 24, 25, 43, 78–91, 92, 94, 95, 96, 113, 123, 165, 191–4, 221, 224, 255, 256
maqāma, 3, 9, 34, 35
marriage, 36, 37, 38, 43, 45, 46, 84, 86, 87, 88, 103, 134, 141, 145, 175, 192, 193, 194, 209, 219, 220, 236, 238, 239, 240, 242, 243, 247, 256
Mary, the Virgin, 139, 140, 176, 180, 181, 226–7, 228, 230, 235
Mecca, 37, 87, 89, 98, 99, 100, 101, 104, 128, 135
Medina, 99, 100, 101
Messiah, 59, 140, 159, 227

messianic, the, 133
  myth, 133, 134
  symbol/allusion, 131, 136; see also Qasim, ʿAbd al-Hakim
  thought, 24, 139
  time, 132
minor literature, 164–5
minority/minorities, 154, 119
  Christian/Copt, 12, 82, 153, 161, 166
  minority/minor discourse, 24, 120, 159
  Egypt's, 154
  identities, 21
  voices, 116, 119, 164
metaphor, 5–7, 47, 66, 67, 80, 193, 194, 196, 199, 207, 212, 235, 238
  metaphorical language, 5–7, 190
modernism
  Islamic, 79
  literary, 89, 116, 119, 124
monophysite, 169
monotheism, 3, 7, 25, 60, 126, 131, 133, 141, 223, 224, 226, 230, 232, 235, 246
  monotheistic belief, 226, 245
  monotheistic myth, 125
  monotheistic religion, 219, 227
  monotheistic tradition, 243
mosque, 39, 44, 61, 64, 67, 83, 89, 93, 94, 129, 130, 136, 139, 146, 192
Muhammad, Prophet, 37, 55, 56, 61, 62, 89, 96, 97–103, 104, 122, 130, 134, 135, 144, 147, 169, 191, 221, 244
Munkar and Nakir (Nakir and Nakeer), 131, 142–3, 146
Musa, Salama, 21
muṣallā, 94
Muslim Brotherhood, 9, 55, 81, 85, 117, 119, 136–8, 139, 153, 154
al-Muwaylihi, Muhammad, 35
  Hadith ʿIsa ibn Hisham, 34, 35–6, 41, 64

al-Nadim, ʿAbdullah, 35
nahḍa, 9, 12, 14, 15, 190, 191
nation-state 10, 78, 83, 85, 88, 135, 172, 181, 254, 255, 259
national allegory, 11, 37, 79ff, 91, 96, 155–6, 169, 255; see also Zaynab; Al-Ayyam, ʿAwdat; the trilogy
national consciousness, 15, 21, 38, 83, 219, 257
national imaginary, 11, 21, 36, 38, 57, 92, 155, 157
nationalism, 8, 10, 13, 21, 22, 26, 38, 44, 59, 60, 78, 92, 113, 159, 172
  as religion, 57, 58–9, 60
  see also liberal nationalism
nationhood, 21, 36, 38, 44, 51, 54, 92, 198, 220, 257
nature, 21, 44, 60
Nestorius, 174, 175–6, 178, 179
novel
  Arabic novel into maturity, 113–16, 119–20
  first Egyptian novelists, 20–2
  historical, 24, 127, 170–1
  incompatible with religion, 8–9
  and intertextuality, 123–6
  and nation, 21–2, 88; see also national allegory
  and religious other, 17–19; see also other
  and secularism/secularity, 10–18, 21, 22, 23, 27, 28, 34, 36, 37, 45f, 64–5, 77, 78, 79, 88, 89, 119, 123, 254–9
  women in the Egyptian novel, 221–2
  see also experimentalism; al-ḥassasiyya al-jadīda; intertextuality; turāth

other (the), 15–19, 20, 23, 51–4, 83, 85, 86, 90–1, 202, 223, 257
  colonial, 19
  religious, 18–19, 51, 56–7, 78, 85, 254

Paradise, 61, 65, 66, 67, 68, 94, 142, 145, 146, 147, 181, 212, 224, 232, 234
patriarchal language, 232–3
patriarchy/patriarchal, 79, 145, 147, 196, 221, 223, 224, 225, 226, 228, 230, 232, 233, 234, 236, 237, 238, 239, 240, 241, 245, 246
pilgrimage, 37, 87, 89, 154, 192
poetry, 7, 8, 26, 27, 116, 122, 128, 199, 209, 211, 226, 232
  Arabic, 3, 4, 115, 125
political imaginary, 38, 131, 135
polygamy, 102, 103, 220, 220, 256
postcolonial studies, 18–19
postmodernism, postmodern, 25, 45, 50, 124, 133, 166, 172
postsecularity, postsecular, 133, 258
prophecy, 134, 135, 144, 147, 174
prophethood, 62, 133, 134

Qasim, ʿAbd al-Hakim, 24, 136, 137, 141, 143, 144, 145, 146, 148, 196, 220, 257
  Al-Mahdi, 24, 136–41, 148, 155, 241

Turaf min Khabar al-Akhira, 24, 141–8, 245
Qur'an, 3, 7, 46, 48, 52, 54, 56, 80, 83, 84, 93, 94, 96, 100, 101, 102, 122, 128, 140, 142, 162, 163, 167, 169, 191, 232–4, 235, 240, 246

reason (rationalism), 4, 5, 7, 9, 10, 13, 55, 56, 57, 77, 119, 131, 135, 136, 195, 201, 210
religious language (also theistic), 43, 46, 53, 85, 86, 89, 104, 130, 232, 233, 242, 245, 256, 257; *see also* Sufi language
religious violence, 24, 137–8, 141, 170, 173, 179–80, 241; *see also* scapegoat
resurrection, 85, 96, 140, 141, 142–3, 146, 161, 227
revelation (religious), 3, 4, 6, 8, 95, 99, 103, 104, 141, 144
Ricoeur, Paul, 4, 6, 17, 97
Ri'fat, Alifa, 25, 246–7, 255
Rumi, 7, 193, 199

Sadat, Anwar, 114, 117, 118, 154
Sa'dawi, Nawal, 25, 177, 221, 222, 223, 226, 227, 228, 230, 233, 234, 235, 245, 246
 Jannat wa Iblis, 25, 230–6, 237, 241, 246
 Mawt al-Rajul al-Wahid, 222
 Suqut al-Imam, 25, 222–30, 232, 233, 236, 237, 241, 242, 245, 246
Said, Edward, 18, 28
saint/s, 48, 57, 61, 90, 133, 134, 135, 168, 178, 190, 199, 244
Sartre, Jean-Paul, 17
Satan, 40, 176–7, 223, 224, 225, 230, 234, 235; *see also* 'Azazil; devil; Jannat wa Iblis
al-Sayyid, Lutfi, 13, 36
scapegoat, 24, 59, 138, 140, 141, 177, 228
scripture, 4, 5, 6, 27, 40, 51, 91, 96, 97, 120, 161, 180, 181, 190, 200, 219, 224, 232, 233, 235, 241
secularism, 9, 13, 14, 17, 21, 25, 28, 34, 37, 38, 41, 45, 46, 49, 50, 51, 58, 62, 64, 77, 82, 85, 156
 Arab, 12–13
 literary, 15, 28, 53, 60, 64–5, 78, 89, 91, 104; *see also* novel and secularism
 and the novel *see* novel and secularism
 secular discourse, 17, 19, 51, 52, 57, 83, 90, 95, 96, 257

vs secularity, 13–14, 28
secularity, 13–16, 17, 27, 28, 38, 45, 46, 51, 60, 61, 64, 65, 77, 78, 79, 85, 89, 104, 119, 255, 257, 258
Sharia, 35, 46, 84, 87, 103, 117, 141, 143, 144, 225, 245; *see also* Islamic law
al-Sharqawi, 'Abd al-Rahman, 18, 23, 90, 91, 95, 96, 97, 98, 99, 101, 102, 103, 104, 144, 156
 Al-Ard, 21, 23, 91–6, 102, 103, 114, 156
 Muhammad Rasul al-Hurrriyya, 23, 91, 96–104
shaykh/s, 48, 64, 77, 83, 93, 94, 95, 136, 143, 198, 201, 223, 233, 243, 256
 'Abd al-Rabbih al-Ta'ih, 206–7, 208–9
 Abu'l-Su'ud, 128–9, 130
 Azhar, 35, 48, 49, 52, 146
 literary shaykh, 63, 254
 Mas'ud, 39, 41, 45, 189
 Mutawalli 'Abd al-Samad, 83, 84, 94
 Sa'id al-Hasiri, 137, 138, 140
 Shinawi, 93–5
 Simhan, 59
 Sufi, 53, 136, 189, 190, 195, 196, 198, 199, 200, 201; *see also* 'Abd al-Rabbih al-Ta'ih
al-Shidyaq, Faris, 12, 17, 34–5
short story, 9, 15, 26–7, 64, 77, 78, 95, 114, 115, 155, 189, 194, 222, 246, 255
Siddiq, Muhammad, 8, 26, 57, 80, 81, 94, 159
sira, 7, 51, 56, 91, 96, 97, 98, 100, 101, 103, 104, 115, 134, 240
sirat dhatiyya, 165, 204, 206; *see also* autobiography
spirituality, 56, 62, 65, 78, 91, 196, 255, 258
stereotype, 18, 54, 65, 87, 120, 221, 240
Sufi/s, 48, 84, 93, 128, 131, 136, 137, 138, 140, 141, 189ff, 254
 Brotherhood, 39, 145, 203, 206
 discourse, 115, 120, 192, 194, 195, 200, 210, 212, 21
 language, 197, 200
 love, 24, 191
 path/way, 24, 129, 131, 168, 191, 193, 194, 195, 200, 207
 poets/poetry (also mystical), 3, 193, 199, 207, 243, 244
 shaykhs *see* shaykhs
 space, 130
 symbolism, 86

Sufi/s (*cont.*)
   text/s, 7, 207
   vision, 24, 117, 202
   voice, 84, 95, 190
   writing, 24, 221
Sufism, 24, 45, 60, 136, 189ff, 255
sukr (intoxication),193, 199, 200

Tahir, Baha', 24, 155
   Khalati Safiyya wa'l-Dayr, 24, 26, 155–8, 159, 168, 169
takiyya, 198, 199, 201
tariqa, 199, 201
Taylor, Charles, 14, 15
theology, 4, 5, 7, 27, 44, 161, 174, 179, 230, 232
tolerance (religious), 12, 24, 160, 162, 169, 170, 171, 172, 173
transcendence (religious), 7, 14, 44–5, 65, 67, 68, 135, 210, 223, 227, 259; *see also* heaven
turāth, 23, 115–17, 120, 124, 125

ᶜulamāʾ, 54, 200

Wafd, 13, 55, 56, 77, 92, 96, 113, 153–4
Weltanschauung 14, 27, 39, 49, 52, 65, 81, 83, 259
Wood, James, 5, 8

zāhir/bāṭin 202, 208
zakat 93, 101
Zaydan, Yusuf 17, 24, 172, 173, 177, 178, 180, 259
   ᶜAzazil, 5, 24, 172–82
Zaynab, Sayyida, 61, 67
   Zulaykha (Potiphar's wife), 25, 40, 235, 236, 240

EU representative:
Easy Access System Europe
Mustamäe tee 50, 10621 Tallinn, Estonia
Gpsr.requests@easproject.com

www.ingramcontent.com/pod-product-compliance
Lightning Source LLC
Chambersburg PA
CBHW052057300426
44117CB00013B/2174